Critical Social Psychology

Critical Social Psychology

An Introduction

2nd Edition

Brendan Gough

Majella McFadden

and

Matthew McDonald

palgrave
macmillan

First edition 2001
This edition 2013
Published by
PALGRAVE MACMILLAN

Palgrave Macmillan in the UK is an imprint of Macmillan Publishers Limited,
registered in England, company number 785998, of Houndmills, Basingstoke,
Hampshire RG21 6XS.

Palgrave Macmillan in the US is a division of St Martin's Press LLC,
175 Fifth Avenue, New York, NY 10010.

Palgrave Macmillan is the global academic imprint of the above companies
and has companies and representatives throughout the world.

Palgrave® and Macmillan® are registered trademarks in the United States,
the United Kingdom, Europe and other countries.

ISBN: 978–0–230–30385–0

This book is printed on paper suitable for recycling and made from fully
managed and sustained forest sources. Logging, pulping and manufacturing
processes are expected to conform to the environmental regulations of the
country of origin.

A catalogue record for this book is available from the British Library.

A catalog record for this book is available from the Library of Congress.

10 9 8 7 6 5 4 3 2 1
22 21 20 19 18 17 16 15 14 13

Printed and bound in Great Britain by
CPI Antony Rowe, Chippenham and Eastbourne

Brendan and Majella: 'For Darcy and Finn'
Matt: 'For Mita'

Contents

List of Boxes

Preface

Since we wrote the original textbook, published in 2001, the world of critical psychology has expanded and diversified. Although there are now many more potential resources for students, including other textbooks covering critical psychology ideas, the range of material available can seem bewildering. Psychology students, socialized into a vision of scientific psychology, traditionally find critical psychology to be a difficult field, and the current wealth and fragmented nature of critical psychology work perhaps makes it even more difficult for students to navigate. We hope this second edition guides students through this complex terrain.

It remains true in 2012 that the majority of social psychology courses are dominated by cognitive–experimental traditions, as evidenced by the preponderance of 'mainstream' (largely North American) mass market texts. And courses dealing with critical social psychology themes often feature in other 'non-psychological' places, such as cultural studies, literary criticism, gender modules or specialist third-level units. Our book represents an effort to consider both perspectives in relation to a range of relevant social psychological topics. It mimics the structure of established mainstream social psychology texts, thereby enabling comparison, but also highlights 'critical' work in each area. In this way students can immediately discern key differences between the traditions and are in a position to assess their relative worth in the context of existing research and 'knowledge'. So, this book can operate as a complementary text for courses informed by cognitive–experimental social psychology and as a core text for courses dedicated to introducing critical social psychology. Although this topic-based structure helps create an accessible text for students, it must be borne in mind that common themes and debates affect each area and these central issues are stressed throughout. For example, the idea of 'knowledge' as social production in critical work is constantly underlined.

Obviously, we have updated the text with references to interesting and important critical work published since 2001. For example, there is more coverage of discursive psychological research, psycho-analytic and psychosocial work, community psychology/participatory action research, and Lesbian, Gay, Bisexual, Transgender and Queer (LGBTQ) material. In addition, we provide two brand new chapters which showcase how critical psychological ideas and methods can be applied to the domains of 'health' and 'work' respectively (Chapters 8 and 9), and we hope these chapters will convince students that critical psychologists can make a difference in the world. We have also decided to merge and rework previously separate chapters on gender and sexuality to avoid repetition (Chapter 7), and to omit a former chapter on aggression to make room for the new chapters.

The book is structured into four main sections, and rounded off with a final discussion and reflections chapter (Chapter 10). Part I comprises three chapters outlining the nature of critical psychology (Chapter 1), a critique of mainstream social psychology (Chapter 2) and a review of research methods which critical psychologists use (Chapter 3). Collectively these three chapters lay the foundations for reading and understanding subsequent chapters, which could then be read in any order. They offer a vision of social psychology as genuinely social, interested in social interaction and the messiness of everyday life, and in highlighting abuse and inequalities which can be challenged. Chapters 4 to 9 then take on a similar format whereby mainstream work on the topic in question is summarized and questioned, followed by a critical psychological take drawing on research examples. Part II considers two classic social psychology topics – social influence (Chapter 4) and prejudice (Chapter 5) – and highlights problems in the theories and methods adopted by mainstream social psychologists before offering alternative perspectives. For example, we show how social influence can be tied to specific contexts and discourses while prejudice and discrimination can often be very subtle in social exchanges, and difficult to rebut. Part III focuses on social identities and relations by first presenting a social view of selfhood (Chapter 6) before concentrating on the social construction of gendered and sexed identities (Chapter 7). These chapters reject the model of the self-contained individual implicit in much social psychological theory while specifying social constraints on individual action and identifications (e.g. with reference to the contemporary sexualization of girls). Part IV then describes how critical psychology can be usefully applied to the health (Chapter 8) and work (Chapter 9) contexts. For example, critical health psychologists move away from biomedical understandings of health and illness to embrace lay accounts and develop alternative discourses (e.g. rejecting medicalized diagnoses such as attention deficit disorder and the accompanying medical treatments). Chapter 9 exposes mainstream work psychology's support and collusion with the owner/ managers of organizations at the expense of workers. In its place it offers an alternative vision for work psychology whose focus is less about 'fixing the individual' and more about calling for workers to have greater freedom and control over the ways in which work is organized in contemporary society. Finally, Chapter 10 summarizes key insights and foregrounds key challenges for critical psychologists, such as the rise of 'positive psychology' and neuropsychology.

This textbook is designed for students taking introductory courses in (critical) social psychology, although it could also feature as a preliminary text for more advanced (critical) social psychology modules. As the title suggests, a key aim is to make students aware of contemporary developments and debates in critical social psychology, with an emphasis on rendering often complex concepts and issues as accessible as possible. In an effort to maximize student understanding we have deployed various devices throughout the text. Each chapter contains:

- 'critical thinking' boxes, which aim to stimulate reflection on the relevant topic with various questions and exercises;
- illustrative material in boxes, which present details of contemporary 'critical' research studies and quotations from theorists on important themes;
- reference to key and new readings in every chapter, carefully selected to provide further insights into pertinent areas.

There is also a glossary at the end of the book, where key terms are defined (students often find the vocabulary of critical social psychology difficult). In summarizing and simplifying the terrain of critical social psychology in this way we are conscious of presenting an account which does not do justice to its breadth and diversity. We do hope, however, that students will use this text as an opening into the world of critical social psychology and we do encourage further reading to garner greater sensitivity to the various strands and debates which exist. However, we must stress that what follows is not an 'objective' or 'neutral' presentation of contemporary social psychology. Rather, our agenda is mainly to promote critical social psychology perspectives as we feel these offer more sophisticated and convincing accounts of social psychological phenomena compared with cognitive–experimental approaches. This agenda is particularly elaborated within the first three chapters, which deal directly with questions of social psychological theory and method and their interconnectedness. However, we also stress that critical social psychology cannot be considered a unified or unproblematic school of thought (see Chapter 10), but that concepts used and issues raised within critical social psychology offer valuable insights into contemporary social life.

In writing this new edition, Matthew has joined us (Brendan and Majella), and we are very grateful for his energy, commitment and intelligence in finessing the text.

We hope you find this book useful.

Introducing Critical Social Psychology

Part I

Critical Social Psychology: An Introduction

This introductory chapter will highlight:

- Diversity within (social) psychology
- Key influences on the development of critical social psychology, including key texts and articles
- Important themes within critical social psychology
- Methods favoured by critical social psychologists

Introduction

Just as the discipline of psychology can be broken down into many different sub-disciplines (developmental, clinical, educational, etc.) and perspectives (cognitive, psychodynamic, humanistic, etc.), so too can social psychology be separated into different fragments. A convenient, though simplistic, way of classifying distinct strands is in terms of approaches which place the individual at the centre of analysis, i.e. psychological social psychology (PSP), and those which emphasize the social dimension to experience, i.e. sociological social psychology (SSP). For example, in studying conformity a PSP approach might focus on 'personality', perhaps devising a scale to distinguish between acquiescent and resistant 'types' of people. On the other hand, an SSP explanation of conformity might focus on aspects of the social situation such as 'peer pressure' as well as wider institutional and cultural expectations such as 'respect for authority'. It is important, however, not to see these two 'camps' as diametrically opposed, since psychological perspectives usually reserve a role for social factors and sociological perspectives often allow for some form of individual or local autonomy. The aim of this text is to contrast these two versions of social psychology, highlighting differences in the explanations offered for various phenomena such as self-identity, gender and prejudice, both between and within the two camps.

In contrast to other textbooks which claim to offer a neutral or 'objective' presentation of the many theories and studies which make up contemporary social psychology, we explicitly argue in favour of a social psychology which stresses the social embeddedness of experience. However, in addition to following an SSP model, we also advocate a social psychology which is 'critical': in other words, a social psychology which challenges social institutions, practices and power relations – including the discipline of psychology – that contribute to forms of inequality and oppression. There is already a history of such critical work in social psychology, as Griffin (1995) notes, including research which has engaged with the impact of unemployment on a community during the 1930s (cited in Jahoda *et al.*, 1972) and research on fascist ideology (e.g. Billig, 1978), but the present day has seen a renewed interest in critical psychology. In studying racism, for example, a critical social psychologist might well highlight and inter-rogate prevailing ideals and claims which locate the 'causes' of racism within the individual (thereby neglecting institutional cultures) or within the minority group in question (blaming the victims for their predicament) (see Howarth & Hook, 2005; Wetherell & Potter, 1992). So, we are promoting a social psychology which gets involved in 'society', which adopts particular positions in important debates on many different issues such as prejudice, violence, mental illness, unemployment, crime – a strange, perhaps alien, departure for students more familiar with the detached 'scientific' stance assumed by many – mainly cognitive–experimental and biological – social psychologists.

The purpose of this chapter is to introduce you to key concepts and debates within what is now known widely as 'critical social psychology' (e.g. Hepburn, 2003; Ibáñez & Íñiguez, 1997; Tuffin, 2004). The term 'critical psychology' is also much used (e.g. Fox & Prilleltensky, 1997; 2009) and is applied beyond social psychology to other areas (e.g. health, developmental, work psychology), spawning other more specific critical offshoots such as 'critical health psychology' (Murray, 2004) and 'critical organizational psychology' (Islam & Zyphur, 2009). For this reason the term 'critical psychol-ogies' is useful, denoting multiple but related critical projects located at the margins of psychology. While still relatively peripheral in the context of mainstream psychology, it is important to note that critical psychologies have blossomed over the past 25 years or so, resulting in many new courses, conferences, websites and assorted publications all around the world. For a snapshot of this global reach, consider the 2005 edition of the *Annual Review of Critical Psychology*, which is devoted to documenting critical psychological work in diverse geo-political regions (Dafermos & Marvakis, 2006).

However, given the relative youth of critical psychologies and, at times, an unfortunate tendency towards complex vocabulary, there is a need for introductory texts such as this to clearly present to a student audience terms and issues which are central to critical social psychologists. The immediate objective of this chapter then is to consider significant influences on the development of critical social psychology, including classic grand worldviews such as Marxism, Feminism and Psychoanalysis, as well as more recent perspectives such as Social Constructionism, Psychosocial Studies and Post-structuralism. It should be noted that each of these fields is complex and diverse; for example, not all feminists agree with each other, and there are consequently different versions of feminism, or feminisms, on offer. In addition, critical psychologists draw upon other theories which focus on particular identity categories and relations; for example, critical race studies focuses on race, postcolonialism on nationality and queer theory on sexuality. Here we will focus on key concepts which have been taken up by psychologists in order to critique mainstream (social) psychological work and to develop alternative understandings of social psychological phenomena. We will then proceed to summarize key themes within critical social psychology. Also, some discussion of methods used within critical social psychology will be presented, with relevant examples provided to give a flavour of what critical social psychologists do in research practice (see also Chapter 3, which is devoted to this topic).

CRITICAL THINKING BOX: (SOCIAL) PSYCHOLOGY

We are suggesting that psychologists should situate themselves and their work within society and develop a critical attitude towards psychological 'knowledge' and its applications. For example, research on sexuality might highlight accounts by marginalized groups (e.g. lesbian women, gay men, bisexual and transgender people) in order to challenge psychological theories which present such groups as 'deviant' or 'abnormal' (see Clarke & Peel, 2007; Kitzinger, 1997). Can you think of any other areas where critical social psychologists might wish to intervene in this way?

Critical social psychology: key influences

As was previously noted critical social psychology emerges from and is informed by a range of other theoretical traditions usually absent from or on the margins of 'scientific' psychology. Marxist and feminist approaches clearly offer critical analyses of social class and gender relations and tend to stress issues of power, conflict and ideology. Also, 'postmodern' and social constructionist ideas have proved very influential, with concepts such as the social constitution of reality, discourse and subjectivity being central. We will now consider each framework in terms of its contribution to critical social psychology.

Marxism

There are many forms of Marxism and differences of interpretation between the various camps but it would not be too controversial to assert that Marxism is about the theory and practice of class struggle. Instead of the psychological focus on the individual, we have the sociological spotlight on relations between groups or social classes within a broader system of economic structures and institutions, i.e. capitalism. As any introductory sociological text will document, this relationship between classes is considered conflictual, where economic conditions are said to sustain competitive and destructive forms of everyday social interactions and relations. In the world of work, it is asserted that the worker is dehumanized and commodified by virtue of the drive for efficiency and profit – the benefits of which are returned mainly to owners and managers rather than to 'ordinary' workers (see Chapter 9 for a more in-depth discussion on Marx's theories of production/work). As Arfken (2011) suggests in his introduction to Marxism and psychology in the *Annual Review of Critical Psychology*, in the wake of the current global financial crisis and vast inequalities in wealth exposed by recent scandals in the UK around banker's pay and bonuses, a Marxist analysis is still clearly relevant to life in the twenty-first century. Within capitalist systems there is little interest or scope for facilitating human needs for social support, creativity, stimulation and identification with work processes and products (see Parker & Spears, 1996; Fromm, 1961/2004). Consequently, there is a tension between the goals of the business, such as profit and shareholder value, and those of the workers, such as fulfilment and the freedom to control the ways in which work is organized, or in other words, a class struggle which manifests itself outside work in society in terms of largely distinct consumption patterns (e.g. a preference for sherry or beer) and leisure pursuits (e.g. a taste for classical or dance music).

This account is greatly simplified, of course, and in contemporary society it could be argued that the boundaries between classes are more difficult to detect, or have even disappeared in the midst of a modern 'classless' society (see Pakulski & Waters, 1996). Nonetheless, the emphasis on power differentials and conflict around class is an important one for critical social psychologists, who are interested in highlighting and challenging inequalities in any form (see Brown, 1974; Ostrove & Cole, 2003). As well as documenting class relations ('reproduction') Marxist approaches also assert a commitment to social change ('transformation'), that is, an effort to resist and overthrow prevailing systems of discrimination and alienation. Again, as Arfken (2011) notes, widespread protests against prevailing economic and political elites, crystallized in the various 'Occupy' camps from Wall Street to the City of London and beyond, recalls the Marxist emphasis on class conflict and social change. This concern and vision about an alternative, oppression-free society is shared by many critical social psychologists. Forms of Marxist theory have also concentrated on 'ideology', loosely defined as 'knowledge' (including psychological theories) which works to obscure exploitation and oppression (see Ingleby, 1972). The notion of aggression and competition as natural and healthy would be one example of an ideological norm which could well be used to justify the subordination of particular individuals and groups ('survival of the fittest', etc.). A Marxist or critical social psychologist might prefer to emphasize competing ideals, for example around solidarity, collaboration and equality. Finally, both Marxism and critical social psychology have in common a project of critical empirical research aimed at exploring local instances of class inequalities and struggles. For further discussion of the relationship between Marxism and psychology, see the edited volume by Arfken (2011), which is the product of the first international conference on Marxism and Psychology in 2010, and free to download at: http://www.discourseunit.com/arcp9/ARCP9. pdf. An earlier edited text by Parker and Spears (1996) is also worth a look, as is Parker's more recent book (see Box 1.1). Notwithstanding the importance of Marxist analyses, critical social psychology is also interested in difference and relations which arise from other social categories and identities, notably gender, as the next section, on feminism, suggests.

CRITICAL THINKING BOX: SOCIAL CLASS

A Marxist analysis highlights differences and inequalities between members of distinct social class groups. To what extent have recent economic problems exposed glaring inequalities in wealth distribution? Which groups have been hit hardest by recent debt problems and subsequent government austerity measures? Why have people been protesting across the world in large numbers, and what effect will this have? Do you think Western governments should limit the power of financial institutions and work towards a fairer society?

Box 1.1 Revolution in psychology: alienation to emancipation (Parker, 2007)

The author uses a Marxist framework to critique mainstream psychology, arguing that it promotes social behaviours and personality traits related to individualism, competitiveness, aggression, ambition, entrepreneurship and flexibility, all of which are required for the capitalist economic system to function effectively. Psychology is therefore one of a number of 'ideological strategies used to divide people from one another and encourage competition in the so-called "free" market' (p. 171). People who do not meet the above set of narrow personality traits and those unwilling or unable to successfully turn themselves into commodities for sale in the marketplace (e.g. the poor, unemployed, homeless, indigenous, disabled, refugees, mentally ill etc.) are marginalized by society and pathologized by psychology. It's no surprise then that life for many in modern capitalist economies is alienating and psychologically distressing, despite the political rhetoric telling us that capitalism is the system that most closely corresponds to human nature. Rather than emancipating people by calling for social change and challenging capitalism's exploitation of social interactions and relations, psychology uses its knowledge to better adapt people to its alienating conditions.

Feminism

Some scholars, notably socialist feminists, have sought to integrate Feminist and Marxist ideas to produce a critique of 'patriarchal capitalism', where the family is highlighted as the nucleus of female subordination and control. Nonetheless, in most classic forms of Marxism, gender is neglected or relegated to secondary status in the analysis of class relations. The importance of feminism lies in its clear, critical and primary focus on gender as a means of organizing social relations and inequalities. Feminists have consistently under-lined the oppression of all women within male-centred heterosexual social institutions and practices (e.g. De Beauvoir, 1962; Millett, 1970; Rich, 1980). For example, sexual violence has been analysed in terms of sustaining male power and control over women generally through producing a climate of fear keeping women 'in their place' (Kelly, 1988a). Women as a group have been presented as second-class citizens across various social spheres, including education, employment and family life, a position justified by ideologies of femininity in which women were defined as mothers, carers and housekeepers.

Through engagement with recent social theory (e.g. post-structur-alism), however, feminism has recognized the often different experi-ences of women from various backgrounds, thereby calling into question the notion of women as a coherent, self-contained group with common issues and goals (see Dua, 2006; Wilkinson, 1986; 1996). Indeed, early forms of feminism have been criticized for reflecting the concerns of mostly white, middle-class women, and as a result contemporary feminism (feminisms or postfeminism) embodies a much more diverse – and sometimes conflicting – range of positions (see Wilkinson, 1996). Further, any particular 'brand' of feminism will itself feature different versions. One key ongoing debate for example revolves around the extent to which women can be considered a unified group – are there some problems shared by all women or do consid-erations of class, race, ethnicity, sexuality, etc. disrupt any claims of universal experiences? For example, one discussion concerns the perspective on heterosexuality, with many lesbian feminists arguing for a rejection of this institution whilst other voices suggest potential ways for women to progress within heterosexual frameworks (see Wilkinson & Kitzinger, 1993). Feminism is a term which is very much contested in contemporary literature, a category which is subject to continuous debate (see Griffin, 1995).

From a critical social psychology perspective, situating the individual within the gendered social relations is an attractive and important move, as is the critical focus on power and gendered inequalities (Segal, 1999). Also, feminist researchers have been at the forefront of critiquing 'scientific' methods in psychology and have advocated more democratic, inclusive and reflexive forms of research which seek to give voice to participants and break down barriers between researcher and researched (Ramazanoglu & Holland, 2002; Stanley, 1990; Wilkinson, 1988; Williams & Lykes, 2003). In general, feminists and gay and lesbian scholars have been among the most cogent and vociferous critics of mainstream psychological theories and methods which have furnished 'norms' around gender and sexuality with scientific authority and contributed to the marginalization of women and homosexuality (e.g. Burman, 1990; Kitzinger, 1987). In fact, the journal *Feminism & Psychology* has provided a key forum for research challenging forms of sexism, heterosexism, racism and class oppression both within and beyond the discipline of (social) psychology (e.g. Bhavnani & Phoenix, 1994; Kitzinger *et al.*, 1992; McDermott, 2006; Walkerdine, 1996). In this sense feminist psychology situates gender and sexuality with respect to other social categories and identities, drawing on interdisciplinary work, including postcolonialism, queer theory and critical race studies (see Box 1.3 and Box 1.4). For example, an interesting article by Scharff (2011) explores young women's rejection of feminism as anti-man, lesbian and unfeminine, showing how women's different identifications in relation to gender, class, race and sexuality influenced this stance in specific, intersecting ways. Also, some feminists working from a gender relations perspective are interested in studying men and masculinity (e.g. Segal, 1990; Wetherell and Edley, 1999. For example, an article by Terry & Braun (2012) explores men's views of vasectomy, arguing that their emphasis on 'heroic' sacrifice and responsibility serves to remind us of, and help perpetuate, women's mundane, ongoing responsibility in this area.

Box 1.2   Feminist psychology (Wilkinson, 1997)

Wilkinson describes feminist psychology as psychological theory and practice which is explicitly informed by the political goals of the feminist movement. Although feminism embraces a plurality of definitions and viewpoints, these different versions of feminism are said to share two common themes (Unger, 1996). Firstly, feminism places a high value on women, considering them as worthy of study in their own right, not just in comparison with men. Secondly, feminism recognizes the need for social change on behalf of women: that is, feminist psychology is explicitly political.

Box 1.3   Lesbian, Gay, Bisexual, Transgender & Queer (LGBTQ) psychology (Kitzinger, 1997)

Kitzinger notes an important shift since the 1970s towards the creation of a lesbian and gay psychology that challenges the whole notion of homosexuality as pathology, investigates the reasons for prejudice and discrimination against lesbians and gay men, develops theoretical and practical responses to lesbian and gay concerns, and attempts to create effective changes in the world such that lesbians and gay men might be spared some of the injustices to which they are currently subjected. Recent work extends to researching the lives of transgendered, queer and bisexual people (see e.g. Clark, Ellis, Peel & Rigg, 2010).

CRITICAL THINKING BOX: GENDER

Feminist social psychologists provide a critical, women-centred focus on gender: is it possible to point to experiences and meanings which all women would share? How might the experiences of poor women living in public housing differ from professional women in owner-occupied suburban houses? Do some women have more in common with some men compared to other women (e.g. because of similar class/race/generational backgrounds)?

Psychoanalysis

In addition to being a form of clinical practice and source of popular psychological discourse concerning individual personality, desire and distress, psychoanalysis offers a range of concepts which can inform critical psychological analysis. Indeed, 'Frankfurt School' Marxist thinkers in early twentieth-century Europe, perplexed by the rise of fascism and the absence of a worker's revolution against capitalist oppression, turned to psychoanalytic theory to help explain such 'irrational' behaviour. A seminal text by Adorno *et al.* (1950) introduces us to the 'authoritarian personality', a tendency towards strict discipline and obedience promoted by traditional nuclear families and reactionary ideologies. Other work by Marcuse (1964/2002) and Fromm (1956/1991) laments the appeal of consumer capitalism which, they contend, provides false solutions to important human needs.

Work in this vein has continued via a range of other prominent social and psychological theorists such as Chris Lasch (1979), Anthony Giddens (1991), R.D. Laing (1967), Jurgen Habermas (1968/1987) and Slavoj Zizek (2000).

Feminist thinkers (e.g. Karen Horney, 1922–37) have also engaged critically with psychoanalytic theory, rejecting some of Freud's more contentious claims as misogynistic (e.g. the Oedipus complex, which suggests inferior female morality), and articulating alternative theories which elevate the status of women. For example, a whole school of Object Relations psychoanalysis attributes primary significance to the infant's pre-Oedipal relations with the mother, in contrast to Freud's emphasis on the primacy of the father during the Oedipal period (e.g. Klein, 1952). More contemporary feminist psychoanalytic thinkers, influenced by Lacan and others, have articulated mature and trans-gressive formations of femininity and sexual desire (e.g. Cixous; Irigary) and relations between men and women (e.g. Benjamin).

In social psychology, particularly in the UK, there has been a critical engagement with psychoanalytic theory around the notion of 'subjec-tivity', or what it means to be a person, and a landmark text here is Henriques *et al.*'s (1984) *Changing the Subject*. More recently, the journal *Subjectivity*, which was established in 2008, features many articles which draw on psychoanalytic theory to understand aspects of contemporary selfhood (e.g. Carlson, 2010 Layton, 2008). Much of this writing blends psychoanalytic concepts with (post)modern social theory, offering a 'psychosocial' perspective. Indeed, psychosocial studies has become a key site for critical work, bringing together psychologists and other social scientists interested in examining how the psychological and the social interconnect in shaping subjectivity (see Frosh & Baraitser, 2008). The first issue of Subjectivity offers a range of perspectives which use – or challenge – psychoanalytic approaches, and all papers can be downloaded for free from http://www.palgrave-journals.com/sub/journal/v22/n1/index.html. In addition, there are a number of useful books on psychoanalytic theory authored by Stephen Frosh (e.g. 1989; 1991; 1999; 2002; 2010), Robert Bocock (1976, 1993, 2002) and Antony Elliott (2002; see Box 1.3).

Box 1.4   Psychoanalytic theorists

Anthony Elliott's (2002) book provides a useful overview of major psychoanalytic theorists and their key contributions from Freud

---

onwards, with the central focus on the relationship between the self, others and society. The relevance of psychoanalysis to social theory is underlined; for example, Freud's notion of repression is located within strict late Victorian values enacted within the family, and several of Freud's books are explicitly concerned with how societies shape personal lives, from *Totem and Taboo* (1913–14) to *Civilization and Its Discontents* (1930). Some of the theories propounded by those influenced by Freud are difficult to grasp, such as work inspired by Jacques Lacan, but they provide provocative and critically interesting perspectives on contemporary selfhood. For example, the concept of narcissism (a concept traditionally applied to the realm of psychiatry, clinical psychology and/or psychotherapy) is reworked by Lasch (1979) to argue that contemporary neoliberal consumerist society has given rise to a narcissistic culture, and a self which has turned inward as a consequence of widespread feelings of social and political alienation. This has led to declines in community participation, a disregard for the poor and disadvantaged, and a lack of concern with social harmony and cohesion. The culture of narcissism is a culture characterized by 'competitive individualism, which in its decadence has carried the logic of individualism to the extreme of a war of all against all, [and] the pursuit of happiness to the dead end of a narcissistic preoccupation with the self' (Lasch, 1979: xv). Reading Lasch's book demonstrates that Freud and his followers were not simply concerned with individual psychology and psychopathology; rather, psychoanalytic theory has much to offer those interested in critical analyses of the individual-in-society (e.g. McDonald *et al.*, 2008; Wearing *et al.*, in press).

Social constructionism

This critique of psychology has also been facilitated by the emergence of a new movement or 'paradigm' called social constructionism. Recent versions of feminism, psychoanalysis and Marxism within social psychology and beyond have been informed by concepts presented by social constructionism. There are various terms currently in circulation which overlap with or which are even used interchangeably with social constructionism, including 'post-modernism', 'post-structuralism', 'deconstructionism'. We will not concern ourselves here with the often subtle and much-debated differences in and disputes over meanings which characterize the theoretical literature (but see

Burr, 2003; Maze, 2001). Rather, we will attempt to convey some key assumptions which frame most contemporary thinking within a broadly defined social constructionist movement.

The first and crucial point to make is that social constructionism represents a 'turn to language' in social theory. In other words, there is an emphasis on representation, meaning and interpretation. This particular focus is hardly new in the social sciences. Indeed, there are many precursors to this linguistic turn, including 'symbolic inter-actionism' (Mead, 1934), which portrays identity as (re-)constructed during social interactions. The other precursor is 'ethnomethod-ology' (Garfinkel, 1967), which focuses on everyday language use as social practice. It is interesting that these theories have histori-cally been presented in other disciplines such as sociology and anthropology and have only recently been taken up within social psychology. In fact, a key moment in the modern development of social constructionism was the publication of Berger and Luckman's (1967) seminal text *The Social Construction of Reality*, in which these sociologists examine the joint creation and negotiation of shared realities between people.

Box 1.5   Language and social construction (Burr, 2003)

Our ways of understanding the world come not from objective reality but from other people, past and present. We are born into a world where the conceptual frameworks and categories used by people in our culture already exist. These categories are acquired by all people as they develop the use of language and are thus reproduced every day by everyone who shares a culture and a language. This means that the way people think, the very categories and concepts that provide a framework of meaning for them are provided by the language that they use.

By placing centre-stage the everyday interactions between people and seeing these as actively producing the forms of knowledge we take for granted and their associated phenomena, it follows that language too has to be more than a way of simply expressing ourselves. When people talk to each other, the world gets constructed. 'Our use of language can therefore be thought of as a form of action, and some social constructionists take this 'performative' role of language as their focus of interest' (Burr, 2003: 8).

Within social psychology, certain landmarks are also identifiable. For example, Gergen's (1973) paper, 'Social Psychology as History', located the discipline within particular cultural and historical settings, thereby undermining claims about scientific objectivity; if the knowledge produced by social psychology makes sense only within specific (Western, individualist) contexts then aspirations of 'truth' and generality can be seen as misguided. Whilst Gergen was writing from the USA, some colleagues in the UK such as Harré and others (Harré, 1979; Harré & Secord, 1972) were also turning to language and its operation in everyday activity. The 1980s and 1990s saw a development of this work with a more 'poststructuralist' flavour, an emphasis on meaning as fluid and unstable. A germinal text here is *Changing the Subject* by Henriques *et al.* (1984), a book which emerged from critical engagements with post-structuralism, psychoanalysis and ideology featured in the since-expired journal *Ideology & Consciousness* (Adlam *et al.*, 1977). This edited volume has proved very influential in the subsequent development of critical social psychology and offers a profound critique of psychology as an individualistic, affirmative enterprise. Drawing principally on the theoretical work of French psychoanalyst Jacques Lacan and French philosopher Michel Foucault, two of the most important figures invoked by critical social psychology, there is a call to re-view 'the subject' (i.e. the individual) as produced or constructed by social and ideological forces.

Other 'critical' key texts focus on 'discourse', and include Potter and Wetherell's (1987) *Discourse and Social Psychology*, and Burman and Parker's (1993) *Discourse Analytic Research*. More recently, different approaches to discursive analysis have been published, including Potter's (2007) comprehensive three-volume set on *Theory and Method*, *Discourse and Social Psychology*, and *Discursive Psychology* respectively, and we now have a textbook which presents a discursive version of social psychology (McKinlay & McVittie, 2008). Parker (2002) has also updated his version of discourse analysis with his edited book *Critical Discursive Psychology* and a more recent paper which assesses the origins and impact of discursive psychology (Parker, 2011). There are clear differences between Parker's and Potter's work, but both can be invoked in challenging standard psychological theory and research. Another useful resource is Wetherell *et al.*'s (2001) two texts on discourse analysis, which outline different theoretical positions and methodological approaches within and outside psychology. Feminist, gay and lesbian, and black social psychologists have produced influential works on discourse, subjectivity and power (e.g. Burman, 1990; Bhavnani & Phoenix, 1994; Wilkinson & Kitzinger,

1995). Recent feminist contributions to critical and discursive work include Weatherall's (2011) critical review of the relationship between feminism and discursive psychology, and Gavey's (2011) personal reflections on 'Feminist post-structuralism and discourse analysis'.

CRITICAL THINKING BOX: LANGUAGE

Social constructionism highlights the role of language in defining ('constructing') reality. This creative use of language is evident when there is more than one version of the same event. Think of three 'objects' (e.g. 'housework'; 'whale hunting'; 'public sector strike'; 'mental illness') and list the different ways in which each is explained or constructed. For example, 'housework' might be defined as 'not proper work' or as 'a valuable contribution to society'. Discuss the reasons for such diverse meanings. Who uses particular constructions, and for what ends?

Critical social psychology: key themes

It is important to stress at this point that, as with any other (sub-) discipline, there are some disagreements and debates within critical social psychology. Indeed, it has been disputed that social constructionism necessarily offers a coherent base for critical social psychology since social constructionist arguments can be used to present a case for relativism, a stance which undermines the authority of 'taken for granted' knowledge, treats all accounts or discourses as equal and renders problematic the connections between language and 'reality' (see Edwards & Potter, 1993; Parker, 1998). This perspective allows us to critically interrogate claims about 'truth' and 'reality' (e.g. in 'scientific' psychology) but can make it difficult to argue *for* a particular or critical version of reality, as some feminist writers point out in their efforts to hold on to a view of social relations centred on the patriarchal oppression of women (e.g. Gavey, 1997; Gill, 1995; Speer, 2000; but see Hepburn, 2000 for a defence of relativism within feminism). More recently, similar debates have emerged concerning the compatibility of feminism and conversation analysis, an approach aligned to discursive psychology which is increasingly influential in sociology and interdisciplinary fields (see Kitzinger, 2002; Wowk, 2007).

Notwithstanding such differences and debates, for the moment we shall limit ourselves to four statements commonly associated with social constructionism which would unite most critical social psychologists:

- the individual is (always, already) located in society;
- the individual is (at least partially) positioned within systems of difference/inequality;
- power is linked to language and representation ('discourse/s');
- research should aim to challenge oppression and promote social change.

The individual and the social

The point here is that it is difficult and perhaps artificial to separate the individual from society (Burr, 2002; Henriques, 1984). It is contended that the individual is constantly connected to the social world in many ways and at various different levels. We can think of 'the social' on at least two levels – the interpersonal and the societal. The former obviously pertains to social interactions and relationships in which the individual is involved, whilst the latter relates to broader social norms, ideologies and practices. Both levels of the social will surround and penetrate the individual, impacting personal identity and public practice.

Consider the example of alcohol consumption. Your experience and presentation of drinking might well be different when with your partner/spouse from when in the company of mates, or with your parents, for example. The place or situation in which drinking takes place could have an impact – the local pub, a cafe-bar, a club, a restaurant, at home, in a park, on the beach, by a river etc.; all present different opportunities and constraints on drinking behaviour (depending on the company too, of course). And then prevailing cultural ideals around gender and class, for example, could frame the drinking event: there is a well-established association between (working-class) masculinity and drinking and fighting in UK culture (but not in Southern European culture), whilst women who drink pints of beer may be seen to contravene traditional definitions of femininity (and subject to unfavourable judgements, even harassment) (see Lyons & Willott, 2008). Even when drinking alone the social is ever-present; in fact, lone drinking is very much constructed as a more 'masculine' pursuit and may be connected to an inability to face one's emotions (again, a traditionally 'masculine' deficiency) or to problems in a relationship or stress at work or college.

Everyday talk and interaction, then, can be seen to rehearse and re-work prevailing cultural ideals. In discussing football, for example, shared norms around gender, sport, competition, etc. are accessed and replayed. When male players are described as 'girls' or 'poofs', this draws on commonly held understandings of masculinity as physical, strong, fearless and so forth (and femininity/male homosexuality as weak, passive and ineffective) (see Plummer, 1999). The pursuit and celebration of victory can even be seen as reproducing capitalist notions of competition, aggression and profit at the expense of 'weaker' others.

These examples highlight the social embeddedness of individual thinking and behaviour; indeed, it challenges the notion of the individual itself as a sovereign entity, standing apart from the social and enjoying total control over her/his actions. This argument is supported further if we examine the historical and cultural variation in individual and social practices. For example, self-expression, individualism and personal responsibility are valued and encouraged in Western societies, whereas self-discipline, self-sacrifice and group responsibility are promoted in Oriental societies, thereby amounting to different customs and forms of interaction in different countries (see Chapter 6). Similarly, social norms and rituals vary across time. Excessive alcohol consumption was previously explained in terms influenced by the nineteenth-century temperance movement, which emphasized individual weakness or lack of discipline, whereas the dominant contemporary account points to the notion of illness with 'alcoholism' deemed beyond the control of individuals. Such variation in ideals and practices across time and place draws attention to the local and transitory nature of what we regard as 'knowledge'.

This is not to suggest, however, that the individual is at the mercy of cultural and historical forces; that would be a deterministic stance which allows for no human 'agency' or autonomy. Most critical social psychologists would suggest that the individual has room to manoeuvre within given social constraints; some women can and do defy conventional expectations by consuming lots of beer and behaving like a 'ladette', whilst many working-class men are not interested in fighting when on a night out. The debate about how much autonomy a person has – and how to conceptualize it – is one which is complex and ongoing within critical social psychology.

CRITICAL THINKING BOX: DRINKING

In researching how alcohol use is defined, critical social psychology points to the impact of social and cultural expectations. Considering your own drinking habits, to what extent do you think that 'social' factors such as gender, class and culture influence these?

The individual and social inequalities

With critical social psychology's focus on social norms comes an interest in power and ideology. It is fairly clear that certain groups in a given society are disproportionately subjected to discrimination, prejudice or abuse and given less access to power. Many examples pertaining to race, gender, class, sexuality, ethnicity, dis/ability, occupational status, etc. can be cited here. As the alcohol example earlier suggests, cultural expectations serve to enable or limit drinking behaviour according to gender, generally tolerating male drunkenness ('boys will be boys') and discouraging female public pleasure ('a woman's place is in the home'). Following a feminist or critical analysis, such gendered notions concerning alcohol consumption can in turn be related to patriarchal social structures and institutions (see Lyons & Willott, 2008; Day, 2000).

If we consider the arena of sexuality, for example, what is 'normal' in most cultures is defined largely in terms of married heterosexuality: that is, a man and a woman engaged in a committed and intimate relationship overseen by the state and usually culminating in children. This 'norm' is supported by institutions such as the family, the law, education, public policy and most religions, and is promoted in advertisements, soap operas and films (e.g. Hyde & Jaffee, 2000). By contrast, gay and lesbian sexualities are marginalized, receiving little or no public acknowledgement, tolerance or rights and are often defined as pathological, deviant, abnormal, etc. (see Clarke *et al.*, 2010; Coyle & Kitzinger, 2001). Consequently, the experiences of gay men and women will be coloured by the way in which they are negatively positioned within society, excluded from mainstream roles and lifestyles and subjected to prejudice, discrimination, aggression and violence. That is not to say that lesbian women and gay men are automatically or completely oppressed by virtue of their sexuality – many may not choose to participate fully in mainstream heterosexist society anyway. The point is that representations of homosexuality as different, sick and dangerous will inevitably curtail aspects of gay men's and lesbian women's lives (e.g. Flowers & Buston, 2001).

Any individual will, at times, face forms of prejudice and discrimination based on the social construction of race, class, sexuality, disability, ethnicity etc. Even white, middle-class men, traditionally granted power and status, can be thought of as vulnerable in some areas for example, immersed in stressful work situations or out of touch with their emotions – although the extent of this 'suffering' is open for debate (see Williams, 2009; Gough & Peace, 2000). The point is that no individual is separate from social relations and systems of difference which serve to position people in various, often inequitable, ways. And social psychology is often implicated in the oppression of particular groups and individuals, as Box 1.5 on the practices of 'abnormal' psychology illustrates.

Box 1.6   A critique of the *Diagnostic and Statistical Manual* (DSM) used to identify mental disorders (Hare-Mustin & Marecek, 2009)

Hare-Mustin and Marecek contend that the *DSM*'s shift to a medicalized frame of reference coincided with the shift to conservatism in national politics in the United States and elsewhere that began in the 1980s and continues to the present. By framing psychological disorders as counterparts of physical illness, it is suggested that the *DSM* focuses clinicians' attention on the individual separated from their social context. Further, it is argued that the *DSM* downplays the potential negative effects of discriminatory treatment, urban disarray, widening social and economic inequalities, and the growing impoverishment of the poor and the working classes. In this way, the mental health professions help conceal the costs incurred to society when wealth is concentrated among a privileged few and when the state relinquishes its commitment to the welfare of the least fortunate members of society.

Discourse/power

For critical social psychology, power is intimately bound up with language, knowledge and representation. In this view, language is active, that is, used to create or 'construct' meanings rather than some neutral reflection of 'reality' – the idea that 'knowledge' produces rather than describes a reality. To proclaim heterosexuality as normal

---

CRITICAL THINKING BOX: SELF IN SOCIETY

Critical social psychology draws attention to the various social positions which people inhabit. One individual will therefore be positioned in many different ways, with some positions more powerful or positive than others. Think about the social identity categories which you 'fit' into (male/female, gay/straight, working/middle-class, ethnic background, able/disabled etc.). Which identities do you think are currently more privileged and which are more oppressed? Why?

---

and homosexuality as alien or deviant, for example, is not to state the nature of things. For example, male homosexuality was the norm in Ancient Greece. Language and knowledge (both of which are a reflection of culture) produce one powerful version of reality within a given society. Moreover, such language and knowledge (e.g. the social sciences) can be used towards certain political and social ends, in this case to criminalize and pathologize gay and lesbian identities and practices. For example, constructions of the military around ideals of heterosexual masculinity can work to exclude women and gay men, etc. from acceptance, access, full participation or promotion. So, any given social construction/interpretation/perspective can be deployed towards certain actions or consequences.

The term 'discourse' is widely used here following the work of Foucault, and is a term which has been usefully defined as a 'set of statements which construct an object' (Parker, 1992: 5). Foucault used the term in his famous historical (or 'genealogical') studies of surveillance and regulation around sexuality, madness and criminality to suggest that language is intimately connected to the operation of power and social control of 'problematic' subjects – perverse, mad, deviant and dangerous individuals. With its power to classify or diagnose and prescribe management techniques and treatments for difficult individuals and groups, psychology was implicated in the disciplinary architecture of modern society (more on Foucault throughout the text).

To illustrate the concept of discourse, think about what it means to be unemployed. A popular discourse around this 'object' relates to notions of individual responsibility, infamously highlighted by 1980s Conservative (neoliberal) un/employment policies which urged people to 'get on your bike' in order to find work. During this era unemployment was re-cast as an individual problem as opposed to a social or economic one. This saw a corresponding shift in public policy away from collective social provision, towards the institution of individual *self-governance*. Welfare or social security for the unemployed required the undertaking of mutual obligations, whereby benefit recipients were required to enter into contracts to become more responsible, productive and competitive individuals (Dean, 2010: 200–203). Under this new discourse unemployment came to be seen as a 'social risk' that the individual was responsible for, as opposed to a social and economic problem.

So, ideas and practices which centre around this 'individualistic' view suggest that the unemployed are to blame for their situation and place the onus on unemployed men and women to find work, show that they are actively seeking employment and that they be willing to subject themselves to 'technologies of agency' (Dean, 2010: 194–197). These technologies include work-for-the-dole schemes, training in emotional intelligence, personality and intelligence testing, time management, personal grooming etc. Within this discourse it becomes easy to position the unemployed as irresponsible, helpless, dependent, lazy, parasitic and unable to adequately manage their own risks. It's no surprise then that many people who find themselves out of work (which can potentially happen to anyone at any time in this era of flexible capitalism) end up feeling ashamed, guilty or desperate. Again, this discourse which defines unemployment as a problem for individuals is but one possible way of presenting this 'object', although again a rather dominant perception in contemporary neoliberal society (Harvey, 2005: 52–54). Nonetheless, there is potential to envisage alternative discourses, such as framing unemployment in terms of economic or global forces or as a positive life choice, discourses which imply radically different images of the unemployed (see Henriques *et al.*, 1984).

CRITICAL THINKING BOX: UN/EMPLOYMENT

As suggested above, prevailing social norms or 'discourses' can largely shape experiences of un/employment. Think about someone you know who is unemployed, or think back to a time when you were unemployed. How do they or how did you explain the situation, and how are they or how were you viewed by others? What other 'discourses' are/were available to explain their, or your situation?

Power/resistance

In light of the above, critical social psychology encourages researchers to examine how discourses are used to subordinate and silence particular individuals and groups in society. Consequently, there is a commitment to social change whereby alternative meanings are marshalled which could be of use to those who are marginalized. The work of feminist, gay and disability scholars can be mentioned here in relation to struggles to challenge conventional notions around femininity/masculinity, heterosexuality/homosexuality and ability/disability, and to present competing discourses, images and practices (see Crawford & Unger, 2004; Clarke *et al.*, 2010; Goodley, 2010, see chapter 6, 'Psychology: Critical Psychological Disability Studies'). In similar ways scholars and activists in the fields of critical race studies and postcolonial studies seek to challenge prevailing images which depict minorities as deficient, passive and problematic and advocate more positive representations depicting activity, creativity and independence.

So, ideas and practices once accepted uncritically as natural, true or proper – 'the man is the breadwinner', 'black people are less intelligent', 'motherhood is the pinnacle of femininity' and so on – are now subjected to critique. Critical social psychologists therefore seek to perform research which challenges and undermines claims to reality or truth, to interrogate taken-for-granted knowledge and to liaise with relevant action groups in the community to promote change. In its 'truest' form, such work is known as 'action research', where participants and researchers engage in dialogue and set the research agenda and practise together (e.g. Fine & Torre, 2006; Kagan *et al.*, 2011; Rheinharz, 1992).

CRITICAL THINKING BOX: SOCIAL CHANGE

Critical social psychology aims to change as well as understand society. Concentrating on a specific area such as work or the family, try to identify current ideals and practices – and their effects. If you feel that any commonly used meanings/practices operate oppressively, what arguments could you use to undermine these and what alternative representations can you imagine?

Critical social psychology: research methods

In general, critical psychologists tend to favour the use of qualitative methods in research. Following the social constructionist argument that all knowledge is constructed, links between theoretical stance and choice of research methods become clear. If a 'natural science' approach is adopted (as it has been by cognitive psychologists, for example) then quantitative methods such as experiments and questionnaires tend to be favoured because they supposedly produce 'objective' or factual knowledge about the phenomenon in question. Critical social psychology, on the other hand, usually adopts an interpretive or constructionist 'epistemology' (theory of knowledge) and highlights the diversity of perspectives and positions presented in talk – and the interpersonal and social functions that particular accounts serve. For example, a study of national identity could question people from different racial and ethnic backgrounds to identify the range of definitions of nationhood on offer and then link these to distinctive political goals and issues. You could imagine that definitions of 'Irishness' would differ between the North and South of Ireland and between religious and political groups within the island. A preference for 'British' or 'Scots Irish' might be attributed to Northern Protestants and Loyalists in the light of their identification with the UK and historical links with Scottish religion, whilst many Catholics and Republicans might well favour 'Irish' or even 'Celtic' given their aspirations towards Irish unification and the celebration of Gaelic culture.

With the emphasis on language, critical social psychology research often amounts to an examination of 'texts', whether these already exist (e.g. newspaper articles, advertisements, etc.) or are produced by the research process (e.g. interview transcripts, diary sheets, etc.). Data collection then can proceed by a variety of methods, including archival searches, interviews, focus groups, diaries, participant observations and so on. The role of the researcher here tends to be much more involved than the 'detached scientists' mode' favoured by cognitive–experimental social psychology. Thus, observation methods tend to emphasize researcher participation rather than distance – the difference between joining in a group's activities and watching from the sidelines. Also, critical social psychology data collection tends towards less rather than more structured formats, thereby enabling participants to (partially) determine the course of the conversation or activity. In general, then, critical social psychology research aims for an inclusive and engaged approach in order to facilitate the gathering of rich data in which participants have a voice.

In terms of data analysis, the popular preference for critical social psychology is discourse analysis (see Potter, 2007; Parker, 2002). Although there are different forms of discourse analysis and debates around this approach (Hook, 2007; see Chapter 3), the main aim is to carefully examine a text, highlight recurrent patterns of talk and to locate such talk within social and political ideals and practices. A study of motherhood, for example, in which new mothers talk about feeling depressed and unable to cope with parenting, might be used to critique the discourse of motherhood which implies that women are naturally equipped to nurture and train children, with fathers notably absent, presumed working. Comments such as 'I don't feel I can live up to the expectations' and 'It looks easy for most other women' would reinforce this analysis (see Sevón's (2011) paper on the transition to motherhood).

This is not to suggest that qualitative, critical research is straightforward or problem-free. On the contrary, there are numerous practical and theoretical issues to be negotiated when undertaking research of this nature. Because the researcher is involved in data collection and is responsible for interpreting data, accusations of bias and subjectivity would be easy to make. There is difficulty in attempting to generalize findings also, since most qualitative studies involve small numbers because data collection, transcription and analysis are so time-consuming. However, such problems arise only if one subscribes to the natural scientific model which emphasizes neutrality and objectivity. It has been argued that qualitative research represents a distinct form of inquiry and as such requires different criteria to assess quality and validity – and that different qualitative methodologies require different sets of quality criteria (see Elliott *et al.*, 1999; Parker, 2004; Willig, 2008, see chapter 9; Yardley, 2000).

Although we provide a 'methods' chapter in this textbook (Chapter 3), we certainly do not wish to reinforce the traditional separation of theory and method. Our rationale is simply presentational – as students you may well be familiar with this format and we wish therefore to encourage critical comparisons with other texts – and we try to emphasize how theory and methods are related throughout the book.

In this vein it has been suggested that 'the personal' inevitably affects the research process (qualitative *and* quantitative research) in terms of choice of topic, methods adopted, forms of analysis and conclusions reached. Consequently, it is recommended that the researcher makes available his/her position so that the analysis can be judged from an informed perspective – a practice known as 'reflexivity' (see

Finlay & Gough, 2003). Similarly, as much detail as possible about the study is presented so that an assessment of procedures and format can be made – a strategy known as 'transparency'. With this in mind, notions of bias and generalization become meaningless. Such issues are developed and discussed further in Chapter 3. On a final note, it must be stressed that critical work does not necessarily stop at research: there is often a concern with social change, with practical interventions aimed at assisting the oppressed (see Fox *et al.*, 2009). To quote Sloan (2009: 333) once again, 'Critical theorizing addresses the social functions of ideas as well as the effects of practices by attending to the ways in which power works in society'.

Box 1.7 The theory–method connection

Within mainstream psychology, choice of research method/s is framed as a technical matter – the research question simply dictates the most appropriate method/s to be used. If the relationship between extroversion and psychological health is to be investigated, a survey study might well be selected whereby relevant questionnaires are administered to subjects and correlations subsequently computed. If the aim is to predict the effect of one variable X on another variable Y, an experiment might be devised where the two variables are isolated, X systematically altered and the impact on Y observed. But social constructionism suggests that the way the research question is framed in the first place presumes a prior theoretical, and methodological, stance. Questions about relationships between variables suggest a natural scientific 'epistemology' (theory of knowledge), whilst those concerning the experience of, for example, being hospitalized presume a humanistic or phenomenological orientation. In other words, the terminology within the research question follows from a particular worldview and tends to imply specific research methods. A study of the experience of hospitalization will inevitably use methods which allow participants to describe their experience, such as interviews and diary methods. The majority of social psychology textbooks, however, devote a discrete chapter to 'methods', a strategy which gives the impression that theory is separate from choice of method. This creates a problem in that theorizing in 'mainstream psychology tends to focus on its relations to data and does not reflect on how its assumptions might be complicit with forces of domination, oppression, or social exclusion' (Sloan, 2009: 332).

Summary

To sum up, critical social psychology can be viewed as a school of thought operating within and against (social) psychology which prioritizes the study of discourse, power and subjectivity. With some precedents in social psychology but more recently influenced by perspectives such as Marxism, feminism, psychoanalysis and social constructionism, there is an emphasis on locating the individual within society in relation to systems of difference and inequality. Also, power tends to be linked to language and representation ('discourse/s); and there is typically a commitment to developing theory and research which strives to challenge oppression and promote progressive social change.

It is hoped that you have acquired a flavour of critical social psychology from this introductory chapter. Don't worry if you have not understood every point here – it is inevitable that a new and unfamiliar terminology will provoke some confusion and anxiety. In the chapters which follow, the concepts and issues discussed in this chapter will be explored in much more detail using relevant and up-to-date examples gleaned from contemporary critical social psychology research, and important issues and debates will also be covered.

Key references

Annual Review of Critical Psychology (1999–), available online at http://www. discourseunit.com/annual-review/
This series of edited volumes features contributions from critical psychologists across the globe on a range of issues. Each volume is focused on a given theme e.g. action research (2000), anti-capitalism (2003), feminisms (2005) and globalization (2006). Although some chapters are a little difficult to follow, overall this series provides a valuable resource for students of critical psychology.

Cherry, F. (2009). Social Psychology and Social Change. In D. Fox, I. Prilleltensky & S. Austin (eds), *Critical Psychology: An Introduction* (2nd edn, pp. 93–109). Thousand Oaks, CA: Sage.
This chapter provides an accessible and up-to-date introduction to 'critical social psychology' with a particular focus on the issues of reflexivity and critical social psychology's commitment to multiple perspectives. This is compared with 'experimental social psychology' via a re-interpretation of some of its classic studies.

Burr, V. (2003). *Social Constructionism* (2nd edn, pp. 1–27). London: Routledge.
See chapter 1, 'What Is Social Constructionism' .
Another accessible introduction, this time on the key themes within and influences on social constructionism, emphasizing the contrast with 'traditional' psychology.

Parker I.A. (2007). *Revolution in Psychology: Alienation to Emancipation*. London: Pluto Press.
Parker's hard hitting critique deconstructs psychology through a predominantly Marxist lens. The final chapter of the book provides an excellent list of further reading and resources for those wanting to deepen their knowledge in this particular area.

New references

Adorno, T. W., Frenkel-Brunswik, E., Levinson, D. J. & Sanford, R. N. (1950). *The Authoritarian Personality*. New York: Harper and Row.

Arfken, M. (2011). Marxist scholarship and psychological practice. *Annual Review of Critical Psychology, 9*, 6–7.

Bocock, R. (1976). *Freud and Modern Society: An Outline and Analysis of Freud's Sociology*. New York: Holmes and Meier.

Bocock, R. (1993). *Consumption*. London: Routledge.

Bocock, R. (2002). *Sigmund Freud* (2nd edn). London: Routledge.

Brown, P. (ed.) (1973). *Radical Psychology*. New York: Harper and Row.

Burr, V. (2002). *The Person in Social Psychology*. London: Routledge.

Burr, V. (2003). *Social Constructionism* (2nd edn). London: Routledge.

Carlson, S. (2010). In defense of queer kinships: Oedipus recast. *Subjectivity, 3*(3), 263–281.

Clarke, V. & Peel, E. (2007). *Out in Psychology: Lesbian, Gay, Bisexual, Trans and Queer Perspectives*. Chichester, UK: John Wiley & Sons.

Clarke, V., Ellis, S., Peel, E. & Riggs, D. (2010). *Lesbian, Gay, Bisexual, Trans and Queer Psychology: An Introduction*. Cambridge: Cambridge University Press.

Crawford, M. & Unger, R. (2004). *Women and Gender: A Feminist Psychology*. London: McGraw-Hill.

Dafermos, M. & Marvakis, A. (2006). Critiques in Psychology – Critical Psychology. *Annual Review of Critical Psychology, 5*, 1–20.

Dean, M. (2010). *Governmentality: Power and Rule in Modern Society* (2nd edn). London: Sage.

De Beauvoir, S. (1962). *The Second Sex* (H. M. Parshley, Trans.). Harmondsworth, UK: Penguin Classics.

Dua, A. (2006). *Feminist Psychology.* New Delhi: MD Publications.

Elliott, A. M. (2002). *Psychoanalytic Theory: An Introduction* (2nd edn). Basingstoke, UK: Palgrave Macmillan.

Elliott, R., Fischer, C. T. & Rennie, D. L. (1999). Evolving guidelines for publication of qualitative research studies in psychology and related fields. *British Journal of Clinical Psychology, 38*(3), 215–229.

Fine, M. & Torre, M. E. (2006). Intimate details: participatory action research in prison. *Action Research, 4*(3), 253–269.

Finlay, L. & Gough. B. (eds) (2003). *Reflexivity: A Practical Guide for Researchers in Health and Social Science.* Oxford: Blackwell Publishing.

Flowers, P. & Buston, K. (2001). 'I was terrified of being different': exploring gay men's accounts of growing-up in a heterosexist society. *Journal of Adolescence, 24*(1), 51–65.

Fox, D., Prilleltensky, I. & Austin, S. (eds) (2009). *Critical Psychology: An Introduction* (2nd edn). Thousand Oaks, CA: Sage.

Frosh, S. (1989). *Psychoanalysis and Psychology: Minding the Gap.* London: Macmillan.

Frosh, S. (1991). *Identity Crisis: Modernity, Psychoanalysis and the Self.* London: Macmillan.

Frosh, S. (1999). *The Politics of Psychoanalysis.* Basingstoke, UK: Palgrave Macmillan.

Frosh, S. (2010). *Psychoanalysis Outside the Clinic: Interventions in Psychosocial Studies.* Basingstoke, UK: Palgrave Macmillan.

Frosh, S. & Baraitser, L. (2008). Psychoanalysis and psychosocial studies. *Psychoanalysis, Culture and Society, 13*, 346–365.

Fromm, E. (1956/1991). *The Sane Society.* London: Routledge.

Fromm, E. (1961/2004). *Marx's Concept of Man* (T. B. Bottomore, Trans.). London: Continuum.

Gavey, N. (2011). Feminist poststructuralism and discourse analysis revisited. *Psychology of Women Quarterly, 35*(1), 183–188.

Giddens, A. (1991). *Modernity and Self-Identity: Self and Society in the Late Modern Age.* Stanford, CA: Stanford University Press.

Goodley, D. (2010). *Disability Studies: An Interdisciplinary Introduction.* London: Sage.

Habermas, J. (1968/1987). *Knowledge and Human Interests* (J. J. Shapiro, Trans.). Cambridge, UK: Polity.

Hare-Mustin, R. T. & Marecek, J. (2009). Clinical psychology: the politics of madness. In D. Fox, I. Prilleltensky & S. Austin (eds), *Critical Psychology: An Introduction* (2nd edn, pp. 75–92). Thousand Oaks, CA: Sage.

Harvey, D. (2005). *A Brief History of Neoliberalism*. Oxford: Oxford University Press.

Henriques, J. (1984). Social psychology and the politics of racism. In J. Henriques, W. Hollway, C. Urwin, C. Venn & V. Walkerdine (eds), *Changing the Subject: Psychology, Social Regulation and Subjectivity* (pp. 60–89). New York: Methuen & Co.

Henriques, J., Hollway, W., Urwin, C., Venn, C. & Walkerdine, V. (eds) (1984). *Changing the Subject: Psychology, Social Regulation and Subjectivity*. New York: Methuen & Co.

Hepburn, A. (2003). *An Introduction to Critical Social Psychology*. London: Sage.

Hook, D. (2007). *Foucault, Psychology and the Analytics of Power*. Basingstoke, UK: Palgrave Macmillan.

Howarth, C. & Hook, D. (2005). Towards a critical social psychology of racism: points of disruption. *Journal of Community & Applied Social Psychology, 15*(6), 425–431.

Hyde, J. S. & Jaffee, S. R. (2000). Becoming a heterosexual adult: the experiences of young women. *Journal of Social Issues, 56*(2), 283–296.

Ibáñez, T. & Íñiguez, L. (1997). *Critical Social Psychology,* London: Sage.

Ingleby, D. (1972). Ideology and the human sciences: some comments on the role of reification in psychology and psychiatry. In T. Pateman (ed.), *Counter Course: A Handbook for Course Criticism,* Harmondsworth: Penguin.

Kagan, C., Burton, M., Duckett, P., Lawthom, R. and Siddiquee, A. (2011). *Critical Community Psychology: Critical Action and Social Change*. Hoboken, NJ: John Wiley & Sons.

Kitzinger, C. (2002). Doing feminist conversation analysis. In P. McIlvenny (ed.), *Talking Gender and Sexuality* (pp. 49–78). Amsterdam: John Benjamins Publishing.

Klein, M. (1952). The origins of transference. *International Journal of Psychoanalysis, 33*, 433–438.

Laing, R. D. (1967). *The Politics of Experience and the Bird of Paradise*. Harmondsworth, UK: Penguin.

Lasch, C. (1979). *The Culture of Narcissism: American Life in An Age of Diminishing Expectations*. New York: W.W. Norton & Company.

Layton, L. (2008). What divides the subject? Psychoanalytic reflections on subjectivity, subjection and resistance. *Subjectivity*, *22*(1), 60–72.

Lyons, A. C. & Willott, S.A. (2008). Alcohol consumption, gender identities and women's changing social positions. *Sex Roles*, *59*, 694–712.

Marcuse, H. (1964/2002). *One Dimensional Man: Studies in the Ideology of Advanced Industrial Society*. London: Routledge.

Hare-Mustin, R. T. & Marecek, J. (2009). Clinical psychology: the politics of madness. In D. Fox, I. Prilleltensky and S. Austin (eds), *Critical Psychology: An Introduction* (pp. 75–92). London: Sage.

Maze, J. R. (2001). Social constructionism, deconstructionism and some requirements of discourse. *Theory & Psychology*, *7*(3), 393–417.

McDermott, E. (2006). Surviving in dangerous places: lesbian identity performances in the workplace, social class and psychological health. *Feminism & Psychology*, *16*(2), 193–211.

McDonald, M., Wearing, S. and Ponting, J. (2008). Narcissism and neoliberalism: work, leisure and alienation in an era of consumption. *Loisir et Societe (Society and Leisure)*, *30*(1), 489–510.

McKinlay, A. and McVittie, C. (2008). *Social Psychology and Discourse*. Oxford: Wiley-Blackwell.

Ostrove, J. M. and Cole, E. R. (2003). Privileging class: toward a critical psychology of social class in the context of education. *Journal of Social Issues*, *59*(4), 677–692.

Pakulski, J. and Waters, M. (1996). *The Death of Class*. London: Sage.

Parker, I. (ed.). (2002). *Critical Discursive Psychology*. Basingstoke, UK: Palgrave Macmillan.

Parker, I. (2004). Criteria for qualitative research in psychology. *Qualitative Research in Psychology*, *1*(2), 95–106.

Parker, I. (2011). Discursive social psychology now. *British Journal of Social Psychology*, DOI: 10.1111/j.2044–8309.2011.02046.x

Plummer, D. (1999). *One of the Boys: Masculinity, Homophobia, and Modern Manhood*. London: Routledge.

Potter, J. (ed.). (2007). *Discourse and Psychology: Theory and Method* (Vol. 1). London: Sage.

Potter, J. (ed.). (2007). *Discourse and Psychology: Discourse and Social Psychology* (Vol. 2). London: Sage.

Potter, J. (ed.). (2007). *Discourse and Psychology: Discursive Psychology* (Vol. 3). London: Sage.

Ramazanoglu, C. & Holland, J. (eds). (2002). *Feminist Methodology: Challenges and Choices*. London: Sage.

Scharff, C. (2011). 'It is a colour thing and a status thing, rather than a gender thing': negotiating difference in talk about feminism. *Feminism & Psychology, 21*(4), 458–476.

Segal, L. (1999). *Why Feminism? Gender, Psychology and Power*. Cambridge, UK: Polity.

Sevón, E. (2011). 'My life has changed, but his life hasn't': making sense of the gendering of parenthood during the transition to motherhood. *Feminism & Psychology, 22*(1), 60–80.

Sloan, T. (2009). Doing theory. In D. Fox, I. Prilleltensky & S. Austin (eds), *Critical Psychology: An Introduction* (2nd edn, pp. 319–334). Thousand Oaks, CA: Sage.

Speer, S. A. (2000). Let's get real? Feminism, constructionism and the realism/relativism debate. *Feminism & Psychology, 10*(4), 519–530.

Terry, G. & Braun, V. (2012). Sticking my finger up at evolution: unconventionality, selfishness, and choice in the talk of men who have had 'preemptive' vasectomies. *Men and Masculinities, 15*(3), 207–229.

Tuffin, K. (2004). *Understanding Critical Social Psychology*. London: Sage.

Unger, R. K. (1996). Using the master's tools: epistemology and empiricism. In S. Wilkinson (ed.), *Feminist Social Psychologies: International Perspectives*, Buckingham: Open University Press.

Wearing, S., McDonald, M. & Wearing, M. (in press). Consumer culture, the mobilisation of the narcissistic self, and adolescent deviant leisure. *Leisure Studies*.

Wetherell, M., Taylor, S. & Yates, S. J. (eds). (2001). *Discourse as Data: A Guide for Analysis* London: Sage.

Wetherell, M., Taylor, S. & Yates, S. J. (eds). (2001). *Discourse Theory and Practice: A Reader*. London: Sage.

Weatherall, A. (2011). Discursive psychology and feminism, *British Journal of Social Psychology*, DOI: 10.1111/j.2044–8309.2011.02062.x

Williams, R. (2009). The health experiences of African-Carribean and white working-class fathers. In B. Gough & S. Robertson (eds), *Men, Masculinities & Health: Critical Perspectives*. Basingstoke, UK: Palgrave Macmillan.

Williams, J. & Lykes, M. B. (2003). Bridging theory and practice: using reflexive cycles in feminist participatory action research. *Feminism & Psychology, 13*(3), 287–294.

Willig, C. (2008). *Introducing Qualitative Research in Psychology* (2nd edn). Maidenhead, UK: Open University Press.

Wowk, M. T. (2007). Kitzinger's feminist conversation analysis: critical observations. *Human Studies*, *30*(2), 131–155.

Yardley, L. (2000). Dilemmas in qualitative health research. *Psychology and Health*, *15*, 215–228.

Zizek, S. (2000). *The Spectre Is Still Roaming Around*. Zagreb: Arkzin.

A Critical Look at Cognitive– Experimental Social Psychology

2

This chapter will highlight the:

- Historical emergence of social psychology
- Humanistic 'crisis' within the discipline
- Rise of cognitive social psychology
- Attempt to produce a distinctive European social psychology
- Analysis of social psychology as social control
- Virtues of a critical social psychology.

Introduction

Having been introduced to critical social psychology, it is important now to place it in the context of social psychology as a whole. As stated in Chapter 1, critical social psychology represents a relatively recent school of thought whilst social psychology as a discrete discipline has been in existence for over a hundred years! Of course, over the years the form/s of social psychology have fluctuated as new perspectives and topics have been taken up and later overtaken by different concerns. Yet, throughout, much social psychological theory and research has been underpinned by common assumptions. For example, a prevailing view in the mainstream is that social psychology is a science which studies the effects of social factors on the individual. According to Baron and Byrne's (1999: 6) definition, for example, social psychology is 'the scientific field that seeks to understand the nature and causes of individual behaviour and thought in social situations'. This echoes an earlier definition put forward by Floyd Allport in his seminal 1924 textbook *Social Psychology*, in which he states: 'There is no psychology of groups which is not essentially and entirely a psychology of individuals' (cited in Hogg & Vaughan, 2005, p. 116). This dominant orientation has informed the largely quantitative research conducted and the emphasis on the individual as the key unit of analysis. For example, experimental studies of 'social facilitation' have sought to measure the effects of the presence of other people on an individual's performance (e.g. Zajonc, 1965).

During the late 1960s and early 1970s many social psychologists became dissatisfied with the discipline's near obsession with quantification and its perceived irrelevance to ordinary people's lives, a period widely depicted as a 'crisis' for social psychology (see Armistead, 1974). There was a subsequent humanistic call for research which would explore the social relations and meanings used by people in daily interaction. Apart from a certain degree of methodological change, however, no great or lasting impact was made on mainstream social psychology, which by this time had embraced the cognitive revolution; more recently social psychologists have been influenced by developments in cognitive neuroscience (see Harmon-Jones & Devine, 2003). Indeed, a European focus on inter-group phenomena, which began by addressing the social dimensions to identity and relationships, proceeded to reduce the level of analysis to cognitive processes. Hence the contemporary focus on 'social cognition', on how the human mind processes 'social' information in predictable (but flawed) ways. This recent history of social psychology is recounted below and the contemporary preoccupation with matters inside people's heads criticized. A critical social psychology analysis is then developed which situates the disciplinary focus on cognition in relation to wider cultural discourses and institutions implicated in social influence and control. The chapter ends by reaffirming the case for a social psychology which is genuinely social and which engages critically with society.

The historical emergence of social psychology

The roots of (social) psychology have been traced back to Greek and Roman civilization, but most writers focus on the modern age, dated roughly from the mid-1600s to the twentieth century (see Jahoda, 2007: Sahakian, 1982; Still, 1996). The philosophy of Descartes (1596–1650) in particular is pinpointed as an important foundation. Briefly, Descartes argued for a separation between mind and body – the 'Cartesian' split – and that human reason and experience can be used to gain knowledge about the world. This call to 'empiricism' (or 'scientific' data collection) has been enthusiastically embraced by modern social psychologists.

A scientific enterprise

(Social) psychology as a separate discipline is typically traced back to the mid nineteenth century, a period characterized as a time of great social and scientific change. The modern or 'enlightenment' philosophy underlying this upheaval centres on scientific reason, progress and liberal humanism (Parker, 1989). In other words, there was a march towards building 'civilization', advancing society beyond the superstition, stagnation and irrationality which was said to characterize earlier 'darker' periods. As Gergen (2010: 68) notes, 'the transformation from the medieval to the "modern" world was dependent upon a radical reconstruction of the concept of the person. In place of spirit or soul, the capacity for rational thought became the focal ingredient of the self.'

The discoveries and successes of the physical (natural) sciences at this time made a great impression on philosophers, who were moved to abandon speculation in favour of a more applied analysis of the human condition. Although 'introspection' – the disciplined examination of one's consciousness (e.g. phenomenology) – was emerging as a tool for investigating the human mind, the rigour and precision offered by the methods of the natural sciences proved irresistible in the quest for knowledge about human behaviour. Indeed, the utilitarian philosopher J.S. Mill positively urged human science to embrace scientific principles and methods (see Hammersley, 1989).

The nascent discipline of (social) psychology was concerned to distinguish itself from 'unscientific' philosophical or everyday thinking, deemed partial, contradictory and inadequate (although the alleged superiority of social psychological terminology is disputed in a recent article by Billig [2011]). For example, note the conflict between the following two proverbs: 'absence makes the heart grow fonder' and 'familiarity breeds contempt'. A primary function advertised by (social) psychology was the capability of 'testing' opposing ideas under scientific conditions in order to establish the circumstances under which specific principles applied. Perhaps it would find 'absence makes the heart grow fonder' more relevant for romantic relationships, and 'familiarity breeds contempt' more appropriate for relationships with work colleagues or family members. At any rate, the rise of 'behaviourism' was set in motion, with a focus on visible, concrete behaviours amenable to observation, measurement and analysis rather than the intangible activities of the mind. Stainton-Rogers *et al.* (1995) speak about a shift from nineteenth-century engineering to twentieth-century 'humaneering'. A study by Norman Triplett in 1898 on the influence of other people on sporting performance is widely cited as the first social psychology experiment (Box 2.1).

So, mainstream social psychology adopted a scientific model and indeed continues to employ quantitative experimental methods to investigate the behaviour of individuals in social situations. Quite often, social psychologists attempt to reproduce specific social scenarios in the laboratory, so that particular variables are more easily isolated and controlled for study. For example, to study conformity, Asch (1952) famously exposed subjects to a condition in which they experienced social pressure to go against the evidence of their senses concerning various comparisons of line length (many 'subjects' were confederates of the experimenter and were instructed to give incorrect answers – see Chapter 4).

Box 2.1   The first social psychology experiment? (Triplett, 1898)

Norman Triplett's (1898) paper 'The Dynamogenic Factors in Pacemaking and Competition' is widely cited as the earliest publication in social psychology. Whilst studying the official bicycle records from the Racing Board of the League of American Wheelmen for the 1897 season, he realized that those cyclists who competed against others performed better than those who cycled alone against the clock. Triplett attributed this phenomenon to the energizing force of competition, a hypothesis which he tested by observing children winding up a fishing reel, both alone and in conjunction with others. He found that, on average, winding time was faster when the children worked side by side rather than alone. This study has proved influential on subsequent 'social facilitation' research, although the effects of other people on performance have been found to be variable (see Zajonc, 1965).

Sometimes social psychologists venture into the 'field' and attempt to manipulate elements of naturally occurring situations. For example, to study altruistic behaviour, a confederate would assume various guises on a train (tramp, businessperson, etc.) and feign some seizure or collapse whilst psychologists recorded the responses of bystanders

(Latane & Darley, 1970). Or studying prejudice at a US summer camp for boys by dividing them into distinct groups and then observing aspects of in-group formation, the development of social hierarchies, inter-group conflict and intergroup integration (Sherif & Sherif, 1953). In each of these research situations, the experimenter controls aspects of the environment and measures or observes the resulting responses of the often unwitting subjects. Experiments remain very popular as a tool for social psychological investigation, although other quantitative (e.g. questionnaires) and qualitative (e.g. interviews) methods are also used, occasionally together.

CRITICAL THINKING BOX: ON SCIENTIFIC PSYCHOLOGY

Since its inception, (social) psychology has attempted to emulate the philosophy and methods of natural science. But can human activities be captured sufficiently by scientific methods (e.g. experiments, questionnaires)? Give examples of human behaviours which can and cannot be measured, predicted and controlled.

The above account clearly emphasizes the dominance of quantitative or experimental traditions within social psychology. Whilst such practices have largely shaped the character of modern social psychology, it is also important to highlight other, more 'social' approaches. The early work of Wundt in the late 1800s, for example, pioneered a form of 'volkerpsychologie', a study of the cultural understandings and practices which informed human consciousness. Dilthey founded the hermeneutic (or interpretative) school, proposing a psychology which examined 'the systems of culture, commerce, law, religion, art and scholarship and the outer organization of society in family, community, church and state' (1976: 90, cited in Still, 1996; see also Richardson & Fowers, 2010). This emphasis on societal relations and systems of meaning was taken up by other prominent figures such as George Herbert Mead and John Dewey during the early decades of the twentieth century. Both Mead and Dewey were forerunners of 'symbolic interactionism' a theoretical approach that gained popularity in sociology and sociological social psychology (Lindesmith et al., 1999: 11–15). As noted in Chapter 1, Sigmund Freud was also interested in psychosexual socialization and his work was adopted to further understand the origins and persistence of fascist ideology (e.g. Adorno et al., 1950). But such contributions were eventually marginalized by mainstream social psychology in favour of a scientific approach to the study of self-contained individuals (Greenwood, 2000). Nonetheless, social psychology has also been interested in exploring, understanding and 'solving' social problems, as the next section suggests.

Addressing social problems

The social psychological pursuit of knowledge could not be accurately described as an impartial, scientific endeavour, for there was and is a great concern with tackling social issues and improving the individual's quality of life. This orientation can be found in Comte during the mid nineteenth century (see Box 2.2), who proclaimed that the then emerging science of 'la morale' would combine biological with sociological knowledge to help explain and provide solutions to moral problems in society. The view that there is nothing as practical as a good theory has often been cited and there have been repeated calls to 'give psychology away' to the people (Miller, 1969). In this sense, there is a departure from a purely scientific or objective approach as particular values (human betterment, equality, etc.) are adopted. This focus is emphasized in textbooks, where a major aim of social psychology is to 'seek out sound knowledge of human nature' in order to 'make social institutions and practices better suited to human needs' (Tiffin *et al.*, 1940: 23), or to consider 'how such (social psychological) knowledge might be used to alleviate some of the problems plaguing us in the world today' (Aronson, 1988: preface) (both cited in Stainton-Rogers *et al.*, 1995). One of the objectives of the Social Psychology Section of the British Psychological Society is to 'Promote social psychological responses to social problems at national and international level' (see http://socpsy.bps.org.uk/socpsy/info/info_home.cfm). If you were to browse issues of major mainstream social psychology journals (e.g. *Journal of Experimental Social Psychology*; *European Journal of Social Psychology*; *British Journal of Social Psychology*) you would encounter research on various social issues, such as immigration, prosocial behaviour, aggression, inter-group conflict, sexism and minority group experiences. The rise of 'positive psychology' (e.g. Seligman & Csikszentmihalyi, 2000; Seligman, 2003) is also worth noting here, a movement explicitly dedicated to enhancing individual wellbeing and the social institutions that support it. Within such initiatives, and in the pages of social psychology textbooks, social agendas are tackled as if they were easy to isolate, measure and resolve by means of scientific methods. Stainton-Rogers *et al.* (1995) liken this 'liberal humanistic' endeavour to missionary evangelizing, in which the social psychologist is depicted as holding or discovering the 'truth' and redeeming society with it.

Box 2.2   Social psychology as moral crusade

Throughout the twentieth century social psychology has painted itself as socially responsive and responsible. According to Gergen (1973), the subject-matter of social psychology has often been dictated by prevailing social issues. For example, the horrors of the Second World War prompted much research on social influence (obedience, conformity, compliance), a key question being how people could be persuaded or coerced to co-operate in the extermination of specific social groups (e.g. Milgram, 1974). Similarly, a research programme on altruism was engendered by media coverage of the lack of public intervention in the course of the murder of a young woman (Kitty Genovese) – 'bystander apathy' (Latane & Darley, 1970). Social issues have figured prominently in the social psychological literature, covering a range of topics, including prejudice and discrimination (racism, sexism, homophobia, etc.), marital breakdown, eyewitness testimony and interpersonal violence. In addition to focusing on addressing social problems, social psychologists are now also engaged in improving positive subjective experiences and positive individual traits (Seligman & Czikszentmihayli, 2000), echoing earlier preoccupations of humanistic psychologists (e.g. Maslow, Rogers). Implicit in such work is the image of the social psychologist as a concerned expert, eager and qualified to 'make a difference' to the world through the application of first-rate 'scientific' knowledge and techniques.

But in studying and accounting for social problems, *individual* factors tend to be emphasized. For example, research on occupational discrimination against woman (lower salaries, less status, etc., compared to men) has focused on women themselves rather than prevailing sexist norms and practices. Thus, women have been found to hold lower career expectations than men, a finding related to numerous other factors, such as:

- women anticipate taking more time off work than men;
- they recognize the 'reality' of unequal pay and conditions more than do men;

- they perceive relatively low levels of pay as more fair than do men, and
- they compare themselves more with other women rather than men. (Jackson *et al.*, 1992)

Somewhat ironically for research on sexism, it is women who are virtually held responsible for inequitable and seemingly unchangeable working practices! The preoccupation with individual factors (expectations, cognitions, etc.) rather than social factors (institutions, norms, etc.) is developed and criticized in the next section.

CRITICAL THINKING BOX: SOCIAL PROBLEMS

Looking at the various topics studied by social psychologists suggests a desire to address social issues such as aggression, racism, stereotyping and stress. Yet research and theories tend to focus on individual characteristics (such as personality traits) and cognitions rather than social, cultural, political or economic factors. Consider one social problem such as aggression or sexism and discuss the various individual and social factors that might be involved. Which explanation/s seem more plausible?

A study of individuals

In the ways social psychology defines and studies 'social' phenomena, society often becomes invisible or constant in favour of a focus on and vocabulary of individual behaviour. The 'social' is reduced to that which can be easily observed or measured, including:

- the presence of others (in altruism research, a key variable is the number of people present which deters the subject from responding altruistically to a person in need);
- the small group (the identification of 'task-centred' and 'people-centred' leaders has proved a popular research project);
- social/cultural categories (many 'traits' and behaviours have been examined in terms of differences between men and women, distinct age groups, nationalities, subcultures, etc.).

Those aspects of society considered too complex or ambiguous to quantify – 'sociological' concepts such as power, ideology, discourse, social relations and institutional practices – are overlooked and projected on to other social science disciplines. In striving to isolate and measure particular concrete aspects of the social situation and individual responses to these, 'social' psychological research manufactures and promotes a de-socialized conception of the individual. As Kvale (1992) notes, culture is taken as accidental and local, while psychological processes are depicted as fixed and universal. The individual is prioritized, but the image of the individual is of a rather passive and simplistic stimulus-response machine.

The following study (Box 2.3) is an example of social psychological research which uses social categories but which fails to analyse the social meanings which impinge on, in this case, gender. Although the testosterone–aggression relationship was found to apply to both sexes, the fact that testosterone is a 'male' sex hormone means that men are more likely to aggress.

Box 2.3 Sex differences in aggression: individual biology over society

Although social psychologists acknowledge the role of social situational factors in explanations of aggression, research continues which also stresses biological influences. In particular, the notion that there are (natural) sex differences between men and women in levels of violence persists. For example, research by Harris *et al.* (1996) investigated the role of 'sex hormones' in aggression. Participants were firstly required to complete questionnaires designed to measure tendencies to behave aggressively and tendencies to be helpful and nurturing in a range of situations. Items used to indicate aggression included: 'I have trouble controlling my temper' and 'If somebody hits me, I hit back', whilst items used to record prosocial behaviour included: 'I often take people under my wing' and 'I like helping other people'. The researchers also obtained two measures of testosterone, a 'male' sex hormone. The results depicted a correlation between testosterone and aggression, with higher levels associated with aggressive tendencies and lower levels with more prosocial behaviours – for both sexes. It was also found that increases in testosterone accompanied instances of aggression, suggesting a causal rather than merely correlational relationship.

But cultural practices and norms around masculinity and femininity are not taken into account, such as the greater power and privilege afforded many men and the reinforcement they receive for being 'tough' and unemotional. Instead, mainstream social psychologists often treat social categories and the alleged differences between them as neutral and constant when, in fact, groups who differ according to gender, race, sexuality, social class, etc. are represented and treated in different and complex ways in society in the first place. Critical social psychology argues that the discourses and practices around social identities need to be acknowledged – and challenged – by social psychologists.

To reiterate, mainstream social psychology has so far been characterized and criticized as a scientific endeavour interested in addressing social issues but doing so from a stance of individualism. The tension between the 'scientific' (technical, value-free) and 'applied' (practical, humanistic) concerns of the discipline have also been highlighted. A debate between these two strands has continued throughout recent times, although the mid-century brought with it some disappointment that theoretical developments were being neglected in favour of pragmatic questions. Brewster-Smith (1983) and Pancer (1997) have argued that the subsequent post-war lapse in applied social psychology in favour of technical and theoretical questions facilitated the image of social psychology as a pure science, a more powerful and privileged position where issues around theory, measurement and methodology were prioritized. But this orientation within the discipline soon generated an amount of dissatisfaction, as the next section discusses.

The humanistic 'crisis'

Although alternative approaches within and outside mainstream social psychology did exist, it was during the late 1960s and early 1970s when criticism became more vociferous and organized, with objections raised in particular about the perceived irrelevance of social psychology to people's lives (see Armistead, 1974; Ring, 1967; Silverman, 1977). This problem was clearly evident in social psychology's failure to account for social forces such as class, discourse and ideology in its understanding of social behaviour. Moscovici (1972) notes:

social class structure, the phenomenon of language, the influence of ideas about society, all appear critically important and claim priority in the analysis of 'collective' conduct though they hardly make an appearance in contemporary social psychology. (20)

There were also concerns about the artificial and highly technical nature of social psychological investigation, the outcome of which was described variously as 'elegantly polished triviality' (Allport, 1968: 29) and, in the words of Toffler (1981: 141–142), 'obsessive emphasis on quantified detail without context, on progressively finer and finer measurement of smaller and smaller problems, leaves us knowing more and more about less and less'. Kline (1988) remarks that the nature of experimental (social) psychology tends to attract neurotic introverts who happily detach themselves from emotional and social contexts! Indeed these criticisms have continued unabated. For example, Hill (2006: 625) questions social psychology's focus on building empirically valid theory when such theory is trivial and does nothing to resolve social problems (see also Pancer, 1997).

As a result of such observations there was something of a clamour for different approaches which could enable the exploration and further understanding of individuals and groups in more natural-istic ways (e.g. Gross, 1974). The focus of this critique then largely centred on method, with orthodox quantitative methods regarded as constraining participants in the push for numerical data. Methods such as experiments and questionnaires were considered to limit individual choice, as subjects were required to select responses from a preordained list or task.

Pausing to reflect on the social psychology experiment, it becomes clear that the typical subject is placed in a strange environment with limited knowledge about the purpose of the study and is instructed to perform often bizarre tasks, the outcomes of which are rarely made known to them. In contrast, the experimenter is aware, active and dynamic in the research process and is in a more powerful position (Jourard, 1972). The subject's own understanding of the situation is neglected and marshalled into the experimenter's cul-de-sac of meanings and measurements (Brannigan, 2004; Brown, 1980). This selective focus on particular variables and their effects led to the charge of 'determinism', i.e. the containment of individual freedom in the experimental situation. The related charge of 'reductionism' referred to the subsequent explanations of behaviour, usually linking complex human phenomena, which are reduced down to a few quantifiable variables. Or put another way, social psychologists sought to under-stand and explain human behaviour by reducing it down to cognitive, physiological or neurological factors (Lindesmith et al., 1999: 23–24).

Consequently, a new improved social psychology was sought. In particular, qualitative methods were advocated as more worthwhile, interesting, relevant and providing greater depth in the understanding social behaviour. Methods such as participant observation, in-depth interviews, role-playing, repertory grids, discourse analysis etc. were favoured as they allowed for a focus on meaning and experience. An interest in studying the rules and roles which people negotiated in real life settings developed under the umbrella of 'ethogenics' (Harré & Secord, 1972; see Box 2.4). Central to this framework is the notion that behaviour, or action, can be explained in terms of the actor's 'social competence', i.e. the knowledge an individual possesses about what is appropriate to do or say in distinct social situations. This approach draws heavily from (micro)sociology (e.g. Garfinkel, 1967; Goffman, 1959) and is concerned to study the conventions adhered to by social actors in their everyday settings. It is the task of the ethogenicist to elicit the nature of the (often implicit) norms which prompt action, typically by examining the actors' accounts. Such accounts are located in various 'texts', including interview transcripts, newspaper clippings, diaries and observational notes.

Box 2.4   An ethogenic approach to football violence (Marsh et al., 1978)

The hypothesis here was that even such apparently disordered behaviour as that perceived on football terraces was structured by underlying rules. A body of accounts was analysed, comprising interviews and conversations with fans as well as video recordings of behaviour on the terraces. Following analysis, two types of account were identified, one stressing disorder and violence, the other order and safety. It was concluded that both types of accounting were necessary for the fans' behaviour: on the one hand an image of excitement and risk could be sustained by stories of aggression, whilst on the other hand talk of safety reinforced the perception that injury was unlikely. With the benefit of the observational data which depicted few scenes of violence, it was argued that the safety account was 'correct', whereas the violence account was merely a constructed version of reality which functioned to promote certain positive images of the fans (as tough, adventurous, etc.).

CRITICAL THINKING BOX: THE SUBJECT-MATTER OF SOCIAL PSYCHOLOGY

The ethogenic approach suggests that social psychologists should direct their attention towards the meanings and practices which people negotiate in everyday life. What are the advantages and disadvantages of this form of research compared to the examination of behavioural responses in a laboratory setting?

However, such work has remained at the margins of the discipline, as concepts such as meaning and perception were assimilated by the burgeoning (social) cognitive approach and reconfigured as internal phenomena ('scripts', 'schemas', etc.) governed by a central processing mechanism. This fact was lamented in the late 1970s when it was recognized that social psychology had largely failed to become more relevant: 'psychology failed for being ahistorical, for not applying to itself the standards it applied to others, for fancying itself value-free, and for continuing indulgence in the Newtonian fantasy' (Leahey, 1992: 481).

The rise of cognitive social psychology

With the advent of computers, (social) psychological attention shifted from behaviour back to mind again and the investigation of mental or cognitive processes. Greenwood (2004a: 239) notes:

> Social cognition (became) the dominant topic of conferences in the late 1970s, and of edited collections in the early 1980s. Fiske and Taylor's definitive text *Social Cognition* came out in 1982. In the early 1980s the journal *Social Cognition* was instituted, along with the 'Attitudes and Social Cognition' section of the *Journal for Personality and Social Psychology.*

This newly instituted cognitive approach did not, however, signal a return to introspective approaches aimed at understanding consciousness; rather, cognitive processes were defined as discrete mental entities such as attitudes, schemas and beliefs, which were made amendable to quantitative measurement using instruments

46

such as questionnaires, tests and experimental tasks. This 'social cognition' approach continues to dominate social psychology in the United States, Canada and Australia as all manner of topics from the self to prejudice and aggression are interpreted in terms of cognitive concepts. Hogg and Vaughan (2005) note:

> It [social cognition] has taught us much about how we process and store information about people, and how this affects the way we perceive and interact with people. It has also taught us new methods and techniques for conducting social psychological research – methods and techniques borrowed from cognitive psychology and then refined for social psychology. (42)

In order to test hypotheses about cognitive processes, subjects are typically presented with information from which they have to make judgements about people and situations. They might be asked to attribute the 'cause' of a particular action (internal or external?), remember as much as they can about a story read some time before (which details are omitted, distorted, etc.?), decide which candidate to employ from a selection of curricula vitae (does gender/race/sexuality, etc. of 'candidate' influence choice?) and so on.

Often this work 'demonstrates' various 'errors' or 'biases' in human thinking which social psychologists attribute to 'cognitive heuristics' or information-processing 'rules of thumb' which we access to make decisions. Brehm *et al.* (2005) provide a table of the main types with accompanying descriptions and examples (see Box 2.5).

Interesting and creative though many of these experiments are, the cognitive model can be subjected to the humanistic criticisms levelled at previous behaviourist-dominated versions of social psychology. The 'scientific' orientation within social cognition again means a preoccupation with measurable responses from subjects who have little awareness of the research aims. This emphasis on method therefore treats individuals and their minds as objects which can be isolated and their activities recorded under various predetermined conditions. In this way cognitive social psychologists subscribe to methodological behaviourism, with the processes of perception often reduced to biological or computational models (see Gergen, 1989).

Also, the overwhelming focus on cognitive biases, shortcuts and errors establishes a contrast between faulty, irrational human thinking and correct, logical scientific thinking. Given that cognitive social psychologists adopt a scientific posture we can presume that they exempt themselves from the mundane mistakes committed by the lay person's mind. Again there is this distinction in operation between 'ordinary' and 'scientific/psychological' reasoning which privileges the latter and therefore helps reinforce the expert status of the discipline (see Stainton-Rogers *et al.*, 1995).

Box 2.5   Evidence of faulty human thinking (Brehm et al., 2005)

In their textbook on social psychology, Brehm *et al.* (2005) outline a number of heuristics or cognitive shortcuts which people are said to use to simplify social perception. Three such heuristics are detailed below.

Representativeness refers to the tendency to assume, despite compelling odds to the contrary, that someone belongs to a particular group because s/he resembles or 'represents' a typical member of that group. For example, a study by Kahneman and Tversky (1973) found that people who read about a conservative man who enjoys maths puzzles and has no interest in social or political issues guess that s/he is an engineer rather than a lawyer – even though s/he was said to be randomly selected from a group containing 70 lawyers and 30 engineers.

Framing refers to the tendency to be influenced by the way something is presented or 'framed'. For example, Levin *et al.* (1988) found that people are more likely to recommend a new medical treatment if described as having a 50 per cent success rate rather than a 50 per cent failure rate.

Simulation refers to the tendency to predict and explain the outcome of an event on the basis of how easy it is to imagine an alternative script or 'simulations' of that event. For example, Miller *et al.* (1990) found that when people hear that a passenger was killed in an airline crash, they find the death more tragic if the person had just switched from another flight ('if only ...') than if they think that the person scheduled for weeks to take the trip.

CRITICAL THINKING BOX: COGNITION

Social cognition research highlights various shortcuts and 'errors' deployed by individuals under specific experimental conditions. But is it important that the human mind is not completely 'scientific' or logical? Discuss!

Critical writers have in fact pointed to the 'language games' deployed by psychologists in the promotion of their work as scientific; many scientists have been found guilty of persisting with beliefs/hypotheses even when the evidence does not support these (see Kuhn, 1970). Finally, the focus on individuals – or individuals' thought processes – makes for a de-socialized discipline where social relationships and practices surrounding the individual are obscured.

This tendency to reduce people to the effects of psycho-biological processes is perhaps most vividly illustrated today by the rise of social neuroscience. The focus here is on areas of the brain and how they are activated in response to individual and social activities, from playing a musical instrument in a band, meditating, kissing a loved one or doing an exam (Harmon-Jones & Devine, 2003; Ochsner & Lieberman, 2001). Neuroscientists use sophisticated brain scanning equipment such as EEG (electroencephalography) and fMRI (functional magnetic resonance imaging) to investigate which elements of the brain 'light up' when people are engaged in a particular activity – and, in the case of neurologically impaired patients, which elements of the brain are damaged. The assumption is that brain processes and structures are intimately involved in shaping behaviours, emotions, and even personality and gender.

This type of research has attracted a lot of media attention in recent years, but also a lot of criticism, both from outside and inside neuroscience (see for example Chapter 7, Box 7.1, Neurosexism). Some critics object to the reduction of complex human activity and behaviour to brain patterns, while others reject the absence of personal responsibility if behaviour can be explained (and excused) in terms of the workings of the brain. Critical psychologists have engaged in these debates, echoing such criticisms but also discussing emerging collaborations between neuroscience and social psychology (see Cromby, 2007; Cromby et al., 2011). Similarly, Gergen (2012: 144–145) argues that the rise of social neuroscience along with the cognitive revolution in psychology, the dominance of experimental methods and disciplinary divisioning are all part of the on-going trend in social psychology to ensure the prioritization of psychological explanations over social ones.

A European social psychology

In the UK and Europe, however, there have been attempts since the 1960s to forge a uniquely Euro-centric social psychology interested in the individual-in-society. Spearheaded by figures such as Marie Jahoda and Henri Tajfel, the ethos of this movement is summed up by Jaspers (1986):

> Social psychology needed another forum, intellectually independent from the one provided by our colleagues in the U.S. ... (3)

> which must include a direct concern between individual psychological functioning and large-scale social processes which shape this functioning and are shaped by it ... (10)

> should not ideas, problems, issues come first? Perhaps this is in part where the difference in focus between European and North American social psychology is to be found. The most noticeable contributions to European social psychology ... took on problems of a much wider scope. (14)

Two influential contributions to this distinctive Anglo–European social psychology are Social Identity Theory (e.g. Tajfel, 1978) and the Theory of Social Representations (e.g. Moscovici, 1981). Both perspectives will be summarized to provide a flavour of apparently more social forms of social psychology, although it will be argued that particular assumptions and methods adopted undermine claims for alternative, social analysis.

Social Identity Theory (SIT)

The theory (e.g. Tajfel, 1978; Hogg, 2006) distinguishes social from personal identity, defining the former as those aspects of self based upon their social group/category membership (e.g. membership of a profession, sporting team, family, school, subculture and/or nationality) with the latter referring to individual traits. It is also assumed that personal and social identities are context-dependent such that they generate diverse forms of action, that is, interpersonal and intergroup activities respectively. Further, it is asserted that everyone has an interest in preserving and enhancing self-esteem and the theory concentrates on how group members work to promote a positive image of their group – and by implication, themselves. Acknowledging that societies contain many groups perceived to occupy different social positions, the theory suggests that membership of 'subordinate' groups will impact negatively on self-esteem, and vice versa. As a result, group members will act to either maintain or improve the status quo, and several strategies are reported.

For example, if social mobility is thought feasible, the individual may attempt to pass into a higher status group. Such an individualistic measure will be encouraged by the dominant group since it leaves the inter-group status quo unchanged – and therefore the superior position of the dominant group. Alternatively, if inter-group boundaries are perceived to be tight, minority group measures such as social creativity may be adopted, whereby inter-group comparison dimensions might be changed (e.g. using sporting prowess instead of economic success) or other social groups chosen for comparison ('at least we're not as poor as them' etc.). Social competition might also be taken on as a strategy and can range from political protest and passive resistance to physical damage and terrorism. In contrast, the dominant group will counter any threats to its position by re-emphasizing traditional justifications of the status quo and deploying fresh defences (see Hogg & Abrams, 1988).

With this inter-group focus, SIT has sought to locate the individual within social processes. However, in many respects the theory can be criticized for perpetuating some of the problems it sought to overcome. For example, an image of the individual as mechanically responding to social conditions and cognitive structures is presented, thereby echoing the determinism inherent in US cognitive–experimental research. And despite a professed interest in the social dimension of identity and experience, much SIT research has been conducted in the laboratory using the 'minimal group paradigm', whereby subjects are arranged into artificial groups and their biased in-group behaviours recorded (e.g. Tajfel & 1973). Jenkins (2008) notes:

> despite Tajfel's original ambitions, 'social identity theory' remains an individualist perspective: groups are, at best, taken for granted as simplified and reified features of the human landscape, actual interaction is largely ignored, and identification appears to take place solely 'inside people heads'. (115)

When relevant work has been conducted in the field, some of the theory's assumptions have been found wanting in the light of social complexity and flexibility. For example, evidence of communal and co-operative behaviour in women's groups casts SIT as a male-centred and simplistic framework (Williams, 1984), whilst research on the Northern Irish conflict points to diverse and inconsistent use of meanings and practices around key 'identities', such as 'British' and 'Irish' (e.g. Gallagher, 1988). In sum, the theory neglects to account for variability and conflict in the words and actions produced by group members in social interaction (see Billig, 1985).

The theory of social representations

In Moscovici's (1984: 948) words, this theory is an attempt to realize the goal of transforming social psychology into an 'anthropological and historical science' by fostering a properly social account of human action and meaning. The term 'social representation' is said to contain two dimensions – abstract concepts and concrete images – which together help define or explain an object. For example, the word 'psychology' can be referenced by concepts such as 'mind', 'psyche', 'personality', etc. and exemplified by a portrait of Freud or the brain or an attitude scale, etc. Social representations are said to circulate in the social world and are drawn upon by individuals to make sense of or make familiar a social phenomenon and to communicate with others. New or difficult concepts are first 'anchored' to existing representations (e.g. 'road rage' is linked to stress) and then 'objectified' or transformed into more concrete images (e.g. a 'crazed' driver, a crash victim). As such, social representations refer to commonsense understandings of academic or abstract ideas. It is assumed that different social groups will apply distinct social representations of an object.

An influential study on the social representations of health and illness in France was conducted by Herzlich (1973). In-depth, semi-structured interviews were carried out with 80 participants, most from the city (Paris) and a few from the countryside. In general, it was found that health and illness were understood as opposites, with health represented as something internal to individuals whilst illness was construed as an external force which can strike at any time. Moreover, illness was commonly associated with city life whereas life in the country was regarded as healthy. However, although much research in this tradition has employed qualitative methods to examine multiple accounts, it has been argued that the theory ignores issues of ideology and power (Jahoda, 1988; Parker, 1987) and that it resorts to cognitive and individualist assumptions. In fact, the individual is presented as possessing the power to select and use those social representations deemed appropriate at a given time, and social representations themselves are situated within individual minds rather than social relations (see McKinlay & Potter, 1987; Parker, 1989). In sum, it has been argued that the work of Tajfel, Moscovici and colleagues have managed to usher in only superficial changes which are easily contained within the existing US-centred experimental–cognitive perspective (Ibáñez, 1990).

But contemporary social psychology within Europe, and especially in the UK (but also in other small pockets in places such as Australia, New Zealand, Canada and South Africa), features a breadth of perspectives and methodologies, from discursive psychology and psychosocial research to the theory of planned behaviour and social identity approaches. This wealth of scholarship is illustrated by the *British Journal of Social Psychology*, which recently published a range of 50th anniversary position papers reflecting developments in social psychology over the years: http://onlinelibrary.wiley.com/doi/10.1111/bjso.2011.50.issue-3/issuetoc. Nonetheless, critical psychological work is still in the minority here: much social psychology proceeds along the lines of experimental–cognitive psychology, adopting concepts and methods to be found in American journals and textbooks.

CRITICAL THINKING BOX: EURO V. US SOCIAL PSYCHOLOGY

As mentioned, there has been a concerted effort to distinguish a European from a US social psychology. Why do you think social psychology has developed (to some extent) differently in Europe (an interest in groups) compared to the US (a focus on individuals)?

Social psychology as social control

Since the late 1960s critics outside the discipline – and more recently within – have challenged the form and functions of mainstream (social) psychology, as evidenced by texts such as *Deconstructing Social Psychology* (Parker & Shotter, 1990), *Social Psychology: A Critical Agenda* (Stainton-Rogers et al., 1995), *Critical Psychology* (Fox & Prilleltensky, 1997/2009), *Critical Social Psychology* (Ibáñez & Íñiguez-Rueda, 1997), *An Introduction to Critical Social Psychology* (Hepburn, 2003), *Social Psychology: Experimental and Critical Approaches* (Stainton-Rogers, 2003) and *Understanding Critical Social Psychology* (Tuffin, 2004). Within this literature social psychology is situated in the wider context of Western capitalism (Fromm, 1956/1991), imperialism (Rose, 1985) and patriarchy (Wilkinson, 1986). This critique is allied with and draws upon various traditions, such as Marxism (e.g. Arfken, 2011, Parker, 2007; Parker & Spears, 1996), feminism (e.g. Wilkinson, 1986) and social constructionism (e.g. Burr, 1995; 2003), which in various ways produce troubling accounts of the modern period and its prevailing values of science, progress and individualism. The critical spotlight is cast on the institutional and disciplinary role of social psychology as bolstering existing inequalities of power by leaving them unexamined. According to this view the social psychologist performs the role of social engineer, helping to maintain the status quo by concentrating the gaze on individuals and not society (see Stainton-Rogers *et al.*, 1995).

A specific and influential critique of (social) psychology was generated in the 1960s by the 'anti-psychiatry' movement (e.g. Cooper, 1967; Laing, 1967). At that time – and indeed currently – psychiatry and clinical psychology were informed by a medical–scientific framework in which patients/clients were viewed as sick or abnormal and subjected to a variety of techniques to cure or control 'problematic' symptoms ('anti-psychotic' drugs, behaviour modification, electro-convulsive therapy etc.). Diagnoses and treatments were directed at the level of individuals and components of individuals (brains, behaviours, etc.), with little or no attempt to understand the individual in social and cultural contexts. In countering the prevailing philosophy, critical theorists and practitioners suggested replacing the notion of 'mental illness' with *interpretations* of strange or disturbing behaviour in terms of language, communication, discourse, ideologies, relationships and cultural factors (e.g. Foucault, 1954, 1961; Lacan, 1968). Szasz (1961) argued that 'mental illness' was a myth, a self-serving creation by dominant academic and professional bodies which fed into establishment concerns about the control of 'deviance'. Within the anti-psychiatry movement, there was a preference for situating problems within families and wider culture rather than locating these inside individuals. For example, Laing (1960) studied communication difficulties within families and linked these to broader material and ideological forces based around capitalism and patriarchy. More recent work by critical psychologists and others have developed critiques of psycho–medical constructions of mental distress, including books such as *Deconstructing Psychopathology* (Parker *et al.*, 1995), *Deconstructing Psychotherapy* (Parker, 1999), *Beyond Help: A Consumers' Guide to Psychology* (Hansen *et al.*, 2003), *Power, Interest and Psychology: Elements of a Social Materialist Understanding of Distress* (Smail, 2005), *Managing the Monstrous Feminine: Regulating the Reproductive Body* (Ussher, 2006), and various book chapters and articles including, Prilliltensky (1999) and Hare-Mustin and Marecek (2009). There are also some websites which cast a critical light on clinical psychology and psychiatry, including the critical psychiatry network: http://www.criticalpsy-chiatry.co.uk/, and Asylum: http://www.asylumonline.net.

> ### CRITICAL THINKING BOX: MENTAL ILLNESS
>
> Clearly there are biological dimensions to 'mental illness'. But do you think medical explanations and treatments have been over used? Discuss other factors that might contribute to 'madness'.

Later feminist critiques connected women's 'madness' with the construction of femininity in the nuclear family and in patriarchal society in general where the female is depicted in a range of conflicting and demeaning ways (e.g. Ussher, 2006, 2011). For example, Wilkinson (1991) highlights the role of psychology in obscuring the socio–political context of women's lives – and the feminist critique of this practice:

> Feminist [social] psychologists have also been critical of the harm that psychology (and the popularisation of psychological ideas) has wrought in women's lives: primarily (but not exclusively) through the location of responsibility – and also pathology – within the individual, to the total neglect of social and political oppression. (8)

More generally, feminist social psychologists have challenged the tendency of (social) psychology to cast women as inferior to men, as:

> inconsistent, emotionally stable, lacking in a strong conscience or superego, weaker, 'nurturing' rather than productive, 'intuitive' rather than intelligent, and, if they are 'normal', suited to the home and family. (Weisstein, 1993: 207)

The force and momentum of anti-psychiatry, feminist and other (black, gay and lesbian, etc.) scholarship and political activity has produced a broader, critical, anti-psychological orientation within and beyond mainstream (social) psychology (e.g. Burman, 1990; Usher, 1991, 2011; Weatherall, 2002; Wilkinson & Kitzinger, 1995). The focus of much contemporary critique tends to be on the use of technical jargon by (social) psychology and the ideological and practical functions this serves.

Discourse/ideology

The 'knowledge' produced by mainstream (social) psychology has been construed as a form of 'mystification', as summed up by Laing

(1967: 52): 'a positive (i.e. scientific) description can only perpetuate the alienation which it cannot itself describe...which it consequently disguises and masks more'. Similarly, Argyris (1975) argues that the model of the person conveyed by psychology presents a de-natured, competitive, rational and gain-oriented individual. The 'knowledge' produced by social psychologists then can be thought of as ideological in its promotion of particular ('objective', 'individualistic') analyses of social phenomena and its suppression of 'other' potential forms of explanation (emphasizing the social embeddedness of self and experience). Another way of regarding social psychological knowledge is as a form of 'fiction', i.e. a particular and partial construction of reality rather than an accurate reflection of reality (see Kvale, 1992; Parker & Shotter, 1990). This point has led some 'post-modern' commentators to argue for the incorporation of fictional accounts into social psychological analyses, a move which repositions social psychology as art rather than science (see Sass, 1992). Indeed, in some of the chapters which follow, we deliberately draw upon accounts from novels as well as social psychological studies in order to illuminate specific points.

Ideologies present as natural or correct ways of thinking and social structures which actually favour the interests of a particular class or group. They are 'systems of widely shared ideas and patterned beliefs that are accepted as truth by significant groups in society...ideologies organize their core ideas into fairly simple truth games that encourage people to act in certain ways' (Steger & Roy, 2010: 11). It could be argued that social psychology has offered social theories and technical solutions to social problems which maintain capitalist (neoliberal), English-speaking, white, male, middle-class interests. This view led some scholars towards a Marxist analysis of the individual-in-society:

> Psychology, like the ruling-class forms of production/distribution it supports, believes in a pessimistic humanity for which 'original sin', 'instinct', or 'inappropriate response' dictate the need for social control. Marxism counters such an attitude with its own view of humanity...transcending the past in the creation of newness...Instead of passive pawns, we become active creators. (Brown, 1974: 165–166, cited in Sapsford & Dallos, 1996)

Foucault (1977) in particular emphasizes the 'governmental' role of the human/social sciences such as social psychology within the institutions and practices of modern life. In light of its individualistic orientation, social psychology is implicated in producing a 'regime of truth' which bolsters dominant Western culture. Of course, defining subjects as a set of measurable variables provides grounds for a range of institutional activities such as personnel selection, academic testing, patient diagnosis, performance appraisal, etc. Foucauldian critics construe such classificatory practices as a form of policing 'problematic', 'deviant' or 'at risk' subjects: 'masturbating children and hysterical women, feebleminded children and recruits to the armed forces, workers suffering fatigue or industrial accidents, unstable shell-shocked soldiers, lying, bedwetting or naughty children' (Rose, 1989: 122). So, the production, nature and application of social psychological knowledge reflects the powerful position of the discipline in the containment of subversive identities, thereby ensuring social control (see Box 2.6).

For example, social psychology played a key role in taming the massive influx of immigrants to North America at the turn of the century. Although useful as workers for the massive industrialization and urbanization projects, the issue of controlling immigrant labour became important. Hence the emergence of Taylorism, or 'scientific management', a regime which advocated the subdivision of work tasks so that performance could be readily monitored and measured (see Parker, 1990). Similarly, Cartwright has pointed to the US government funding of research in the wake of the Second World War on numerous research topics, including: 'building civilian morale and combating demoralisation; domestic attitudes, needs, and information; enemy morale and psychological warfare; military administration; international relations; and psychological problems of a wartime economy' (1979: 84).

The discipline of social psychology does not simply impose its knowledge and techniques on a docile public. Rather, as Foucault has pointed out, power is not possessed by privileged groups – it is dispersed among the population in often complex and subtle ways. Over the past 30 years or so, power has been analysed in terms of ideology or discourse (e.g. Parker, 2002; Billig et al., 1988). Instead of conceiving ideology as a system of beliefs external to individuals designed to obscure the 'truth' of class inequalities (thus inflicting people with 'false consciousness'), Althusser (1984) presents ideology as a set of relationships between individuals and social worlds within which we negotiate meanings and identities about ourselves and others. For example, individuals discover themselves as students, husbands, fathers, etc. by being recognized as such by other people and society in general, as all these roles are already established and

Box 2.6   Psychology, consumerism and advertising

In addition to assisting in the taming of the migrant population in the US to become hard working efficient 'producers', psychology in the early twentieth-century was instrumental in educating the population to become 'consumers' by applying its theories and techniques to advertising. Business leaders and politicians at the time came to the realization that mass production would not survive without a corresponding mass consumption, which was necessary to stave off the ever present threat of economic stagnation. Rather than allowing workers the freedom to control the means of production, business leaders and politicians, with the assistance of psychologists, promoted the self-actualization of workers through the consumption of products and services (Ewen, 2001: 189). Psychologists that contributed to this movement included Walter Dill Scott, John Watson and Edward Bernays. Scott authored two highly influential books *The Theory and Practice of Advertising* and *The Psychology of Advertising* published in 1903 and 1908 respectively. Watson left his academic post at Johns Hopkins University to join the J. Walter Thompson advertising agency (eventually becoming Vice President) where he applied his ground breaking research in behaviourism to advertising and marketing. Edward Bernays (nephew of Sigmund Freud) pioneered techniques in public relations, advertising and marketing in order to influence public opinion in support of consumer lifestyles. Bernays applied theories and research from social psychology (crowd psychology, persuasion) and psychoanalysis (the unconscious) to further corporate and political aims of turning the US population into consumers.

Psychology's long running and intimate relationship with advertising was summed up in a recent article published in *The Psychologist* (the monthly publication of the British Psychological Society) on the psychology of advertising, which noted that 'Psychology and the advertising industry have always had a close "personal" relationship' (Florance *et al.*, 2011: 462). Since the turn of the twentieth-century psychology has successfully linked people's desires, passions, hopes, fears and anxieties, with material comfort, pleasure and therapy (Cushman, 1995; McDonald *et al.*, 2008; McDonald & Wearing, 2012; Miller & Rose, 1997). While psychology is keen to promote the application of its knowledge to advertising the lack of debate or concern about its often pernicious effects, particularly on children, is of concern to critical psychologists.

familiar. Ideology therefore helps to (dis)locate people in the world through providing identity slots which individuals fill with little or no choice in the matter. This reading of ideology obviously introduces more complexity to identity by linking it with social structures in a dynamic, multifaceted way (see Chapter 5). With Foucault, the power/discourse dimension is complemented by an equal emphasis on resistance that subjects are produced by ideology but can also position themselves outside particular representations.

One of the most pervasive discourses in contemporary society of concern to critical psychologists relates to psychologization i.e. a relentless, exclusive focus on individual 'personality' and behaviour (De Vos, 2012). In a psychotherapeutic culture such as the one we have in the West (Parker, 1997), individuals are held responsible for their actions and encouraged to seek solutions to problems through personal projects, psychological approaches (e.g. cognitive behavioural therapy), and displays of commitment, willpower and motivation. For example, the 'positive psychology project' (Seligman, 2003) has been criticized for adopting a version of American individualism and political economy which promotes self-improvement and self-fulfilment while downplaying the social contexts and circumstances which constrain individual capacities for change (Becker & Marecek, 2008; Christopher & Hickinbottom, 2008; McDonald & O'Callaghan, 2008). Issues concerning psychologization are discussed in a special issue of the *Annual Review of Critical Psychology* (Gordo & de Vos, 2010). This special issue was introduced in the following way:

> This issue of *Annual Review of Critical Psychology* represents a collaborative effort to continue unravelling the modern, and ever expanding, tendency to manage non-psychological issues in psychological terms. The most important challenge, here, lies in probing the boundaries between the non-psychological and the psychological and exploring ways to transcend them…. Psychologisation and, by extension, psychology may be conceptualized as an outcome, a central feature of neoliberalism or, alternatively, as a process rather than a steady condition…. Are we lost in psychologisation? Is there no outside of psychology and psychologisation? (3–7)

This issue can be downloaded in full for free at http://www.discourseunit.com/annual-review/arcp-8-psychologisation-under-scrutiny/

CRITICAL THINKING BOX: ON IDEOLOGY AND SOCIAL CONTROL

Do you agree that social psychology has played a role in the oppression of particular groups and the maintenance of the social order? What can social psychologists do to resist the discipline of social psychology?

Revisiting critical social psychology

To reiterate, critical social psychology is concerned to contest the knowledge and practices which characterize mainstream experimental–cognitive social psychology. As Chapter 1 suggests, critical social psychology emphasizes the 'social construction of reality' and is sceptical of scientific social psychological claims of neutrality and fact-finding. Instead, the aims, methods and outcomes of social psychology are highlighted as ideological, as producing forms of knowledge which obscure and therefore reinforce power differentials in society. This point is emphasized by Wilkinson (1991) in relation to the (social) psychological formulation of women, but can also be applied to other groups subordinated in terms of race, ethnicity, social class, (dis)ability, sexual orientation, etc.:

> psychology's theories often exclude women, or distort our experiences – by assimilating it to male norms or man-made stereotypes, or by regarding 'women' as a unitary category, to be understood only in comparison with the unitary category 'men'... Similarly, psychology [screens out] ... the existence and operation of social and structural inequalities between and within social groups (power differentials are written out). (7–8)

Whether the focus is on individuals or groups, social relations, differences and conflicts are not recognized or held constant, so that the ensuing 'knowledge' is stripped of relevance and insight. When devising and measuring 'internal' entities such as 'personality', 'attitude', 'motivation', 'intelligence', 'need for achievement', etc., and comparing different social groups on these dimensions, social psychology paints a rather simplistic, static and de-socialized picture of the phenomenon in question. In contrast, critical social psychology points to social complexity, contradiction and construction, thereby disrupting social psychological narratives of 'objectivity' and 'progress'. As Wetherell (1996) puts it:

> I want to argue for a 'critical social psychology' which takes the term 'social' very seriously indeed. We are not isolated individuals but social beings. Our dreams, hopes, fears and expectations may be the products of solitary reflection but they also tell us a great deal about the ways in which we are inserted into society. Social psychology should be a social science, not an imitation natural science. We belong with disciplines such as sociology, politics and cultural studies rather than physics, chemistry and astronomy. Our methods, research aims and theories should reflect the particular nature of social action, difficult though this is. We should work with and study the ambiguities, fluidity and openness of social life rather than try to repress these in a fruitless chase for experimental control and scientific respectability. (11)

But critical social psychology does not seek to replace one form of social psychology with another – it seeks to undo, un-define, deconstruct those (powerful) presentations of nature, fact and essence within social psychology and wider culture. In the chapters which follow, we hope to illustrate and develop the critique of experimental–cognitive social psychology as applied to a number of relevant topics and to show how critical concepts such as discourse, ideology and power can be brought to bear on such material.

Summary

In this chapter we have situated mainstream social psychology within a modern Western philosophical context where values of science, progress and individualism are embraced. We then described how the social psychological preoccupation with scientific measurement which subsequently developed came to be criticized during the late 1960s and early 1970s in what is often referred to as a time of 'crisis' for the subdiscipline. The drive for increased relevance led some social psychologists towards humanistic approaches while many in Europe articulated a more group-centred focus to counter the perceived dominance of North American individualistic approaches. But, as we stressed, such 'alternative' directions have not made a huge impact on social psychology; in fact, the 'cognitive revolution', which social psychologists turned into 'social cognition' has overtaken social psychology in the past 40 years, has dictated the agenda so that mental phenomena are given priority, even within apparently social perspectives such as Social Identity Theory. We then discussed more fundamental critiques offered by a range of theorists both within and outside social psychology which highlighted the role of the discipline in perpetuating 'knowledge' in the service of dominant political/ business aims and social inequalities. The turn towards examining the social functions of theory – and discourse in general – is one of the key features of critical social psychology, an approach which concentrates on power relations, difference, ideology and the social construction of meaning.

Key references

Armistead, N. (1974). Introduction, *Reconstructing Social Psychology*. Harmondsworth: Penguin.
This introductory chapter gives a flavour of the disillusionment felt by many social psychologists with the discipline at the beginning of the 1970s.

Gergen, K. J. (2012). The social dimension of social psychology: A historical analysis. In A. W. Kruglanski & W. Stroebe (eds), *Handbook of the History of Social Psychology* (pp. 137–157). Hove, UK: Psychology Press.
In this chapter Gergen traces the historical relationship and tension (or divide) between the 'psychological' and 'social' understandings of social behaviour in social psychology.

Greenwood, J. D. (2004a). *The Disappearance of the Social in American Social Psychology*. Cambridge: Cambridge University Press.
Greenwood charts the history of social psychology in the US arguing that its founders embraced a concept of the social that was broad ranging and inclusive. However, by the mid twentieth century these social concepts were abandoned by social psychologists in favour of a de-limited understanding of social behaviour that emphasized individual cognition in social contexts. For a more condensed outline of Greenwood's thesis see his article published in the *Journal for the Theory of Social Behaviour* (Greenwood, 2004b).

Sapsford, R. (ed.) (1996). chapters 10 and 11, *Issues for Social Psychology*. Buckingham: Open University Press.
The two final chapters present a range of objections to the theories and applications of cognitive–experimental social psychology.

Shotter, J. & Parker, I. (eds). (1990). *Deconstructing Social Psychology*. London: Routledge.
An edited collection where several critical psychologists take aim at aspects of social psychology in a conscious update of the Armistead (1974) text.

Tuffin, K. (2004). *Understanding Critical Social Psychology*. London: Sage.
The first two chapters of Tuffin's book provide a useful critical overview of the
history and philosophy of mainstream social psychology.

New references

Arfken, M. (2011). Marxist scholarship and psychological practice. *Annual Review of Critical Psychology, 9*, 6–7.

Becker, D. & Marecek, J. (2008). Positive psychology: history in the remaking? *Theory & Psychology, 18*(5), 591–604.

Billig, M. (2011). Writing social psychology: fictional things and unpopulated texts. *British Journal of Social Psychology, 50*(1), 4–20.

Brannigan, A. (2004). *The Rise and Fall of Social Psychology: An Iconoclast's Guide to the Use and Misuse of the Experimental Method.* Piscataway, NJ: Aldine Transaction.

Brehm, S. S., Kassin, S. M. & Fein, S. (2005). *Social Psychology* (6th edn). Boston, MA: Houghton Mifflin.

Burr, V. (2003). *Social Constructionism* (2nd edn). Hove, UK: Routledge.

Christopher, J. C. & Hickinbottom, S. (2008). Positive psychology, ethnocentrism, and the disguised ideology of individualism. *Theory & Psychology, 18*(5), 563–589.

Cooper, D. (1967). *Psychiatry and Anti-Psychiatry.* London: Paladin.

Cromby, J. (2007). Integrating social science with neuroscience: potentials and pitfalls. *BioSocieties, 2*(2), 149–170.

Cromby, J., Newton, T. & Williams, S. J. (2011). Neuroscience and subjectivity. *Subjectivity, 4*(3), 215–226.

Cushman, P. (1995). *Constructing the Self, Constructing America: A Cultural History of Psychotherapy.* Cambridge, MA: Da Capo Press.

De Vos, J. (2012). *Psychologisation in Times of Globalisation.* London: Routledge.

Ewen, S. (2001). *Captains of Consciousness: Advertising and the Social Roots of Consumer Culture* (Rev edn). New York: Basic Books.

Florance, I., Mullensiefen, D. & Carter, S. (2011). How to get ahead in the psychology of advertising. *Psychologist, 24*(6), 462–465.

Foucault, M. (1954). *Mental Illness and Psychology* (A. Sheridan, Trans.). Berkeley, CA: University of California Press.

Foucault, M. (1961). *Madness and Civilization: A History of Insanity in the Age of Reason* (R. Howard, Trans.). London: Routledge.

Fox, D., Prilleltensky, I. & Austin, S. (eds). (2009). *Critical Psychology: An Introduction* (2nd edn). Thousand Oaks, CA: Sage.

Fromm, E. (1956/1991). *The Sane Society.* London: Routledge.

Gergen, K. J. (2010). Beyond the enlightenment: relational being. In S. R. Kirschner & J. Martin (eds), *The Sociocultural Turn in Psychology: The Comtextual Emergence of Mind and Self* (pp. 68–87). New York: Columbia University Press.

Gergen, K. J. (2012). The social dimension of social psychology: A historical analysis. In A. W. Kruglanski & W. Stroebe (eds), *Handbook of the history of social psychology* (pp. 137–157). Hove, UK: Psychology Press.

Gordo, A. & De Vos, J. (2010). Psychologism, psychologisation and de-psychologisation. *Annual Review of Critical Psychology, 8,* 3–7.

Greenwood, J. D. (2000). Individualism and the social in early American social psychology. *Journal of the History of the Behavioral Sciences, 36*(4), 443–455.

Greenwood, J. D. (2004a). *The Disappearance of the Social in American Social Psychology.* Cambridge, UK: Cambridge University Press.

Greenwood, J. D. (2004b). What happened to the 'social' in social psychology? *Journal for the Theory of Social Behaviour, 34*(1), 19–34.

Hansen, S., McHoul, A. & Rapley, M. (2003). *Beyond Help: A Consumers' Guide to Psychology.* Ross-on-Wye, UK: PCCS Books.

Hare-Mustin, R. T. & Marecek, J. (2009). Clinical psychology: the politics of madness. In D. Fox, I. Prilleltensky & S. Austin (eds), *Critical Psychology: An Introduction* (2nd edn, pp. 75–92). Thousand Oaks, CA: Sage.

Harmon-Jones, E. & Devine, P. G. (2003). Introduction to the special section on social neuroscience: promise and caveats. *Journal of Personality and Social Psychology, 85*(4), 589–593.

Hepburn, A. (2003). *An Introduction to Critical Social Psychology.* London: Sage.

Hill, D.B. (2006). Theory in applied social psychology: past mistakes and future hopes. *Theory & Psychology, 16*(5), 613–640.

Hogg, M. A. (2006). Social identity theory. In P. J. Burke (ed.), *Contemporary Social Psychological Theories* (pp. 111–136). Stanford, CA: Stanford University Press.

Hogg, M. A. & Vaughan, G. M. (2005). *Social Psychology* (4th edn). Harlow, UK: Pearson.

Jahoda, G. (1988). Critical notes and reflections on 'social representations'. *European Journal of Social Psychology, 18*, 195–209.

Jahoda, G. (2007). *A History of Social Psychology: from the Eighteenth-Century Enlightenment to the Second World War.* Cambridge, UK: Cambridge University Press.

Jenkins, R. (2008). *Social Identity* (3rd edn). London: Routledge.

Lacan, J. (1968). *The Language of the Self: the Function of Language in Psychoanalysis* (A. Wilden, Trans.). Baltimore, MA: John Hopkins University Press.

Lindesmith, A. R., Strauss, A. L. & Denzin, N. K. (1999). *Social Psychology* (8th edn). Thousand Oaks, CA: Sage.

McDonald, M. & O'Callaghan, J. (2008). Positive psychology: A Foucauldian critique. *The Humanistic Psychologist, 36*(2), 127–142.

McDonald, M. & Wearing, S. (2012). *Social Psychology and Theories of Consumer Culture: A Political Economy Perspective.* London: Routledge.

McDonald, M., Wearing, S. & Ponting, J. (2008). Narcissism and neoliberalism: work, leisure and alienation in an era of consumption. *Loisir et Societe (Society and Leisure), 30*(1), 489–510.

Miller, P. & Rose, N. (1997). Mobilizing the consumer: assembling the subject of consumption. *Theory, Culture & Society, 14*(1), 1–36.

Moscovici, S. (1972). Society and theory in social psychology. In J. Israel & H. Tajfel (eds), *The Context of Social Psychology* (pp. 17–68). London: Academic Press.

Ochsner, K. N. & Lieberman, M. D. (2001). The emergence of social cognitive neuroscience. *American Psychologist, 59*(9), 717–734.

Pancer, S. M. (1997). Social psychology: the crisis continues. In D. Fox & I. Prilleltensky (eds), *Critical Psychology: An Introduction* (pp. 150–165). Thousand Oaks, CA: Sage Publications.

Parker, I. (1987). Social representations: social psychology's (mis)use of sociology. *Journal for the Theory of Social Behaviour, 17*, 447–470.

Parker, I. (ed.). (1999). *Deconstructing Psychotherapy.* London: Sage.

Parker, I. (ed.). (2002). *Critical Discursive Psychology.* Basingstoke, UK: Palgrave Macmillan.

Parker, I., Georgaca, E., Harper, D., McLaughlin, T. & Stowell-Smith, M. (1995). *Deconstructing Psychopathology.* London: Sage.

Richardson, F. C., & Fowers, B. J. (2010). Hermeneutics and sociocultural perspectives in psychology. In S. R. Kirschner & J. Martin (eds), *The*

Sociocultural Turn in Psychology: The Contextual Emergence of Mind and Self (pp. 113–136). New York: Columbia University Press.

Ring, K. (1967). Some sober questions about frivolous values. *Journal of Experimental Social Psychology, 3,* 113–123.

Seligman, M. E. P. (2003). *Authentic Happiness: Using the New Positive Psychology to Realize Your Potential for Lasting Fulfillment.* Sydney: Random House.

Seligman, M. E. P. & Csikszentmihalyi, M. (2000). Positive psychology: an introduction. *American Psychologist, 55*(1), 5–14.

Silverman, I. (1977). Why social psychology fails. *Canadian Psychological Review, 18,* 353–358.

Sherif, M. & Sherif, C. W. (1953). *Groups in Harmony and Tension: An Integration of Studies of Intergroup Relations.* Oxford: Harper & Brothers.

Smail, D. (2005). *Power Interest and Psychology: Elements of a Social Materialist Understanding of Distress.* Ross-on-Wye, UK: PCCS.

Stainton-Rogers, W. (2003). *Social Psychology: Experimental and Critical Approaches.* Maidenhead, UK: Open University Press.

Steger, M. B., & Roy, R. K. (2010). *Neoliberalism: A Very Short Introduction.* New York: Oxford University Press.

Tuffin, K. (2004). *Understanding Critical Social Psychology.* London: Sage.

Ussher, J. (2011). *The Madness of Women: Myth and Experience.* London: Routledge.

Weatherall, A. (2002). *Gender, Language and Discourse.* London: Routledge.

Doing Critical
Social Psychology

3

This chapter will highlight:

- The turn to language in critical social psychology
- Forms of discourse analysis
- Narrative and psychosocial research
- Action and participatory action research
- Reflexivity

Introduction

The methods and practices of critical social psychologists differ widely from those of mainstream or 'positivist' social psychologists. As the previous chapter argued, there are many problems associated with experimental–cognitive social psychological research. To reiterate, conventional quantitative methods have been criticized for:

- reducing complex human phenomena to measurable variables and simplistic categories;
- presenting 'subjects' as naive stimulus–response machines and 'society' as invisible or constant;
- providing 'knowledge' which is technical, mystifying and uncritical;
- helping to perpetuate social relations of inequality;
- obscuring significant personal and contextual features of the research;
- facilitating the myth of social psychology as a science that will one day uncover the set of universal laws governing social behaviour.

As noted in Chapter 1, critical social psychology, in contrast, has been influenced by a range of critical traditions such as Marxism, feminism, psychoanalysis, social constructionism etc., and follows markedly different assumptions and practices about research. The focus is often on language, in line with a general shift in social theory towards an analysis of 'discourse' (e.g. Burman & Parker, 1993; McKinlay & McVittie, 2008; Parker, 2002; Potter, 2007; Potter & Wetherell, 1987; Wetherell, 2003; Wilkinson & Kitzinger, 1995). This critical focus on discourse incorporates the meanings people negotiate in social interactions and relations (the interpersonal level), and more broadly, the ways in which everyday talk is structured or framed by prevailing cultural norms, ideologies or discourses (the sociocultural level). These two levels of analysis are interrelated – people use language to communicate but the terms and assumptions they draw upon are provided by the surrounding culture. So, two men having a conversation about football might work to preserve a joint identity as 'football fans' but they will also be reproducing cultural norms about gender and sport (masculinity-football-sexism, etc.). Although language is spoken or written, there is an emphasis on the latter, a turn to 'text', since speech tends to be transcribed for ease of analysis. So, an infinite variety of 'texts' can be studied, such as interview transcripts, newspaper reports, online discussion forums, political rhetoric, field notes from observations, diaries, blogs, magazine articles, recordings of actual conversations, film scripts, etc.

Such texts may be analysed in a quantitative fashion using 'content analysis' (e.g. Krippendorff, 2004), for example, whereby superficial features can be identified and frequency counts conducted. For instance, a content analysis of a wrestling magazine might categorize units into different types (advertisements, interviews, features, etc.) and produce a table displaying the relative frequency of key terms such as 'strength', 'reputation', 'aggression'. Whilst such analyses can present a useful indication of important themes in the text, critical social psychology tends to favour qualitative forms of data analysis, although there are examples of quantitative methods being re-worked and used 'critically' within critical social psychology (see Lubek, 1997; Unger, 1996) and, of course, a summary of quantitative data can provide a helpful reason for further qualitative analysis. In light of the preoccupation with language, however, most forms of 'critical' research involve qualitative, and often discursive, forms of analysis. Discourse analysis is an umbrella term that covers a complex family of approaches; these include:

- 'discursive psychology' (e.g. Potter; 2007; 1996; Wiggins & Potter, 2008), which analyses construction, variation and function in relation to psychological terms (thoughts, feelings, memories) in talk;
- 'membership categorisation analysis' (Stokoe, 2010), which studies how identity categories (masculine, mother, nurse etc.) are employed in social interaction;
- 'conversation analysis' (Kitzinger, 2000; Wilkinson & Kitzinger, 2008), which focuses on the sequential, 'turn-taking' organization of talk.

Other forms of discourse analysis are less interested in detailed analysis of talk and more interested in the broad cultural discourses which structure talk; these include:

- 'critical discourse analysis' (Fairclough, 2010; Parker, 2002), which explores language in relation to ideology and power;
- 'Foucauldian discourse analysis' (Arribas-Ayllon & Walkerdine, 2008; Willig, 2008a: 112–128; Hook, 2001), which investigates relatively well-bounded areas of social knowledge (e.g. psychology, sociology, anthropology, criminology, medicine, psychiatry) and the ways in which they subjugate certain elements of the population (e.g. the mentally ill, unemployed, homosexuals, single mothers, migrants, criminals, patients).

All of these varieties of discourse analysis have been used for critical purposes. Other qualitative methods which can be deployed critically included psychosocial and psychoanalytically-informed research (e.g. Midgely, 2006), narrative analysis (e.g. Crossley, 2000; Andrews *et al.*, 2008; Williams *et al.*, 2003) and phenomenological methods (e.g. Langdridge, 2007).

In contrast to traditional positivist models of research, critical qualitative research in general is informed by social constructionism, a contemporary school of thought which presents 'knowledge' as a social product (or construction), the outcome of specific relationships and practices within the research context (see Chapter 1). Theoretical orientation and research practice are regarded as interconnected, as mutually influential, which is why some critical writers resist the practice of separating out theory from method in journal articles and books. The fact that we are here presenting a visibly distinct chapter on methods is somewhat ironic of course, but we see this as a useful resource for students of social psychology who may already be familiar with reading about and writing discrete methods sections. Nonetheless, we continually link research method with theoretical positions throughout this chapter and urge students to bear in mind the ways in which the whole research process is framed by researcher (and participant) ideals and values.

Indeed, the researcher's ideas and feelings about the research topic dismissed as 'bias' from the perspective of conventional mainstream or positivist research is re-viewed as an inevitable occurrence within qualitative research and, moreover, is often considered a positive resource in informing the research process (see Finlay & Gough, 2003; Gough & Madill, in press). As a result, any research report is considered a construction, i.e. an account from one perspective of the study in question, one which is always open to alternative inter-pretations through differing theoretical perspectives. For this reason one has to strive to provide persuasive arguments and supporting textual evidence to bolster one's analysis; otherwise the quality of the analysis will be called into question. Hence critical researchers tend to be as 'transparent' and 'reflexive' as possible concerning the steps taken in the research and the part they played (including their own personal background) in conceiving, conducting and re-presenting it. As you would expect by now, the aims of critical social psychology research revolve around highlighting and challenging taken-for-granted thinking around psychology, discourse/s, power relations and practices implicated in the oppression of individuals and groups. In short, compared to the above features of mainstream psychological research, 'critical' research usually sets out to:

- 'denaturalize' taken-for-granted thinking in psychology; emphasize the variation, complexity and often contradictory qualities in human experience and social behaviour;
- situate individuals/research participants within wider social and (inter-)personal contexts;
- offer knowledge which is partial, incomplete and critical;
- challenge aspects of existing inequalities in society;
- make visible pertinent personal and contextual elements within the research;
- deconstruct the myth of (social) psychology as a natural science, and challenge its key assumptions which underpin its authority and relevance to contemporary social behaviour.

These features will be discussed below as this chapter highlights forms of critical research in relation to different types of data. This is not a (qualitative) methods chapter which describes in detail how to collect data and analyse it; rather, the emphasis here is on illustrating forms of critical inquiry. For more thorough advice on methods of qualitative data collection and analysis you can consult other texts, such as Banister *et al.* (1994; 2011), Hayes (1997), Smith (2007), Willig (2008a) and Willig and Stainton-Rogers (2008).

In this chapter, we will first introduce forms of discourse analysis, highlighting key themes and debates, and presenting some examples. We then move on to other methods, specifically 'narrative' and 'psychosocial approaches', again providing some research examples. Modes of 'action research' are then covered, where researchers and community members work together towards shared goals, before we consider a key issue in critical qualitative research in 'reflexivity'.

Discourse analysis

There is no one or definitive brand of discourse analysis to which all 'critical' social psychologists subscribe (see Wetherell *et al.*, 2001) and, to make matters worse, a variety of terms are often used interchangeably with little or no consensus on meaning. Some of these include discourse, text, narrative, theme, story, repertoire, etc. For students (and researchers), concepts and debates can appear rather abstract, which may inhibit or discourage attempts at understanding. At the same time, efforts such as this to simplify the literature are open to charges of reductionism or simplification. Nonetheless, a key aim of this chapter is to clarify and illustrate forms of discourse analysis to facilitate awareness and stimulate critical research practice. An important point to make from the outset is that discourse analysis is not an automatically critical endeavour – some researchers who present themselves as discourse analysts could not be said to be doing critical research (see Burman, 1991; McKinlay & McVittie, 2008). However, the analysis of discourse is a common activity within critical social psychology and although many different strands exist, two broad approaches are normally distinguished. These approaches emerged in the UK during the late 1980s and 1990s and have influenced much critical work since.

Subjects as discourse users

One tradition influenced by post-structuralism, microsociology (e.g. ethnomethodology – Garfinkel, 1967) and the sociology of science emphasizes the 'performative' qualities and 'action orientation' of conversational and linguistic activities (e.g. Billig *et al.*, 1988; Potter & Wetherell, 1987). This 'bottom-up' approach attends to the rich and varied use of language as it is produced in interactions, and highlights the rhetorical strategies people use to achieve particular ends such as justifying one's position or defending a friend from perceived slander. In order to present self, others and the world in specific ways, people are said to draw upon 'linguistic (or interpretative) repertoires', which 'consist of sets of recurrent and coherently related stylistic, grammatical and lexical features, including seminal metaphors and tropes or figures of speech' (Wetherell, 1997: 162). For any given 'object' ('men'; 'parenthood'; 'football' ...) there will be a range of repertoires from which people draw, and the same person may well use different, even conflicting, repertoires at different points, depending on the conversational context and the (inter)personal goals. For example, members of a sports team or street gang might variously describe the group in terms of:

- family – everyone is a 'brother'/'sister';
- army – defending perceived group rights against designated enemies;
- body – where each member is an integral part/arm of the central figure/whole;
- religion – when faith in and devotion to the group's abilities is expressed;
- sanctuary – shelter/escape from everyday existence/hassle, etc.

The three key features of talk emphasized within this tradition are variability, construction and function (Potter & Wetherell, 1987). Discourse analyses of texts often highlight the multiple and conflicting ways in which people account for something. For example, a child speaking about family might present it as supportive at one point (e.g. talking about pocket money received) and prohibitive at another (e.g. talking about family rules). The second feature, construction, refers to the use of language to produce a given account in conversation. The categories and strategies used by people to create meaning are drawn from those existing in surrounding culture. The concept of 'family', for example, will have a number of understandings or representations in a given society at a given time, some of which will be negative (e.g. 'family as controlling') and some positive (e.g. 'family as nourishing'). Finally, the third feature of function refers to the social effects of such 'speech acts' (Austin, 1962). Continuing with the example, a 'family as controlling' repertoire used by a child or adolescent might serve to position the child as a victim of unreasonable family restrictions and help justify some 'rebellion', whilst employing a 'family as nourishing' repertoire would emphasize a more positive family image and perhaps work towards attracting favours or concessions from parents. The repertoires chosen and functions served would of course be understood in relation to the context in which they were used, whether as part of a family discussion at home, an interview with a researcher, or talk at school with friends, and so on.

This approach has developed into what is now widely known as 'discursive psychology' which is primarily concerned with rethinking (social) psychological phenomena, such as attitudes, emotions and memory, as constructed in interaction rather than residing somewhere inside the person (e.g. Potter, 2007, 2012; Edwards & Potter, 2005). This work contributes to the critique of mainstream (social) psychology by arguing convincingly that 'cognitive' structures and processes are better understood as having a public or social, rather than private reality, i.e. in the language used to construct such phenomena. As Edwards (2005: 260) argues the main thrust of discursive psychology 'is to avoid psychological theorizing in favour of analysis based in the pragmatics of social action'. Willig (2008: 164) outlines six main points that characterize discursive psychology, they include:

- emerged from ethnomethodology and conversation analysis;
- is concerned with discourse practices;
- emphasizes the performative qualities of discourse;
- emphasizes the fluidity and variability of discourse;
- prioritizes action orientation and stake;
- asks, 'What are participants doing with their talk?'

According to Parker (1992), this form of analysis is rarely extended to comment on the political implications of individualistic and mentalistic discourse within (social) psychology and wider culture generally, although Potter (1997) suggests that studies of discourse and rhetoric should not always or exclusively deal with social critique. Despite these debates, however, much research in this tradition has investigated the ideological dimensions to everyday talk (e.g. Wetherell & Potter, 1992; Billig, 1992 – see Box 3.1). Indeed, Wetherell et al. (1987) use the term 'practical ideologies' to convey how people deploy various rhetorical methods in order to present a particular view as factual or natural – and other views as incorrect or unnatural: 'the often contradictory and fragmentary complexes of notions, norms and models which guide conduct and allow for its (inequality) justification and ration-alisation' (1987: 60).

Presenting a personal view as factual or 'the way things are' helps resolve what Edwards and Potter (1993) call the 'dilemma of stake'. For example, a government politician would be expected to defend policies, but to make the defence more credible and deflect potential criticisms of stake or interest ('you would say that'), the speaker might refer to statistics ('facts') or demonstrate a 'bias' on the part of opposition politicians in order to authorize or reinforce the account or they may choose to denigrate a group of people who challenge their policies by saying are 'un-British', 'un-American' or 'un-Australian'. Of course, positivist psychologists are faced with the same dilemma and are often at pains to stress the 'objectivity' of the research and sophistication of the statistical analysis. And efforts to protect state-ments or actions from being undermined are to be found frequently in everyday conversations, with the speaker presenting self as rational and the other as emotionally involved, for example ('I did what was logical, but you overreacted').

Box 3.1   Ideology as common sense: talking of the Royal Family (Billig, 1992)

According to Billig, everyday understandings of the British monarchy present an important opportunity to study 'ideological thinking in practice', since an uncritical acceptance of monarchy amounts to an acceptance of social inequality based on class/status differences. Although written texts tend to be favoured by discourse analysts, Billig emphasizes the value of studying actual conversations in naturalistic settings. Consequently, the project on the monarchy involved a researcher visiting 63 families from a range of socio–economic backgrounds in order to record their conversations on this topic.

Billig also argues that perspectives on the Royal Family (or any topic) will be varied and often contradictory, indicating a 'dilemmatic' quality to common sense and ideology (see Billig *et at.*, 1988). For example, in the family discussions, the 'royals' were frequently urged not to be too 'ordinary' ('they're quite different, really they have to set standards') – nor to be too 'royal' ('they're just human, after all'). Similarly, the institution of the monarchy was presented both as the 'priceless' heritage of the nation and as a significant source of revenue from tourists. The examples above perhaps relate to a broader 'ideological dilemma' between 'history as national progress' and 'history as national decline'. According to the former account, old differences in power and prestige between individuals and groups (e.g., between 'ordinary' people and the 'royals') had largely been eroded such that people enjoyed a better quality of life today. In contrast, another story drawn upon presented a conflicting picture, one where respect for valued traditions such as the Royal Family had diminished, to the detriment of society. This oscillation between two positions between speakers – and often with the same speaker – supports the contention of ideology as fragmented, negotiated and fluid.

To sum up so far, the above approach to discourse analysis attends closely to the 'repertoires' deployed in everyday conversation. It is assumed and frequently illustrated that speakers will draw upon a wide range of (sometimes competing) metaphors, images and idioms in different conversational contexts; indeed, the same speaker may well use conflicting repertoires during one social encounter. Although discourse analysis in this vein is not always or necessarily used for 'critical' ends, there are many examples of research projects which examine links between common sense and the ideological mainte-nance of inequalities. Such analyses are often sophisticated exposi-tions of the complex and contradictory workings of discourse/ideology as reproduced in everyday talk.

Subjects as structured by discourse

Another distinct but related form of discourse analysis is more explicitly concerned with discourse/s as producing and maintaining people ('subjects') within particular positions and relationships (e.g. Arribas-Ayllon & Walkerdine, 2008; Hook, 2001; Parker 2002; 2011). This is a more 'top-down' approach as it concentrates mainly on broad historical and cultural representations advertised within dominant institutions (medicine, law, government, mass media) and the ways in which people are constrained within and/or resist these frameworks. This work has a more macro-sociological flavour and is influenced by social theorists such as Althusser and Foucault, who were interested in language, ideology, power and subjectivity.

Foucault's work became familiar to (social) psychology in the late 1970s and reflects concerns with the historical representations and practices around madness, punishment, confession and the self used to contain and control populations (see Hook, 2007; Parker, 1992). Following Foucault (1972), who characterized discourses as 'practices that systematically form the objects of which they speak' (1972: 49), Parker (1992: 5) defines a 'discourse' as 'a set of statements which construct an object'. For example, a 'medical' discourse will produce representations of unusual behaviours in terms of illness or disease.

An important conceptual framework utilized by discourse analysts within this tradition is the 'psy-complex' (Rose 1985; 1999). This refers to the contemporary preoccupation with and promotion of psychological or individualistic 'objects' (attitudes, personalities, etc.) and explanations embedded in a range of cultural texts and practices (soap operas, government policies, sport, etc.) (see Gordo and de Vos, 2010; de Vos, 2012). But these and other discourses can be resisted and there is a particular interest here in developing and articulating alternative 'counter-discourses', after Foucault (e.g. 1980). In line with the three features outlined by Potter and Wetherell (1987) – variability, construction and function – Parker (1994) suggests the Foucauldian triad of contradiction–constitution–power. Although sympathetic to the former system, he argues that these latter three concepts attached to discourse analysis signal a more explicitly critical endeavour. As opposed to variability, the first concept of contradiction between discourses is said to imply struggle, fragmentation and social conflict. The notion of constitution rather than construction is presented as emphasizing structural constraints on individual activity – 'our ideas are constituted within patterns of discourse that we cannot control' (1994: 290), although meaning as contestable remains a theme. The preference for power over function stresses the force of discourses in positioning individuals in complex and often constraining ways (see Box 3.2).

Lastly, more recent attempts to invoke Foucault's concepts of discourse analysis in social psychology have come from Hook (2001, 2007), who is critical of previous attempts at understanding and employing Foucault's ideas as a methodology. Hook argues that discourse for Foucault is a less a linguistic system and more of a method for understanding the ways in which 'knowledge', 'materiality' and 'power' are used to construct and discipline subjects. 'It is exactly the omission of these three dimensions of analysis that so undermines the epistemological strength, the explanatory power and the political abilities of both Parker's (1992) and Potter and Wetherell's (1987) approaches' (Hook, 2007: 132).

Box 3.2   A discourse analysis of instructions for using children's toothpaste (Parker, 1994)

Parker considers the text presented on a tube of children's toothpaste to highlight the versatility of discourse analysis as well as the cultural structuring of such 'innocent' material. The 'MAWS PUNCH & JUDY TOOTHPASTE' is accompanied by pictures of Punch and Judy and provides the following directions:

Choose a children's brush that has a small head and add a pea-sized amount of Punch & Judy toothpaste. To teach your child to clean teeth stand behind and place your hand under the child's chin to tilt head back and see mouth. Brush both sides of teeth as well as tops. Brush after breakfast and last thing at night. Supervise the brushing of your child's teeth until the age of eight. If your child is taking fluoride treatment, seek professional advice concerning daily intake. Contains 0.8% Sodium Monofluorophosphate.

After explaining the steps in and assumptions of his analysis in some detail, Parker goes on to identify four discourses in the Foucauldian tradition: 'rationalist' – implying an ability to follow procedures, make judgements, etc.; 'familial' – where children are 'owned' and supervised by parents; 'developmental–educational' – which stresses teaching the child until a developmental milestone is reached; 'medical' – linking the use of toothpaste to hygiene, professional supervision and chemical composition.

  He proceeds to argue that such discourses function to reinforce the institutions of the family and of medicine, which are interconnected; medical authorities have often sought to advise parents on best practices (Donzelot, 1979). The image of Punch and Judy, on the other hand, provides a conflicting symbol of family in that it represents bad parents but also suggests revolt against the forces of discipline and order. In sum, parents and medics are positioned as powerful subjects whilst children are their subordinates, under their surveillance and control. Parker goes into much more detail in presenting and arguing for this form of analysis and acknowledges potential criticisms (e.g. implying that discourses are constructed, external and static; see also Antaki *et al.*, 2003).

In practice, many discourse analysts draw on both broad approaches in their work and there have been calls for more eclectic, integrationist methods (Wetherell, 2007; 1998). Since there are many different practices and disagreements within this broad area, it is difficult to produce a formal set of procedures for conducting discourse analysis. However, several authors have provided useful guidelines and worked examples (e.g. Potter, 2007; Antaki *et al.*, 2003; Wetherell *et al.*, 2001; Willig, 2008). As you might expect, discourse analysis requires close, careful reading of the texts in question. Next, the coding of relevant material is undertaken, with care taken not to be too selective or exclude too much text. This process is complex and the identification of discourses fraught with uncertainty and revision. The important point is that your interpretations must be grounded in textual evidence, but there must also be an openness to and acknowledgement of potential alternative interpretations. Once fairly confident that you have identified the main discourses employed in the text, it might be fruitful then to discern the functions which these serve. Discursive functions can be understood or read in terms of the interpersonal context (justifications, accusations, etc.) as well as the wider sociocultural climate (how the phenomenon is constructed in society). For example, if 'men as victims' has been identified as a common discourse, this could be related to the research context (e.g. a gathering of unemployed men) and/or wider social trends (e.g. a backlash against feminism) (e.g. Gough & Peace, 2000). Throughout this process it is important to consider the variability as well as consistency in talk, as even short extracts can yield complex and contradictory positions (see the appendix to this chapter for further details).

As mentioned, discourse analysis may be applied to a wide range of 'texts', and various journals provide excellent examples of critical discourse analytic work, including *Discourse and Society, Feminism and Psychology* and *Qualitative Research in Psychology*.

Narrative and psychosocial research

Qualitative research methods have multiplied over the years and are rising in prominence in psychology (see Madill & Gough, 2008; Willig & Stainton-Rogers, 2008). There are now a wealth of textbooks, journals and other resources where students and researchers can learn about many different methodologies. However, many quali- tative researchers and qualitative research traditions do not claim to be undertaking critical work; indeed some (e.g. phenomenological) approaches are interested mainly in individual experiences and perceptions rather than the societal discourses and structures which may shape and constrain these. In addition, some qualitative approaches assume that there is a direct relation between what people say (e.g. in research interviews) and what they are thinking/feeling/experiencing. In contrast, critical (social) psychologists are concerned with situating individual and group experiences within salient social and cultural contexts – and interrogating those discourses which may be contributing to inequalities and marginalization of particular communities.

But there are also many varieties of critical research, and methodologies not normally thought of as critical can be used for critical purposes. For example, Langdridge (2004, 2007, 2008) makes a case for phenomenological and narrative methods as having the potential for critical social psychological contributions. Phenomenology is concerned with the nature of subjective experiences, with the person viewed as a conscious actor who constructs meaning. Narrative analysis focuses on the content and structure of personal stories and suggests that experience is meaningfully conveyed in narrative form. Drawing from major theorists in hermeneutic, phenomenological and narrative traditions (e.g. Polkinghorne, 1988; Ricoeur, 1984; Sarbin, 1986), Langdridge (2007: 129–152) proposes a 'Critical Narrative Analysis' which respects the research participant's accounts, is open to observing politically significant aspects of experience and can call upon theoretical categories not mentioned by the participant to help situate experience and challenge wider discourses informing those accounts.

Similarly, Squire and colleagues (e.g. Andrews *et al.*, 2008) advocate a critical narrative approach, and have developed a Centre for Narrative Research: http://www.uel.ac.uk/cnr/. A key concern at this centre revolves around social change:

> Narrative research in the social sciences searches out, analyses and works with stories that relate significantly to people's lives. Many argue that this increasingly popular qualitative approach can offer understandings of social change. Narratives themselves can be important components of social change, and narrative research may contribute to such change. Researchers have worked successfully with narrative to address medical, social and educational problems, to build communities and resolve crises, to aid reconciliation and to improve understanding in situations of conflict and change.

http://www.uel.ac.uk/cnr/
NarrativeandSocialChange.htm

In their 2008 text, these authors cover critical approaches to narrative, for example by usefully distinguishing experience-centred and culturally oriented approaches to narrative (Squire), and by discussing the relevance of critical theorists such as Foucault (Tamboukou) to narrative research (see Andrews *et al.*, 2008).

Other researchers also apply narrative approaches critically. For example, Crossley (2000) engages with critical and discursive psychology to develop a narrative approach which she has employed to explore experiences of trauma, such as child sexual abuse and living with HIV. Similarly, Murray (e.g. 2002; 2003; 2007) has developed a social approach to narrative research which involves group/community narratives as well as personal stories. Murray (2007) notes:

> the study of narrative breaks down the traditional psychological/ social distinction and develops a more complex psycho-social subject. The narrator is an active agent who is part of a social world. Through narrative, the agent engages with that world. Through narrative analysis, we can begin to understand both the narrators and their world. (116)

Smith and Sparkes (e.g. 2011) use narrative methods to study how former rugby players cope with severe disability, locating personal stories within gendered and medicalized contexts. Stephens (2011) calls for more narrative research in health psychology as a means for understanding inequalities in health. Hall (2011) adopts a critical, feminist application of narrative methods in the context of trauma recovery, specifically on success and thriving in women who had suffered childhood maltreatment.

Narrative also plays a role in some psychosocial research. There is a concern within psychosocial approaches that discourse-based theory and analysis does not provide an adequate understanding of subjective experience (e.g. Blackman *et al.*, 2008; Hollway & Jefferson, 2000) and so an important feature of psychosocial work is a focus on subjectivity. Subjectivity is understood in relation to biographical as well as social influences, so life stories (narratives) become important here (see Emerson & Frosh, 2009). As mentioned in Chapter 1, much psychosocial work is informed by psychoanalytic theories, so there is an emphasis on the unconscious and early experience as important influences on personal choices, valued identities and relationships with others. Other work labelled as psychosocial steers away from psychoanalytic concepts and views the subjective in terms of personal engagement with cultural discourses, individual histories and significant relationships (see Finn & Henwood [2009] for a broad psychosocial analysis of interviews involving first time fathers).

A useful research example which both highlights a psychoanalytically informed psychosocial approach and which identifies points of opposition to it concerns an article by Hollway and Jefferson (2005) and associated commentaries. Here the authors document their psychoanalytically informed analysis of a case study ('Vince'), who had experienced difficulties at work and a psychosomatic illness. Hollway & Jefferson portray Vince as a divided psychosocial subject, influenced by unconscious conflict and defences as well as social forces. One of the commentaries is by Wetherell (2005), an important figure in UK (critical) social psychology and in the discourse analysis community. Her own position could be described as psychosocial – but without employing psychoanalytic concepts. In response to Hollway and Jefferson's psychoanalytically inclined analysis of 'Vince's' interview data, she makes her position clear:

> I assume a reflexive actor embedded in relationally and inter-subjectively organized flows of practices, partly subject to pre-existing discursive resources, but endlessly mobilizing and reworking these (170)...

> I prefer forms of psychosocial analysis which stay with the patterns in the accounting itself – the discursive resources available to Vince which organize his narratives, which create his dilemmas and which in this case are almost unliveable. (172)

Clearly there is a debate here concerning the theoretical concepts which can best account for Vince's actions: both the psychoanalytic and the discursive stances summarized here locate Vince within relevant social circumstances and contexts, but disagree on the source of and motivations for his actions (unconscious v proactive 'choices'). There are other psychosocial researchers who attempt to blend psychoanalytic and discursive approaches together (e.g. Gough, 2009; Frosh *et al.*, 2002), although this marriage has been questioned by some (e.g. Edley, 2006). Whichever position one favours with these debates, a key point is that psychosocial work on subjectivity clearly rejects mainstream psychological theories which present the self as unitary and rational (see Chapter 6); instead, the self is socially and biographically situated and engaged in efforts to negotiate through a range of competing and sometimes contradictory subject positions.

Action research

Action research typically involves the researcher/s working in partnership with a particular group or community in order to facilitate positive changes in social position and experience. Action research is more an 'orientation to inquiry' than a particular research method, as such it 'attempts to combine understanding, or development of theory, with action and change through a participative process, whilst remaining grounded in experience' (Kagan *et al.*, 2008: 32). It is especially attractive to critical researchers committed to raising awareness of inequalities and attempting to bring about social change and justice. No one research method dominates, and projects may use a range of methods and data collection techniques such as 'narrative inquiry' (e.g. Williams, Labonte & O'Brien, 2003), 'semi-structured interviews' (e.g. Siddiquee & Kagan, 2006) and 'focus groups' (e.g. Bostock & Freeman, 2003). As a form of research it attracts those who are interested in improving things for specific groups and communities, informed by particular agendas, including feminism, socialism, gay rights and anti-racism. Rheinharz (1992) refers to 'action-in-research' and helpfully specifies five relevant tasks/goals:

Action research	the obvious but nonetheless crucial requirement of a research project working towards desirable change;
Participatory/ collaborative research	a democratic research process is favoured where participants have an equal say in decisions concerning data collection and analysis – the term 'co- researchers' is often used in this context;
Prevalence and needs assessment	instead of being defined in advance by researchers, participant needs and issues are identified during the initial stages of the research through open discussions, etc.;
Evaluation research	to assess the effectiveness of actions instituted within the research process and decide between competing strategies for further use;
Demystification	refers to knowledge gained during action research as prompting change – the greater the awareness of the situation, the greater the capacity for action.

So, the key theme of action research is intervention in a situation perceived to be 'problematic' in some way/s. An action research 'spiral' is summarized by Elliott (1991):

- select the general area; discuss, observe, read and decide on your first action;
- take your action (and monitor the action);
- examine the information you have collected;
- evaluate processes and outcomes;
- plan next action;
- take next action;
- continue.

Banister *et al.* (1994) describe a hypothetical example of action research. The 'problem' a youth worker identifies upon firstly arriving at a new centre concerns the relative lack of young women using the centre. The next step is then to gather information and develop research questions by engaging with the relevant research literature, discussing the issues with colleagues and centre-users and studying local documents regarding that particular centre. Having completed these tasks, a course of action might be devised, such as organizing women-only activities and discussions. In the midst of such action male domination and sexual harassment might well arise as a deterrent to the women's attendance at the centre. Further action here might be to continue the women-only sessions if desired by the users, observe whether this support group is having any demonstrable effects on participation in centre activities and perhaps take formal action to ensure equal access to facilities, such as the pool table. All the while the effects of in/action would be monitored and more actions planned and initiated, depending on the time constraints of the project. The action research should then be written up, preferably in conjunction with users, and written for lay as well as academic audiences. All stages in the research process should be documented (a reflexive diary is useful here; see below) and the final analysis should be returned to participants for further comment and possible revision. Critical qualitative research in general tends to emphasize 'critical subjectivity', or reflexivity, in order to interrogate the values and interactions which have created the research and its outputs.

Another variation on the 'action research' orientation is Participatory Action Research (PAR). PAR stemmed initially from research conducted by the social psychologist Kurt Lewin and radical educationist Paulo Freire. There are three main tenets that define PAR; they include: (1)

research typically originates in communities and with populations that have been exploited or oppressed in some way, (2) it works to address specific concerns of the community with the purpose of achieving positive social change and (3) it is a process of research, education and action that all community members are given an opportunity to play a meaningful role (Brydon-Miller, 1997: 660–661). PAR is 'critical' because it seeks to release communities living under unjust power relations and to contest and reconstitute unjust, and/or unsatisfying (alienating) ways in which others may interpret and describe their world, ways of working and ways of relating to others (Kemmis & McTaggart, 2005: 567; see also Box 3.3). Two examples of PAR are provided by Fine and Torre (2004) in their article on PAR in public institutions. Firstly, they report on a longitudinal mixed methods study of the impact of college in prison on the women students, the prison environment, prisoners' postrelease outcomes and civil society. The second study concerns another mixed methods study focusing on how race, ethnicity, class, and academic opportunities and outcomes are (inequitably) distributed in public schools. Here there is a concern to document the struggles of marginalized groups, a focus on inequalities and a desire to facilitate social change. Given the significant benefits that accrue from using PAR, it has become a popular means for assisting a range of different communities such as young adults using psychiatric services (Delman, 2012), people in community aged care (Ottmann et al., 2011), and indigenous peoples living in rural and remote area communities (Wearing et al., 2010).

Box 3.3   Critical community psychology and action research (Kagan et al., 2011)

In their book *Critical Community Psychology* Kagan et al. provide a highly useful and practical guide for the budding student or practitioner wishing to conduct some form of action research. By using an action research approach informed by critical theory, the authors aim to provide their readers with a 'powerful set of practical-theoretical tools' which they can apply to 'social phenomena to try and get a more thorough understanding that can help foment progressive social change' (12). The authors define critical community psychology as a framework for working with groups marginalized by existing social systems that lead to a critical consciousness and value-based participatory work that functions by forging community alliances. 'It is a way of working that is pragmatic and reflexive, whilst not wedded to any particular orthodoxy of method' (24). In part two of their book the authors outline four key 'action' strategies for promoting positive social change; they include:

1. Creating a critical consciousness (or 'conscientisation') – This aspect is designed to expand people's knowledge, understanding, beliefs and critical reflections on their world and experiences (186–198);
2. Creating new social relations and/or settings – In this part people and organisations with similar interests are brought together in order to secure resources and to creatively devise new insights and possibilities for wider change (198–207);
3. Development of alliances and counter-systems – The focus here is on expanding and maxmising the resources by making partnerships with new groups and organisations in order to spread social change beyond the local issue or content. There is also a commitment here to developing alternatives to the existing social order (210–224);
4. Accompaniment, advocacy and analysis of policy – In this part of the process researchers walk alongside, listening to and witness the lived realities of marginalised communities; this is referred to as 'accompaniment'. There is also an emphasis on providing advocacy where this is required and an analysis of social policy formulation and implementation that threatens equality and wellbeing (224–240).

Reflexivity

As stated above, critical social psychologists work mainly with qualitative data, and this can range from data gathered by researchers such as interviews, participant observations and focus group discussions, to data which already exist in some form, such as media features (e.g. newspaper articles, radio and television interviews), political speeches and online discussion forums. All such data sources are well represented in published books and articles, and in the rest of this book you will find examples of many different studies. This diversity of methodologies generates issues and debates concerning quality criteria – how can we evaluate the 'validity' of different qualitative research studies? There have been attempts to develop quality criteria which cover all or most qualitative methods (Lincoln & Guba, 1985; Henwood & Pidgeon, 1992; Yardley, 2008), and these are usually contrasted to established standards for judging quantitative research (objectivity; replicability; reliability etc.). For example, 'transferability' is a concept which is used in relation to qualitative research and can be contrasted with 'generalisability' in quantitative research. Qualitative researchers accept that all research situations are to some extent unique, but suggest that findings can nonetheless be cautiously applied to other, similar, samples and situations, while acknowledging any variations between the original research cluster and other sites. 'Triangulation' is another quality check that is used by qualitative researchers whereby multiple methods and/or analysts can be used for comparison purposes. Denzin and Lincoln (2005) note that triangulation:

> Reflects an attempt to secure an in-depth understanding of the phenomenon in question... [using] the combination of multiple methodological practices, empirical materials, perspectives, and observers in a single study... that adds rigour, breadth, complexity, richness, and depth to any inquiry. (5)

Qualitative researchers may also employ a technique known as 'consensual validation', whereby two or more researchers independently analyse a set of interview transcripts or other textual data and then compare their sets of themes with each other to see where there is similarity and difference. The independent analysis is then combined, providing a richer analysis overall then would have been the case if only one person had conducted the analysis. This process however is not without its drawbacks. For example, a focus on agreement and shared themes may well neglect the different interpretations that analysts necessarily bring to datasets – messy, idiosyncratic views may well be swept under the carpet. All qualitative analysis involves a degree of creativity and subjectivity (as well as systematic procedures, rigour and discipline), and the concept of 'reflexivity' has been developed to account for researcher influence, which we will come to shortly. In addition, there are important differences between qualitative methodologies, and even particular fields will feature different versions of methods (e.g. discourse analysis), so it is also essential that such differences are recognized – and that distinctive quality criteria can be conceived and applied to particular methodologies and particular research projects. This point is made clear by Parker (2005) in his book *Qualitative Psychology: Introducing Radical Research*, where he argues that criteria should be open and flexible, and that core principles or apprenticeship, scholarship and innovation should override any set of criteria when conducting and evaluating research. Another important principle which links to diversity and complexity in research practice is reflexivity, which we will now look at more closely.

Reflexivity is signalled by the researcher's incorporation of information relating to the research context and to relevant 'personal' thoughts and feelings into the research report. In contrast to positivistic psychology, where researcher detachment and neutrality are cherished, it is thought inevitable that the perspectives of researcher and participants and their interrelationship will impact the research and, moreover, that such influences should be documented to further contextualize the research (see Finlay & Gough, 2003). In feminist work, for example, the suppression of the human researcher is viewed as a particularly masculine practice, rather than some universal or necessary scientific norm, and a more participative and open stance is advocated (Wilkinson, 1988). Making public one's interpretative resources and processes renders the researcher more accountable for the analysis and places the reader of the research report in a better-informed position from which to situate and assess the research as a whole.

In a much-cited piece, Wilkinson (1988) notes three distinct, but inter-related, forms of reflexivity: personal, functional and disciplinary:

- *Personal reflexivity* requires that the researcher make visible their individuality and its effects on the research process. There is an attempt to make visible those motivations, interests, attitudes, etc. which the researcher has imported to the research process and to reflect on how these have impacted the research. Such subjective factors are typically construed as 'bias' or 'interference' within 'scientific' research, but recognition of the (inter-)personal dimension to research is heralded as enriching and informative by qualitative researchers.
- *Functional reflexivity* relates to one's role as a researcher and the effect this might have on the research process. It focuses attention on the different identities presented within the research and the interactions between researcher and participants. In this case a key issue concerns the distribution of power and status within the research process; although many qualitative researchers are

committed to democratic forms of inquiry where the voices of participants are encouraged and respected, it is virtually impossible to escape researcher–participant relationships structured by inequalities (see Parker, 1992). After all, it is the researcher who principally develops an idea, formulates the research questions and organizes the format of the research.

- Finally, *disciplinary reflexivity* involves a critical stance towards the place and function of the particular research project within broader debates about theory and method. It suggests outlining those existing concepts and traditions which have been important in shaping the research and requires some discussion of the potential contribution of the research to a particular literature. This dimension of reflexivity is enthusiastically endorsed by feminist and critical researchers interested in challenging the findings of conventional (usually quantitative) social science research (see Stainton-Rogers *et al.*, 1995).

A common way of tracking the impact of the researcher and research context is to keep a diary or journal which documents the researcher's thoughts and experiences before, during and after data collection and analysis (Banister *et al.*, 1994; 2011). Notes concerning why certain choices and decisions were made, about changing directions, personal reactions, etc. can be used to inform a 'reflexive account', which in turn will inform the research report. The question of how to incorporate this narrative into one's writing-up is indeed difficult, with many authors preferring to simply provide information about researcher and participant subject positions (gender, age, social class, race) and perhaps hazarding some speculation towards the end of the paper on the effects of these factors on the research outcomes. But there are examples of more ambitious forms of reflexive writing which entail disrupting the narrative flow of the text, for example with commentaries at the end of each section contrasting the academic analysis with more personal reporting, thereby highlighting the fragmented positions of the researcher and the status of the text as constructed (see MacMillan, 2003; Lather, 1992). But even when engaging in such adventurous and creative forms of writing up research, certain problems plague the notion of reflexivity, as discussed below.

The observation and reporting of subjective thoughts and feelings germane to the research rests on some dubious assumptions. Prevailing definitions and practices around reflexivity do tend to presume a conscious subject with unproblematic access to their 'intentions', 'motivations' and 'feelings' and the ways in which these shaped the data collection and research as a whole (Bishop & Shepherd, 2011): a reflexive stance implies 'honesty' about presenting one's position. But can we be sure that we know what prompts us to choose a particular research project, to ask certain questions, to respond in specific ways? To accomplish such an onerous task would require a 'superhuman self-consciousness', which may be attainable only (if at all) through an intensive programme of psychoanalysis, according to Seale (1999). Compounding this problem of self-awareness is the post-modern deconstruction of subjectivity as socially constructed, fragmented and contradictory (e.g. Blackman *et al.*, 2008; Shotter & Gergen, 1988; see also Chapter 6). How can we pin down a self which is multifaceted, dynamic and embedded in language and social relationships? Indeed, there is an emerging consensus that our identities are multiple, fluid and dispersed across time and place, subject to negotiations within sets of relationships at home, at work and at leisure (Wetherell & Mohanty, 2010; Wetherell & Maybin, 1996). Consequently, reflexivity must be re-viewed as similarly complex and tenuous (see Bishop & Shepherd, 2011; Gough, 2003).

A fruitful way of exploring the complexity of positions and relationships within the research process is to turn to the text, whether this constitutes interview transcripts, field notes, or diary entries and so on. Close reading of the text will highlight the multiple and shifting positions of the researcher during the data collection phase and perhaps enhance reflexivity through identifying positions not consciously adopted at the time. For example, the researcher could describe themselves as 'feminist', presenting details about self and existing theory which justify this self-identification, whereas a study of the interview transcripts could throw up instances where anti-feminist talk was ignored or even encouraged by the researcher. The point is, it is impossible and simplistic to presume a fixed, knowable researcher-subject in advance when diverse and conflicting positions may well become apparent upon retrospective analysis. Therefore, it is important for qualitative researchers to acknowledge a potentially numerous range of possibly competing interests and to return to the transcripts a number of times in order to achieve this end. And the reader of the research report will similarly be in a position to relate claims about subjectivities and relationships between researcher and the researched to the textual evidence and to make judgements about the persuasiveness of the reflexive analysis. So, it is important to sustain an openness to the possibility that one's research aims and stated orientation may be complicated or compromised during inter-actions with participants and in the subsequent presentation of the research 'findings'. But it should be borne in mind that reflexivity can slide into self-referential analysis if the focus shifts from the account/s and potential critical analyses to the researcher's construction of the account/s (Gough & Madill, in press; Burman & Parker, 1993).

Summary

Critical social psychological research follows from concerns to highlight and challenge forms of oppression and exploitation in contemporary society, a concern which often entails a focus on discourse and subjectivity, and potentially involving a range of different methodologies, from discursive and narrative approaches to psychosocial and action research projects. It is important to recognize that critical research projects can take many different forms, from case studies to community action projects, and can be used to serve a variety of purposes, from challenging mainstream psychological theories to advocating social change on behalf of a particular marginalized group. In contrast to much social psychological work, critical psychologists tend to be involved in the research process, whether through selecting topics of personal significance, working with a community towards shared goals, or emphasizing particular aspects of the research for different audiences. This personal dimension requires careful management, which is why a reflexive stance is important: documenting and analysing the researcher's own investment in, and influence on, the research process will help to place the research in context for readers. On a final note, it must also be stressed that critical activities need not be confined to research. As Nightingale and Neilands (1997) suggest, a 'critical' attitude can be usefully deployed in the services of charitable organizations (telephone counselling, befriending schemes, etc.) and political groups (anti-sexist, environmental campaigns, etc.) (see also Prilleltensky *et al.*, 2002). Similarly, many critical writers stress the importance of resisting abuses of psychology in practice – in the areas of therapy, health and education, for example (see Parker, 1999). The boundaries between critical research and practical activities are of course blurred in forms of 'action research'.

Key references

Andrews, M., Squire, C. & Tamboukou, M. (eds). (2008). *Doing Narrative Research*. London: Sage.
A range of contributions on narrative research with critical purpose.

Crossley, M. L. (2000). *Introducing Narrative Psychology: Self, Trauma and the Construction of Meaning*. Buckingham UK: Open University Press.
Crossley's book provides an introduction to narrative inquiry with a particular focus on the way in which people construct a sense of self-identity through the stories they tell themselves and others. These stories of self-identity are shaped and influenced by historical, discursive and socio-cultural structures. Crossley then provides two examples of narrative psychological studies on the topics of childhood sexual abuse and people living with HIV.

Finlay, L. & Gough, B. (eds). (2003). *Reflexivity: A Practical Guide for Researchers in Health & Social Sciences*. Oxford: Blackwell Science.
Chapters cover theories on reflexivity, reflexive practices in research and writing reflexively.

Hollway, W., & Jefferson, T. (2005). Panic and Perjury: a Psychosocial Exploration of Agency. *British Journal of Social Psychology*, 44, 147–163 (plus commentaries).
Provides a useful summary of key debates between psychoanalytic and discourse analytic approaches, with a focus on an interesting case study.

See the *Journal of Community and Applied Social Psychology*, Volume 13, Number 6, which contains eight articles on the topic of 'action research'.

Parker, I. (2005). *Qualitative Psychology: Introducing Radical Research*. London: Routledge.
A provocative critique of established qualitative methods and call for innovative, critical projects.

Wetherell, M., Taylor, S. & Yates , S.J. (eds). (2001). *Discourse as Data: A Guide for Analysis*. London: Sage/Oxford University Press.
Very useful resource documenting a range of discourse analytic approaches involving 'real' data.

New references

Andrews, M., Squire, C. & Tamboukou, M. (eds). (2008). *Doing Narrative Research*. London: Sage.

Antaki, C., Billig, M., Edwards, D. & Potter, J. (2003). Discourse analysis means doing analysis: A critique of six analytic shortcomings. *Discourse Analysis Online, 1*(1).

Arribas-Ayllon, M. & Walkerdine, V. (2008). Foucauldian Discourse Analysis. In C. Willig & W. Stainton-Rogers (eds), *Sage Handbook of Qualitative Research in Psychology* (pp. 91–108). London: Sage.

Banister, P., Bunn, G., Burman, E., Daniels, J., Duckett, P., Goodley, D., Lawthom, R., Parker, I., Runswick-Cole, K., & Sixsmith, J. (2011). *Qualitative*

Methods in Psychology: A Research Guide (2nd edn). Maidenhead, UK: Open University Press.

Bishop, E. C. & Shepherd, M. L. (2011). Ethical reflections: examining reflexivity through the narrative paradigm. *Qualitative Health Research, 21*(9), 1283–1294.

Blackman, L., Cromby, J., Hook, D., Papadopoulos, D. & Walkerdine, V. (2008). Creating subjectivities (Editorial), *Subjectivity 22*, 1–27.

Bostock, J. & Freeman, J. (2003). No limits: doing participatory action research with young people in Northumberland. *Journal of Community & Applied Social Psychology, 13*(6), 464–474.

Brydon-Miller, M. (1997). Participatory action research: psychology and social change. *Journal of Social Issues, 53*(4), 657–666.

Crossley, M. L. (2000). *Introducing Narrative Psychology: Self, Trauma and the Construction of Meaning.* Buckingham, UK: Open University Press.

Denzin, N. K., & Lincoln, Y. S. (2005). Introduction: the discipline and practice of qualitative research. In N. K. Denzin & Y. S. Lincoln (eds), *The Sage Handbook of Qualitative Research* (3rd edn, pp. 1–32). Thousand Oaks, CA: Sage.

Delman, J. (2012). Participatory action research and young adults with psychiatric disabilities. *Psychiatric Rehabilitation Journal, 35*(3), 231–234.

de Vos, J. (2012). *Psychologisation in Times of Globalisation.* London: Routledge.

Edley, N. (2006). Never the twain shall meet: a critical appraisal of the combination of discourse and psychoanalytic theory in studies of men and masculinity. *Sex Roles, 55*, 601–608.

Edwards, D. (2005). Discursive psychology. In K. L. Fitch & R. E. Sanders (eds), *Handbook of Language and Social Interaction* (pp. 257–273). Mahwah, NJ: Lawrence Erlbaum.

Edwards, D. & Potter, J. (2005). Discursive Psychology, mental states and descriptions. In H. te Molder & J. Potter (eds) *Conversation and Cognition.* Cambridge: Cambridge University Press.

Emerson, P. & Frosh, S. (2009). *Critical Narrative Analysis in Psychology* (Revised edn). Basingstoke, UK: Palgrave Macmillan.

Fairclough, N. (2010). *Critical Discourse Analysis: the Critical Study of Language* (2nd edn). Harlow, UK: Longman.

Fine, M. and Torre, M. (2004). Re-membering exclusions: participatory action research in public institutions. *Qualitative Research in Psychology, 1*, 15–37.

Finlay, L. & Gough, B. (eds). (2003). *Reflexivity: A Practical Guide for Researchers in Health & Social Sciences.* Oxford: Blackwell.

Finn, M. & Henwood, K. (2009). Exploring masculinities within men's identificatory imaginings of first-time fatherhood, *British Journal of Social Psychology*, DOI: 10.1348/014466608X386099.

Frosh, S., Phoenix, A. & Pattman, R. (2002). *Young Masculinities: Understanding Boys in Contemporary Society*. Basingstoke: Palgrave Macmillan.

Gordo, A. & De Vos, J. (2010). Psychologism, psychologisation and de-psychologisation. *Annual Review of Critical Psychology, 8*, 3–7.

Gough, B. (2003). Shifting researcher positions during a group interview study: a reflexive analysis and re-view. In Finlay, L. and Gough. B. (eds) *Reflexivity: A Practical Guide for Researchers in Health and Social Science*. Oxford: Blackwell Publishing.

Gough, B. (2009). A psycho-discursive approach to analysing qualitative interview data, with reference to a father-son relationship, *Qualitative Research, 9*(5), 527–545.

Gough, B. & Madill, A. (in press). Subjectivity in psychological science: from problem to prospect, *Psychological Methods*.

Hall, J.M. (2011). Narrative methods in a study of trauma recovery, *Qualitative Health Research, 21*(1), 3–13.

Henwood, K. & Pidgeon, N. (1992). Qualitative research and psychological theorizing, *British Journal of Psychology, 83*(1), 97–111.

Hollway, W. & Jefferson, T. (2005). Panic and perjury: a psychosocial exploration of agency. *British Journal of Social Psychology, 44*, 147–163.

Hook, D. (2001). Discourse, knowledge, materiality, history: Foucault and discourse analysis. *Theory & Psychology, 11*, 521–547.

Hook, D. (2007). *Foucault, Psychology and the Analytics of Power*. Basingstoke, UK: Palgrave Macmillan.

Kagan, C., Burton, M. & Siddiquee, A. (2008). Action research. In C. Willig & W. Stainton-Rogers (eds), *The Sage Handbook of Qualitative Research in Psychology* (pp. 32–53). London: Sage.

Kagan, C., Burton, M., Duckett, P., Lawthom, R. & Siddiquee, A. (2011). *Critical Community Psychology: Critical Action and Social Change*. Hoboken, N.J.: John Wiley & Sons.

Kemmis, S. & McTaggart, R. (2005). Participatory action research: community action and the public sphere. In N. K. Denzin & Y. S. Lincoln (eds), *The Sage Handbook of Qualitative Research* (3rd edn, pp. 559–603). Thousand Oaks, CA: Sage.

Kitzinger, C. (2000). Doing feminist conversation analysis. *Feminism & Psychology 10*(2), 163–193.

Krippendorff, K. (2004). *Content Analysis: An Introduction to Its Methodology* (2nd edn). London: Sage.

Langdridge, D. (2007). *Phenomenological Psychology: Theory, Research and Method.* Harlow, UK: Pearson.

Langdridge, D. (2008). Phenomenology and critical social psychology: directions and debates in theory and research. *Social and Personality Psychology Compass, 2*(3), 1126–1142.

Lincoln, Y. S. & Guba, E. G. (1985). *Naturalistic Inquiry.* Newbury Park, CA: Sage.

MacMillan, K. (2003). The next turn: reflexively analysing reflexive research. In Finlay, L. & Gough, B. (eds). (2003). *Reflexivity: A Practical Guide for Researchers in Health & Social Sciences.* Oxford: Blackwell.

Madill, A. and Gough, B. (2008). Qualitative research and its place in psychological science. *Psychological Methods, 13*(3), 254–271.

McKinlay, A. & McVittie, C. (2008). *Social Psychology and Discourse.* Oxford, UK: Wiley-Blackwell.

Murray, M. (2002). Connecting narrative and social representation theory in health research. *Social Science Information, 41* (4), 653–673.

Murray, M. (2003). Narrative psychology and narrative analysis. In P. Camic, J. E. Rhodes & L. Yardley (eds), *Qualitative Research in Psychology: Expanding Perspectives in Methodology and Design* (pp. 95–112). Washington, DC: American Psychological Association.

Murray, M. (2007). Narrative psychology. In J. A. Smith (ed.), *Qualitative Psychology: A Practical Guide to Research Methods* (2nd edn, pp. 111–132). London: Sage.

Ottmann, G., Laragy, C., Allen, J. & Feldman, P. (2011). Co-production in practice: participatory action research to develop a model of community aged care. *Systemic Practice and Action Research, 24*(5), 413–427.

Parker, I. (ed.). (2002). *Critical Discursive Psychology.* Basingstoke, UK: Palgrave Macmillan.

Parker, I. (2005). *Qualitative Psychology: Introducing Radical Research.* Buckingham, UK: Open University Press.

Parker, I. (2011). Discursive social psychology now, *British Journal of Social Psychology,* DOI: 10.1111/j.2044–8309.2011.02046.x

Polkinghorne, D. (1988). *Narrative Knowing and the Human Sciences.* Albany, NY: State University of New York Press.

Potter, J. (ed.). (2007). *Discourse and Psychology: Theory and Method* (Vol. 1). London: Sage.

Potter, J. (2012). Discourse analysis and discursive psychology. In H. Cooper, P. M. Camic, D. L. Long, A. T. Panter, D. Rindskopf & K. J. Sher (eds), *APA Handbook of Research Methods in Psychology: Research Designs: Quantitative, Qualitative, Neuropsychological, and Biological* (Vol. 2, pp. 119–138). Washington, DC: American Psychological Association.

Prilleltensky, I., Nelson, G. & Geoffrey, B. (2002). *Doing Psychology Critically: Making a Difference in Diverse Settings.* Basingstoke: Palgrave Macmillan.

Ricoeur, P. (1984). *Time and Narrative* (K. McLaughlin & D. Pellauer, Trans. Vol. 1,2 & 3). Chicago: University of Chicago Press.

Rose, N. (1999). *Governing the Soul: The Shaping of the Private Self* (2nd edn). London: Free Association Books.

Sarbin, T. (ed.) (1986). *Narrative Psychology: The Storied Nature of Human Conduct.* New York: Praeger.

Siddiquee, A. & Kagan, C. (2006). The internet, empowerment, and identity: an exploration of participation by refugee women in a Community Internet Project (CIP) in the United Kingdom (UK). *Journal of Community & Applied Social Psychology, 16*(3), 189–206.

Smith, J. A. (ed.). (2007). *Qualitative Psychology: A Practical Guide to Research Methods* (2nd edn). London: Sage.

Smith, B. & Sparkes, A. (2011). Multiple responses to a chaos narrative. *Health: An Interdisciplinary Journal for the Social Study of Health, Illness & Medicine, 15*(1), 38–53.

Stephens, C. (2011). Narrative analysis in health psychology research: personal, dialogical, and social stories of health. *Health Psychology Review, 5(1)*, 62–78.

Stokoe, E. (2010). Gender, conversation analysis, and the anatomy of membership categorization practices. *Social and Personality Psychology Compass 4*(7), 428–438.

Yardley, L. (2008). Demonstrating validity in qualitative psychology. In J. A. Smith (ed.), *Qualitative Psychology: A Practical Guide to Research Methods* (2nd edn, pp. 235–251). London: Sage.

Wearing, S., Wearing, M. & McDonald, M. (2010). Understanding local power and interactional processes in sustainable tourism: exploring village-tour operator relations on the Kokoda Track, Papua New Guinea. *Journal of Sustainable Tourism, 18*(1), 61–76.

Wetherell, M. (2003). Paranoia, ambivalence and discursive practices: Concepts of position and positioning in psychoanalysis and discursive psychology. In R. Harre & F. Moghaddam (eds). *The Self and Others: Positioning Individuals and Groups in Personal, Political and Cultural Contexts.* New York: Praeger/Greenwood Publishers.

Wetherell, M. (2005). Unconscious conflict or everyday accountability? *British Journal of Social Psychology, 44*(2), 169–175.

Wetherell, M. (2007). A step too far: discursive psychology, linguistic ethnography and questions of identity. *Journal of Sociolinguistics, 11*(5), 661–682.

Wetherell, M. & Mohanty, C. T. (eds). (2010). *The Sage Handbook of Identities*. London: Sage.

Wetherell, M. & Potter, J. (1992). *Mapping the Language of Racism: Discourse and the Legitimation of Exploitation*. NewYork: Columbia University Press.

Wetherell, M., Taylor, S. & Yates, S. J. (eds) (2001). *Discourse as Data: A Guide for Analysis*. London: Sage/Open University Press.

Wiggins, S. & Potter, J. (2008). Discursive psychology. In C. Willig & W. Stainton-Rogers (eds), *The Sage Handbook of Qualitative Research in Psychology* (pp. 73–90). London: Sage.

Wilkinson, S. & Kitzinger, C. (2008). Conversation analysis. In C. Willig & W. Stainton-Rogers (eds), *The Sage Handbook of Qualitative Research in Psychology* (pp. 54–72). London: Sage.

Williams, L., Labonte, R. & O'Brien, M. (2003). Empowering social action through narratives of identity and culture. *Health Promotion International, 18*, 33–40.

Willig, C. (2008a). *Introducing Qualitative Research in Psychology* (2nd edn). Maidenhead, UK: Open University Press.

Willig, C. (2008b). Discourse analysis. In J. A. Smith (ed.), *Qualitative Psychology: A Practical Guide to Research Methods* (2nd edn, pp. 160–185). London: Sage.

Willig, C. & Stainton-Rogers, W. (eds). (2008). *The Sage Handbook of Qualitative Research in Psychology*. London: Sage.

Classic Social Psychology Topics Revisited

Part II

Social Influence

4

This chapter will highlight:

- Social cognition perspectives on social influence
- Theoretical and methodological limitations of such approaches
- Foucauldian notions of social influence as socially constructed and managed activities
- Re-workings of conformity and obedience as potential sites of social control
- Concepts of agency and resistance

Introduction

In crowds, do we disintegrate into untamed animals, or function as passive recipients of others' knowledge, even when that knowledge defies our perceptions? These are two images of what happens to the individual in the presence of other people that have, until recently, enjoyed currency in social psychology. Many people continue to draw on these accounts today, citing examples of the seemingly mindless violence of football hooligans, instances of ethnic cleansing or rioting in response to government austerity measures in the wake of economic recessions. This chapter reviews the classic studies and theoretical explanations of social influence processes, including the work of Le Bon (1895) and Asch (1952). By raising questions about the theoretical framework and the content of this work, alternative insights into how and why people behave in the presence of others are offered from the perspective of critical social psychology.

Historical context

The pursuit of answers to the question of whether the presence of others enhances or inhibits individual performance dates back to the nineteenth century. Early work by Triplett (1898) investigating the effect of others on the racing times of cyclists suggested that the presence of others enhanced individual performance, with those cycling in groups achieving faster times than those cycling alone or against pacers. As Triplett (1898: 533) noted, 'the bodily presence of another contestant participating simultaneously in the race serves to liberate latent energy not ordinarily available'. Later researchers such as Zajonc (1965) pursued and consolidated this idea, incorporating it in a theory of 'social facilitation'. Historically, though, the bulk of experimental work conducted on social influence processes has concentrated on the negative impact that the presence of others has on the activities of the individual. Primary among such studies is Le Bon's (1895) work on crowd behaviour. His observations were based on events he witnessed during the French Revolution in 1872 when, as a member of the ruling classes, he was dismayed at what he perceived as the erosion of traditional standards accompanying 'modernity' (briefly defined as a socio–political project emerging around 1770 with the triple aims of replacing irrational thought with reason, replacing superstition with scientific truths and promoting human betterment). The lower classes were viewed as the source of decay, endangering civilized society. The keystone of this work was that in crowds people lose their rational, human capacities, regressing to more primitive, irresponsible and infantile states of mind leading to violence and other forms of animalistic behaviour (Graumann, 2001: 11–13).

The work of Le Bon (1895) sowed the seeds of later work in social psychology on conformity by suggesting that when in crowds, people suffer 'collective hallucinations which are distortions of the external world suffered by people in crowds as a result of processes of "contagion" and "suggestibility"' (Stainton-Rogers et al., 1995: 79).

'Classic' experiments

Sherif's (1935) autokinetic effect

Sherif (1935) set out to investigate the nature of 'distortions' that individuals experienced in the presence of others. To do so, he employed the autokinetic effect, a perceptual illusion whereby in a darkened room a stationary point of light appears to move. Firstly, individuals in isolation were asked to estimate how far the light moved. Despite wide individual variation, when individuals came together in a group, estimates of movement converged to produce a 'group norm'. Conversely, Sherif found that when people firstly estimated the movement of light in groups and were then asked in subsequent trials to estimate movement individually, in the second instances estimates made as part of the group seemed to influence those made when alone.

Asch (1952) and conformity

One of the major concerns with Sherif's experimental design was that he had effectively based it around an illusion, and thus many argued that the inherent ambiguity weakened any conclusions that could be drawn about the impact of others on the performance of the individual. This was addressed in the work of Asch, who used objective stimuli, the lengths of different lines, to assess whether individuals experienced distortions in the presence of others. This experiment went as follows. Subjects were asked to compare sets of two or three lines and to judge which of the lines was most similar in length to a comparison line. An easy enough task we hear you say! However, unknown to the 'naive' subject, the others present (usually up to seven) had been employed by Asch (as confederates) to perform the task of deliberately choosing lines that were not the most similar to the comparison line. So, we have a naive subject participating in what has been described as a study on perceptual judgement, sitting at the end of a table with people providing verbal responses to the comparison task. On the first two trials all 'subjects' agreed on the appropriate line as they called out their choice. However, on the next and subsequent trials, the seven confederates called out what was clearly the wrong choice. And what did the subject do? Asch found that 5 per cent of subjects conformed to obviously wrong estimates of line size on all trials, 33 per cent conformed on half or more of the trials, and 25 per cent did not conform on any trials.

Throughout the trials the disbelief and discomfort of the naive subjects was visible, and in interviews following the experiments many of those who according to Asch had conformed to the incorrect majority view, talked about not wanting to be different or believing that the others in the group had a clearer view of the lines. Theoretical explanations for the activities witnessed in the above studies centre around the dual concepts of normative and informational pressure, coined by Deutsch and Gerrard (1955). In the Asch (1952) studies, naive subjects who answered incorrectly on trials are believed to have done so from a need for social approval and acceptance: that is, out of a desire to be liked and wanting to seek harmony in the group and to avoid conflict. In contrast, Deutsch and Gerrard (1955) suggest that those converging towards a group norm in the Sherif (1935) experiments did so as a result of informational pressure: that is, on uncertain territory subjects used other people as sources of objective information about the situation and so conformed from a desire to be right.

The Milgram experiment: obedience

Events witnessed during the Second World War raised new questions about how others can influence the behaviour of the individual. In particular, the concept of obedience took centre-stage, embodied in Milgram's (1974) empirical studies into the psychological mechanisms underlying obedience. Milgram advertised for volunteers to participate in a study at Yale University on the effects of punishment on learning. Over one thousand volunteers were to perform either as teacher or pupil, roles that were assigned randomly. 'Teachers' were to aid learning by giving electric shocks of increasing voltage each time 'pupils', situated in a separate room, answered incorrectly. Voltage levers were labelled from mild up to 450 volts (Danger: Severe shock), and teachers were instructed to progress with shocks by the experimenter standing beside them. The disturbing findings showed 62 per cent of the teachers inflicting shocks to the maximum voltage, despite their own discomfort and the cries of pain coming from pupils.

Explanations for why people were prepared to unexpectedly shock other people to 450 volts centred on the pervasiveness of social power and status; that, in the presence of authority figures, individuals lose their capacity for rational, moral thinking and succumb to the authority of the powerful 'other'. Milgram illustrated that obedience is related to situational pressure, a finding that was extremely novel for psychology in the 1960s, as previous explanations of destructive obedience had centred on character traits and certain types of people (e.g. 'The Germans are different' hypothesis).

Common themes in classic social psychology

Although Le Bon's (1895) work could be described as a naturalistic inquiry, and that of Sherif, Asch and Milgram as experiments, they share a number of common themes. Firstly, the focus of this work was on the power of one or more persons to change and shape individual behaviour. For Le Bon, observations made during the French Revolution, and for Milgram the events of the Second World War, narrowed the focus further to concentrate on the presumed negative influence that others could have on the behaviour of the individual. Secondly, each shared a vision of the individual in his (or her) natural state of existence, that of the rational moral being existing separately from an objective social world. Finally, each shared similar epistemological origins: the classic works are, as Stainton-Rogers *et al.* (1995) describe, products of an historical force, 'modernity', whereby social science sought to provide universal truths relating to human behaviour in the belief that such knowledge would ultimately promote human betterment (see also Stainton-Rogers, 2003: chapter 1 'What Is Social Psychology'). It is through unpacking these common themes and assessing their influence on the knowledge derived from the classic works that many authors are increasingly sceptical about what experimental social psychology has actually told us about social influence processes (see Brown, 1996; Harré & Secord, 1972: 79).

The individual and the social

Understandings of social behaviour offered by classic experimental studies on conformity and obedience are based on a particular mechanistic formula regarding the origins of people's activities:

behaviour = the sum of individual + the situation

However, for the formula to be of use to social psychologists, certain givens are assumed about the nature of each of the components in the equation. Firstly, behaviour is presented as an outcome response by the individual to a specified situation. It is assumed that human behaviour is observable and measurable and can be explained using knowledge of the individual and specified stimuli they have been exposed to. Secondly, the individual is defined as *self-contained*, an entity existing independently of social contexts and circumstances. All individuals are viewed as possessing states that are internal and stable – attitudes, cognitions, personalities, to name a few. These have become the bread-and-butter of psychology, with human activities explained in relation to how these states are influenced by and affect social contexts and situations. The third part of the equation, situational influences, is also viewed as objective and malleable. It is assumed that a singular reality, a *real world*, exists which all humans experience and react to universally. In the work of Sherif and Asch, the social is defined as the presence of others, and their impact on the activities of individuals explored in isolation from the other issues, such as the identity of participants, historical practices, cultural contexts, political pressure, economic circumstances and differences in power and social status. Yet the influence of such factors was ever present in Asch's later work and that of subsequent researchers. In the various permutations of his original experimental design, Asch illustrated that the presence of even one ally who went against the majority view reduced conformity among the 'real' participants (as opposed to confederates). Furthermore, the influence of historical–cultural contexts was highlighted in later replications of Asch's studies by Larsen (1974), Perrin and Spencer (1981) and others (see Box 4.1).

Box 4.1   Replications of Asch's studies

Alternative interpretations of Asch's original experiments have been generated in light of replications that emphasize the influence of sociocultural factors in the behaviour of research participants. Larsen (1974) recruited American students in his replication finding significantly lower rates of conformity than Asch found. Perrin and Spencer (1981) draw attention to differences in the historical climate when this work was conducted: that is, the post-hippie era, when independence and freedom of expression were vehemently guarded, in contrast to the 1950s McCarthite America of Asch, where deviance from norms and values was tinged with accusations of Communism.

Perrin and Spencer (1981) replicated Asch's design using British engineering, mathematics and chemistry students, and found that across trials these students remained independent, reporting correct line comparison even in the face of a majority who repeatedly gave incorrect answers. As Brown (1996) notes, the academic culture of these individuals and the nature of the task may have combined to encourage confidence in their ability to judge lines correctly.

Experiments/groups

Following on from the above equation of human behaviour, the assumed certainties that it enshrines about an objective reality and the nature of the individual promote the experiment as the logical method to explore the impact of certain social stimuli on the behaviour of the individual. However, one of the most resounding criticisms of the work of Sherif, Asch and Milgram is their use of the experimental paradigm to explore conformity and obedience. Many question the ecological validity of the autokinetic effect, the comparison of lines and the learning paradigm used. Take for example the events of the Second World War, with Germany, a previously economically and politically unstable country, steeped in the propaganda of a dictator promising worldwide domination through the extermination of Jewish populations and other marginalized groups. Does administering (fake) electric shocks to volunteers in the safety of Yale University, with its academic kudos, equate with the gross acts of inhumanity witnessed in Germany in the 1930s and 1940s? In arguing against such comparisons, critical social psychologists point out that Milgram's work was conducted in surroundings unfamiliar to participants, where individuals responded in isolation, and was also a short-term activity. In contrast, the inhumanity witnessed in camps such as Auschwitz and Belsen occurred over many years, and were the result of a complex interplay of historical, political and economic forces, not to mention 'psychopathology, avarice, careerism, and ignorance', explanations rarely explored in the mainstream social psychology literature (Mastroianni, 2002: 170). The systematic murder of Jews, homosexuals, Romani, communists and others occurred in contexts that were familiar, and where many carrying out such acts believed the fate of Germany in the 1930s and 1940s was due directly to the subversive influence of these groups, which was fed to them in daily Nazi propaganda (Housden, 1997). This led to a belief by a significant minority of the population in an 'eliminationist anti-Semitism' as the only practical solution to Germany's problems (Goldhagen, 1992 cited in Mastroianni, 2002: 168). Drawing on the work of Daniel Goldhagen (author of *Hitler's Willing Executioners: Ordinary Germans and the Holocaust*) Mastroianni (2002: 168) argues that Milgram's 'situationist' perspective 'narrowly defined in terms of the transient conditions that can be manipulated in a social psychology laboratory' does not possess the power to explain 'the horrific actions recorded during the Holocaust'.

Harré (1989) suggests that the omission of the wider, more complex social and cultural fabric in experiments is a fundamental flaw in experimental paradigms of human social activity. Danziger (2000) adds:

Psychological experiments, almost without exception, had been limited to the investigation of a very limited range of effects. In particular, they had been limited to exploring *effects that were local, proximal, short term, and decomposable*. Effects were local in the sense that they were observed at a particular place and time. I use 'proximal' to refer to effects that resulted from the immediate presence of some effective agent, known as a 'stimulus'. (333–334)

Like others, both Harre and Danziger berate experimental social psychology for ignoring that which is fundamental to understanding human social behaviour – the humanness – people's identities, cultural structures and practices. Wetherell (1996b) sums this up as follows:

Social relationships are complex and multi-layered. The lines of influence from one person to another are intertwined and difficult to disentangle. The controlled experiment has never been adequate to this task. The patterns involved are much more complex than the linear laws of experimental (*cause and effect*) social psychology suggest. (11–12)

Further questions relating to the design of social influence experiments arise from assumptions embodied in the work of Sherif (1935) and Asch (1952). Sherif and Asch talk of the collections of people participating in their work as groups, but is this a legitimate perception? Many, including Wetherell (1996b), would suggest not, as collections of people with no shared history or experience does not constitute a group. The impact of established group membership is further highlighted in Williams and Sogon's (1984) replication of the Asch study, where among Japanese participants a higher error rate was recorded for intact groups (sports club members), and a lower rate for unacquainted students.

Social influence as negative

As a starting point, let us remind ourselves of what Sherif, Asch and Milgram were attempting to uncover about human social behaviour. If we think back to the paradigm of human behaviour extolled by Le Bon (1895), two strands emerge: firstly the assumption that in the presence of others the 'normally rational civilized' behaviour of the individual in some way changes, and secondly that the nature of this change is negative (Le Bon talked of how in crowds the rational and moral basis of individuality is shattered, exposing the savage beneath). In this sense the expectations of Sherif, Asch and Milgram about what they would find were pre-formed by the Western doctrine of individuality and the way this had historically been enshrined as a truth within the discipline of psychology.

So, what was it that these experiments showed us about human social activity? Firstly, the Sherif, Asch and Milgram studies did indicate that in certain situations social influence occurs. However, where many contemporary psychologists diverge from the historical narrative embodied in this work is in relation to the ways these findings have been reported and the implications about human social activity that have been drawn. Let us take Asch's findings for example. Asch illustrated that 5 per cent of subjects conformed to obviously wrong estimates of line size on all trials, 33 per cent conformed on half or more of the trials and 25 per cent did not conform on any trials. But what do these statistics really tell us if, say, people were asked to choose between X, Y and Z washing powders and that over a period of 40 washes 33 per cent of consumers used X for half or more washes. Would you accept this as a basis for believing that a preference for X was a universal behaviour and be happy to conclude that we are a nation of X users? We think not, yet Asch's work instilled beliefs that in the presence of others, people, regardless of class, age, background, ethnicity, or situation, conform to perceived pressure from others – that they are prepared to change their beliefs due to a desire to be right (informational influence) or to be liked (normative influence). In addition, as Brown (1996: 19) comments, later replications of Asch's work reported in Box 4.1 indicate 'that there is no universal way in which individuals respond to group pressure when there is a discrepancy between their own perceptions and those of other group members'. They show that participants will be affected by the *meaning* a situation has for them which itself may be influenced by *cultural* variables which have a bearing on how we relate to groups.

So how do we explain the widespread currency of Asch's work in psychological explanations of human social activity? To do so, again we must return to the historical basis of psychology as a scientific discipline and the ingrained assumptions about the nature of the individual, the social and behaviour. Social psychology, since the nineteenth century, has been, as Stainton-Rogers *et al.* (1995) describe, on a *humaneering mission*. In response to the shifting intellectual and social structures of Western societies in the nineteenth century and the subsequent anxieties relating to the so-called degeneracy of the lower classes and, ultimately, the social and moral fabric of civilized existence, psychology has historically positioned itself as the procurer of objective truths about the nature of human social activity. This knowledge is offered as something that can contribute to the protection and indeed enhancement of the moral and social underpinnings of civilized society (as defined in nineteenth-century rhetoric). In order to produce such knowledge, concrete definitions of the nature of the individual, society and behaviour are essential, as from such foundations universal codes relating to human activity may be formulated and actions taken to make improvements (see Danziger, 1997; Rose, 1985). In many ways, Asch's studies did not rock the theoretical boat, so to speak, as he produced concise experimentally based evidence that reinforced the existing narrative about the negative influence of groups on individual performance and placed explanations for such phenomena solely at the feet of the individual – as a result of their desire to be liked or right. In doing so, there was no need for psychology to ask any messy questions about either the social mechanisms through which conformity and obedience are secured or the political purpose of such mechanisms. The avoidance of these questions in social psychology has been achieved by maintaining research designs (such as experiments) which aspire to an illusion of certitude by claiming to discover universal truths about social behaviour. They do this by asking relatively simplified research questions, necessarily made so, to be methodologically manageable. Thus, under the banner of evidence and 'good science' we find operationally delimited definitions of conformity and obedience that reside firmly within the psyche of the individual (see Box 4.2).

Box 4.2   The 'pop psychology' of psychological experiments

Since Milgram's original experiments (first begun in 1961) a number of films, documentaries, media depictions, replications and variations of his study have been carried out. Replications of his experiment include the documentaries *The Milgram Re-enactment* (2002), *The Tenth Level* (1975), films such as *Atrocity* (2005), *The Heist* (2006) and *How Violent Are You* (2009). There has even been a French game show called *The Game of Death* (2010). For the most recent fully fledged academic replication see Burger (2009). Given the limitations of psychological experiments as discussed above, one wonders why they have become so popular, not only for students and film makers but also the public at large? There are three main reasons for this: (1) psychological experiments provide relatively simplistic explanations for complex social behaviours, making it easier for an audience to digest and understand, (2) audiences perceive that psychological experiments (even replications) carry 'scientific authority', so their findings can be relied upon and (3) audiences are led to believe that psychological experiments are predictive of social behaviour in settings outside the laboratory or the film/television studio where they are conducted.

Rethinking social influence

Within critical social psychology, insights into social influence (conformity, compliance to requests, obedience) are based on understandings of the *individual constituted by society*. Conformity and obedience are understood as discursive practices (representations of social ideas and codes of practice in language and everyday talk), in contrast to mainstream (social) psychology, where such practices are analysed at the level of the individual, as internal desires or motivations resulting in specific behaviours (think back to Asch's work – 'the desire to be liked and the desire to be right'). Consequently, the theoretical assumptions framing the work of experimental social psychologists such as Asch and Milgram are revised. This section maps out these revisions.

Social influence processes are not viewed as behaviours which people do (or do not) perform but rather, as Burr (2002) points out, are viewed from the social practices that people engage in and the interactions that take place between people (see Box 4.3). Activities acquire meaning in the social processes that people participate in and, as such, give rise to social phenomena such as conformity and obedience. For example, consider the interactions between people during a social psychology lecture in a university. I (Majella) as the lecturer prepare my lecture in advance, produce overhead slides, lecture notes and relevant reading materials. The students indulge (I hope!) in active listening and make relevant additional notes, and opportunities to ask questions are created by me at certain intervals throughout the process. These weekly classes are shaped by the wider academic context in which we are situated and produce knowledge relating to the legitimate conduct of such sessions (as well as the penalties incurred should this not take place). From my position as the lecturer these penalties include negative appraisals from my employers and/or the students, while students who do not participate in an acceptable manner may face disciplining from the lecturer or, even worse, from their fellow students. As such, the practices of the lecturer and/or students are not dictated by individuals who desire to be 'liked' or 'right', but rather by the wider social interactions, norms and identities.

Box 4.3   Group anorexia: the deadly way women bond
(*Cosmopolitan*, September 1993: 33–35)

The article in *Cosmopolitan* describes the way in which groups of women influence each other's eating behaviours. The main theme to run through the article is the pressure on women to achieve and maintain the ideal size-10 body and the dangerous activities (vomiting, laxatives, excessive dieting and exercise) many women indulge in to attain such a body. One of the case studies presented is that of Emily, a final-year student at university, who vomits to 'stay a neat size 10, just like all her flatmates' (p. 33). The article describes how Emily had a normal attitude towards food and no hang-ups about her body before leaving home for university.

'But, life in a shared house changed all that. Just weeks into her first term at university, she and her new friends were comparing their bodies, swapping slimming tips and sharing paranoias. The subject of food loomed over them constantly and, soon, it was a common enemy. Eating disorders were not far behind. "Leaving home had a lot to do with it," admits Emily now, "Suddenly food mattered. Sizes were *so* important. We'd try on each other's clothes and notice which bits were too big and which were too small, and say do I look fat in this? The cruellest thing you could do was try on someone else's outfit and say it was too big. In the supermarket, we'd look in each other's trolleys and count the calories. You couldn't even eat a bar of chocolate without the others focusing on it, making comments like, oh you're so brave"' (pp. 33–34).

CRITICAL THINKING BOX: COLLECTIVE IDENTITIES

Read Box 4.3, and in small groups, discuss the explanations offered for the development of communal eating patterns. Then consider the following questions: Do friends influence how you relate to food? If so, how? Why do you think this happens? Are there other activities where you conform to group ideals (e.g. dress, social or sexual activities)? Why might this be? Can group influences be resisted?

The historical, social and political theorist Michel Foucault (1978; 1988) provides insights into the construction of the socially legitimate person and the practices this person could indulge in. Through his consideration of the progressive regulation of what are traditionally thought personal properties or activities (e.g. the body, sexuality, reproduction), Foucault (1978) illustrates the construction of norms relating to a wide range of human activity and explicates the mechanisms through which conformity and obedience among people is achieved. For Foucault, human social activities such as obedience and conformity are not situated either in the desires of individuals or the authority of powerful figures. Rather, Foucault suggests conformity and obedience are produced by, and are products of, evolving social organizations and the interactions of people within these. Foucault tracks the evolution of social organizations from religious dictates to state regulation, through to a multiple network of sites of social control, new forms of knowledge about the human activity. Primary among these mechanisms are social sciences like psychology (as well as sociology, criminology, anthropology etc), whose knowledge and practices are used as strategies to discipline the conduct of individuals (Hook, 2007; Rose, 1998). The function of this discipline according to Foucault (1988: 59) 'is to create useful subjects, men and women, who conform to a standard, who are certifiably sane or healthy or docile or competent, not free agents who invent their own standards'.

Power relations are the key concept in this organization and in particular how these function in different historical, political and social contexts to generate frameworks of norms. Foucault points to the rise of science in the nineteenth century whereby, historically, bodies such as psychology through its scientific knowledge and investigation generated social norms and codes relating to normal/abnormal/healthy, etc. In Foucault's work, the production and generation of the self and activities prescribed for the care and maintenance of this self situates the body and soul at the centre of a diverse collection of philosophical, religious and (later) scientific discourses. For example, the Greek philosopher Epictetus describes man's (sic) care of the self as a moral duty, the activity that separates man from animal. In his writings, man is presented as:

the being who was destined to care for himself. This is where the difference between him and other creatures resides. The animals find 'ready prepared' that which they need in order to live, for nature has so arranged things that animals are at our disposal without them having to look after themselves, and without our having to look after them. Man, on the other hand, must attend to himself: not however as a consequence of some defect that would put him in a situation of need and make him in this respect inferior to animals, but because the god (Zeus) deemed it right that he be able to make free use of himself; and it was for this purpose he endowed him with reason. (Foucault, 1988:49)

Foucault underlines the complex regimes that have accompanied the care of the self, including abstinence, health regimes, physical exercise and so forth, and the continued embodiment of these activities in a range of nineteenth- and twentieth-century medical and religious discourses. He emphasizes the complex nature of such regulation and the collusion of individuals in their own subjection when he concludes: 'Now there is a new subjection, which creates and legitimizes new subjects – not the carriers of rights but of norms, the agents and also the products of moral, medical, sexual, psychological (rather than legal) regulation. Our interest shifts, because the action shifts, from the singular state to a pluralist society' (1988: 54). That is, in accepting the authority of specialized bodies of knowledge, by seeking counselling, or treatment, people submit themselves to scrutiny, regulation and discipline. It is this active role for the individual, the seeking and legitimizing of authority that is interesting in Foucault's work as it conceptualizes the individual as inseparable from the social context. In Foucault's vision, the person is simultaneously shaped by and shapes the social context. Consequently, simplistic notions of the exercise of power as a top-down process are challenged, and Foucault presents a more diffuse and fluid view of power relations. Power is not something that is held by one set of people, but rather:

power is exercised from innumerable points. Power is employed and exercised through a netlike organisation...individuals circulate between its threads; they are always in a position of simultaneously undergoing and exercising power. They are not only its inert or consenting targets; they are also elements of its articulation. (Foucault, 1988: 54–55)

By drawing attention to the socio–political context Foucault sought to highlight how behaviour is constituted by specific periods of 'time' (history) and 'space' (geography). As Foucault (1980: 252) noted 'space is fundamental to any exercise of power'; therefore its planning, design, organization and management play an important role in social influence. By adhering to an atemporal and aspatial worldview mainstream social psychology treats space as a set of external variables that affects self-contained individuals who are antecedent to the environment/context they find themselves in. In this formula the environment is treated as a 'stimulus' that elicits a 'response' from the individual based on their individual differences (personality) or group memberships (social identity). For mainstream social psychologists space and people are viewed as distinct entities that are deemed separate from one another for the purpose of making research more manageable.

In contrast, Foucault conceptualized space, whether it be a building, courtyard, park or laboratory, as a dynamic and socially produced entity. This view of space has the potential to expand our understanding of social influence because it views space as the product of a complex interplay of historical, social, cultural, political and economic forces. If we use this view of space to understand social behaviour in the psychological laboratory then it alerts us to the different power relations that may exist in this highly unusual context, and the way in which power is inscribed into its setting and the meanings this holds for the people who use it. For example, in the Asch experiments student participants conformed or didn't conform for reasons other than those put forward by Asch. One of these was the power inequalities that existed between the student participant's taking part in the experiment and their desire to meet the requirements of the experiment as set down by their lecturers/professors (Burr, 2002). As a result, the experience of the student participants would likely be different if conducted in spaces outside the laboratory and the university where different power relations are likely to exist. Burr (2002) notes:

One might reasonably expect that participants in these experiments are struggling with a number of implicit questions: What is the experimenter trying to prove? How can I be a good subject? How am I supposed to behave? Will I spoil the experiment if I agree/disagree with the others? What will the experimenter think of me if I agree/disagree? What will the others think? Will their opinions have consequences for me? (40–41)

Box 4.4 Alternative reading of conformity and obedience

In contrast to the work of Sherif (1935) or Milgram (1974), Foucault (1978: 88) argues that conformity and obedience are not universal behaviours: instead they fluctuate in different historical, cultural and social contexts. Thus, Foucault provides an important rationale for exploring the meaning and status of knowledge and the importance of the socio–political context in which such knowledge is produced. Explanations for the popularity and power of experimental studies on social influence must then surely also include an understanding of the scientific status and values underlying such research as well as the impact of the overarching socio–political contexts on the researcher's expectations of human social activity.

It is such influences that Brown (1996) highlights when she argues that the very language psychologists use reveal underlying value judgements: 'Asch certainly viewed conformity as deplorable and perhaps did not emphasise enough that in his experiments it was a minority response....Asch describes conforming subjects as "yielding" when he might have referred to these subjects as trusting other people. Those who did not succumb to group pressure he refers to, approvingly, as independent' (Brown, 1996: 25).

In her work with young adolescent women, Sue Lees (1993: 98) describes how women's conformity to specific understandings of femininity is achieved through a collection of linguistic and social practices subscribed to by both men and women. Terms such as 'slag', 'slut' and 'bitch' are highlighted as key mechanisms through which young women's activities and social reputations are controlled to the advantage of men: 'The term "slag" can be seen as part of a discourse about behaviour as a departure, or potential departure from, in this case, male conceptions of female sexuality which run deep in the culture' (1993: 23). Lees (1998) points out that the term 'slag' is used in a multitude of ways, not only in relation to young women's sexual activities but to their appearance, how they talk, how they relate to boys and even their future aspirations. In addition, Lees (1993: 98) notes that despite an awareness among her young female participants of the unfairness of these controls on women's sexual and social behaviour, many of the young women conformed to socially prescribed behaviours rather than incur the negative social penalties of being called a slut or slag. As Lees (1998: 22) states, 'The crucial point about the label slag is that it is used by both girls and boys as a deterrent to nonconformity. No girl wants to be labelled bad and slag is something to frighten any girl with. The effect of the term is to force girls to submit voluntarily to a very unfair set of gender relations.'

What is a 'slag'?

As discussed, Lees (1993) suggests that the term 'slag' is used in a variety of ways to control identities and activities of many young women. Women can earn the label of 'slag' by virtue of the way they dress: wearing too much make-up or not being interested in their appearance and thereby appearing dirty and unkempt, wearing clothes that are too tight or tops that are too low and so on. Yet as Lees (1993) notes, there are no definitive guidelines on what constitutes too much make-up or how low a top can acceptably be. Rather, this is something that young women learn through their negotiations with others, and for many this can be a risky and painful learning curve. A good example of this can be seen in a recent study conducted by Carey *et al.* (2011). The authors interviewed girls aged 14–15 years about their concerns around body image and the influence that attending an all-girls High School had on this. The authors found that students 'policed' each other most often through gossip to conform to popularly accepted styles of appearance such as those found in women's magazines. This gossip about body image was found by the authors to function as a form of self-surveillance over one's own and other student's bodies.

Returning to the term 'slag' we can see how the power and pervasiveness of such derogatory terms function to ensure young women's conformity to socially constructed and frequently contradictory representations of femininity. In a series of interviews conducted with a group of 30 heterosexual women in Northern Ireland McFadden (1995) found that when women talked about their sexuality, it conjured up the image of a tightrope walker. It was found that in their everyday activities they were required to negotiate the thin line between appearing as a slag or a drag (i.e. frigid). These young women presented a range of complex strategies (see Box 4.5) including self-surveillance and censorship of and by others, which they used to get it (femininity) right.

Box 4.5   How nice girls behave (McFadden, 1995)

Lesson one: nice girls don't talk about sex

From interviews conducted with the 30 women, norms relating to how young women talked and behaved in mixed company emerged. These women indicated that talking about sex or even commenting on someone's appearance in the company of men was a no-go area. Zoe described the reactions of male friends when she stayed outside the boundaries and commented on a passing male: '... like men are really funny. For example I was walking down the road with male friends and I saw this really nice guy and I said "He's nice", and they were all, "What are you talking about?", "Don't be such a slapper", and things like that. They got really annoyed. They're really funny. Girls aren't expected to do things like that.'

Similarly Stephanie describes the negative consequences if a woman was to talk about sex in front of men: '... like I think a lot of fellas would be put off by a girl who talked about sex, probably think that she was some kind of slut or something'.

Lesson two: nice girls don't carry condoms

Nice women definitely do not carry condoms unless in a steady relationship. Of the 30 women, 25 described in derogatory terms women who carried condoms and who they knew were not in a relationship. For example, while in principle Marilynne thought it was OK for women in light of AIDS to carry condoms, she goes on to say '... but if I saw a girl with condoms in her handbag and I knew she wasn't in a steady relationship I'd think she was a bit of a slag. I know it's an awful way to think but...that's what I think.'

Jenny voiced similar opinions: 'If they're in a steady relationship...that's fair enough, but if they're [women] Just going out for the night with a packet of condoms in their pocket, I don't think that's on. It's really low.'

The social penalties that single women who carry condoms may face was further elaborated on by Tess, who suggested that '... If a woman was to do that [sleep around, using condoms] people would talk about her and say that she was dirty and that she'd probably got all types of diseases'.

Lesson three: nice girls don't do it on a first date

'Women aren't supposed to have sex on the first night, like even girl really liked a boy, if she wanted to go with him again she wouldn't sleep with him on the first night because he might get the wrong idea' (Dot, aged 17).

'... a girl would get called a slut for doing it [having sex] on the first night and a fella doesn't get called anything. I think that's why a lot of girls would prefer to wait until a steady relationship...they're afraid of getting a bad name' (Emma, aged 18).

Lesson four: nice girls don't have too much of a sexual history

These young women's narratives about femininity in the 1990s related to how much information you disclose about sexual activity. For most of the women interviewed this was a task that had to be carefully negotiated. Among female friends, talk of sex did take place, but disclose too much and you risk being labelled as a slut, even by close friends. This was a risk Marilynne was well aware of: 'Well women do talk about sex but I suppose there are some of my friends that it would be hard to let know that I had sexual experience, they'd probably talk about me...think that I was a bit of a slag or loose or something. I suppose you do have to be careful who you tell whereas among men when they talk about who they've slept with it's all boasting.'

Daisy described how there were clear rules about how much sexual experience was alright and when you were in danger of being passed over by men or thought of as low. Although these rules had not been formally recognized, women are aware of the consequences of transgressing them, to the extent that according to Daisy women lie about their sexual histories: 'It [denying sexual experience] would be because of social pressure...you know all men want to marry a virgin...so it's easier to let on that you're sexually inexperienced ....I know a lot of people [women] who have lied about their experience for fear of what their friends might say. Like no one wants their friends distancing themselves because they think you've got a bad name or calling you a slut or something behind your back.'

Experimental social psychology has traditionally been concerned with identifying how internal and external processes influence the behaviour of the individual. Within this paradigm both the 'individual' and the 'social' are understood in specific ways. It is assumed that in his or her 'natural' state the individual exists separately from his or her social world, and that all individuals share internal states (motivations, desires, drives, instincts) which are impacted upon by external factors in stable and predictable ways (McGhee, 1996). Similarly certain assumptions are made about the structural nature of the social world in experimental social psychology. It is assumed that a single objective reality exists, that social forces can be isolated and their effects on the individual monitored and understood. Think back to the work of Asch and his explanations for the conformity witnessed among those participating in his experiments.

CRITICAL THINKING BOX: CONFORMITY AND GENDER

To what extent do the above discourses on femininity still constrain women's behaviour in the twenty-first century?

In experimental studies of social influence, it is suggested that the subjects involved conformed as a result of the 'desire to be right' among fellow subjects or the 'desire to be liked'. The social world is understood simply in terms of the 'presence of others' without any recognition of the cultural and social contexts in which the experiments are undertaken or the characteristics of the participants (e.g. age, ethnic background, socio–economic status). In contrast, critical social psychology views the person as a product of, and enmeshed within, diverse social, historical and cultural contexts. Take for example the baby in its mother's womb. Prior to its birth it is recognized within the social order as a foetus; this term elicits different understandings of its status depending on the viewpoint of the speaker (e.g. a collection of cells, or a human being from the moment of conception). After birth, the child's experiences may differ from others depending on its gender, ethnic background, current parenting philosophies and so on. Within critical social psychology, rather than being viewed as born in the possession of a set number of personality traits the person is understood as being gradually constructed through her or his social interactions, relations and actions. Kirschner and Martin (2010) note:

> Such perspectives envision psychological processes, such as mind and the self, as phenomena that are socioculturally constituted – that is, actually made up within, as opposed to merely facilitated by, culture and society. These constitutive approaches to psychology understand cognition, emotion, memory, identity, personality, and other psychological constructs as relational entities that emerge out of interactions with others within a sociocultural context. (1)

This doesn't mean, as Wetherell (1996) points out, that we do not have our own dreams, expectations and hopes but rather challenges understandings of how these are shaped as well as assumptions that these are universal and stable.

Similarly, critical social psychology challenges the taken-for-granted notion of the social that is embedded in experimental social psychology. Rather than understanding the social as, for example, the presence of others and exploring the impact that the presence of one or more persons has on an individual's behaviour, a broader definition of the social is developed. In critical social psychology the structure and content of a person's social world is central to understanding human behaviour. The social world of the individual is viewed as complex and dynamic, influenced by their physical environment, economic structures, language, representations and ideologies. New questions then emerge about human behaviour, such as where and how the person is placed within the existing social order, the factors that contribute to this positioning (e.g. gender, ethnicity, class), and how social positioning can change during and as a result of social interactions.

Box 4.6 Experimental psychology and body image research

Sylvia Blood's (2005) book *Body Work: The Social Construction of Women's Body Image* argues that findings from experimental social psychology have become the dominant explanation for girls and women's distress in relation to 'body image disturbance' and 'body image dissatisfaction'. These explanations have become popularized through the mass media, in particular women's magazines, which offer advice and psychological treatments. The manner in which the mass media functions in modern society illustrates its powerful social influence on the way girls and women think about and experience distress in relation to body image. Of particular note here is the manner in which the media uses 'scientific truths' taken from research conducted by experimental social psychologists.

These 'truths' impact upon women through the process of subjec-tification. Via popular women's magazines, a discourse of body image problems is woven into the fabric of everyday experience. The 'truth' about women's body image problems is presented in a persuasive, compelling, plausible manner. Information about body image is presented to women as something all women 'have', as something that can be identified and measured according to scientific 'norms' and as something women should know and be concerned about .... These 'findings' of experimental psychology's body image research, reproduced in popular women's magazines, have damaging social implications for women's lives, in particular, for the ways women can experience embodiment. (2005: 1–2)

Blood's analysis indicates that experimental social psychology inadvertently shifts the problem of body dissatisfaction away from the perverse social and cultural pressures that women experience in modern Western society, on to women themselves, blaming them for their psychological reactions to the ways in which they view and evaluate their bodies. From this perspective the problem of body image disturbance and/or dissatisfaction becomes one of 'individual pathology' as opposed to 'societal pathology'.

CRITICAL THINKING BOX: CONFORMITY

Think about an experience you have had when you feel you may have conformed. Why did you do this? Look at your reasons and compare them with the explanations offered by mainstream social psychology and by critical social psychology. Which fits most comfortably with your understanding?

Critical social psychology does not offer a neat, universal explanation of why people conform or obey on the basis of internal states, nor even a grand theory on social influence. Rather it reintroduces what Armistead (1974) described as the 'humanness' in explanations of social activity, focusing on the meaning of a situation for those involved and how this meaning may be mediated in relation to a variety of influences including identity, class, race, gender and culture. As such, explanations centring on socially constructed norms and the contexts in which these are produced and reproduced become more complex and diverse than those traditionally offered. In particular, power relations and ideologies become central to understandings of why people 'conform to' or 'obey' social dictates. For example, Wilkinson and Kitzinger (1994) trace the psychological creation of heterosexuality as a normative identity. They highlight the dominant view of heterosexuality as 'natural' and as detrimental to other identities, which are then seen as 'deviant' or 'abnormal'. An exploration of the ways in which heterosexuality is constructed through established relations of power within many Western societies is, the above authors suggest, central to an understanding of the ways in which people are produced as, and reproduce, heterosexuality. In addition to exploring the construction of heterosexuality as the norm in a variety of powerful nineteenth-century historical, psychological and political discourses, Wilkinson and Kitzinger (1994) highlight a number of social sites where the privileged position of heterosexuality continues to be preserved:

> men and especially women are coerced through a variety of forces including rape, child-marriage, sexual harassment, pornography and economic sanctions. For most of those who are not heterosexual the coercive nature of heterosexuality is everywhere apparent. But for many heterosexuals, their heterosexuality feels 'natural' and 'innate' or freely chosen and often – in both cases – enjoyed as a pleasurable experience. Others feel *excluded* from heterosexuality because of their failure to conform to sex-role stereotypes or to conventional ideas of able-bodied attractiveness. (309; emphasis added)

In the above quotation the discursive production of heterosexual identities is made explicit, and consequently researchers are required to deal with multiple influences to explain how and why people are produced as, and reproduce, heterosexuality. The historical, social and political contexts for heterosexuality require examination as well as differences in experience mediated through class, gender, race and age. Consequently the meaning of this social phenomenon becomes more diverse and complex.

In addition, setting activities such as conformity and obedience within such contexts introduces to a further level of analysis absent from traditional accounts – the function of conformity and obedience. Many writers within the social constructionist traditions explicitly talk about such activities in the language of social control. In his writings on the care of the self, introduced earlier in this chapter, Foucault concludes that the regimes prescribed relating to the maintenance of the body and mind are exercised with a series of aims and objectives, in particular to establish sophisticated sets of social regulations that structure relations between the individual and his or her body as well as generate channels of communication with others, e.g. medical profession, psychology, legal bodies, etc.

Critical social psychologists explicitly identify as problematic the view of the person as a passive recipient of her or his experiences inscribed in much traditional social psychological theorizing. Rather, the individual is represented as actively negotiating her or his social activities. It is recognized that such negotiations are not, strictly speaking 'free choices', but may be constrained by various social and cultural processes, including gender, class, historical context and ethnicity (Smith, 1988). Viewing the person as an agent demands that psychologists explore the ways that people resist dominant representations and understandings, and so provides additional information for piecing together the complex picture of human social activity. Again, the social theorist Foucault (1978: 95) stressed the centrality of resistance for accounting for the diverse and changing social positions individuals occupy and the social actions they perform: 'Where there is power, there is resistance, and yet or rather consequently, this resistance is never in a position of exteriority of power.' As an example Foucault (1978) cites the resistance of many homosexual men earlier in the twentieth century to representations of themselves as biological deviants in the writings of sexologists such as Freud (1908) and Ellis (1913). In challenging such perceptions, homosexual men not only gained public visibility but also began to articulate alternative representations of homosexuality. Yet, while at the same time gaining a recognizable identity, the activities of homosexual men came under the scrutiny of many kinds of specialized knowledge, including medicine, psychology and law.

Although the activities and identities of the young women in both Lees (1993) and McFadden (1995) were regulated by a variety of punitive linguistic and social processes, this is not the end of the story. Understanding these young women's attempts at resisting notions of how they should dress, behave, etc. provides important insights into the changing and diverse nature of feminine identities and practices and highlights the emergence of new understandings regarding how young women negotiate socially constructed ideas of what 'woman' means. Many of the young women interviewed used diverse ways to challenge others' expectations of how they should act or behave (see Box 4.7).

A recent and high profile example of women subverting derogatory terms related to female sexual behaviour was the SlutWalk. SlutWalk was a series of worldwide rallies held in 2011 protesting against the view that what a woman wears should act as an excuse for sexual harassment and assault. The first SlutWalk took place in Toronto, Canada after a senior Canadian police officer speaking at the University of York (Canada) commented that 'women should avoid dressing like sluts in order not to be victimized'.

Box 4.7 Strategies of resistance

Strategy one: inverting the term 'slag'

In response to the question 'is it more acceptable for men to have sex outside of a steady relationships?'

'I personally don't think it is but it seems so because they can't get pregnant or anything so it's just easy for them to do it [have sex] quickly and walk away. I don't think it's acceptable though, like girls get called sluts and I would still call a man a slut if he was doing it...Like it's unusual but I would still say he's a slut.'

In this extract, Jenny makes visible the double standards that exist around the sexual behaviours of women and men. However, she challenges such differences by turning the socially constructed notion of a slag on its head and applying it to men who behave in particular ways.

Strategy two: subverting the term 'slag'

'I mean some people look down on women who carry condoms. In fact among my friends I'm the only one who carries condoms, yet most nights my female friends come up to me and ask for a condom...I have come across people, both men and women, who have thought of me as a bit of a slag, but if being a slag means you have sex when you want and you can protect yourself, then fine, I'm a slag.'

In this extract Gillian redefines the term 'slag', from someone who does not follow social regulations to someone who is satisfying her own desires and taking responsibility for her own sexual safety.

CRITICAL THINKING BOX: AGENCY

Using Boxes 4.4 and 4.5 as examples, can you think of any times that you have behaved in ways other than were expected. If so, what did you do and why did you do this? What were the consequences for you of doing this?

Summary

Theories of social influence based on the classic studies are critiqued in relation to definition of the individual and social, methodologies employed and the universal status of analysis undertaken. In addition, the influence of socio–political context on psychological research is highlighted. Critical social psychological understandings of social influence processes, such as conformity and obedience, as social actions produced and reproduced in a variety of discourses, are introduced. Consequently, the need to extend the parameters of explanations for conformity and obedience to include a consideration of the meaning and function of social influence processes within historical, social and political contexts is argued. Finally, the concept of agency, absent from traditional explanations of social influence, is introduced.

Key references

Brown, H. (1996). Themes in experimental research on groups from 1930s to the 1990s. In M. Wetherell (ed.), *Identities, Groups and Social Issues*. London: The Open University.
This chapter provides a detailed outline of experimental research on groups and discusses the limitations associated with these approaches for understanding human social practices in their full complexity.

Lees, S. (1998). The policing of girls in everyday life: sexual reputation and the social control of girls. In S. Lees, *Ruling Passions: Sexual Violence, Reputation and the Law*. Milton Keynes: The Open University Press.
This chapter is based on the finding from a three-year research study with young women (aged 15–16). It highlights the complex ways in which women's sexualities are produced and constrained within varying social and cultural contexts.

Stainton-Rogers, W. (2003). *Social Psychology: Experimental and Critical Approaches*. Maidenhead, UK: Open University Press.
This unique text book explores the two main theoretical approaches taken in social psychology – 'experimental' and 'critical'. It explores their histories and methodologies discussing both their benefits and drawbacks. It brings into sharp relief the key questions facing social psychology as it moves into the twenty-first century by asking what social psychology is and how it should be studied as it moves into the future.

Tuffin, K. (2005). *Understanding Critical Social Psychology*. London: Sage.
Chapter 1 of Tuffin's book 'Experimentation and the Social World' provides a wide-ranging critique of experimental social psychology from both a methodological and ethical perspective.

New references

Blood, S. K. (2005). *Body Work: The Social Construction of Women's Bodies*. London: Routledge.

Burger, J. (2009). Replicating Milgram: would people still obey? *American Psychologist, 64*(1), 1–11.

Burr, V. (2002). *The Person in Social Psychology*. London: Routledge.

Carey, R. N., Donaghue, N. & Broderick, P. (2011). 'What you look like is such a big factor': Girls' own reflections about the appearance culture in an all-girls' school. *Feminism & Psychology, 21*(3), 299–316.

Danziger, K. (1997). *Naming the Mind: How Psychology Found Its Language*. London: Sage.

Danziger, K. (2000). Making social psychology experimental: a conceptual history. *Journal of the History of the Behavioural Sciences, 36*(4), 329–347.

Foucault, M. (1980). *Power/Knowledge: Selected Interviews and Other Writings, 1972–77*. London: Harvester Press.

Graumann, C. F. (2001). Introducing social psychology historically. In M. Hewstone & W. Stroebe (eds), *Introduction to Social Psychology* (3rd edn, pp. 3–22). Malden, MA: Blackwell.

Hook, D. (2007). *Foucault, Psychology and the Analytics of Power*. Basingstoke, UK: Palgrave Macmillan.

Housden, M. (1997). *Resistance and Conformity in the Third Reich*. London: Routledge.

Kirschner, S. R. & Martin, J. (2010). The sociocultural turn in psychology: an introduction and invitation. In S. R. Kirschner & J. Martin (eds), *The Sociocultural Turn in Psychology: the Contextual Emergence of Mind and Self* (pp. 1–27). New York: Columbia University Press.

Mastroianni, G. R. (2002). Milgram and the holocaust: a re-examination. *Journal of Theoretical and Philosophical Psychology, 22*(2), 158–173.

Rose, N. (1985). *The Psychological Complex: Psychology, Politics, and Society in England, 1869–1939*. London: Routledge & Kegan Paul.

Rose, N. (1998). *Inventing Ours Selves: Psychology, Power, and Personhood*. Cambridge, UK: Cambridge University Press.

Stainton-Rogers, W. (2003). *Social Psychology: Experimental and Critical Approaches*. Maidenhead, UK: Open University Press.

Triplett, N. (1898). The dynamogenic factors in pacemaking and competition. *American Journal of Psychology, 9*, 507–533.

Prejudice in Practice

5

This chapter will highlight:

- Strengths and limitations of traditional social psychological explanations of prejudice
- Critical readings on prejudice that emphasize the importance of social, cultural and political concepts
- New forms of indirect prejudice

Introduction

Prejudice against others because of their gender, colour, religion, etc. has engaged the discipline of social psychology for much of the twentieth century and beyond. This chapter reviews explanations of prejudice proposed by traditional social psychology and introduces recent theoretical accounts of prejudice emerging from critical social psychology that argue for the need to understand prejudiced activities in terms of language, culture and ideology.

Traditional social psychological theories of prejudice

Prejudice as errors in thinking: social cognition approaches

Walter Lippman (1922/1965), in his book *Public Opinion*, provided a theoretical explanation of prejudice centred on distortions in the cognitive processes of the individual. Within this theory, the analogy of a computer is invoked to describe how the individual makes sense of the multitude of social information he or she encounters. To negotiate this complexity Lippman argued that people turn to solace in simplistic explanations.

> For the real environment is altogether too big, too complex, and too fleeting for direct acquaintance. We are not equipped to deal with so much subtlety, so much variety, so many permutations and combinations. And although we have to act in that environment, we have to reconstruct it on a simpler model before we can manage with it. To traverse the world men must have maps of the world. (20)

Recognizing the growing complexity of a globalizing world, the exponential increase in information and the limited cognitive capacities of the human mind, the individual is perceived as simplifying this task by generating 'general categories' relating to self and others (on the basis of colour, race, age, sexuality, etc.). By doing so, Lippman and others (e.g. Fiske *et al.*, 2010) suggest that the overloading of our limited cognitive processes is prevented, and thus categorization is presented as generally an advantageous cognitive process. Social cognition theorists, however, point out that at times this system of filing can short-circuit, and certain 'faulty categorizations' can be introduced, with people forming stereotypes about members of groups (see Box 5.1).

A stereotype is defined by Wetherell (1996: 189) as 'a selective over-generalization which prejudges any individual member of a group'. Common stereotypes include representations of Irish people as 'stupid' or 'bog trotters' or Asian people as 'money-grabbing owners of corner shops'. Within the social cognition perspective, it is suggested that stereotypic schemata/scripts can bias the encoding of new knowledge about individual or group members, as people will pay more attention to activities that confirm their pre-formed beliefs (Hamilton & Trolier, 1986). Much of the research within this tradition has focused on the content of stereotypes, the role of socialization in the development of stereotypes and, perhaps more controversially, how stereotypes can be changed (see Brown & Hewstone, 2005). Hamilton and Trolier (1986) suggest that in addition to information that reinforces stereotypes being salient, when perceived members of certain groups behave in ways other than those expected such information is likely to impress and be remembered by those observing.

The final strand of this approach consists of research suggesting how psychologists might work with people to challenge stereotypes. These remediation strategies include the 'book-keeping effect', with people gradually changing their accounts of certain groups based on new, inconsistent information (Rothbart, 1981). In general, then, within the social cognition tradition, prejudiced activities are viewed as the unfortunate by-products of limitations on our rational mental organization (Billig, 1985), and remediation strategies include having sufficient contact with those we have stereotyped to counter prejudicial views (see Brown & Hewstone, 2005).

Box 5.1   A classic social cognition experiment

Synder and Uranowitz (1978) conducted a study based on homophobic stereotypes. They argued that people are more likely to remember information about another person which is consistent with their stereotype of a social group or category. In their study, subjects were asked to read a case history about a woman called Betty. The case study described Betty's childhood, her education, career, social life, etc. Subjects returned a week later to carry out a recognition memory test on various details of Betty's life. Prior to the test, however, half the subjects were told that Betty was now living in a happy and successful lesbian relationship and the other half told that she was in a happy and successful heterosexual relationship. The study found that the new information on Betty had a significant impact on the results of the memory recognition test. Subjects centred their memories and recall of information around the respective categories of 'lesbian woman' and 'heterosexual woman' – thus suggesting that people use category information to interpret information and recall memories.

CRITICAL THINKING BOX: STEREOTYPES

Read the following extract from Jeanette Winterson's (1985) *Oranges Are Not the Only Fruit*. Are you familiar with the representations of homosexual people presented by the mother character? In small groups discuss whether you think social cognition theory provides an adequate explanation for the prejudice illustrated in this account.
My mother wanted me to move out, and she had the backing of the pastor and most of the congregation, or so she said. I made her feel ill, made the house ill, brought evil into the church. There was no

escaping this time I was in trouble. ... It seems to hinge around the fact that I loved the wrong sort of people. Right sort of people in every respect except this one romantic love for a woman was a sin. 'Aping men,' my mother had said with disgust. Now, if I was aping men she had every reason to be disgusted. As far as I was concerned men were something you had round the place, not particularly interesting, but quite harmless. I had never shown the slightest feeling for them, and apart from my never wearing a skirt, saw nothing else in common between us. Then I remembered the famous incident of the man who'd come to church with his boyfriend. At least, they were holding hands. 'Should have been a woman that one', my mother had remarked (pp. 125–126).

Despite the currency of social cognition accounts of prejudice, this approach has been increasingly criticized by those within the discipline of critical social psychology along the following lines:

- *Individualistic orientation*: Wetherell and Potter (1992) question the image of the individual in social cognition theories. The individual is represented as a solitary figure, encoding information, sometimes erroneously, about others on the basis of perceived similarities and differences. The production of prejudiced cognitions does not have a logic to explain why only certain individuals perform prejudiced activities nor why, historically, certain groups have been the victims of racist thinking. Rather, the suggestion is that as all human minds function in similar ways it is possible that any one of us could develop stereotypes of anyone else in our social domain. As such, prejudiced thoughts and feelings are represented as universal traits, part of the conditions of being human. As Dixon and Levine (2012: 6–7) note much of the research on prejudice conducted by social psychologists has the individual, and their processes of cognition and personality, serving as the primary cause.
- *De-contextualized accounts*: The representation of the social or society in social cognition theorizing has also been criticized as simplistic and reductionist. An objective physical reality is assumed to exist that people perceive or misperceive in linear ways, regardless of their individual, social, cultural and historical origins. So, for example, this theory would suggest that the religious and social conflict that has dogged Northern Ireland for

decades is the result of misperceptions of 'Protestant' or 'Catholic' individuals or groups and is unaffected by cultural reinterpretations of historical events, political ideologies or material inequalities between communities. As Wetherell and Potter (1992: 41) suggest, the underlying assumption within the social cognition tradition is that 'a collection of individuals produce the same judgements, not because they talk and communicate with each other, but because each person faces the same set of stimuli with the same inbuilt cognitive limitations'.

- *Remediation strategies*: One of the most contentious aspects of social cognition theory relates to the 'contact hypothesis' – the idea that if individuals or groups can have sufficient contact with others about whom they hold stereotypic and prejudiced views, in time sufficient inconsistent information will be experienced to erode erroneous beliefs. The implication here is that if only the gay man, black person, etc. would behave in *better ways* and offer images of their groups which contradicted stereotyped views, then the prejudiced views of individuals may be in some way altered. Apart from evidence that contact may in fact increase stereotyping and prejudice (e.g. Smith *et al.*, 2006), what many find unacceptable about such an explanation is that it places responsibility on those experiencing homophobia, sexism, racism, etc. to prove they are 'different' and naturalizes the prejudiced views held as simply problems with information processing. As Julian Henriques (1984: 74) concludes:

> the black person becomes the cause of racism whereas the white person's prejudice is seen as a natural effect of their information processing mechanisms. (This works as a subtle double exoneration of white racism, no doubt all the more effective because it is not conscious).

Prejudice as personality traits: psychodynamic approaches

The work of Adorno *et al.* (1950) produced a theory of prejudice that attempted to explain its social and emotional dimensions. Such work, since developed by Frosh (1997, 2002), recognizes that prejudiced activities are not simply cognitive, but for many are unconscious, accompanied by intense emotions (predominately a fear of the 'Other') and influenced by socio–political circumstances. In trying to understand where such emotions originate and the diverse ways in which such feelings are manifested, this tradition draws on Freudian psychoanalysis. In addition, Adorno *et al.* (1950), aware of individual differences in prejudiced activity, set out to explain why, at certain historical times, political ideologies appeal to different people to varying degrees. In particular, Adorno and colleagues were interested in the psychological processes shared by those who were attracted by anti-democratic, conservative ideologies such as fascism. A complex theory was proposed that considered the impact of conscious and unconscious activities, as well as parenting practices and social circumstances on the development of personality. This theory suggests that there is a certain type of personality – the authoritarian personality – that is attracted to anti-democratic, conservative ideologies. The origins of this personality were not perceived by the above authors as being attributable to chance but rather to lie in particularly harsh childhood experiences. Parenting practices associated with the development of the authoritarian personality are also situated more widely within patriarchal, capitalist societies.

Through empirical research, Adorno and colleagues suggested that authoritarian personality types shared a number of recurring features, including:

- being conformist;
- conventional (not only in terms of political beliefs but also in relation to family life, sexual relations, etc.);
- locked into stereotypical thinking;
- organized and obedient;
- respect perceived strength;
- dislike perceived weakness, intolerance of ambiguity;
- defer to authority.

In the language of psychoanalysis, a type of dualistic world is experienced by such individuals where one part of their world is over-idealized and the other structured by excessive negativity. Within this theoretical perspective, strict but often inconsistent parental discipline produces children who learn readily to obey authority but who fear expressing their own needs/feelings. As a result of such interactions, some children may become masochistic, believing themselves to be 'bad' and striving to meet parental norms and expectations, and who, at the same time, learn the importance of obedience. 'An authoritarian personality is thus based on a sado-masochistic personality structure which finds comfort in submission to authority whilst displacing aggression onto out-groups who are made blameworthy for society's ills' (Durrheim *et al.*, 2009: 200). In psychoanalytic terms, children experiencing such parenting internalize the standards of parents, especially the father, developing a strong, punitive superego or conscience.

In lay terms, then, these children are constantly judging themselves according to harsh social or cultural standards. Furthermore, the initial instilling of beliefs about the importance of obedience and respect for authority persist in adulthood. Other authority figures (teachers, group leaders, political figures) substitute for the parents and an exaggerated respect is shown to those who are perceived to be as strong and disciplined as the parents. However, harsh parenting and excessive deference to authority also produces excessive resentment that cannot be vented at parents or other authority figures. In order to ease the psychic tensions experienced, Adorno *et al.* (1950) suggest that such individuals unconsciously employ defence mechanisms – projecting their resentment on to those perceived as weaker, inferior or Othered within the overarching political and economic climate. Frosh (1997: 216) suggests that projection 'creates a world full of hated objects, thus confirming the racist's (or fascist's, in terms of *Authoritarian Personality*) vision of being ensnared in a dangerous situation in which the other has to be wiped out for the self to survive'. The theory of the authoritarian personality argues against the contact hypothesis because the process of racist ideation is one in which unwanted, feared or hated objects of the self are projected onto the prejudiced Other. As a consequence contact is likely to reinforce or indeed inflame existing prejudices (Frosh, 2002: 105–106).

This theory has been acclaimed by many authors, including Wetherell and Potter (1992), for its attempt to incorporate the ways that ideologies, such as fascism, in certain socio–economic situations, can psychologically engage or appeal to certain individuals. In contrast to the social cognition perspective discussed earlier, this theory produces a complex theoretical explanation of prejudice that combines individual internal mechanisms and the social context. Within this theory prejudiced activities are linked to identity and individuals are conceived as fragmented and shaped by conflicting desires, desires to be both submissive and powerful. This representation of the individual stands in stark contrast to the unified individual presented in social cognition accounts of prejudiced activity:

> The chain of cause and effect is complex – from the mores and habits of certain social circumstances, to parent-child interactions,

to the formation of personality, to the expression of political ideology, which then once more sets the scene for the reproduction of these personality forms in another generation. (Wetherell and Potter, 1992: 50)

There is also some correlational evidence linking scores on authoritarian personality scales to prejudice (e.g. Duckitt, 1992; Heaven & St Quintin, 2003) and linking racist attitudes between parents and children (e.g. Duriez & Soenens, 2009). However, others such as Pettigrew (1958) and Billig (1978) have indicated that this perspective provides a limited explanation of prejudiced activity. Firstly, it is suggested that this theoretical perspective links racism too narrowly with child-rearing practices and so cannot cope with the multiple contexts and diverse content of prejudiced activities. For example, the work of Minard (1952) with black and white miners stressed the variability in racist activities among this group, with racism occurring above ground but not below in the mines. Thus the context in which interactions occur is highlighted as significant for understanding prejudiced activity. Secondly, the authoritarian personality approach is criticized as oversimplifying the complex links between the internal world constructed by the individual and the external social world (Wetherell, 1996). Pettigrew's (1958) work illustrated how the prevalence of authoritarian personalities remained constant across Western societies and across southern and northern regions of the United States, yet instances of racism varied widely in different societies and between these regions in the United States. Such instances suggest a more complex interplay between the individual and her or his social worlds than Adorno et al. (1950) can account for. In addition the methodological approach adopted by Adorno and colleagues has been critiqued (see Wetherell and Potter, 1992, for further discussion).

Prejudice and group membership

This third theoretical approach to prejudiced activity suggests that the earlier works on cognitive processes and personality structure are too rigid to explain prejudiced activities and instead focus on the effects of group membership on the psychology of individuals. Central to this perspective is the Realistic Group Conflict Theory (Sherif & Sherif, 1969) and Social Identity Theory (Tajfel & Turner, 1979).

Sherif and Sherif (1969) rejected what they considered to be the overly simplistic analogies between human and animal social aggression that had been noted by earlier theorists (Lorenz, 1966), arguing that animal aggression lacked the organization and diversity of human social aggression, prejudice and group conflicts. Sherif and Sherif presented the processes underlying animal social aggression, witnessed in defensive behaviours relating to territory and resources, as mediated through straightforward chemical and visual discrimination, the 'sniffing out' of unfamiliar opponents. In contrast, they argued that prejudiced activities among humans were more complex, mediated through the cultural meanings of perceived territory (or homeland) and the rights that accompanied this. Theirs is a strongly environmental account of prejudiced activity where the immediate social situation (membership of a group and the group's relations with others) causes the psychological states involved in aggression. Central to the 'realistic group conflict theory' is that the positioning of groups, for example in relation to scarce resources or particular goals, causes the various psychological states that characterize intergroup relations. To quote Wetherell (1996: 204), 'People's perceptions of those who belong to their own group and to the other group, their emotions, identifications or lack of identification will fall in line with the state of relations between the groups.' Sherif and Sherif (1969) illustrated their theoretical ideas with a series of experiments conducted in a boys' summer camp (see Box 5.2).

Based on the evidence collected from the summer-camp experiments, Sherif and Sherif (1969) claimed to demonstrate a clear link between the objective relations between groups and the psychology of individuals. In phase three of the experiments, where the groups competed in the tournament, in-group identification and loyalty were consolidated and hostility towards members of the perceived out-group intensified. Behavioural and emotional indicators of prejudice were evident in the name-calling and stereotyping that occurred. Later experimental research (Tajfel & Turner, 1979) supported the findings of Sherif and Sherif (1969).

Box 5.2   The summer-camp experiments

Sherif and Sherif (1969) set up a summer camp over a two-week period. The boys who participated were unaware that they were part of the experimental research and all were selected for their 'normal' characteristics. The researchers set up four social situations. Firstly, the boys were allowed to mix freely, and spontaneous friendship groups emerged. The second phase occurred a few days later and involved the establishing of two groups. Although the groups appeared to the boys to be chosen arbitrarily, the researchers established them to cut across established groups and allegiances. The two groups worked separately on activities and quickly new friendships emerged, to the extent that the boys developed their own codes of behaviours and names such as the Bulldogs and Red Devils.

During the third phase of the study, the groups were brought together and a tournament announced. Each group could compete to earn points for their own group. Initially the points for each group were kept artificially equal. At this stage norms of good personship were discarded and open hostility emerged between the groups and in-group loyalty became evident. The final stage involved the groups working towards mutual superordinate goals (e.g. solving problems with the camp water supply). Over time, indulging in co-operative activities reduced intergroup hostility, which was further reduced by the introduction of a third group of boys from a nearby camp (common enemy). This period introduced a climate in the summer camp that resembled that in the first phase.

CRITICAL THINKING BOX: METHODOLOGY

Read the experiments described in Box 5.2. What do you consider are the limitations of such experiments for exploring prejudiced activities?

Although Sherif and Sherif (1969) acknowledged that real-life incidences of intergroup conflict were more complex than those illustrated through the summer-camp experiments, various limitations of the 'realistic group conflict theory' have been discussed:

- *Intergroup conflict as a natural response to conflicts of interest*: Wetherell (1996) suggests that such a conclusion carries serious moral and political implications for understanding prejudiced activities. If prejudice is a natural response to group conflict then how can it possibly be problematized; rather, it is simply a predictable outcome based on a conflict of interests. So, for example, is it sufficient to say that racism in the UK is as a result of competition over jobs, and that by creating more jobs, racism could be eliminated? In many ways such an explanation obscures the diversity and pervasiveness of prejudiced activities and ignores historical representations of particular groups in societies and the ways such discourses are used to legitimize prejudiced activities (see Dixon & Durrheim, 2003). Also, if prejudiced activities are viewed as a natural response to group conflict, how do we define someone involved in such activity in terms of personal accountability?

- *Prejudice as a universal trait*: The suggestion that membership of a group will affect people in stable, predictable ways has been heavily criticized. Such an approach neglects important issues such as the history of the development of perceived groups, social positioning and how this affects access to resources, culture and ideology. It fails to explain variation in prejudiced activities and to explore why specific groups in society are discriminated against.
- *The invisible third group*: The work of Billig (1976) draws attention to methodological considerations, in particular the role of the experimenter(s). Billig challenges the taken-for-granted scientific understanding of the experimenter as a neutral observer and instead draws attention to her or his social position and power in experimental contexts. In the summer camp experiments, Sherif and associates effectively formed a third 'authority' group, instrumental in creating the social structure within which the activities of the boys were framed. They instigated the establishment of two distinct groups, defined competitive and superordinate tasks and, perhaps more important, intervened when competition between the boys took place at 'unexpected' stages of the experimental process. The lack of analysis of the influence of the experimenter(s) and competition between the boys even when they were not directly in competitive situations calls into question the theoretical validity of Sherif's work for understanding 'real-life' instances of intergroup hostility and conflict (for a fuller discussion see Billig, 1976).

Tajfel's experimental work in the 1970s (e.g. Tajfel, 1978) concentrated further on the identification that occurs within group situations and the consequences of the psychological changes this identification involves. Tajfel believed that group contexts introduced specific psychological changes in the ways individuals identify both themselves and others. In contrast to the work of Sherif and Sherif (1969), Tajfel argued that the processes of group identification would result in intergroup conflict in the absence of competition for resources or the attainment of some goal. Tajfel conceptualized behaviour in terms of a continuum. At one end he visualized 'interpersonal behaviour', that is the behaviours and characteristics that are manifested when we act as individuals. When perceiving oneself as a unique individual, Tajfel suggested that we relate to others as individuals, viewing and evaluating them in terms of their unique characteristics or personality. At the other end of the continuum is intergroup behaviour, the characteristics and behaviour we indulge in when we perceive ourselves as a group member (e.g. student, teacher, even our family). Again, Tajfel viewed this as having consequences for our relations with others, in particular the tendency to overgeneralize the characteristics attributed to other groups, leading to perceptions and evaluations of others as homogeneous masses. Tajfel acknowledges that these behaviours in their purest form rarely exist and that factors such as cultural context will also influence how we understand situations and react to them.

Tajfel (1981) explored the processes of identification with an interesting series of experiments known as the minimal group experiments. In contrast to Sherif and Sherif's (1969) work, where competition between two groups was deliberately fostered, Tajfel's subjects were randomly assigned to two groups under the pretence of a preference for the paintings of artists such as Klee and Kandinsky. The students participating were not aware of the group others were assigned to, and for the rest of the experiment subjects performed individually in cubicles. Students were presented with matrices and asked to divide points worth money between the two groups. The matrices contained code numbers for individuals and the subjects were asked to assign points to individuals in each group, never to themselves. Despite the fact that the groups shared no history or contact and were not in a situation of direct competition (in contrast to the summer camp experiments), the results indicated signs of in-group favouritism and discrimination against those perceived as out-group members (see also Kinder & Kam, 2009). These minimal group experiments have been frequently replicated, with similar outcomes (e.g. Wilder, 1990; Ben-Ner et al., 2009).

Tajfel and Turner (1985) suggested that the results of the minimal group experiments could be explained in terms of the changes to personal identity that result from group membership. They suggest that when individuals perceive themselves as members of groups (working-class, Catholic, Asian, etc.), they categorize their social world according to their group's characteristics and beliefs. These changes, they propose, occur through a three-stage psychological process theorized in social identity theory. This theory links the negative processes such as stereotyping and the inequitable allocation of resources illustrated in the earlier experimental work, with the individual's desire for a positive self-image. Firstly, Tajfel and Turner suggest a change in cognitive processing within group contexts whereby categories based on the salient features of groups emerge which structure the individual's view of her or his social world. It is argued that similarities within groups are accentuated and differences with other groups emphasized. This, Tajfel and Turner argue, promotes a change in self-definition. Identification with a group erodes individuality as the person begins to define herself or himself in line with the characteristics, beliefs and traits of the in-group. Turner (1982) described this process as depersonalization, with the social identity of the group providing an important basis for self-esteem. The final process of social comparison is, according to these theorists, vital for a positive social identity and self-esteem, and provides the final key to understanding collective actions. As Wetherell (1996: 213) points out, 'self-esteem, according to this logic will be tied to the position of one's groups *vis-à-vis* other groups. To think well of ourselves, it is necessary to think well of our groups.'

Consequently, if people compare their group with others and do not feel highly valued they will feel dissatisfied. If the relationship between themselves and the other group(s) is seen as legitimate, individuals will accept this and attempt to move to the more favourable group(s). If however, the intergroup relationship is perceived as illegitimate, group members will take collective action or individual action to improve their social identity and enhance self-esteem. So, for example, collective action has taken the form of the violence in Northern Ireland in the past, with various terrorist groups (e.g. IRA, UVF, etc.) fighting for the rights of their so-called communities (Catholics, Protestants). Or on an individual basis, if one identifies oneself as 'working class', self-worth and self-esteem may be achieved by focusing on characteristics such as being down-to-earth, honest, hard-working, etc. and the perceived characteristics of the 'middle class' (such as pretentious, snobbish, artificial, etc.) that maximize difference may be emphasized. According to social identity theory it is these psychological processes that not only lead to intergroup conflict but also maintain it (see Brown, 2007; Jenkins, 2009: 112–117).

In many ways this latter account of social identification, categorization and comparison could be considered a more social account of the causes of prejudiced activities than the other perspectives discussed earlier in this chapter. The social context is emphasized as central to understanding group conflict and resulting discriminatory practices. From a critical social psychology perspective, however, a number of fundamental anomalies underlie social identity theory, two of which are discussed below:

- *The 'individual' and the 'social':* This theory attempts to explore the interface at which aspects of the individual (cognitions, motivations, identities) and the organization of the social (groups/categories) combine and result in prejudiced activities. However, Wetherell and Potter (1992) argue that for the theory to hold, certain representations of the individual and the social need to pre-exist. Individuals within this theory are conceptualized as self-contained units sharing sets of internal processes (cognitions, motives) that function in some universal way (categorization, comparison, differentiation) regardless of individuals' social, cultural and historical contexts. Consequently, prejudiced thoughts, emotions and activities are seen as residing within the individual with no theoretical exploration of their social origins or the diverse socially constructed ways in which these are legitimized and manifested. The social in this theoretical perspective is represented as a collection of discrete and simplified groupings (class, religion, gender, minority, majority, etc.), and a social reality is assumed which the individual visibly perceives and processes in particular ways. The processing of such social stimuli in turn produces observable, predictable forms of social action such as racism, sexism, homophobia, etc. However, as Billig (1978, 1996, 2002) points out, the diverse cultural, social, political and legal representations of identities mediated through institutional representations/language and everyday talk are an absent level of analysis in such accounts. Instead the ever-present dynamic socio–historical reminders of 'who we are' and how we are situated in relation to others are theorized as a universal and static backdrop to activities, existing as 'traditions' (religion, race, sex) that are conceptualized as having some type of naturally existing status.
- The problem with such assumptions has been highlighted through work on the minimal group experiment in a variety of cultures. In her work with Pacific Island Maori and white European New Zealand children, Wetherell (1982) illustrated differences in the strategies chosen by the children that reflected the social and cultural meanings of group relations. Unlike the European white

New Zealand children, who chose strategies similar to those subjects in the original minimal group experiments, the Pacific Island children consistently chose to maximize the joint profit of both groups even on occasions where their group would receive considerably less than the out-group. As Wetherell (1996: 217) concluded, 'this behaviour makes sense in terms of the cultural and social frameworks of Polynesian societies and the emphasis these societies place on generosity to others as a marker of high status'. This example would provide evidence to argue against the notions of universal cognitive processing offered by Tajfel and Turner (1985) and also calls into question the concept of an objective, observable social reality. Rather, what appears to be important is the ways in which people in groups interpret and make sense of intergroup relations in line with the social and cultural frameworks shaping their worlds.

- *Prejudice as a cognitive by-product*: Despite its emphasis on the social context, social identity theory, like the social cognition perspective, has been criticized for its representation of prejudiced activity as an inevitable product of perceptual processing (see Brewer, 2001; Duckitt, 2003). Presenting the individual as a processor of information, structured in this instance within the context of social groups and categories, in order to maximize self-esteem, implies that racism, sexism etc. are unfortunate by-products of universal perceptual systems. As Wetherell and Potter (1992 :47) suggest, 'because these types of group phenomena are expressions of a universal psychological dynamic, racism is more likely to persist than not, and, if racism did disappear, it would simply be replaced by some other grounds for group differentiation'.

Box 5.3 Social Identity Theory (SIT), conflict and Northern Ireland

In the 1980s, Northern Ireland, with its two large independent groups and their associated power differentials seemed to offer a natural laboratory for SIT. Much work relating to the influence of social identity on intergroup conflict and discrimination was conducted (Cairns & Mercer, 1984; Kremer et al., 1986). Although producing many interesting findings, Gough et al. (1992) suggest that this work was confined by the limitations of SIT. The previous authors highlight difficulties with the assumption that groups can be objectively defined, in this case on the basis of religion; as such definitions are

---

contested depending on the criteria adopted. For example, in terms of a simple head-count and using socio-economic criteria, Catholics are often classified as the minority group. Within Ireland as a whole, Protestants are the minority, and in the United Kingdom both Catholics and Protestants in Northern Ireland would be perceived as minority groups. Thus the permanence of terms such as majority and minority underlying much research on prejudice is called into question. In addition, variations in group affiliations depending on the context (Waddell & Cairns, 1986) and regional differences in prejudice and discrimination (Kremer *et al.*, 1986) that could not be fully explained within the context of SIT, were highlighted, leading Gough *et al.* (1992: 638) to conclude that:

> it is dangerous to assume that situations can be readily and objectively defined. In reality, people will actively interpret situations according to their own needs and existing cognitions. SIT theorists have focused on more global processes of social categorization and social comparison without detailing how these processes impact at an individual level.

Identities, discourse and ideology: critical readings of prejudice

Social constructionism offers an understanding of prejudice that begins with a rejection of the dualistic concept of 'the individual and the social' embodied in the perspectives discussed previously. The individual as the possessor of internal psychological states (cognitions or motivations) linked to particular social actions is destabilized by representations of selfhood as multiple and fragmented (see Chapter 6). The identities in which individuals engage are perceived as neither unitary nor stable but rather are inextricably linked with sociocultural contexts. In more contemporary work on prejudiced activities, identity is perceived not as a static, consistent concept but rather is fluid, constructed and reconstructed through the interactions that occur. Talk, as Wetherell (1996) stresses, does not occur in a vacuum but is formed within a culture and directed at an assumed audience that fundamentally influences what is said and how it is presented. The accounts that are presented reflect how we interpret our historical, social and cultural positions as well as how we position others.

Much critical work on prejudice emphasizes the social construction of such activities by highlighting the changing content of prejudice talk and actions. Billig (1988) in his work on racism refers to new, more subtle types of racist activities, where in cultures such as the UK blatant racism is on the decline, but where now people often present racist sentiments but deny their own prejudice at the same time (see Box 5.5). Billig (1988) illustrates 'new racisms' by drawing attention to the diverse ways in which people present, for example, racist content while actively attempting to avoid being labelled as 'racist' in multi-cultural societies (see also Van den Berg et al., 2003). This is achieved through a denial of one's prejudice and a justification for treating others differently, not on the basis of colour but by using broader arguments relating to employment, housing, equality, law and order, etc. This pattern can be found in talk about immigration and asylum-seeking where, for example, speakers convey their opposition to asylum in 'rational' terms (e.g. economics) rather than 'irrational' (racism). This 'discursive deracilaization' (Every & Augustinous, 2007) has been noted in campaign material from the UK conservative party which claimed their anti-asylum and immigration policy was based on 'common sense' rather than race (Capdevila & Callaghan, 2008). Deracialization is also accomplished in the process of 'talk-in-interaction'. In this process the parties involved share the labour of doing racism through 'innuendo, irony and implication, making implicit associations between race categories and racial attributes' (Durrheim, 2012: 196). These implicit associations obscure direct racist talk allowing the speaker(s) or author to avoid the opprobrium associated with it.

Indeed, recent research suggests that the norm against prejudice is being undermined, since members of majority groups can cite the taboo on prejudice as a means of suppressing their freedom of speech (Goodman, 2010), while people can hesitate to attribute racism to others since racism is now associated with extreme instances and can therefore be rejected (van Djik, 1993). In a recent discursive analysis of asylum-seeking discussions online, Burke & Goodman (2012) highlight the complexity of argumentation around race issues (Box 5.4).

Apart from critical research which investigates sites where issues of race are central, such as internet groups discussing asylum-seeking or researcher-directed interviews about race, discursive research has also considered other situations where other matters are prioritized but where race nonetheless is made relevant. For example, Stokoe and Edwards (2007) analyse naturalistic data from two sources – telephone complaints to a mediation service about nuisance

Box 5.4   Asylum-seeking, Nazis and Facebook: a discursive analysis

In this study Burke and Goodman (2012) analyse posts on Facebook relating to asylum-seeking and immigration in the UK. They note that supporters of asylum-seekers present opponents as Nazis who, in turn, construe accusations of Nazism as constraining free speech. The extract below from a Facebook campaign group description, where the author orients to accusations of being racist and questions the legitimacy of asylum seekers so as to present opposition to them as being based on economic factors.

Extract 5: I'm NOT racist, just concerned about mass immigration! Group description

1. This group is for all people who are fed up of being branded a racist or fascist
2. for being concerned about the amount of immigrants entering this
3. country. This group does not condone the removal of all immigrants but the
4. ones we don't need, the so called asylum seekers and the visa overstayers
5. are not welcome to use the British taxpayer as a never ending cash reserve
6. which they can exploit whenever they like.

In the authors' analysis, this account explicitly responds to accusations of prejudice linked to opposing immigration. The position is then clarified and made to sound reasonable by only calling for the removal of immigrants that are 'not needed', asylum seekers and 'visa overstayers' (line 4), and questioning their legitimacy by referring to them as 'so called' (line 4) (see also Lynn & Lea, 2003: 432). The argument then is that opposition to asylum is based on practical and economic factors rather than on any unreasonable prejudices (e.g. Goodman & Burke, 2011). The authors suggest that the account orients to the contemporary norm against prejudice (Billig, 1988) by explicitly denying that opposition to asylum is racist (note the emphasis of 'NOT' in capital letters); the term discursive deracialization (Augoustinos & Every, 2007) is also relevant here since as the account justifies opposition to asylum via non-prejudiced reasons (e.g. economic factors) and rationality (see Goodman, 2008).

neighbours, and police interviews with those suspected of disturbing neighbours – where racist talk was noted. The authors take a conversation analytic approach, focusing on how racial insults are enacted, and how they function, in conversations pertaining to neighbourhood disputes. For example, it was observed that racial insults are often delivered as two-word formulations (e.g. 'Paki bastard'; 'Irish twat'; 'bitch Somali'); this pattern had previously been observed by Guimarães (2003) in relation to complaints as recorded by police officers in Brazil. Stokoe and Edwards also found that the swear-word component of the two-word formulation ('bastard'; 'twat'; 'bitch') was often replaced with a generic term by the speaker, rendered as 'nigger this: nigger that', 'gyppo this', 'white this' etc., which may function to distance the speaker from the kinds of things racists say, thereby protecting them from any accusations of or associations with racism (and maintaining the focus on an accused other). The authors also note that racial insults tend to include 'localizers' (e.g. 'go home'; 'go back to your own country'; 'get out of here'), and contend that such statements feature so routinely in theirs and other data that they can be understood as idiomatic, and that they serve to exclude others from the implied national category (e.g. 'English' or 'British') (see also Baker, 2000; Billig, 1995). Another observed feature concerned 'generalizers' (e.g. 'white this, white that *and stuff like that*'; 'black this *an all this nonsense*'; 'such as Paki family *etcetera*'), which work to construct the suspect of uttering not one but several, repeated racist remarks (see also Jefferson, 1990; Overstreet, 1999). The article also shows how reports of racism are treated (differently) by mediators and police officers, and argue that it is possible and important to study mundane enactments of racism (and other social problems) in situations in which other issues are ostensibly foregrounded (see also Zimmerman, 2005).

Discursive analyses have provided interesting and valuable insights into the subtleties of contemporary prejudice, but critical work extends beyond discourse analysis and discursive psychology. For example, discursive research has been criticized for paying insufficient attention to political and material dimensions of prejudice (e.g. Burman, 2003; Hook, 2001), discriminatory practices ranging from psychiatric diagnoses, police stop-and-search actions, and school exclusions, which disproportionately affect minority groups, cannot be challenged by discursive research (Callaghan & Lazard, 2011). Critical psychologists have also been influenced by critical race scholars and postcolonial theorists in their attempts to understand, and intervene in, racist phenomena (e.g. Hook, 2011). In a recent position paper, Adams and Salter (2011) outline their version of a 'critical race psychology', incorporating:

- *Race as epistemological position* i.e. race is not to be treated as a topic separate from other 'psychological' topics but as a lens with which one can view any topic, regardless of how immediately relevant the issue of race may appear;
- *Identity consciousness* i.e. recognizing the role of identity and racialized subjectivity in constructing 'reality' and 'knowledge', since race and other identity categories are often neglected or obscured in mainstream psychological work. This critical, reflexive stance deliberately departs from the conventional detached position of the psychologist–scientist;
- *Critical methodology* i.e. a rejection of traditional scientific methods which mask the operation of race privilege and a preference for more qualitative, reflexive and narrative forms of inquiry which attend to relevant historical and contemporary contexts.

These central features recall those of critical psychology, and indeed the authors go on to cite both critical (e.g. Howarth & Hook, 2005) and discursive psychology (e.g. Augustinous *et al.*, 2005) as key influences on critical race psychology. They also refer to:

- Black Psychology – since the civil rights protests in the 1960s, a Black Psychology movement has sought to challenge orthodox psychological theories and research which makes claims about the superiority of white, Euro-centric groups over black and minority ethnic groups (e.g. White, 1970; Jones, 1991).
- Multicultural Counselling – this form of practice advocates sensitivity to race identities and relations in the therapeutic relationship, encouraging (white) therapists to attend to their own race privileges and to appreciate aspects of the client's experience informed by racism (rather than simply individual biography) (e.g. Ancis & Syzmanski, 2001; Whaley, 1997).
- Liberation Psychology – this movement was founded by Ignacio Martin-Baro (Aron & Corne, 1994) in the postcolonial context of El Salvador and promotes the application of psychology to social justice for marginalized groups in collaboration with members of those groups as a form of action research (see also Burton & Kagan, 2005) .
- Cultural Psychology – psychologists interested in culture have sought to understand indigenous cultural phenomena from the

perspective of the native culture – without imposing Western psychological norms on their analyses. At the same time, cultural psychologists have endeavoured to expose 'universal' psychological processes as ethnocentric formulations (e.g. Okazaki & Abelmann , 2008; Adams & Salter, 2007).

Prejudice is also tied up with versions of history as well as politics and economics. For example, in their analysis of Maori–Pakeha relations in New Zealand, Wetherell and Potter (1992) note that in describing the position of the Maori people, the middle-class Pakeha sample not only talk about current relations but also try to make sense of their history and the colonialism that occurred in the mid-nineteenth century. Similarly, McCreanor (1996), in his review of anti-homosexual discourse in New Zealand, illustrates how the diverse range of historical and contemporary representations of homosexuals presented acquire meaning within a society that constructs heterosexuality as normal/natural and devalues homosexuality (see also Blackwell et al., 2003: 207–214). Participants drawing on historical anti-Semitic images of Jews intensify the fear of contamination and the further destabilizing of moral and social order 'poisoning the well'.

Institutions can also be implicated in the maintenance of prejudice. For example the charge of 'institutional' racism has been levelled at the Metropolitan Police in the UK following the Stephen Lawrence inquiry (McPherson report, 1999; see also Hattenstone, 2012). In his report McPherson defined institutional racism in the following way:

> the collective failure of an organisation to provide an appropriate and professional service to people because of their colour, culture or ethnic origin [which can] be seen or detected in processes, attitudes, and behaviour, which amount to discrimination through unwitting prejudice, ignorance, thoughtlessness, and racist stereotyping, which disadvantages minority ethnic people.

Many different institutions have been accused of prejudice against minority groups, including health services, psychiatry, educational establishments and so on. Foucault's (1978) work on the power–knowledge couplet is an important dimension in understanding how prejudiced activities are produced and maintained by and within institutions. He stresses the network of power bases that historically have defined human existence through the production of knowledge (medicine, law, philosophy, science etc.), producing definable categories of people and structuring social relations (1978: 88). With respect to women, Guillaumin (1995) and other feminist scholars stress how historically knowledge about women's *nature* has been produced by men in positions of power (e.g. sexologists such as Ellis, 1913, and Freud, 1923) to structure social relations (e.g. marriage), to justify their exclusion from public arenas and their confinement to certain activities such as child production and the servicing of men's needs. Blakemore *et al.* (1997) illustrated the persistence of such representations of women in the institutions in the 1990s in their study 'Exploring the Campus Climate for Women Faculty'. This study illustrates how such ideas continue to shape women's existence and reproduce power relations on a daily basis. The women participating in this study recounted stories of professional devaluation and differences in promotion and tenure opportunities existing between them and male colleagues. Similar differences were enacted by students who addressed male staff using professional titles (Professor, Dr, etc.) while frequently referring to female staff as Miss or Mrs. Furthermore, sexual harassment, exclusion from social networks and demeaning remarks based on gender were reported by the female participants. Other critical work has examined sexism and heterosexism. Gough's (1998) study on the reproduction of gender inequality by a group of university-educated men explores some of these issues (see also Box 5.5).

Box 5.5   New sexist discourse

In this study, Gough (1998: 44) highlights 'the deployment of "new sexist" discourse...a form of talk where liberal values are called upon to present the speaker in a positive light and enable the intimation of sentiments which can be viewed as sexist such that censure is discouraged'.

This is illustrated in the following extract where prejudiced talk is framed by an expressed tolerance. For example, Kevin describes many feminist activities as being 'fair enough' but simultaneously criticizes these with his remark that 'at the same time they [feminists] take it too far'. Again, similar constructions are reproduced in Kevin's talk on equal employment opportunities. He begins by expressing liberal values on women in the workplace – 'I mean women obviously should be allowed to have jobs and stuff' – and then furthers his justifications for why women's access to jobs should be limited by representing women as biologically inferior to men: 'but there are some jobs they gotta accept they can't do, like you get bloody women pilots and stuff, they just can't make the fitness don't you think?'

Discursive analysis of prejudiced talk can be persuasive and insightful. However, some researchers working from a psychosocial perspective (see Chapter 1) draw on psychoanalytic as well as discursive concepts in order to understand contemporary prejudice (e.g. Frosh, 2002; Wetherell, 2003). In Gough's (2004) article, for example, 'masculinity' is presented as defensive as well as discursive; the psychoanalytic (Kleinian) concept of projection is used to help interpret instances of homophobic talk. Many of the male participants in focus group discussions drew on dominant discourses of heterosexuality as the normal/natural sexuality to depict homosexuality as perverse and as a danger to the normative heterosexual society. However, Gough suggests that unprompted emotional and irrational elements of the talk signal unconscious anxieties about masculinities shared by the men. Consider the following extract:

> *Martin:* ... I've always tolerated it but what annoys me is when you see these gay marches, they're all dressed up in these perverted leathers, whatever it is, bondage gear – if they wanna do that in their own home then that's alright, but I think they're gettin' themselves a bad name when they all turn up dressed as transvestites and they've got tights on like the Rocky Horror Show and they're all walkin' down the street; you look at them and you think what are they? and they look like monsters. If they're dressed fairly conventionally, just say 'look I'm a homosexual, accept me', I'd have no problem with that whatsoever – you're not tryin' to rape me, you're not tryin' to force it on me, I accept it, but it's that perversion that they seem to put over, not all of 'em, I mean it's a public minority, but it's that that I don't accept. If it was a heterosexual march and everybody was like in bondage gear and handcuffs, it's not on this... you can't have this walkin' down the street. It goes off, you know it happens, you accept that... but for them to force that on people, now whether they're dressin' to that extent to make a point, this is what you gotta accept. (Gough 2004: 254)

Here, Martin compares gay marchers to monsters and constructs gay men as potential rapists, and justifies this on the basis of perceived 'normal' behaviours and styles of dressing. Heterosexuality is equated with privacy and restraint, the implication being that homosexuality is bound up with unacceptable public displays and, as stated more explicitly later in the extract, should be controlled. In his interpretation of this extract, Gough (2004: 254) proposes that '... unprompted allusion to the possibility of male rape by gay men connects with discourses which construct gay men as immoral and promiscuous, but the images and vocabulary mobilized here are imbued with threat ("for them to force that on people") and horror ("that perversion they try and put over"), as if unconscious fears are surfacing through discourse'.

CRITICAL THINKING BOX: HOMOPHOBIA

List the similarities and differences between popular representations of gay men and women. Why are they different?

Cash (2002) provides us with another example of how psychoanalytic concepts can be used to interpret prejudice. He argues that the troubles in Northern Ireland represent a struggle over discourse and its influence on political subjectivity. He uses the example of the unionist movement to illustrate the ways in which an 'exclusivist' and 'inclusivist' discourse shape and is shaped by different sets of unconscious rules. These unconscious rules shape the different group identities that exist within the unionist movement (e.g. Ulster Unionist Party and Democratic Unionist Party) and the psychic defences each group deploys when defending their own policy positions. As Cash (2002) argues:

> a great deal of political conflict is intragroup conflict within the nominal community. Of course such intragroup conflict is concerned, exactly, with the issue of which set of discursive rules should be drawn upon to think, feel, construe and act properly within the field of intergroup relations. (93) (See also Box 5.3.)

Box 5.6   Cultures of prejudice (Blackwell et al., 2003)

In their book *Cultures of Prejudice: Arguments in Critical Social Science* the authors analyse the ways in which culture, discourse and ideologies are designed to prejudice certain groups of people (e.g. those living in poverty, migrants, people on welfare, women, homosexuals etc.) in order to maintain existing power relations in society. Each of the book's chapters analyse the rhetoric and 'truth claims' that are deployed in order to support prejudicial beliefs and attitudes. For example: 'the welfare state rewards laziness', 'feminism is no longer relevant', 'homosexuality is unnatural', 'abortion is murder', 'unions are too powerful: they are detrimental to the economy', 'everybody is a racist, it is a part of human nature', 'freemarkets pave the way for social development'. The authors argue that social science is at its best when it confronts, deconstructs and refutes the 'cultures of prejudice'.

Summary

In this chapter, theories of prejudice from the 1920s to the more contemporary accounts of critical social psychology in the 2000s have been critically reviewed. We then dealt with traditional social cognition accounts that frame prejudice in terms of limitations on cognitive processes (that is, the ways in which people categorize and group stimuli together). Understandings of prejudice based on character structure, and the authoritarian personality, were then examined, with proponents of this approach suggesting that personality (as a result of childhood development) is central to understanding whether or not people indulge in prejudiced activities. Finally, the 'realistic group conflict' theory and 'social identity' theory were discussed. These theorists argue that group situations, in particular intergroup relations, fundamentally influence individual psychology and lay at the heart of explanations of prejudiced activities. As Hepburn (2003: 21) notes, the topic of prejudice illustrates what is both good and bad about mainstream social psychology: 'it is motivated by a concern with human welfare and improvement, but it works within an individualist notion of social organization'.

We proceeded to argue that people's identities and social positioning are fundamentally influenced by the social and ideological contexts in which they are situated. The social positions that different individuals or collectives of people occupy are not perceived as natural, observable phenomenon but rather are constructed and re-constructed through the social interaction in which they are engaged. Critical social psychologists suggest that the possibilities for identity negotiation are not finite but rather are limited by social and ideological constraints. Consequently prejudiced activities are constructed within the struggles over representation and identity that individuals or collectives of people go through and are fundamentally linked to conflicts of interests and power inequalities.

Key references

Brown, S. D. (2007). Intergroup processes: social identity theory. In D. Langdridge & S. Taylor (eds), *Critical Readings in Social Psychology* (pp. 133–162). Maidenhead, UK: Open University Press.
In this chapter Steven Brown reviews social identity theory (SIT) in relation to race and ethnicity. He then contrasts this with the work of Michael Billig who critiques the SIT model for its failure to account for the role that emotion, power and ideologies play in prejudicial thinking.

Dixon, J., & Levine, M. (eds). (2012). *Beyond Prejudice: Extending the Social Psychology of Conflict, Inequality and Social Change.* Cambridge, UK: Cambridge University Press.
Drawing on Margaret Wetherell's phrase, the 'prejudice problematic', this edited book evaluates the concept of prejudice in an attempt to move beyond some of the mainstream social psychological approaches to the concept. Chapters 1 (Dixon and Levine), 8 (Wetherell), 9 (Durrheim) and 10 (Condor and Figgou) will be of most interest to critical social psychologists.

New references

Adams, G. & Salter, P.S. (2007). Health psychology in African settings: a cultural-psychological analysis, *Journal of Health Psychology*, *12*(3), 539–548.

Adams, P. & Salter, P. (2011). A critical race psychology is not yet born. *Connecticut Law Review*, *43*(5), 1355–1377.

Ancis, J.R. & Szymanski, D.M. (2001). Awareness of white privilege among white counseling trainees, *Counseling Psychologist*, *29*, 549–550.

Aron, A. & Corne, S. (eds). (1994). *Ignacio Martín-Baró: Writings For A Liberation Psychology.* Cambridge, MA: Harvard University Press.

Augoustinos, M. & Every, D. (2007). The language of 'race' and prejudice: a discourse of denial, reason, and liberal-practical politics. *Journal of Language and Social Psychology 26*, 123–144.

Baker, C.D. (2000). Locating culture in action: membership categorization in texts and talk. In A. Lee and C. Poynton (eds) *Culture and Text: Discourse and Methodology in Social Research and Cultural Studies* (pp. 99–113). London: Routledge.

Ben-Ner, A., McCall, B.P., Stephane, M. & Wang, H. (2009). Identity and in-group and out-group differentiation in work and giving behaviours: experimental evidence, *Journal of Economic Behaviour and Organization, 72*, 153–170.

Billig, M. (1985). Prejudice, categorization and particularization: from a perceptual to a rhetorical approach. *European Journal of Social Psychology, 15*, 79–103.

Billig, M. (1995). *Banal Nationalism*. London: Sage.

Billig, M. (1996). Remembering the particular background of social identity theory. In W. P. Robinson (ed.), *Social groups and identities: Developing the legacy of Henri Tajfel* (pp. 337–358). Oxford: Butterworth-Heinemann.

Billig, M. (2001). Humour and hatred: the racist jokes of the Ku Klux Klan, *Discourse & Society 12*, 267–289.

Billig, M. (2002). Henri Tajfel's 'cognitive aspects of prejudice' and the psychology of bigotry. *British Journal of Social Psychology, 41*, 171–188.

Blackwell, J. C., Smith, M. E. G., & Sorenson, J. S. (2003). *Cultures of Prejudice: Arguments in Critical Social Science* (2nd edn). Peterborough, Canada: Broadview Press.

Brewer, M.B. (2001). In-group identification and intergroup conflict: when does in-group love become out-group hate? In R. Ashmore, L. Jussim & D. Wilder (eds) *Social Identity, Intergroup Conflict and Conflict Reduction*. New York: Oxford University Press.

Brown, S. D. (2007). Intergroup processes: social identity theory. In D. Langdridge & S. Taylor (eds), *Critical Readings in Social Psychology* (pp. 133–162). Maidenhead, UK: Open University Press.

Brown, R. & Hewstone, M. (2005). An integrative theory of intergroup contact. In M. Zanna (ed.) *Advances in Experimental Social Psychology, 37*, 255–343.

Burke, S. & Goodman, S. (2012). 'Bring back Hitler's gas chambers': asylum-seeking, Nazis and Facebook – a discursive analysis, *Discourse & Society, 23*(1), 19–33.

Burman, E. (2003). Discourse analysis means analysing discourse. *Discourse Analysis Online*, http://extra.shu.ac.uk/daol/current/

Burton, M., & Kagan, C. (2005). Liberation social psychology: learning from Latin America. *Journal of Community & Applied Social Psychology 15*(1), 63–78.

Callaghan, J. & Lazard, L. (2011). *Social Psychology*. Exeter: Learning Matters.

Capdevila, R. & Callaghan, J. (2008). 'It's not racist, it's common sense': a critical analysis of political discourse around asylum and immigration in the UK. *Journal of Community and Applied Social Psychology, 18*, 1–16.

Cash, J. (2002). Troubled times: changing the political subject in Northern Ireland. In V. Walkerdine (ed.), *Challenging Subjects: Critical Psychology for a New Millennium* (pp. 88–100). Basingstoke, UK: Palgrave Macmillan.

Dixon, J.A. & Durrheim, K. (2003). Contact and the ecology of racial division: some varieties of informal segregation, *British Journal of Social Psychology*, *42*, 1–24.

Dixon, J., & Levine, M. (2012). Introduction. In J. Dixon & M. Levine (eds), *Beyond Prejudice: Extending the Social Psychology of Conflict, Inequality and Social Change* (pp. 1–23). Cambridge, UK: Cambridge University Press.

Duckitt, J. (1992). *The Social Psychology of Prejudice*. Westport, CT: Praeger.

Duckitt, J. (2003). Prejudice and intergroup conflict. In D.O. Sears, L. Huddy & R. Jervis (eds) *Oxford Handbook of Political Psychology* (pp. 559–601). New York: Oxford University Press.

Duriez, B. & Soenens, B. (2009). The intergenerational transmission of racism: the role of right wing authoritarianism and social dominance orientation. *Journal of Research in Personality, 43*(5): 906–909.

Durrheim, K. (2012). Implicit prejudice in mind and interaction. In J. Dixon & M. Levine (eds), *Beyond Prejudice: Extending the Social Psychology of Conflict, Inequality and Social Change* (pp. 179–199). Cambridge, UK: Cambridge University Press.

Durrheim, K., Hook, D., & Riggs, D. W. (2009). Race and racism. In D. Fox, I. Prilleltensky & S. Austin (eds), *Critical Psychology: An Introduction* (2nd edn, pp. 197–214). Thousand Oaks, CA: Sage.

Every, D. & Augoustinos, M. (2007). Constructions of racism in the Australian parliamentary debates on asylum seekers. *Discourse & Society, 18*(4), 411–436.

Fiske, S.T., Gilber, D.T., & Lindzey, G. (eds). (2010). *Handbook of Social Psychology* (5th edn). New York: Wiley.

Frosh, S. (2002). Racism, racialised identities and the psychoanalytic other. In V. Walkerdine (ed.), *Challenging Subjects: Critical Psychology for a New Millennium* (pp. 101–110). Basingstoke, UK: Palgrave Macmillan.

Goodman, S. (2008). Justifying the harsh treatment of asylum seekers on the grounds of social cohesion. *Annual Review of Critical Psychology, 6*, 110–124.

Goodman, S. (2010). 'It's not racist to impose limits on immigration': constructing the boundaries of racism in the asylum and immigration debate. *Critical Approaches to Discourse Analysis across Disciplines, 4*(1), 1–17.

Goodman, S. & Burke, S. (2011). Discursive deracialization in talk about asylum seeking. *Journal of Community and Applied Social Psychology, 21*(2), 111–123.

Gough, B. (2004). Psychoanalysis as a resource for understanding emotional ruptures in the text: the case of defensive masculinities. *British Journal of Social Psychology, 43*(2), 245–267.

Guimarães, A.S.A. (2003). 'Racial Insult in Brazil', *Discourse & Society*, *14*, 133–151.

Hattenstone, S. (2012). Stephen Lawrence verdict does not end debate on police racism. *Guardian*, 6 January. Retrieved 15 May 2012, from http://www.guardian.co.uk/commentisfree/2012/jan/06/stephen-lawrence-verdict-police-racism.

Heaven, P.C.L. & St Quintin, D. (2003). Personality factors predict racial prejudice. *Personality and Individual Differences*, *34*, 625–634.

Hepburn, A. (2003). *An Introduction to Critical Social Psychology*. London: Sage.

Hook, D. (2001). Discourse, knowledge, materiality, history: Foucault and discourse analysis, *Theory & Psychology*, *11*(4), 521–547.

Hook, D. (2011). *A Critical Psychology of the Postcolonial: the Mind of Apartheid*. Hove, UK: Psychology Press.

Howarth, C. & Hook, D. (2005). Towards a critical social psychology of racism: points of disruption, *Journal of Community and Applied Social Psychology*, *15*(6), 425–430.

Jefferson, G. (1990). List construction as a task and resource. In G. Psathas (ed.) *Interaction Competence*. Lanham, MD: University Press of America.

Jenkins, R. (2009). *Social Identity* (3rd edn). London: Routledge.

Jones, R.L. (ed.) (1991). *Black Psychology*. Berkeley, CA: Cobb & Henry.

Kinder, D.R. & Kam, C.D. (2009). *Us against Them: Ethnocentric Foundations of America Public Opinion*. Chicago, IL: University of Chicago Press.

Lippman, W. (1922/1965). *Public Opinion: An Important Work on the Theory of Public Opinion in Relation to Traditional Democratic Theory*. New York: Free Press.

Lynn, N. & Lea, S. (2003). A phantom menace and the new apartheid: the social construction of asylum-seekers in the United Kingdom. *Discourse & Society*, *14*(4), 425–452.

McPherson, W. (1999). The Stephen Lawrence Inquiry: Report of an Inquiry by Sir William Macpherson of Cluny. London: The Stationery Office.

Okazaki, S., & Abelmann, N. (2008). Colonialism and psychology of culture. *Social and Personality Psychology Compass*, *2*(1), 90–106.

Overstreet, M. (1999). *Whales, Candlelight, and Stuff Like That: General Extenders in English Discourse*. Oxford: Oxford University Press.

Smith, R., Miller, D.A., Maitner, A.T., Crump, S.A., Garcia-Marques, T. & Mackie, D.M (2006). Familiarity can increase stereotyping, *Journal of Experimental Social Psychology*, *42*, 471–478.

Stokoe, E. & Edwards, D. (2007). 'Black this: black that': racial insults and reported speech in neighbour complaints and police interrogations, *Discourse & Society, 18*(3), 337–372.

Van den Berg, H., Wetherell, M. & Houtkoop-Steenstra, H. (eds). (2003). *Analysing Race Talk: Multidisciplinary Approaches to the Interview.* Cambridge: Cambridge University Press.

van Dijk, T.A. (1993). Denying racism: elite discourse and racism. In J. Solomos & J. Wrench (eds) *Racism and Migration in Western Europe* (pp. 179–193). Oxford: Berg.

Wetherell, M. (2003). Paranoia, ambivalence and discursive practices. concepts of position and positioning in psychoanalysis and discursive psychology. In R. Harre & F.M. Moghaddam (eds), *The Self and Others: Positioning Individuals and Groups in Personal, Political and Cultural Contexts* (pp. 99–120). Westport, CT: Greenwood Publishing.

Whaley, A.L. (1997) Ethnicity/race, paranoia, and psychiatric diagnoses: clinician bias versus sociocultural differences, *Journal of Psychopathology and Behavioural Assessment, 19*, 1–17.

White, J. (1970). *Toward a Black Psychology, Ebony* magazine.

Wilder, D.A. (1990). Some determinates of the persuasive power of in-group and out-groups: organization of information and attribution of independence, *Journal of Personality & Social Psychology, 59*, 1202–1213.

Zimmerman, D.H. (2005). Introduction: conversation analysis and social problems, *Social Problems, 52*(4), 445–448.

Self in Society

Self, Identity, Subjectivity

6

This chapter will highlight:

- The psychological concept of 'personality'
- Social roles
- The impact of culture on the self
- The self as fragmented and de-centred
- Societal and discursive constraints on identity
- The problem of subjective experience

Introduction

In most Western societies, we are used to thinking about ourselves as unique, as different from other people. We may admit some family resemblances ('I'm a bit like my dad') and make generalizations about members of a particular group ('Call men' are pathetic), but we tend to emphasize individual differences above all. We are fascinated by the latest surveys on personality which categorize the self into different types ('which type of lover/boss/driver/parent/husband/ wife are you?'). Our language provides us with many terms for differentiating between people – assertive/passive; anxious/calm; lazy/ productive, introverted/extraverted – which we may also use to predict an individual's behaviour. After all, if we label Linda as 'quiet' then this implies that she will normally be quiet, and this is 'knowledge' which is helpful when we anticipate encountering her in the future (we will not be surprised by Linda's quietness and will 'know' to direct the conversation, for example). In other words, the term 'personality' is used to suggest those 'core' characteristics thought to 'capture' a person's being. Of course, such ideas have been present(ed) in psychology for much of this century, where it is proposed that personality can be clearly defined and measured; most people are familiar with Eysenck's Personality Inventory (1952), which is used to calculate extroversion–introversion and stability–neuroticism.

However, this assumption that personality is fixed and amenable to measurement has been questioned both within and beyond (social) psychology. Within sociology and sociological social psychology, for example, the psychological focus on the individual is, predictably, criticized for ignoring how society shapes people in various ways (e.g. Shotter & Gergen, 1988; Oishi et al., 2009). Role theory is used to highlight the impact of social expectations and situations on the self; for example an interviewee will hardly appear in casual clothes and refuse to answer questions, nor will mourners at a funeral tend to dress colourfully or speak disrespectfully of the deceased in public. There is a sense, then, in which the self must be managed, at least in certain situations, in order to fulfil social norms and obligations (see Goffman, 1959). Such an analysis points to a self which is flexible and dynamic, adopting and discarding 'multiple roles' as the situation demands – a fragmented rather than a unitary self. The argument that people are responsive to local rules and conventions has been extended to cultures, where different values related to the individual have been noted between nations and societies. For example, Eastern countries such as Japan tend to encourage self-effacement, in that individual needs and desires are secondary compared to the requirements of the family, the organization, the club, etc., in contrast to the Western promotion of self-expression and self-interest (Smith et al., 2006; see also Ratner, 2006).

With the emergence of critical social psychology, this latter sociological–pluralistic view of selfhood is favoured over the psychological–unified stance, although there are many debates concerning the extent to which an individual is moulded by societal and cultural forces (see Parker, 1992; Potter & Wetherell, 1997). Critical social psychology considers the various representations of self on offer in a given culture and examines how these are taken up, re-worked or even resisted by people in the way they talk about themselves (Burman & Parker, 1993; Potter & Wetherell, 1997). For example, a gay man might wish to refuse an effeminate identity in favour of more traditionally 'masculine' positions (strong, rational, etc.), thereby challenging the discourse which associates male homosexuality with femininity and weakness. Moreover, as critical social psychology is concerned also with issues of power and inequalities, questions about the functions which certain ideals are pushed to serve would be asked. For example, it has been argued that the Western capitalist spotlight on individuals rather than societies facilitates a politics where individuals are blamed for problems which might otherwise be conceived in terms of social factors (see Parker, 1992; Sampson, 1993; Smail, 2005). So that when people in contemporary Western society seek to account for the likely origins of their own experiences of ill-health, disempowerment and inequality they typically have a propensity to 'discount the harmful effects of those social and material adversities with which they may be struggling, and instead attribute their problems to their own apparent lack of will power, or internal moral resolve' (Moloney & Kelly, 2008: 280).

The riots that broke out in London in August 2011 (and other large cities in England) are a case in point. Politicians, social commentators and journalists were quick to blame the riots on a handful of 'immoral' 'feral' individuals, or as some put it, individuals with 'defective personalities' who had been raised by 'defective families'. While there is certainly no denying that certain individuals were responsible for terrible acts of violence, arson and theft that occurred during the riots, very few commentators were prepared to ask *why* it was that these particular young people in England (the majority under the age of 24) would behave in such a violent and destructive way towards their own poor communities (Jones, 2011b). In the weeks following the riots a more considered commentary began to look at the possible causes in more depth and to ask questions of what it was about the social and cultural environment that contributed to the violence, and what could be done to prevent it happening again in the future. Some of the issues raised in this commentary included the penal system and its methods of rehabilitation (many of the rioters had previous criminal records), the massive gap between rich and poor in England's largest cities (the majority of the rioters came from poor deprived areas), and the lack of educational and employment opportunities that some young people experience growing up in these areas.

So, this chapter presents a critical view of the traditional psychological (and 'commonsense') position which presents the self as a stable, measurable essence or object set apart from social relationships. Instead, critical social psychology uses terms such as 'subjectivity' and 'identities' to suggest a fluid, multiple process embedded in social practices, institutions and discourses, but not completely determined by these – identity is constructed, negotiated and defended in relation to other people and in the light of prevailing values and conventions. Such ideas are developed below.

CRITICAL THINKING BOX: PERSONALITY

Psychologists have popularized the concept of personality, which assumes a stable and consistent self. But how do different people you know describe your 'personality'? Do their assessments agree? What factors influence how *you* think about yourself?

Deconstructing the psychological self

As mentioned above, individualist societies like most Western societies promote a culture where the self is visible, distinctive and personally responsible. We talk constantly about 'personality', debating those 'types' of person most likely to engage in 'road rage', those that are able to confidently interact with others, collect stamps, obsess about football, take drugs, surf the net and so on. We assume that the cause or one of the main causes of such behaviours resides within the person, in their personality, in their genetic makeup, so that only those predisposed towards aggression will submit to road rage and that only certain weak or pathological individuals will seek narcotic stimulation. When we resort to such explanations we echo personality theorists and assume that personality is:

- identifiable (and measurable);
- stable over time (i.e. fixed);
- internally consistent (all characteristics fit together);
- the (main) cause of behaviour.

Let us take a closer look at these assumptions. Firstly, we take it for granted that people possess a unique set of personal characteristics, or 'traits', which corresponds to their 'core' or 'essence', their personality. In psychology, much time and effort has been invested in producing thousands of personality tests which claim to measure such traits as 'authoritarianism', 'need for achievement', 'androgyny', 'emotional stability' and 'attributional style' – the list is endless!

To give you a flavour of such instruments, the form of the Attributional Style Questionnaire (ASQ) is detailed in Box 6.1. The theory behind the scale proposes that individuals differ in their attributional or explanatory style. Attributions refer to our accounts or 'causal explanations' pertaining to particular situations. For example, in considering why you were late for work your boss might focus on the personal (an internal cause, such as 'laziness', 'lack of responsibility') whereas you might point to an external cause (e.g. 'the train was cancelled'). You might also suggest it was a one-off event (unstable cause) whereas your boss might suspect future tardiness (stable cause). You might console yourself with thinking that at least you are not late for other events, such as a 'date' or a doctor's appointment (a specific cause) while the boss might wonder whether you are late for everything (a global cause). The ASQ attempts to assess how you think in terms of these three attributional dimensions: internality/externality, stability/instability and globality/specificity.

**Box 6.1 'Attributional style questionnaire'
(Peterson et al., 1993: 156)**

Instructions:

Please try to vividly imagine yourself in the situations that follow. If such a situation happened to you, what would you feel would have caused it? While events may have many causes, we want you to pick only one – the cause if this event happened to you. Please write this cause in the blank provided after each event. Next we want to ask you some questions about the cause. To summarize, we want you to:

1. Read each situation and imagine it happening to you.
2. Decide what you feel would be the major cause of the situation if it happened to you.
3. Write one cause in the blank provided.
4. Answer three questions about the cause.

At this point the subjects are presented with six 'bad' events (your friend is hostile; you can't make a work deadline, etc.) and six 'good' events (a success at work, in a relationship, etc.). The task is to discern the cause of each event on 7-point scales according to internality/externality, stability/instability and globality/specificity. And for each cause, the subjects respond to three questions:

1. Is this cause due to something about you or something about other people or circumstances?
2. In the future will the cause again be present?
3. Is the cause something that influences this situation or does it also influence other areas of your life?

Scores for the three dimensions – internality, stability and globality – are collated for the good and bad events separately. Often an overall, composite score for 'explanatory style' is calculated.

In general, two main explanatory styles have been identified. On the one hand there are people who explain positive outcomes in terms of internal, stable and global factors ('my success in the exams is down to me, I am wonderful') and negative outcomes as external, unstable and specific to the situation ('my failed exam was down to a bad paper, I did well in other exams'). On the other hand, some people are said to exhibit a reverse pattern where positive events are construed as external, unstable and specific and negative events viewed as internal, stable and global: in short, people who show signs of depression (Peterson *et al.*, 1993).

However, the problem with such questionnaires is that they oblige you to select a limited option (in this case, the major 'cause') when, in fact, your response to the item might have otherwise been much more complex and nuanced. There is just no room for responses like: 'Well, I'm not quite sure, I did well on that paper because I worked hard, although it was a pretty fair exam and I did buy the recommended texts whereas others didn't.' Similarly, when thinking about the selected cause in terms of the three dimensions it might well be difficult to select numbers on a scale because of the potential number of competing explanations for an outcome (as above). Moreover, the exercise feels not a little artificial: you are asked to respond in a limited way to a set of predetermined items and scenarios and the 'causes' you select for the experiment might well reflect the situation and your status within it. There is little scope for the subject bringing his or her own interpretations to bear on the material – definitions of 'good' and 'bad' events are likely to vary between people. Indeed, there has been much work on 'demand characteristics' and 'social desirability' (Orne, 1962) which suggests that subjects' responses are sensitive to the dynamics of the test situation. In avoiding or dismissing such influences, the complexity in people's social interactions is foreclosed and the portrait of the individual based on overall score surely simplistic and one-dimensional.

When we categorize someone as, say, neurotic we imply that they have always been this way and always will; in other words, a person's character remains stable throughout life the second assumption. After all, if we thought that someone fluctuated a lot in their behaviour then personality terms which suggest stability would become meaningless. In psychological and popular parlance it is sometimes further assumed that personality is at least partially preordained by biology. Body shape itself was originally linked to personality (Kretschmer, 1925) although subsequent theories pointed to neural wiring (Eysenck, 1952). Commonsense ideas frequently focus on family resemblances ('like father like son', etc.) with a typical claim that such similarities are due to genetic inheritance. Hormonal systems are highlighted to suggest personality differences between men and women, with the former identified as more aggressive by virtue of greater testosterone levels (e.g. Goldberg, 1977) and the latter deemed more nurturing because of oestrogen effects (Rossi, 1977) (see Box 2.3, Chapter 2).

CRITICAL THINKING BOX: BIOLOGY AND 'PERSONALITY'

A range of biological 'causes' have been used by psychologists to explain 'personality' (e.g. genetics, hormones, neurochemistry). Do you believe biology plays a role in fixing the way you are? How far can biological influences be overcome?

But such theories do not seem to recognize that people change, that quiet children may become loud adults, that sullen adolescents may develop into contented grown-ups. Apart from changes brought about by life stage, people may also vary their behaviour according to the situation, as in a teacher being efficient and disciplined at work but getting drunk and dancing at weekends, or a therapist prone to excitability when not being professionally detached.

The third assumption of personality-talk is that the different aspects of someone's self necessarily fit together into a neat, consistent package. For example, if we describe a person as outgoing, we may also guess that she or he is talkative, has a good sense of humour, enjoys novel situations and challenges, and that traits such as passivity and neuroticism do not feature. The notion of personality, then, implies that a person cannot be both extroverted and introverted at the same time, as this would be inconsistent – the categories are mutually exclusive. Again, this way of thinking does not do justice to the variation in behaviour witnessed in daily interaction. A friend or partner can be sensitive and caring one day and cold and aloof the next, depending on mood, context or events (see Burr, 2003).

Finally, personality is commonly used as a means of accounting for someone's behaviour, held up as the reason or cause. Hence, criminal activity is explained in terms of violent or antisocial personalities, good performance at school is attributed to intelligence, watching lots of television is construed as laziness, etc. The problem here is one of circularity, where both the alleged cause and the outcome amount to much the same thing (criminal behaviour is due to a criminal personality; academic excellence is due to academic qualities; lazy behaviour is due to lazy people). So, much the same terms are used to describe the behaviour and its cause (personality), a case of tautology (see Potter & Wetherell, 1987).

So, the main problem with personality theories is that a whole host of factors outside (but connected to) the individual are not considered as valid explanations for behaviour, such as the social situation, cultural and historical forces, interpersonal relationships. This point has been emphasized in social psychology by social learning theory (e.g. Bandura, 1977; Mischel, 1966) in which the 'situation specificity' of behaviour is the key assumption. How we present ourselves in a given set of circumstances will depend on what we have learned from previous comparable situations. For example, if a child has been rewarded ('reinforced') in the past for asking permission to leave the dining table then this behaviour is likely to be repeated; rather than some personality trait accounting for this behaviour ('politeness'? 'respect for authority'?), the 'cause' is located in the particular context. If a person carries out a criminal act, for example, it could be because they have been forced to by other people, because they need money to feed a family, because they have ingested alcohol or drugs, because it may earn some respect from peers, and so on. Moreover, those making judgements on the case will inevitably vary in the weight they grant to the different accounts so that the 'real' reason for the criminal act will likely not be found, only competing versions of the 'truth'. It is clear, then, that a number of problematic issues are raised when the definitions and uses of the concept of personality are probed. The principal objection here relates to the simplistic categorization of a person in terms of a few broad traits, a practice which neglects the dynamic and complex ways in which people present themselves across different contexts.

In considering how personality is deployed within (social) psychology, it has been proposed that the focus on the measurement of the individual acts as a form of social control. According to Stainton-Rogers et al. (1995) and Rose (1996), the emergence of psychology as the scientific study of the individual served to define and 'treat' persons in the interests of securing a stable and successful society. That is, (social) psychology sets out to market the discipline as the only proper and effective technology for selecting staff to do particular jobs, screening out dangerous parents, identifying which children will benefit from academic education and so on (see Hollway, 1989; Rose, 1999). The use of personality tests therefore functioned to define, explain, predict and, if necessary, control 'problematic' subjects (see Chapter 2). Nonetheless, there has always been a branch of (sociological) psychology which has preferred to understand the self as embedded within society, as subject to various roles.

CRITICAL THINKING BOX: SITUATIONAL SELVES

The critique of 'personality' suggests that people are actually difficult to categorize once and for all, that different selves are presented for different occasions. One self or many selves – what do you think? To what extent do you present different 'faces' in different environments?

The sociological self

Not surprisingly, sociological social psychologists have been more inclined to locate the individual within social structures and processes. This idea is expressed in role theories (e.g. Dahrendorf, 1973), where people are said to conform to expectations placed on them by various social forces, such as family, work, gender, age, etc. Roles which may be relevant could relate to marital status, profession, political affiliation, sport teams supported, nationality, voluntary work, etc. Within this perspective, then, the self is distributed across different, social arenas rather than limited to a space within the person and is connected to multiple roles rather than one central core.

As traditionally conceived, roles were thought to be enacted in a largely mechanical, conformist fashion – the individual as fixed into place by social institutions (Parsons, 1954). But theorists such as Goffman (1959) allowed the individual more agency with the idea that roles were performed, sometimes in a conscious, strategic way. The 'presentation of self' could be manipulated to achieve particular ends, such as avoiding embarrassment or blame, or attracting praise or material rewards. For example, a child might resort to tears upon falling down ('playing the victim') in the hope that chocolate might be forthcoming from father or mother; a lecturer might attempt a few references to youth culture to dispel the stereotype of the ivory tower academic and so forth. The language of theatre is used by Goffman – the 'dramaturgical metaphor' – to suggest the world is a stage in which people act out their lives according to various roles and scripts provided by society.

But objections to this public, superficial view of self have been raised, mainly by humanistic or experiential psychologists (e.g. Stevens, 1996). They argue that 'behind' the facade of the social roles played out by an individual lies the 'real', 'true' or 'inner' self, much in the same way as a director shapes the action in a film off screen. In other words, a distinction between public and private selves is set up, with the latter deemed more 'authentic' and significant. This latter self is deemed more authentic because it is seen to be uncontaminated by social and other expectations, which require us to conform in ways that are counter to our true nature. Consequently, therapeutic activities informed by such humanistic or 'person centred' conceptions of self attempt to 'uncover' and develop one's true inner self, as characterized by notions like 'self-actualization' (Maslow, 1954), or via therapeutic techniques that call for the therapist to show 'genuineness', 'empathy' and 'unconditional positive regard' in order to assist the client to discover their true values, beliefs and passions which have been hidden away deep inside the self (Rogers, 1961). However, as with the concept of 'personality', the construct of an authentic self marks a separation of the individual (self) from society (roles) and privileges psychological explanations of (social) phenomena. Instead of looking at the self-in-society, causes of action are framed in terms of internal motivations or cognitive processes (see Potter & Wetherell, 1987).

The concept of social roles, then, provides us with one explanation for variability in behaviour, but rather than see the roles we play as merely superficial or even false (although some may not be that central for us), it is perhaps more useful to regard our main roles as important for identity (Burr, 2003; 2002). It is likely, for example, that the role of 'breadwinner' is taken seriously by many men (and, increasingly, women) and the same goes for other key roles (parent, Anglican, school governor, team manager). But when the demands of one role compete with those of another, especially those roles we regard as major, then experiences of tension and conflict often ensue. For example, playing for the local pub football team on a Wednesday night might become difficult during half-term when you are faced with childcare obligations, and difficult decisions have to be made (do you let the team down or leave the children with friends promising future treats?). Managing such incompatible expectations and desires is part of most people's lives which the notion of a coherent, unified personality cannot accommodate; instead, we must locate identity within the social arena with concepts such as roles in order to account for the complex negotiations which characterize the making of identities.

CRITICAL THINKING BOX: SOCIAL ROLES

Clearly there are many roles which people play in everyday life. Think about the many roles which you perform. Which ones are most fulfilling? Give examples of conflicting roles and discuss with a partner how you might reconcile these.

The cultural self

CRITICAL THINKING BOX: MY SELF

Write down 20 responses to the question 'Who am I'? as quickly as possible (i.e. 1. 'I am...; 2. 'I am ...' etc.). There are no 'correct' answers – include whatever responses you think are relevant. This – exercise is called the 'Twenty Statements Test' (see Bond & Cheung, 1983).

We have commented on the multiple roles available in a given society. But if we compare different societies, as recent research has done, it becomes apparent that cultural norms and practices also have a bearing on how the self is presented and understood. Indeed, in some 'collectivist' cultures (Asia, Africa, Latin America) the very notion of a self-contained independent individual so dominant in the West does not figure prominently. Instead, identity is defined in terms of relationships with other people, such as family members, work colleagues, friends, acquaintances or kin/tribal groupings in the case of indigenous peoples. What this cultural variation means, of course, is that the Western ideal of personality, where people are seen to possess a natural, essential, unique self, is but one (perhaps limited) way of conceptualizing person-hood. This contrast between individualist/independent and collectivist/interdependent models of the self is illustrated below.

These broad cultural differences are reflected in everyday practice, in the ways that people perceive and relate to self and others. For example, rather than resort to a vocabulary of abstract personality traits, Asian cultures tend to favour concrete descriptions of people embedded in the surrounding community. According to research cited in Shweder and Bourne (1982), Indian subjects prefer more 'holistic' accounts of behaviour, such as 'she brings cakes to my family on festival days' (as opposed to simply generalizing to 'she is generous') or 'he has trouble giving things to his family' (instead of 'he is mean'). So, such descriptions function to situate the behaviour in a specific context and do not suggest any consistency or stability beyond the particular instance – an individual who does something nice one day may well do something nasty the next.

One of the most vivid examples of a collectivist culture is the various tribal groupings that make up Australian Aboriginals, whose history is thought to span as far back as 40,000 years. Traditional Australian Aboriginals had no concept of an individual self. They saw themselves first and foremost as part of their tribal or language group (e.g. Ngunawal, Bunurong, Tharawal). So strong was this bond with the group (the collective) that notions of individual property rights did not exist in the same way they do in Western capitalist societies. So that what belonged to the individual belonged to the tribe (ALRC, 1987). We can see in this example that collectivist cultures do not restrict the focus to individuals, a point vividly reinforced by some interesting research by Semin and Rubini (1990) on the variation in favourite insults used between Northern Italy (characterized as individualist) and Southern Italy (deemed more collectivist) (Box 6.2).

Clearly, it is not damning enough to slight the target individual in collectivist cultures; the reputation of the family (or other group) must be undermined for the insult to achieve maximum impact. The importance in choosing the culturally appropriate type of insult is supported by Bond and Cheung (1983), who noted that Hong Kong students reacted more to slights directed at their group than those directed at them as individuals.

Box 6.2   Insulting differences between cultures (Semin & Rubini, 1990)

Semin and Rubini (1990) asked students from Sicily (South) and Bologna and Trieste (North) to give examples of the types of insults they had experienced or used. Whereas insults in the North targeted the perceived offender, Southern people extended the insult to include relations:

Individualist insults (Northern Italy)

You are stupid; You are a cretin; Swear words referring to religious figures; Swear words referring to sexual nouns.

Collectivist insults (Southern Italy)

I wish cancer on you and all your relatives; You are queer and so is your father; You are a Communist; Insults relating to incest.

Another difference concerns the importance attached to self-expression as opposed to self-discipline. Whilst US therapists encourage open communication about self as a way to psychological health, Japanese therapists advocate suppression of emotions and impulses as beneficial. Similarly, Hindu men realized their identity more through fulfilment of social roles than emotional expression. This cultural obligation to subordinate individual desire in favour of group roles and responsibilities is reflected in the common sense of collectivist societies, as the following proverbs illustrate:

'If a nail sticks up, hammer it down' (Japan); 'If one finger is sore, the whole hand will hurt' (China).

Such thinking extends even to the realm of emotions. US subjects tend to select personal events as provoking anger (indicating independence) whereas Chinese subjects indicate events which had happened to other people (suggesting engagement with others) (see Smith *et al.*, 2006).

Of course, we must be careful not to categorize cultures simplistically in terms of the individualist–collectivist or tightness–complexity dimensions (see Triandis, 2001), as most contemporary societies boast both individualist and collectivist aspects. It is not difficult to produce examples of collectivist behaviours in Western societies, such as patriotism during times of war and loyalty to a sports team, when individual needs often become secondary. Moreover, examples of interdependence are often located within subcultures, ethnic minorities and assorted marginalized groups. In the UK, for example, the importance of connectedness with family and others is stressed especially by Asian and Afro–Caribbean communities whereas notions of group belongingness and even sacrifice are present in religious, sports and even criminal settings. It is also pertinent to note that past historical periods have witnessed more communal social organization in Western societies, as in pre-capitalist agricultural communities characterized by the sharing of resources such as food, space, etc. Conversely, there is evidence of individualistic pursuits in collectivist cultures. In an interesting study by Bond and Cheung (1983), Hong Kong students came out as less collectivist than Japanese peers and less individualist than North Americans in their self-descriptions. Obviously Hong Kong society has been influenced by both Chinese and British ideologies.

CRITICAL THINKING BOX: CULTURE AND SELFHOOD

Consider your responses to the Twenty Statements Test above. How many of your responses can be labelled 'individualist'? How many 'collectivist'? Compare your results with peers and discuss reasons for similarities and differences.

Multicultural identities

When we consider those people/s who have migrated from one country or community to another, complexities and ambiguities in identity are vividly illustrated. The concept of 'diaspora' conveys identities which are framed by and situated in different locations and highlights the increasing multiculturalism of many cities and communities. Immigrants to the UK from Asia, for example, may recruit aspects of both their original and adopted country to forge an identity; indeed, it has become popular to mix aspects of different cultures to produce eclectic and innovative styles in music, fashion, cinema, etc. But this fusing of two (or more) cultural traditions is by no means a straightforward process, as a recent newspaper profile of Anglo–Indian musician Nitin Sawhney suggests:

> Beyond Skin (his acclaimed third album) is Nitin Sawhney's attempt to come to terms with the fact that, while he was raised as an outsider in England, the motherland of his parents is no longer available to him as an innocent spiritual alternative, because it no longer exists. As such, it is about the identity of an individual and the becoming of two cultures, two nations: 'I'd love to be able to gain back what my parents left in terms of their heritage, but you can't', he is saying, 'I go back to India, and I'm a stranger, and I accept that. But I'm still a stranger here too' (in the UK). (Andrew Smith in *The Guardian*, 19 September 1999: 13–17)

This sense of being 'homeless' or not belonging in any particular community is perhaps something you have experienced upon moving to another country or region, whether for work, university or family commitments. For example, 'working-class' individuals may well encounter difficulties in the face of predominantly middle-class institutions such as higher education where the culture and values may mitigate against academic success. In such circumstances, any sense of self as coherent and unified will most certainly be undermined as the 'homeland' is left behind and a new location taken up. In an article by Joseph O'Connor, contemporary Irish novelist and journalist, he reflects on the meaning of 'home' and identity from the perspective of an Irish 'exile' in London, capturing the contradictions, difficulties and advantages of a dichotomous existence (see Box 6.3). You may recall that critical social psychologists are content to consider accounts from existing texts, for example from journalism, literature, film or theatre instead of or in conjunction with accounts from research participants. This practice is consistent with the view that social psychological texts, as with texts from other disciplines and sources, may be regarded as constructed, partial or even fictional (see Kvale, 1992).

Box 6.3   Ireland in exile (O'Connor, 1996: 150–159)

'You might be coming home for a family celebration or a funeral. Or to see a friend. Or you might be coming home for Christmas. You would meet your friends the night you got home, the people who stayed behind in Ireland to tough it out. And…your friends resented you a little for going, and if the truth be told you resented them a little for staying, although you could never really put your finger on why. When you used the word "home", for instance, or "at home", your friends sometimes didn't know where exactly you meant. Sometimes you didn't know yourself.'

'Somehow, despite the crack, something is wrong. You're home in Ireland but you're not home really. Your heart is in London or New York or Paris. But the rest of you is in Ireland.'

CRITICAL THINKING BOX: MULTICULTURAL IDENTITIES

Have you had any experience of inhabiting two (or more) different, perhaps conflicting, cultures? Have you felt 'out of place'? How have you managed to negotiate such diverse influences on identity?

The 'death of the subject'

Evidence of cultural (and historical) diversity and complexity in conceptions of selfhood poses problems for deciding which models of self provide better or more useful insights. The growing consensus amongst researchers and theorists of identity is that the Western individualist view is somehow inferior, as the anthropologist Clifford Geertz (1974) stressed:

> The Western conception of the person as a bounded, unique, more or less integrated motivational and cognitive universe, a dynamic centre of awareness, emotion, judgement and action, organized into a distinctive whole and set against a background of other such whole and against a social and natural background, is, however incorrigible it may seem to us, a rather peculiar idea within the context of the world's cultures. (229)

The critique of dominant Western conventions governing the self has gathered pace in recent years. Markus and Kitayama (1991) agree that the Western de-socialized notion of the self is not an adequate description of selfhood. The charge here that the Western view is misleading suggests that identity is often bound up in relationships with others and is framed by broader cultural constraints. Some critics (Parker, 1989; Sampson, 1993) go even further to suggest that an ideology of individualism originates from and serves to promote the interests of elites which typically comprise white middle-class males. Within capitalist patriarchal structures the fostering of competition between individuals obscures differences in power and prestige whilst subjecting people to personality tests in order to differentiate between the chosen/healthy/successful and the subordinated others (see Parker, 2007).

The resistance of oppressed groups (women, gay and lesbian people, ethnic minorities, transgender, people with disabilities etc.) has contributed to the critique of the dominant Western view of self as independent and detached from society. The emergence of 'identity politics' from the 1960s counter-culture zeitgeist made visible a range of diverse positions previously regarded as secondary or 'other' by mainstream society. Feminism, for example, has provided a platform where women's voices are presented and respected, often arguing for forms of identity which are inclusive and communal as opposed to self-centred and separated from society (e.g. Gilligan, 1982). Indeed, it is argued that individualism has flourished precisely because alter-native ideologies of selfhood have been suppressed.

This point highlights the connection between identity and difference – that any particular form of identity is defined in relation to, or against, other competing forms. Some 'essentialist' feminists, for example, opted to reclaim a repressed unique female identity which was nurturing and maternal in opposition to a dominant male identity perceived as destructive (Daly, 1978). Indeed, mascu-linity and femininity are often understood as opposing tendencies (cold/warm; hard/soft; rational/emotional; strong/weak). But such 'binary oppositions' do not usually contain two equal-status terms, for the 'masculine' term is usually more culturally valued: head over heart, culture over nature, etc. (Cixous, 1975). As are personality traits identified as masculine such as extraversion, independence, and competitiveness. The same goes for classifications of race (white over black), sexuality (straight over gay), social class ('higher' over 'lower') and so on, all cultural constructions which have been under-mined by various social movements. In the past 30 years or more, the 'otherness' of marginalized identities has been celebrated. But if we accept a dispersed, interdependent view of identity, does this mean that we abandon our cherished concept of self as unique and personal?

CRITICAL THINKING BOX: OTHERNESS

Think about the social categories that you occupy (e.g. heterosexual, Asian, middle-class). How are these identities defined in relation to 'others' (e.g. homosexual, white, working-class)? Which identities are privileged/subordinated?

De-centred selves

To reiterate, the position expressed above that identity is tied to social and cultural ideals suggests that the self as a discrete object that is owned and treasured by the individual is nothing but a fantasy, a myth brought about by a set of institutions (including psychology) which has been shattered by contemporary theory. In other words, 'personality' is regarded as a cultural construct which, although persistently popular in Western societies, amounts to a rather strange and flawed way of thinking about selfhood. As expressed by Freeman (1993: 8): 'how are we to escape the conclusion that we ourselves are ultimately fictions? The self, after all, is not a thing: it is not a substance, a material entity that we can somehow grab hold of and place before our very eyes.'

To claim that we possess knowledge and control over our 'selves' is merely to reproduce a dominant cultural myth founded on a rather arrogant, detached individualism. The gathering consensus, meanwhile, proposes a decentralized version of identity where the individual is dispersed amidst a variety of social relationships and cultural expectations. The metaphor is one of distribution, destabilization, a disrupted, fragmented being-in-the-world. Gergen (1991) suggests a 'saturated' self, a subject bombarded with images, ideas and values from the surrounding culture which are absorbed and debated. The spotlight is on the surface, on the language of a sign-obsessed society and its processing by individuals, rather than on some deep core or authentic self nestled somewhere deep within the person. By virtue of contemporary technology, Gergen argues that the voices and representations of others assail us from every direction, via mobile phones, e-mail, the internet, newspapers, magazines, film, television, radio, video, and contribute to the fragmentation and mutability of self. In other words, the relationships we have with others are framed and derive from many, often transitory, disembodied interactions and emphasize the immersion of self in the surrounding social world. As Gergen (1991) himself notes:

> Emerging technologies saturate us with the voices of humankind – both harmonious and alien. As we absorb their varied rhymes and reasons, they become part of us and we of them. Social saturation furnishes us with a multiplicity of incoherent and unrelated languages of the self. For everything we 'know to be true' about ourselves, other voices within respond with doubt and derision. (6)

Although Gergen's argument has been criticized for depicting the experiences of middle-class elites (see Smith, 1994), the emphasis on the deconstruction of (the unified, stable) self in the contemporary world is shared by many other theorists of identity. For example, Giddens (1991: 146) argues that self-identity in late modernity has become less anchored to proximally close interactions, relationships and places due to the influence of global events, ideas, ideologies and fashions that now dominate everyday life.

Box 6.4   The social psychology of globalization

One of the problems with mainstream social psychology is that it fails to adequately engage with broader social trends such as globalization and its effects on the self. This criticism was initially pointed out by Sampson (1989) who argued that social psychology needed to move away from a theory of the person based on enlightenment ideas such as liberalism and individualism – a theory narrowly focused on inner experience and personal preferences – towards a theory of the person that recognizes a more fluid and changeable self that is constituted by social and cultural interactions and relations. Chiu and Cheng (2007) and McKenna and Bargh (2000) argue that globalization (and in particular information and communication technologies) influence our day-to-day lives to a much greater extent so that we are influenced by events, fashions, voices and ideologies from all over the world, and at a pace never before imagined. The result of all this 'interconnectedness' is that people today have much greater opportunities to engage in the enhancement and enlargement of self-identity.

CRITICAL THINKING BOX: CONTEMPORARY SELFHOOD

Think of the interactions you have in a typical day/week. To what extent are these mediated by technology? Describe instances where you have experienced social saturation.

Self as process

It is difficult, admittedly, to stop thinking of the self as just that, a real object. The concept of roles is useful for exploding this 'object' into fragments, but there is perhaps a sense that roles are preordained slots which have a certain order or logic to be grasped with little or no room for manoeuvre on the part of the individual. After all, people can and do rebel against or re-work the way they have been presented in a situation. However, in his later work, Goffman (1959) abandons a description of self in terms of differing substances in favour of a more flexible notion of self as social process, a changeable formula for managing oneself during events. Perhaps it is helpful to think about identity in terms of life projects, ongoing negotiations within a complex web of relationships and practices, to regard the self as emergent, as always in the process of construction during social inter-action. To this end many discursive psychologists examine the ways in which identity is produced in talk in social encounters. Shotter (1993a/b), for example, speaks of 'joint action' to indicate the co-pro-duction of identities in the course of an interaction, a process which is open, incomplete and given to misunderstandings (Box 6.5). From this example the complex and often fraught nature of social inter-action can be witnessed as both parties struggle to construct meaning from words and action and, by extension, to fashion identities for self and other (and both, as a couple).

The work of McKinlay and McVittie (2008) and Potter and Wetherell (1987) uses a discourse analytic approach to explore the dynamic and at times difficult (re)working of identities which frequently features in everyday social interaction. The image of the person as 'discourse-user' is prominent here, whereby speakers draw upon a range of strat-egies and 'interpretative repertoires' to achieve particular goals in conversation (see Chapter 3). If a couple are having an argument, for example, there is often a struggle towards presenting the other as transgressor and self as victim and the person who manages to manoeuvre into a morally virtuous position (thus constructing the other as blameworthy) will indeed be satisfied. Such discourse dynamics are frequently on show in political language where politi-cians seek to equivocate, defend positions, gain applause, emphasize the logic of their own views/policies, and to persuade the public that one's opponents are misguided, irresponsible or even ridiculous (Billig, 2003; Bull, 2007; Rapley, 1998). For example, arguments for greater government expenditure on defence could be framed in terms of protecting the nation, with those against this policy projected as jeopardizing the future of the nation, whereas a call to divert defence monies to health and education could be presented as more ethical, with those against cast as irresponsible hawks sacrificing improved services for the population.

As Billig *et al.* (1988) have suggested, a position or argument is always voiced in opposition to another 'inferior' counter-stance: there is usually an eye fixed on potential criticisms of your position and a move on your part to undermine the other position. For example, a claim by Sue that Jack watches too much sport on television could be seen to position Jack as lazy and uninteresting, which he could attempt to resist by recasting this activity as a form of relaxation or release from the pressures of work, thereby regaining a more morally positive position for himself. In turn, Sue may suggest an alternative,

---

Box 6.5 Self as emergent, negotiated, incomplete
(Shotter, 1987: 228, cited in Radley, 1996)

Witness the making of sexual approaches. 'I'm just off to the cinema', says a woman in the vicinity of a man she is attracted to, in the hope that he will respond as she desires. The significance of her utterance is not yet complete, however. If he says, 'Oh, can I come too?' then he has completed its significance as an invitation, and she is of course happy to accept it as having been as such. If he just says, however, 'Oh, I hope you enjoy the film', then he completes it simply as an 'informative statement'. Embarrassment has been avoided by her not having to issue a direct invitation, which might risk a direct refusal.

But if he did turn her down, was it because to go to a film at that time was truly impossible for him, or because he truly did not want to be with her? Clearly, the situation between them is still somewhat vague, and thus requires further practical investigation between them if they are to clarify it further. Let us imagine that he did accept her invitation, and as they walk out of the cinema after the film, she then says 'Would you like to come back for a coffee?' He says, 'Oh, yes please!' and goes to put his arm around her. But she draws back and says, 'Whatever gave you that idea?' He is taken aback. He knows what gave him the idea. It was the whole way she offered the original 'invitation': it seemed to imply an invitation to greater intimacy, but at the same time, as both he and she were aware, it did not explicitly request it. The character so far of the relationship they are in is 'open' to such reversals as these; while perhaps unexpected they are not unintelligible.

---

more active or healthy stress-relieving pursuit, such as jogging or using the local gym, a move which undermines Jack's former justification and returns him to his previous (negative) position of slob. Of course, he could defend his sport-watching further by framing the alternatives in a critical light ('jogging is boring'; 'the gym is full of preening air-heads'), and the debate could go on until some mutually satisfactory resolution is achieved or one party capitulates or storms off so that this particular language game is postponed until another time. Negotiating subject positions with another need not be so conscious, strategic or hostile, but the example serves to illustrate the dynamic, interconnected and often combative qualities which such activities involve.

Power and subjectivity

But Potter and Wetherell (1987) also accept that the form and content of self-construction will inevitably be subject to local language; how we may speak of ourselves is constrained by the linguistic norms of the relevant community. Prevailing discourses will make available a limited number of 'subject positions' from which individuals forge identities (see Davies & Harré, 1990; Henriques et al., 1984; Parker, 1992). In the words of Shotter and Gergen (1989: ix), 'persons are largely ascribed identities according to the manner of their embedding within a discourse – in their own or in the discourse of others'. This means that the possibilities for self-formulation are far from infinite, so that despite the opportunities that globalization has opened up for the enlargement of the self various constraints still operate to oppress particular identities. Many examples spring immediately to mind: Jewish identities in Nazi Germany, Black identities in apartheid South Africa, homosexual identities in the military, female identities in Moslem cultures. This focus on how individuals are positioned within discourse/s is most commonly associated with the work of Foucault (e.g. Foucault, 1972 – see Chapter 3; Parker, 1992).

The oppression of particular groups and individuals is engendered by the use of discourses which re-present certain categories of person as somehow inferior, abnormal, illegitimate or dangerous. For example, historical constructions of the Irish in UK culture as unintelligent, feckless and prone to violence and drunkenness can be linked to instances of discrimination and hostility in this society. Indeed, the construction of immigrants as uncivilized, work-shy and alien has precipitated restrictive legislation and even violence against foreign visitors, as witnessed in California, USA (see Santa Ana, 1999). So, discourses within which we are inscribed or in which we define ourselves will shape relationships with others and produce concrete consequences. Research on the discursive representation of others and the connection to prejudice is covered in detail in Chapter 5.

Other examples based on gender, sexuality, employment status, appearance, social class, regional background, etc., are not difficult to produce. You can imagine or may have experienced situations in which women, gay men, street cleaners, obese individuals, people with disabilities and the working-class have been discriminated against on the basis of conventional stereotypes or discourses. Jones's (2011a) recent book *Chavs: The Demonisation of the Working Class* is a good case in point. Jones argues that over the past 30 years once-proud working class communities have become the target for political rhetoric and middle class opprobrium aimed at portraying these communities as council housed, welfare dependent, bad parents, violent, degenerate and feckless.

Other examples include the way motherhood is culturally presented as the pinnacle of femininity, which has been used to criticize women who work or who do not find parenting pleasurable or easy (see Woodward, 1997). The associations between 'fat' and ill-health and gluttony offer a means of judging people who are overweight when medical rather than 'personality' factors may well account for this situation. Of course, there is often more than one representation of a particular 'object' in circulation, so that 'career women' and 'women as consumers' may coexist with 'women as mothers' (to which many 'women's' magazines testify) and alternative discourses can be drawn upon to resist dominant positionings – a decision not to have children or to place them in a nursery at an early stage can be justified from a 'career woman' position. But how this action will be perceived will depend on which discourses are currently more powerful in a given culture. The continued promotion of motherhood for women by various institutions (church, state, soap opera, etc.) may well cause difficulties and tensions for women attempting to pursue a career as well as bring up children. Moreover, other discourses, such as those around fatherhood, work, etc., will impinge upon the positions adopted and how these are experienced.

One of the most powerful discourses in circulation today, aimed primarily at girls and women, is the way in which the media, marketing and advertising industries tie identity to their body image (Bordo, 1993). This discourse plays on women's emancipation from their traditional roles inside the home by promoting an image of women as independent and seeking to assert their sexuality in more prominent ways, using this to gain power over men (Gill, 2008). This discourse seeks to emancipate women by celebrating their greater economic independence from men and their newfound freedom to express and assert themselves in new and novel ways (particularly in the consumption of goods and services). However, women's identities in this discourse are still constrained by a male hegemony. For example, women's identities continue to be dominated by a heterosexual worldview in which a women's agency is subjugated to masculine desire. In this discourse women are disciplined to conform to a specific body type conceived to suit the desires and sexual fantasies of men. This can be seen in advertising images, film, television, magazines etc. which promote the idea that a women's greatest achievement is in gaining approval for their physical attributes and fashions from men.

CRITICAL THINKING BOX: SUBJECT POSITIONS

Think about a time when you have been judged because of some social category you inhabit. What were the ideas reinforcing this assessment? How did/could you resist the position in which you were cast?

The problem of subjective experience

Whilst this view of the self as a collection of subject positions within discourse has enabled a critical relocation of the individual within the social realm, there is a danger that the psychological or personal dimension to identity is overlooked (Burr, 2003). Indeed, several theorists sympathetic to social constructionism have nonetheless lamented the absence of ideas on 'subjectivity', or the actual experience of selfhood. There is little work on how individuals feel about the various subject positions they inhabit or the personal meanings attached to these. To adopt the position of 'househusband' within a discourse of 'the new man' is perhaps to be marginalized in a society still obsessed with the ideal of a nuclear family, but how does this feel for a man in the twenty-first century? Similarly, how does it feel for a women to be positioned as a single mother in contemporary society, or to be positioned as unemployed, elderly or disabled? Although these various positions can be analysed in terms of their relative status and historical production, a discourse analysis cannot convincingly get at the experience of identifying with (or resisting) a given position. To be fair, the whole notion of experience is called into question by social constructionism (something which is mediated or framed by language and convention) but this does not satisfy many critics who believe in some connection between language and 'reality' (see Chapter 3). This critique is summed up by Henriques *et al.* (1984):

> In this [post-structuralist] view the subject is composed of, or exists as, a set of multiple and contradictory positionings or subjectivities. But how are such fragments held together? Are we to assume, as some applications of post-structuralism have implied, that the individual subject is simply the sum total of all positions in discourses since birth? If this is the case, what accounts for the continuity of the subject and the subjective experience of identity?

What accounts for the predictability of people's actions, as they repeatedly position themselves within particular discourses? Can people's wishes and desires be encompassed in an account of discursive relations? (204)

As a result of this critique, some feminist and critical social psychologists have returned to psychoanalysis in order to complement discourse analysis. Social psychologists such as Walkerdine (1987), Hollway (1983; 1989), Billig (1999), Cúellar (2010) and Frosh (1993) focus on the (unconscious) desires and anxieties which people invest in particular speaking positions. Of course, much ('unacceptable') desire is routinely repressed in social interaction, so it becomes important to consider what is repressed and how it is defended in talk. Thus, discourse analysts are encouraged to use psychoanalytic concepts such as repression, splitting and projection in addition to the more familiar tools (multiplicity, construction, contradiction, power) in their work. In contrast to Freud, however, these psychoanalytic concepts are applied *between*, rather than within, individuals – a form of 'relational dynamics'. According to Hollway (1989), one of the key tasks in social interaction is to present oneself in ways which protect and/or enhance the ego, a task which (following Klein) is often accompanied by anxiety and which will typically involve defensive moves.

As feminist social psychologists have been prominent in interrogating the preoccupation with language in discourse analysis and social constructionism, psychoanalytically informed analyses have concentrated mainly on gendered subjectivity (a key focus for psychoanalysis also). For example, psychoanalysis as well as discourse analysis can be applied to the study of masculinities. The conventional discourse which constructs men as rational and dispassionate (i.e. not feminine or irrational) ensures that feelings of vulnerability experienced by men will produce anxiety which then pushes the emotion out of awareness – and often projected on to women (hence the prevalence of sexism, misogyny and anti-feminism in much male discourse and practice). Indeed, this is further evidenced by reports that in certain discreet situations, such as visiting a prostitute or during fantasy, men will gladly relinquish prevailing expectations (see Friday, 1980). Accounts that are presented in talk, then, will depend on those discourses which are culturally available but also on the relationship with other/s, the context of interaction and the power to present preferred alternatives (see Jefferson, 1994). Although there are difficulties associated with attempts to integrate psychoanalytic theory (often seen as essentialist) and social constructionism, the turn to psychoanalysis is interesting and could be developed fruitfully to complement the broader discourse analytic approach to subjectivities.

Summary

The Western individualist concept of 'personality', the 'self-contained' individual or the 'unitary, rational subject', has come under a wide-ranging critique in this chapter. This psychological focus, which presents selfhood as stable, consistent and universal, is rejected by sociocultural approaches such as role theories where the person is construed as taking on different roles according to what is expected in particular situations. Such approaches promote an image of the self as multifaceted, decentred and fluid. These social roles are largely determined by social norms, practices and trends (such as globalization), a point emphasized by research cited on cultural variation which shows markedly different self-conceptions, notably between Western (individualist) and Eastern (collectivist) societies. As most societies today could be understood as multicultural and technological, a huge range of 'identities' are potentially on offer, a situation which can be both liberating and overwhelming. Critical social psychologists would, however, stress constraints on identity 'choices', as it can be difficult to take on subject positions within discourses which define you as 'other' (e.g. for a woman to assume 'masculine' positions or a man to assume 'feminine' positions). The critical focus on subjectivity as determined by discourse, however, has recently been challenged by social psychologists influenced by psychodynamic theory. In analysing subjectivity in terms of the investments which individuals make to specific discourses within social contexts, an (inter-)personal dimension to subjectivity is recovered.

Key references

Burr, V. (2002). *The Person in Social Psychology*. London: Routledge.

Burr's highly accessible book takes the reader on a journey through some of social psychology's most iconic studies (e.g. Muzafer Sherif's Robber Cave experiments, Stanley Milgram's obedience studies) challenging their traditional theoretical models which assume the self has an already existing nature which is subject to influence from various environmental variables.

Sloan, T. (2009). Theories of personality. In D. Fox, I. Prilleltensky & S. Austin (eds), *Critical Psychology: An Introduction* (2nd edn, pp. 57–74). London: Sage.
For a number of years now Tod Sloan has been criticizing mainstream social psychology's narrow conception of the self. In this chapter he critiques mainstream Western theories of personality which locate responsibility at the level of the individual. In its place he argues for a critical approach which promotes agency on the part of the individual to resist or change those social relations that maintain injustice and inequality.

Stainton-Rogers, W. (2003). *Social Psychology: Experimental and Critical Approaches.* Maidenhead, UK: Open University Press.
Chapter 8 of Stainton-Rogers chapter titled 'Selves and identities' reviews both mainstream and critical social psychological concepts of the self.

Wetherell, M. & Maybin, J. (1996). The distributed self: A social constructionist perspective. In R. Stevens (ed.), *Understanding the Self* (London: Sage/ Open University Press).
A comprehensive chapter which explores the role of culture and language in shaping selfhood.

New references

Australian Law Reform Commission (ALRC). (1987). Traditional Aboriginal society and its law. In W.H. Edwards (ed.), *Traditional Aboriginal Society: A Reader* (pp. 189–202) Melbourne: Macmillan.

Billig, M. (1999). *Freudian Repression: Conversation Creating the Unconscious.* Cambridge, UK: Cambridge University Press.

Billig, M. (2003). Political rhetoric. In D. O. Sears, L. Huddy & R. Jervis (eds), *Oxford Handbook of Political Psychology* (pp. 222–251). Oxford, UK: Oxford University Press.

Bordo, S. (1993). *Unbearable Weight: Feminism, Western Culture, and the Body.* Berkeley, CA: University of California Press.

Bull, P. (2007). Political language and persuasive communication. In A. Weatherall, B. M. Watson & C. Gallois (eds), *Language, Discourse and Social Psychology* (pp. 255–275). Basingstoke, UK: Palgrave Macmillan.

Burr, V. (2002). *The Person in Social Psychology.* London: Routledge.

Burr, V. (2003). *Social Constructionism* (2nd edn). Hove, UK: Routledge.

Chiu, C.-Y., & Cheng, S. Y. Y. (2007). Toward a social psychology of culture and globalization: some social cognitive consequences of activating two cultures simultaneously. *Social and Personality Psychology Compass, 1*(1), 84–100.

Cúellar, D. P. (2010). *From the Conscious Interior to An Exterior Unconscious: Lacan, Discourse Analysis and Social Psychology.* London: Karnac Books.

Gergen, K. J. (1991). *The Saturated Self: Dilemmas of Identity in Contemporary Life.* New York: Basic Books.

Giddens, A. (1991). *Modernity and Self-Identity: Self and Society in the Late Modern Age.* Cambridge, UK: Polity Press.

Gill, R. (2008). Culture and subjectivity in neoliberal and postfeminist times. *Subjectivity, 25*(1), 432–445.

Jones, O. (2011a). *Chavs: the Demonization of the Working Class.* London: Verso.

Jones, O. (2011b, September). The poor against the poor: feral underclass or economically excluded. *Le Monde Diplomatique* (English Edition), pp. 12–13.

Maslow, A. (1954). *Motivation and Personality.* New York: Harper & Row.

McKenna, K. Y. A., & Bargh, J. A. (2000). Plan 9 from cyberspace: the implications of the internet for personality and social psychology. *Personality and Social Psychology Review, 4*(1), 57–75.

McKinlay, A. & McVittie, C. (2008). *Social Psychology and Discourse.* Malden, MA: Blackwell.

Moloney, P., & Kelly, P. (2008). Beck never lived in Birmingham: why cognitive behaviour therapy may be a less helpful treatment for psychological distress than is often supposed. In R. House & D. Loewenthal (eds), *Against and for CBT: Toward a Constructive Dialogue* (pp. 278–288). Ross-on-Wye, UK: PCCS.

Oishi, S., Kesebir, S., & Snyder, B. H. (2009). Sociology: a lost connection in social psychology. *Personality and Social Psychology Review, 13*(4), 334–353.

Parker, I. (2007). *Revolution in Psychology: Alienation to Emancipation.* Ann Arbor, MI: Pluto Press.

Rapley, M. (1998). 'Just an ordinary Australian': self-categorization and the discursive construction of facticity in 'new racist' political rhetoric. *British Journal of Social Psychology, 37*(3), 325–344.

Ratner, C. (2006). *Cultural Psychology: A Perspective on Psychological Functioning and Social Reform.* Mahwah, NJ: Lawrence Erlbaum.

Rogers, C. (1961). *On Becoming a Person: A Therapist's View of Psychotherapy.* Boston, MA: Houghton Mifflin.

Rose, N. (1996). *Inventing Ours Selves: Psychology, Power, and Personhood.* Cambridge, UK: Cambridge University Press.

Rose, N. (1999). *Governing the Soul: the Shaping of the Private Self* (2nd edn). London: Free Association Books.

Sampson, E. E. (1989). The challenge of social change for psychology: globalization and psychology's theory of the person. *American Psychologist, 44*(6), 914–921.

Smail, D. (2005). *Power, Interest and Psychology: Elements of a Social Materialist Understanding of Distress.* Ross-on-Wye, UK: PCCS.

Smith, P. B., Bond, M. H., & Kagitcibasi, C. (2006). *Understanding Social Psychology across Cultures: Living and Working in a Changing World.* London: Sage.

Triandis, H. C. (2001). Individualism-collectivism in personality. *Journal of Personality, 69*(6), 907–924.

Gendered and Sexed Identities

7

This chapter will highlight:

- Biological explanations
  - Sex differences
  - Heterosexuality: naturalizing male dominance–female submission
  - Homosexuality as deviance
- Sex roles and individual choice
  - Social learning theory
  - Androgyny
  - Liberal–humanistic standpoint
- Critical, feminist and queer perspectives
  - Diversity
  - Social constraints
  - Intersections

Introduction

Historically, psychology has preferred biological explanations concerning behaviours presumed to be gender-related and/or sexuality-related. For example, men and women have been regarded as fundamentally different in their 'psychology', and these differences have been explained in terms of biological processes and substances (evolution, hormones, anatomy etc.). In addition, heterosexuality has been viewed as 'natural' and 'normal', featuring male dominance and female submission, while homosexuality has been treated as unnatural, deviant and abnormal, a condition requiring psycho–medical intervention. For example, it was not until 1973 that homosexuality was removed from the *Diagnostic and Statistical Manual for Mental Disorders* (Spitzer, 1981).

More recently, however, social accounts of gender and sexuality have gained currency, and notions of choice and individuality have flourished. For example, any one individual may display both 'masculine' and 'feminine' attributes (an 'androgynous' type) – regardless of biological sex. Sex 'roles' are seen as learned during socialization, from role models such as parents, peers and through the mass media, rather than hard wired. Similarly, sexual orientation can be viewed as a lifestyle choice informed by one's upbringing, rather than determined by genes, hormones or brain regions. However, such 'social' accounts often neglect the influence of cultural values, power relations and expectations which may constrain 'choice' – masculinized attributes such as rationality and independence are still frequently preferred over feminized attributes such as emotionality and inter-dependence, while heterosexism and homophobia may not be so visible in the twenty-first century, such discourses continue to manifest themselves in more subtle ways. Critical perspectives, largely drawing from feminist and 'queer' theory, emphasize the social construction of gender and sexuality, highlighting issues of power, discourse and resistance, as well as complexity and fluidity in gendered and sexed identities and relationships. This chapter will summarize key ideas around gender and sexuality which have been prominent in mainstream (social) psychology before presenting alternative critical perspectives.

Biological explanations

Sex differences

The nature–nurture debate within (social) psychology and feminism has structured much of the literature on sex/gender differences. Indeed, many social and cognitive understandings of gender tend to rely on the notion of natural and fixed differences between the sexes (see Callaghan & Lazard, 2011: 134–154, for an overview). To this end, studies of sex differences have invoked a range of neuro–anatomical and physiological factors, including hormones, genetics, brain lateralization and even brain size. For the most part, research has studied the effects of biological processes on female activity and, moreover, has tended to emphasize negative consequences. For example, much research has focused on the influence of reproductive hormones (e.g. oestrogen) on women's performance and behaviour, often emphasizing detrimental outcomes, such as mood swings, irritability and unreliability (see Choi, 1994). Such research continues despite evidence that the relationship between hormones and mood is complex (e.g. Ussher, 2006) and feminist analyses which point to the absence of premenstrual 'symptoms' in non-Western cultures (e.g. Johnson, 1987). While biological interpretations of sex differences waned for a period during the twentieth century, they have become popular once again as Walter (2010) notes:

> The current fashion for biological determinism purports to rely on new directions in scientific research. Over the last few years there has been a deluge of research studies on the possible biological basis for sex differences, emanating from psychology to linguistics to neuroscience departments of universities, and those studies that seem to back up biological explanations for stereotypes are picked up with enormous enthusiasm throughout the media. (144–145)

A good example of this is the notion that men and women have differently wired brains (see Box 7.1). Baron-Cohen (2005) has proposed a theory which suggests that women's brains are structured for empathy and emotional communication while men's brains are built for systematic and rational thinking. Other books purporting similar theories include *The Female Brain* and *The Male Brain* both by Louann Brizendine (2008, 2011).

Box 7.1 Neurosexism

Cordelia Fine's (2010) latest book, *Delusions of Gender: How Our Minds, Society and Neurosexism Create Difference*, critiques much of the research linking gender to neurological differences. Fine argues that historical, cultural and social factors in the West promote gender stereotypes, and that these stereotypes prime research participants to think and behave in expected ways when observed under experimental conditions. It is these gender-specific behaviours however which are often interpreted by psychobiologists as evidence that gender differences are hard wired in the brain, so that women are naturally more suited to nurture children and domestic work. These overly simplistic assumptions represent attempts by science to progress what Fine refers to as 'neurosexism'. 'It is for this reason that we can't understand gender differences in female and male minds – the minds that are the source of our thoughts, feelings, abilities, motivations, and behaviour – without understanding how psychologically permeable is the skull that separates the mind from the sociocultural context in which operates' (Fine, 2010: xxvi). See also Hines (2005) *Brain Gender* and Jordan-Young (2011) *Brain Storm: The Flaws in the Science of Sex Differences*.

Where male biology has been investigated, there has been much reliance on animal studies (an area of research known as 'comparative psychology'), making generalizations to humans problematic. Such research has tended to find a correlation between testosterone levels (which are higher in males) and aggression, but this conclusion has been challenged by studies involving humans, where the evidence is mixed (see Archer, 2004). Other studies have considered cases where opposite sex hormones have impacted the foetus. For example, Imperato-McGinley *et al.* (1979) studied a group of individuals with 'five alpha-reductase deficiency', whereby the penis and scrotum remain underdeveloped until puberty, and found that all individuals in the study, most of whom were raised as female, pursued a male identity when the external sex organs became visible. The fact that 'biological' men may pass as women suggests that social definitions of gender have a great impact on identities ascribed to individuals from birth. Such evidence also undermines the biological view that gender is fixed from birth.

Within sociobiology (e.g. Wilson, 2000), sex differences in various behaviours such as aggression and promiscuity are asserted and interpreted in terms of evolutionary advantage. For example, men are 'naturally' more aggressive because it enables them to go out and hunt/work in order to provide for their families, whilst women are regarded as biologically suited to nurturance and hence childcare. Although this argument is often used to justify sexism (women are not *naturally* suited to work or combat roles in the armed forces, etc.), some feminist theorists have drawn upon biological 'essentialism' in order to promote women's 'superior' nature. In contrast to 'malestream' psychobiological theories, women and femininity are associated with protecting children and nature, with peace rather than 'male' aggression and war (e.g. Daly, 1978).

Feminist social constructionists however reject the notion that sex differences and inequalities are somehow fixed by nature and therefore unchangeable (see Fine, 2010; Gergen, 2001; Kitzinger, 1994; Oyama, 1997). Most feminists and social psychologists prefer accounts of gender which include the concept of socialization and which tend to suggest an interaction between nature and nurture. Despite having been rejected by cognitive–experimental social psychology, psychoanalytic accounts of gender provide interesting and provocative analyses that emphasize an interplay between biological and socio–cultural forces (Chodorow, 1990, 2002). Freud's writing can be said to be more directly concerned with sexuality, which we discuss below.

> **CRITICAL THINKING BOX: BIOLOGY**
>
> Describing men and women as 'naturally' different can serve both feminist and anti-feminist goals. Discuss the ways in which feminists and non-feminists may use biology to support their views.

Sexual orientation as innate

The sociobiological perspective

> Since sex is often referred to as one of our more animal instincts, perhaps we should 'naturally' turn to biology for an explanation of our sexuality. (McFadden & Sneddon, 1998: 41)

There is a long tradition of work that views various aspects of human sexual and social behaviour from within a wider biological context. The origins of this work lie in a much-respected body of research exploring the reproductive arrangements of non-human species (Gould & Gould, 1989). From the 1970s, there have been various attempts to understand human sexuality within a similar framework, but the success of such theoretical forays remains a contentious issue (Lees, 1993; Mahony, 1985; Miller & Fowlkes, 1980; Sahlins, 1977).

Within the sociobiological tradition (Hutt, 1972; Wilson, 2000), sex and sexuality are depicted as determined through the mechanism of hormonal activity and shaped by parental investment which is based on Darwinian ideas of natural selection. Individuals are assumed to be driven to maximize the number of offspring that they successfully produce but because of differences between males and females, the sexes approach this task differently. Describing 'reproductive strategies' in terms of differences in the size of the female ova and male sperm, sociobiologists argue that women have a greater investment in the embryo, and eventual child, than men. Thus females are best served by, firstly, being selective about the males with whom they mate, and secondly, ensuring the survival of any offspring produced. In contrast, sociobiologists argue that as males invest less reproductive material (sperm) than their female counterparts, their most successful strategy is to compete for, and reproduce with, as many females as possible. Depending on the environmental contexts in which species are situated, male polygamy or promiscuity is proposed as the most effective biological means of servicing the survival of male genetic material.

Furthermore, within this paradigm hormonal activity is treated as sex-specific and linked directly to the physiology and behaviour of the sexes. Hutt (1972) suggests that the sexes differ physiologically and behaviourally from birth due to the effects of different sex hormones. The male hormone plays a critical role in the sexual and social development of males, inducing behaviours such as aggression, ambition and drive. In contrast the female hormone is inextricably geared towards reproduction and the behaviours this incorporates (e.g. Campbell, 2008; Taylor *et al.*, 2000).

Despite the popularity of this theoretical perspective for understanding sexual behaviour and gender differences across the animal kingdom, it has been dismissed by many as an inadequate explanation of the range and diversity of human sexuality. For example, Mahony (1985) suggests that the aggression that Hutt (1972) associated with boys was probably learned and subsequently reinforced within a society where aggression pervades perceptions of masculinity (e.g. Connell & Messerschmidt, 2005). Whitehead (2002) also notes that the testosterone–aggression link cannot explain violence perpetrated by those with low levels of the hormone, such as prepubescent boys. Other theorists have questioned the primary assumption within this perspective that the sole function of sex is the production of offspring and that males and females have different forces driving them to this end. As McFadden and Sneddon (1998: 43) note, 'It is but a short step from making this assumption to viewing non-reproductive sex as aberrant, and to prescribing different roles to males and females.'

The science of sexology

Since the late 1800s, research into and understandings of sexual identity and sexual practices have been informed by the discipline of sexology. Predominant among this tradition is the work of psychologists such as Freud (1933) and Ellis (1913, 1936). Freud viewed sexuality as a lifespan development, starting from infancy and progressing through a series of age- and sex-related phases. His theory intertwined the influence of the psychic (unconscious drives), biological and social factors on sexual development. Freud envisaged female and male infants as initially sharing common development until the phallic phase. However, according to Freud the primary factor in the acquisition of masculine and feminine sexualities is the differential resolution of the Oedipus complex experienced during the phallic phase. This complex is perceived as occurring when the child becomes aware of others (especially the father) and how they impinge upon her/his exclusive relationship with the mother (who is, according to Freud, the primary object of the child's love).

For the young boy, the awareness that the father shares a relationship with the mother leads to a bitter hatred for the father. Indeed the son fantasizes about killing the father and securing the love of the mother for himself. However, Freud points out that at the same time, the young boy is also aware of the power of the father and fears he will be punished by the father if he challenges him. For the young boy at this stage in his development, his sexual drive is satisfied through mastur-bation and he fears that the father will punish him by removing this treasured part of his anatomy. The anxiety experienced by the young boy in relation to the removal of his penis is what Freud refers to as castration anxiety. This anxiety is further fuelled by the young boy's recent awareness that his female counterparts are lacking a penis and according to Freud he experiences these young girls as 'mutilated creatures'. Castration anxiety motivates the young boy to repress his desire for the mother and to identify with the father. This identifi-cation requires the young boy to respect not only the father but that which he represents on a societal level – law and morality. Through the processes of identification, the young boy acquires not only a masculine identity but, with development of the superego, a place in the societal structure.

For the young girl, Freud presented the resolution of the Oedipus complex as more problematic. Indeed throughout his writings Freud consistently muses over the enigma that is female sexuality. This is reflected most clearly in the following quotation from his 1933 lecture on femininity: 'Throughout history people have knocked their heads against the riddle of femininity. Nor will you have escaped worrying over this problem – those of you who are men; to those of you who are women this will not apply – you are yourselves the problem' (Freud, 1933: 224).

For the young girl, then, the resolution of the Oedipus complex is perceived as complicated and disappointingly incomplete. Like the young boy, the girl becomes aware of the presence of others (especially the father) in the relationship with her primary love object, the mother. Again, like the young boy, the girl becomes enraged by the mother's desire for the father and wishes to kill him. However at this stage the girl becomes aware of differences in her primary source of satisfaction, the clitoris, and that of her male counterpart. This results in what Freud (1933: 225) calls penis envy: 'girls hold their mother responsible for their lack of penis and do not forgive her for their being thus put at a disadvantage'. In despair she turns to the father in the hope of winning back that which all women desire, the penis. At this stage the girl's object of love changes from being that of the mother, to the father. However, the girl soon realizes that she cannot possess the father (and the penis) and, accepting her loss, reluctantly identifies with the mother. Completion of this phase, Freud suggests, occurs when the girl substitutes her desire for the anatomical penis and what it symbolizes (identity, power and a place in human culture) with that for a (male) baby: 'if woman can positively wish for a baby as a substitute source of power and identity, so much the better for the quality of her femininity' (1923: 231).

In Freud's writing it is clear that the young girl encounters more hurdles and conflicts in her development towards adult sexuality, often with negative consequences. Freud argues that because girls do not experience castration anxiety, they lack the psychic energy necessary for the development of a strong supergo, or sense of morality. As a result, women are presented as passive human beings rather than active human subjects. The wound of inferiority resulting from the realization that she lacks a penis means the young girl limps into adulthood feeling incomplete: 'They will feel seriously wronged, often declare that they want to "have something like it too", and fall victim to "envy for the penis", which will leave ineradicable traces on their development and the formation of their character' (Freud, 1923: 226), resulting in a character structured by jealously, insecurity and masochism. It is not surprising, then, that Freud views the task of building civilization as the domain of 'mankind' characterized by rationality, moral strength and emotional security. Nor is it surprising that many traditional psychoanalysts view femininity as spawning a variety of neuroses (see Figes, 1970; Minsky, 1996).

CRITICAL THINKING BOX: FREUD

What contribution do you think Freud has made to our understanding of psychosexual development? In what way does his work continue to shape our understanding of sexuality in the twenty-first century?

The work of Ellis also emphasizes sex as biologically determined. His ideas on male and female sexuality are couched in the language of survival and reproduction; sex is described as being like a biologically orchestrated dance, with the dance partners occupying distinct biolog-ically based positions. In relation to female sexuality, Ellis perceives women, like men, as possessing biological instincts or impulses that motivate them to indulge in sex. In volume 1 (1936: 69) of his work he expands on the nature of female sexual impulses by employing notions of modesty: 'The female's primary role in courtship is the playful but serious one of the hunted animal who lures her pursuer, not with the aim of escaping but of finally being caught.' He refers to women as psychologically characterized by an instinctive fear or reluctance to indulge in sex, which he links to the instincts of animals, who in oestrus are not physiologically ready for mating. He does acknowledge that the situation in humans is more complex, as women do not have designated biological times when they are available for sex. However, this modesty is key to the act of courtship, as Ellis (1936: 1) explicitly links female reluctance and male sexual arousal.

The second major theme of Ellis's work proposes that women's sexuality includes natural experiences of pain and violence. Ellis suggests that, for men, the inflicting of pain and use of force are necessary to conquer the women's natural inhibitions towards sex and moreover that these are the by-products of different instinctive impulses characterizing masculinity and femininity. Ellis, like Freud, suggests that women have masochistic tendencies and enjoy being taken by surprise and force. Indeed, in the writings of Ellis, force appears key to women's sexual pleasure; as Jackson (1994) points out, Ellis goes to extraordinary lengths to claim that women need pain in order to experience sexual pleasure. Pain and pleasure, Ellis continues, are indistinguishable in women; 'the normal manifesta-tions of a woman's sexual pleasure are exceedingly like pain' (1936: 84). Furthermore Ellis asserts that the use of force is a reflection of a man's desire for a woman and indeed that women feel sexually wanted through the use of force by a male partner.

Thus, within the writings of Ellis, heterosexual sex is presented as a mutually sadomasochistic act between man and woman. Male sexual impulses are presented as innocent, but violent, and are aroused by the complementary sexual coyness of the female. Finally, Ellis, like Freud, suggests that different social positions and practices for men and women are the natural outcome of sexual desires and practices. Ellis refers to motherhood as a woman's supreme function and something that required all her energies: 'The task of creating a man needs the whole of a woman's best energies' (Ellis, 1936: 7). Thus Ellis berated political groups such as the Women's Movements as drawing women away from their natural reproductive duties (Jackson, 1994).

However, both theories' contribution to understandings of sexuality remains a highly contested issue. For many psychologists, both theorists were trailblazers, constructing the foundations of modern sexuality and generating powerful insights into gender inequality. In supporting the account offered by psychoanalysis Juliet Mitchell (1974) argued that Freud's account of sexual difference should be read as a critique of the psychic roots of patriarchy in modern society, not as a justification for it. In this respect Freud's account of sex differences were descriptive as opposed to prescriptive. As Elliott (2009: 192) notes, Freud's account of womanhood – masochism, penis envy, jealously, a weak superego – should be understood as a 'consequence of women's subjection to patriarchal law, and not as innate psychological attributes'. For other critical feminist social psychologists, the conceptualization of sexuality in the work of Ellis and Freud and their research philosophies are viewed as extremely problematic on many levels (Figes, 1970; Jackson, 1994; Jeffreys, 1986; McFadden & Sneddon, 1998; Weeks, 1981).

Many commentators have suggested that Freud and Ellis did not provide objective scientific accounts of sexuality as they claimed, but rather maintained and reproduced notions of male supremacy (Faderman, 1991; Jackson, 1989; Penelope, 1992). Both theorists have been criticized for failing to challenge stereotypes of masculinity and femininity in relation to both sexuality and social roles. Weeks (1977) draws attention to tensions in Ellis's writings on women's sexuality. On the one hand Ellis advocates a distinct sexuality for women which they should be able to control, yet on the other argues that women's sexuality is expressed most naturally (and satisfactorily) in motherhood. In addition, many feminist theorists argue that the representations of female sexuality (linked to male orgasm and motherhood) emerging from the writings of Freud and Ellis are inextricably linked to increasing calls from the Women's Movement, in the late nineteenth century and early twentieth, for female sexual and social autonomy (Jackson, 1989; Jeffreys, 1986).

Also, central concepts in the writings of Freud and Ellis have been subjected to critical scrutiny. Commentators such as Cixous (1975) and Frosh (1987) suggest that Freud's insistence on femininity as a riddle indicates the male agenda underpinning his work and has also meant that female sexual identity and practices are not explored, nor the social consequences of femininity investigated. Similarly, Ellis's representation of sex as a natural pleasure–power couplet has been challenged as obscuring the negative sexual and social implications of biologically determined definitions of masculinity and femininity. Jackson (1984a) notes that Ellis's descriptions of female modesty and male aggression as natural merely legitimized and maintained male power (and control) over women. In an attempt to make visible the negative social consequences of a female sexuality based on inferiority and anatomical mutation, Horney (1924a,b) dismissed Freud's notion that girls experience penis envy during the phallic stage. Instead she suggested that young girls do not desire the anatomical penis but the social penis – the power and identity that the possession of the phallus seems to provide her male counterparts, in society.

Inversion and fixation: homosexuality

In the writings of Freud and Ellis, homosexuality was pathologized, defined as a developmental or genetic abnormality, an illness that endangered the stability of both the individual and society as a whole, and therefore was something that needed to be cured. For example, in the work of Ellis, lesbian women were defined as sexual inverts and perceived as being in some way biologically abnormal. Indeed, according to Ellis, although sexual inverts may maintain the clothes and appearance of 'normal' women, their innately masculine characteristics and practices, especially their lack of female modesty (and therefore sexual attractiveness), were telltale signs. Ellis (1936), describes the lesbian as follows:

> When they still retain female garments, these usually show some traits of masculine simplicity, and there is nearly always a disdain for pretty feminine articles of the toilet. Even when this is not obvious, there are all sorts of instinctive gestures and habits which may suggest to female acquaintances the remark that such a person ought to have been a man. The masculine straightforwardness and sense of honour, and especially the attitude towards men, free from any suggestion of either shyness or audacity, will often suggest the underlying psychic abnormality to a keen observer. (250)

A further dimension to Ellis's thesis on lesbianism was the detrimental impact of such women on society. Ellis linked lesbianism to various forms of social instability including feminism and the demise of heterosexual marriages, and in particular through his explicit reference to the 'pseudo-homosexual'. This phrase denoted instances when a naturally heterosexual woman was temporarily seduced into an immoral lesbian lifestyle by a real lesbian woman. For Freud, an overly possessive and seductive mother who rejects her son's attempts at independence precipitated the development of male homosexuality in boys. For girls, lesbianism resulted from their failure to resolve the Electra complex, to repress their more masculine, active sexual desires and accept the more passive sexual practices that constituted femininity.

Many 'queer' and feminist theorists have challenged such essentialist accounts of gay men and lesbian women. Penelope (1992) and Faderman (1991) believe that Ellis's pseudo-homosexual was heavily influenced by the changing social and sexual contexts of the early twentieth century. Faderman (1991) notes that through the eighteenth and nineteenth century intimate relationships (sometimes involving physical or genital contact, sometimes not) between women were tolerated, often viewed as a way of training women for the skills they would require to sustain a successful marriage. However, the twentieth century witnessed an attack on 'romantic friendships' with such relationships increasingly talked about in the language of lesbianism (abnormality, inversion, etc.) and redefined as a danger to the moral fabric of society. In addition, Jeffreys (1984) highlights the disdain of sexual theorists such as Freud and Ellis for the burgeoning women's movement by drawing attention to the links between feminism and lesbianism within their writings. Turning away from psycho–biological explanations, many social psychologists and social scientists were attracted to the concept of 'sex roles', which we now describe.

Sex role theories

Most commentators agree that Talcott Parsons, an influential sociologist writing in the 1940s and 1950s, was responsible for originally developing the concept of sex role. Based on his studies with small groups, he came up with the terms 'instrumental' and 'expressive' to classify the two orientations thought necessary for social cohesion (Parsons, 1954). The former category neatly maps on to 'masculine' capacities such as reason and physical labour, whereas the latter connotes 'feminine' domains of emotion and nurturance, etc. The two forms of orientation were deemed complementary, working together in order to ensure the smooth functioning of society (hence 'functionalism', the name given to the broader theory which assumes that different parts of society work together to promote stability).

Parsons also drew on elements of Freudian theory to help explain how people became socialized into sex roles, notably the Oedipus complex wherein young boys and girls come to identify with the same-sex parent and hence internalize 'sex-appropriate' attributes (see above). This focus on early family dynamics qualifies Parson's account as genuinely social, although the reliance on unobservable, untestable Freudian constructs gradually attracted much criticism from sociological and psychological quarters which were increasingly concerned to flag their 'scientific' status. This drive towards quantification in the pursuit of scientific respectability culminated in a widespread rejection of psychoanalysis and, with it, Parson's functionalism.

Social learning theory

Consequently, within (social) psychology in the 1960s and 1970s, social learning theory (Bandura, 1977; Mischel, 1966) became the dominant approach to sex role socialization. Deriving from basic behaviourist principles propounded earlier by theorists such as Watson and Skinner, the focus here is on overt, measurable behaviour and how it is learned by a combination of observation, imitation and reinforcement. Also drawing on psychoanalytic principles, individuals are said to be encouraged to behave in 'sex-appropriate' ways through identifying with significant others of the same sex (parent, athlete, cartoon character, etc.) and by virtue of social rewards and punishments issued by appropriate socializing agents (Bussey & Bandura, 1999).

There is a wealth of evidence documenting how a range of agents, popularly known as 'role models' (parent, teachers, peers, media figures), reinforce traditional sex roles. For example, Fagot (1974) found that parents typically promote assertiveness in boys by responding to their demands whilst ignoring and therefore discouraging equivalent behaviour from girls. Similarly, many studies indicate that in the classroom boys attract more praise for the intellectual quality of their work whereas girls receive more attention for the neatness of their work (see Renzetti & Curran, 1992). Conversely, children are frequently reprimanded – and indeed caution their peers – for engaging in activities deemed to be 'inappropriate' or 'deviant' for one's sex (boys playing with dolls, girls climbing trees) (e.g. Garvey, 1977). From a very early age, then, many children are proficient at recognizing, realizing and regulating norms around masculinity and femininity.

CRITICAL THINKING BOX: SEX ROLES

Reflecting on your own experience, list those people who have had an impact on your personal development and identity. Which figures have been the most influential? Are there more examples of same-sex 'models'?

This modelling explanation became popular in academic circles and the general public. It was often raised in debates around the sexualization of children, especially young girls who were increasingly exposed to images of half-dressed celebrities and to an increasingly influential pornified culture more generally, which became a mainstay of the mass media and advertising (see Gill, 2012 and Walter, 2010 for a critical overview of these debates). The modelling explanation has also been cited in cases of violence and criminal activity, where evidence concerning the impact of media violence on boys and girls has found little to no gender differences (e.g. Huesmann & Eron, 1986; Huesmann et al., 2003).

Indeed, the research literature on sex differences in general has not delivered much convincing evidence of sex role socialization. A comprehensive review of sex difference research in the 1970s suggests that only small differences could be claimed on a few variables, such as visual–spatial ability and mathematical ability, which have since disappeared (see Baumeister, 1988; Maccoby & Jacklin, 1974). Tellingly, feminist writers have pointed out that this literature only tends to publish research where significant differences are demonstrated, thus failing to take into account many studies which show little or no variation between the sexes (see Segal, 1990). This research has often been used to interpret why fewer women are interested in studying subjects like maths, pure science and engineering and why they are underrepresented in allied professions. These interpretations continue to be used despite the fact that research now indicates that girls are beginning to outperform boys in these traditionally male areas (e.g. mathematics, physics and chemistry) (see Kimball, 1994; Hiatt, 2010; Hunt, 2011; Walter, 2010: 174–180).

The notion that gender stereotypes need not impinge upon an individual's identity or behaviour has been actively pursued since the 1970s when Sandra Bem, a liberal feminist social psychologist, introduced the concept of 'androgyny'.

Androgyny

It was only in the 1970s that social psychologists recognized that 'masculinity' and 'femininity' were social constructs that did not have to equate with biological sex. This assumption is inherent, for example, in Terman and Miles's (1936) Masculinity–Femininity scale, which assessed the degree to which men and women embodied their 'natural' roles, that is, to be a task-oriented breadwinner (men) or a domesticated carer (women). Bem (1974) rejects the idea propounded by sex role theories and related research that individuals automatically and unproblematically assume gender identities consistent with traditional expectations. Rather, masculinity and femininity could be viewed as independent orientations such that any individual could display aspects of both. Of course, an individual could just as well embody traditional ideals ('sex-typed') but the focus switched to 'androgynous' people, those who scored highly on both masculinity and femininity; those with low scores on masculinity and femininity attracted the dubious label of 'undifferentiated' (see Bem, 1974; and Box 7.2). Bem's hypothesis is consistent with Jungian psychology which suggests the presence of two complementary archetypes within the individual psyche – the anima (feminine) and the animus (masculine) (see Johnson, 1976). Characterizations of these archetypes correspond closely to gender conventions: the animus is defined by 'active achievement, cool reasonableness, mastery, penetration', whilst the anima comprises the 'primeval and oceanic, instinct, unity, relationship and relatedness...' (see de Castillejo, 1973: 57). Both approaches claim that a combination of the masculine and the feminine within the individual make for a more advanced, psychologically healthy subject (see Bem *et al.*, 1976), although feminists argue that possessing 'masculine' characteristics is more important for both sexes because these tend to be more highly valued in society (see Wilkinson, 1986).

Bem's work was undoubtedly valuable for questioning the rigid equation between biological sex and gender identity promoted by social psychology and widely accepted in the general public, and it therefore contributed to the feminist challenge to existing gender norms. However, Bem's approach has been criticized for locating gender at the level of the individual and ignoring societal factors such as power and ideology. In other words, it is up to individuals to decide which 'sex-role orientation' to adopt, as if free choice were possible and not constrained by differential access to power due to social positions of class, race, education, etc. (see Wetherell, 1997). According to Hollway (1989: 99), Bem's 'feminist intentions were subverted by the methods and assumptions she reproduced uncritically as a result of her training as a social psychologist [within] the atheoretical, empiricist tradition of Anglo-American psychology'. This liberal, idealistic and individualistic approach continues to inform much apparently feminist social psychology in the United States, as embodied by journals such as *Sex Roles* (see Connell, 1987). From a critical social psychology perspective, the ideals and approaches of mainstream social psychology – which do not theorize societal relations of gender –remain intact.

Box 7.2   Bem sex-role inventory (Bem, 1974)

From an initial list of 200 attributes, Bem asked groups of under-graduate students to rate the items according to how 'desirable' they were for a man or woman in order to elicit gender norms or stereotypes. Based on the results, 20 items were identified as more appropriate for men, 20 for women and a further 20 which did not differentiate between the sexes. 'Masculine' and 'feminine' items are listed below.

Masculine items	Feminine items
acts as a leader	affectionate
aggressive	cheerful
ambitious	childlike
analytical	compassionate
assertive	does not use harsh language
athletic	eager to soothe hurt feelings
competitive	feminine
defends own beliefs	flatterable
dominant	gentle
forceful	gullible
has leadership abilities	loves children
independent	loyal
individualistic	sensitive to the needs of others
makes decisions	easily shy
masculine	soft-spoken
self-reliant	sympathetic
strong personality	tender
willing to take a stand	understanding
willing to take risks	warm
	yielding

College students were then asked to specify the degree to which each trait described themselves. Low correlations were found between masculinity and femininity scores, thus confirming Bem's hypothesis that these dimensions referred to independent traits rather than a continuum. Also, the results suggested that rigid gender stereotypes were not necessarily or automatically internalized by the 'appropriate' sex. Using a slightly different test, the Personal Attributes Questionnaire, Spence *et al.* (1974) confirmed these findings.

CRITICAL THINKING BOX: ANDROGYNY

Select 10 items from Box 7.2 which you think best describe your 'personality'. Using the Bem sex-role inventory (BSRI) system, and categorize your choices as 'masculine' or 'feminine'. How androgynous do you appear? Are there specific situations when your more 'masculine' traits emerge? How about 'feminine' traits?

'Just like us': liberal–humanistic explanations of homosexuality

Other non-biological accounts emphasize individuality over socially determined gendered or sexed roles. Within psychology, representations of homosexuality as socially deviant and an illness were challenged in the 1960s and 1970s backlash against essentialist theories of sexuality and replaced by understandings of homosexuality situated within liberal–humanistic paradigms (Kitzinger, 1987). Within this context, the social stigma associated with gay identities was challenged through representations of gay and lesbian people as normal individuals who had made a personal choice that was as healthy and normal as that made by their heterosexual counterparts. In addition, representations of such individuals as a danger to moral and social instability were contested through the emphasis on their 'personal choice' and 'private lifestyle'. Such representations of gay and lesbian identities were embraced by many who had lived with pathologized understandings of their identities, and theorists who had challenged the persuasiveness of essentialist definitions of lesbianism and homosexuality. For many others, liberal–humanistic definitions were also viewed as problematic. For example, rather than liberating lesbians, Kitzinger (1987) believes that the reduction of lesbian identities to a matter of personal choice denies the opportunity for many women to define themselves in socio–political terms. In particular, couching lesbianism in the language of personal choice and equating it with heterosexuality renders invisible other important discourses around lesbianism, as, for example, a source of empowerment (Kitzinger & Wilkinson, 1997b), or pleasure (Dancey, 1994) or as resistance to heterosexuality (McFadden, 1995: see Box 7.3). The lives of lesbian, gay, transgendered and bisexuals are now being researched from a position of respect for diversity (see Clark et al., 2010; Clark & Peel, 2007).

Box 7.3   It's more than a personal choice: alternative experiences of lesbianism (McFadden, 1995)

In the following extract, Molly talks about how she feels about being lesbian:

I just find being a lesbian – and that's across-the-board, not just how I express myself sexually – very liberating. I think lesbians have [pause] greater opportunities for self-expressions and just developing confidence that the parameters of heterosexuality don't either allow or encourage. And I think there's some strain in heterosexual relationships to do with the power imbalance. [pause] I'm trying to think of friends who are straight and who are excited and fulfilled by their relationships [laugh]. I just can't think of any, like I know some of these people really enjoy sex with men but I don't know on the wider level how satisfied they are in their relationships with men. I kinda feel that women and men communicate differently and [laugh] I don't know what that says but I think they have different understandings of words and expressions and to that end I think women in relationships are more likely to speak the same language. They have the same understandings of things like support or companionship or just needin' to let off steam or whatever; you know men, they're just not in the same head-set as women. So to that end I think that women are one step up when in relationships with other women [pause] I mean most women I know would say that it's in their relationships with other women that they have most expression and intellectual stimulation. It's not like hard work.

CRITICAL THINKING BOX: SEXUAL IDENTITY

Explore the language in Box 7.3. Consider how Molly experiences being lesbian? What aspects of heterosexuality does she identify as problematic? Is lesbianism for Molly simply a personal choice as suggested in liberal–humanistic perspective introduced in the above section?

Towards a critical/feminist/queer social psychology of gender and sexuality

Gender

Contemporary critical and feminist analyses of gender and sexuality typically deploy terms such as diversity, conflict, ideology and power. Within this broad perspective, the social construction of gender is emphasized, where representations of masculinities and femininities are regarded as cultural, multiple, dynamic, interrelated and influential on self-definition. As feminists have pointed out, meanings around masculinity have been traditionally privileged over all things feminine. For example, the common social practice of favouring 'masculine' over 'feminine' activities and characteristics is referred to as the 'plus male, minus female' by Spender (1980). This phenomenon extends to instances where the same behaviour performed by men and women is differentially evaluated (men are assertive and strong, women are pushy and bitches; men are studs, women are sluts etc.).

CRITICAL THINKING BOX: GENDER INEQUALITIES

Consider again the list of BSRI items above. On a scale of 1 to 5, rate each attribute on its social importance, i.e. the value placed on possessing the characteristic in society (1 = not important; 2 = limited importance; 3 = neutral; 4 = fairly important; 5 = very important). Now compare the mean ratings for 'masculine' and 'feminine' items. Did you rate 'masculine' items as more important? Why (not)?

This point has been used to criticize theory and research propounded by liberal feminist social psychologists such as Bem, who point to the damaging effects of gender stereotypes and emphasize personal choice and development in the formulation of one's gender identity, with a preference towards androgynous identities. Concepts such as choice and internalization, however, do not address social relations of difference and inequality between men and women and between constructs of masculinity and femininity. For example, the capacity for a woman to play rugby or drink lots of beer will be constrained and framed by wider social understandings of gender which define femininity outside particular sports and leisure pursuits. Similarly, the capacity for a man to take an interest in sewing or nursing will be mediated by prevailing ideals of masculinity which identify such activities as unmanly, effeminate, soft, etc. Box 7.4 describes work by Hall and Gough on how 'metrosexual' men present their interests in conventionally feminine practices around appearance – in masculine terms.

Box 7.4 Metrosexual men and contemporary masculinities

Hall and Gough (2011) have researched the phenomenon of 'metrosexuality' online, via discussion forums. Metrosexuality is a term coined by Simpson (1994) to define an emerging breed of men who take an interest in their appearance, investing in historically feminized beauty practices including self-tanning, eyebrow plucking and the application of cosmetics. The authors were interested in how self-identified metrosexual men accounted for these kinds of rituals. It was found that, almost universally, men who referenced beauty regimes displayed concern with appearing 'masculine', for example by citing a heterosexual payoff in terms of greater attention from women. Another popular account dismissed men who were disinterested in their appearance as lacking self-respect. These themes are exemplified in the following extract, from 'Rafael', a contributor to a discussion thread on metrosexuality:

Robert, just like you think now, once I thought that metrosexual was a gay guy that dresses like a man, or something too delicate to be a man. Later I found out, I was a metrosexual myself. A man that does care for his looks, the way he smells, the way he behaves, the way he approaches women and a man that goes to the gym trying to keep his looks up. I am 32 and I can say I have been successful with woman my entire life never needing to pay for one to please me, like some real man as they think they are with their rugged manly grossness need to do, because a sane sexy woman cannot take his bee rand tobacco smell unless they pay her to do it. I am married now, I am the father of a beautiful girl and the husband of a stunning woman I love, and you know what guys, I am still a metro.

Hall and Gough suggest that such accounts reinforce the delicacy involved for men in presenting themselves as interested in feminized practices, and the continued influence of 'hegemonic' or powerful forms of masculinity which emphasize sexual success, self-respect and paternity. More broadly, it is argued that traditional forms of masculinity are not so much being challenged as recalibrated and repackaged for business profit in a consumer-driven, body-conscious society. Evidence for this can be seen in recent television advertising where male subjects like actor Matthew Fox, who typically play characters best described as 'rugged individuals', promote the purchase of 'men's only' cosmetics.

Women who aspire or attempt to move into 'non-traditional' arenas (e.g. driving a truck/lorry, working in construction, playing rugby , displaying sexual assertiveness, drinking lots of beer) are often subjected to ridicule and abuse (verbal and physical attacks, lower pay, harsher conditions, etc.). Research consistently uncovers deep resentment and a multitude of barriers which act to preserve male dominance, typically warranted by claims that 'it isn't natural for women to demand equality' or 'women have gone too far' (see Faludi, 1992; Ford, 1985). Women are thus caught in a double bind: to adhere to the norms of femininity is to remain a second-class citizen (excluded from public life, etc.) whereas to struggle for equal rights often means enduring much psychological and physical suffering. Within radical, Marxist and socialist schools of feminist theory, sex roles are situated in 'patriarchal' society where established social structures and relationships favour men. Instead of concentrating on encouraging individuals to become more androgynous, a strategy which ignores the deep structural constraints which inhibit free movement, the concern here is to challenge the wider (patriarchal) social, economic and historical structures which conspire to cement traditional gender relations (see Segal, 1987).

The gender picture is more complicated still when other systems of difference are acknowledged. It is relatively easy to imagine various limitations on number and type of roles practised depending on social class, sexual orientation, ethnic background and occupational choice. For example, it is often difficult for gay and lesbian individuals to 'come out' and fulfil this role in a heterosexist society. Similarly, a working-class single mother may well find it difficult to hold down a full-time job or register for a course because of childcare responsibilities and/or lack of transport. Conversely, those individuals defined as heterosexual or middle class will probably encounter fewer obstacles and will have more opportunities to take on and enjoy a range of roles. Socialist and post-modern (or social constructionist) forms of feminism highlight issues of diversity, conflict and fluidity in relation to gendered identities. A feminist social psychological analysis would seek to identify the range of gendered roles or positions available, examine any difference and/or conflicts between these representations and highlight their implications for gender relations. Recent articles in the journal *Feminism & Psychology* have featured debates on social diversity and politics in relation to (hetero)sexuality, race and social class (e.g. Fine, 2012; Sevon, 2012; Muise, 2011).

CRITICAL THINKING BOX: SEXISM

Considering the examples below, identify relevant popular images/representations:

female rugby players; male nurses;
male hairdresser;
women in the armed forces;
female bouncers; single mothers;
male flight attendants; unemployed men.
How do traditional ideals around gender influence how we see these identities?

Rather than fixing masculinity or femininity as a property or structure within individuals, a contemporary critical feminist approach to gender tends to locate it as a social construct and examines the meanings attached to gender within various (textual) presentations (speeches, magazine features, advertisements, interview transcripts). Contemporary feminist writing on femininity highlights multiple and contradictory discourses where 'postfeminist' neo-liberal notions of choice, assertiveness and individuality co-exist with traditional and often constraining expectations based around appearance, maternity, nurturance and so on. In a study on appearance pressures in an Australian high school, Carey *et al.* (2011) describe how young girls negotiate a range of expectations within a gendered school culture (Box 7.5).

The analysis of language has provided an important focus for feminist and critical researchers interested in challenging gender ideals. Seminal work by Cameron (1992), for example, suggests that women are subordinated more often in talk through being addressed by their first name (rather than Mrs, Ms, Dr, etc.) or through terms of

Box 7.5 Appearance culture in an all-girl school

Carey *et al.* (2011) interviewed nine girls about appearance-related expectations and practices at their school. The rationale for the study cites high rates of body image concern among adolescent girls (e.g. Jones *et al.*, 2004), especially in single-sex schools (Shroff & Thompson, 2006). The girls stressed the importance of image, and the negative impact this culture had on bodily self-confidence:

What you look like is such a big factor. (Emily)

So like being skinny and, like what you look like is really important, especially at an all girls' school, and everyone just cares a lot about what they look like. (Ella)

The more like popular kind of people are more careful about how...they look...they're really concerned about the way they look and they always want to impress, like, everybody else. (Charlotte)

The work involved in maintaining an acceptable appearance was highlighted by interviewees, including diet regimes, weight monitoring and the frequency of body-related conversations with peers:

...like everyone's pretty healthy but I guess lots of people talk about dieting heaps, that's so often talked about, and not eating to lose weight and stuff – like my friends are, have a modelling thing on this weekend, have to wear bathers, so they're like 'oh, I'm not gonna eat dinner all week'... (Ella)

Especially like the group of girls, like in our group, we'll go yeah, I'm...doing a diet do you wanna diet with me, like yeah okay we'll diet together. (Emily)

The girls also talked, often critically, about the school's efforts to confront body image concerns:

A big one is the way that the school focuses on eating disorders and while it's good to discuss them and talk about them, I think they also need to talk about healthy options...they need to find a balance...like I don't remember talking about healthy eating last year...but I remember talking about...bulimia and anorexia and that's what stayed in my mind. (Isabella)

The authors thus underline the pervasiveness of appearance-centred culture at the school, echoing other feminist analyses which lament the destructive over-emphasis on girls' and women's bodies (Jeffreys 2005), and which critique the linking of beauty to health, morality and success (e.g. Bordo, 1993). They also pick up on the girls' criticism of the school's interventions, and argue that culture-based, rather than individual-centred, initiatives which recognize the pressures faced by girls on a daily basis have a better chance of success, as Burns *et al.* (2009) have demonstrated. The authors also point to online resources designed to enable exploration of body-related issues e.g. by emphasizing appearance as performance rather than individual essence (e.g. www.fashionista.com).

endearment ('love', 'dear', etc.). Equally significant work by Spender (1980) has critically examined 'man-made language', the most obvious example being the widespread use of generic words such as 'man' to refer to all people. The use of compliments by men directed at women's bodies can also be thought of as reinforcing female subservience: 'they serve as a reminder that a woman's appearance is available to be commented upon and that the person giving the compliment is in a position to pass judgement' (Swann, 1992: 31–32).

More specifically, however, much critical social psychology work concentrates on 'discourse/s' (see Chapters 2, 3). The (male) bread-winner can be regarded as a discourse, a traditionally powerful one which is signalled by a range of interconnecting 'statements' or assumptions, such as 'men at work', 'women's place is in the home', 'a man must provide for his family' and 'women love shopping', etc. As Pleck (1987) notes, another role (or discourse) construes fatherhood in terms of involvement, closeness and emotional support. So, at any given historical moment there will be more than one understanding of fatherhood (or any other 'object' for that matter) which a particular culture makes available. Further, following Foucault's (1972) notion that discourses exist in relations of power and knowledge, it is usual that one discourse will be socially dominant at any one time. In the case of fatherhood, one could argue that the traditional 'bread-winner' discourse remains ascendant despite the evolution of alternative discourses. For example, Finn and Henwood (2009) studied contemporary fatherhood by conducting in-depth interviews, which they analysed using critical psychosocial theory. Despite the changes in discourse that have occurred in the past 30 years around the notion of fatherhood (e.g. fathers as more caring and emotionally expressive) a number of the men continued to identify with traditional masculine discourses such as instilling their children with courage, strength and self-reliance. Rather than simply identifying and describing the range of roles/discourses present in society, there is an additional effort to study how discourses are re-presented (or 're-produced') in everyday talk and, significantly, how dominant discourses are resisted or re-worked (there is no assumption here that socially powerful ideals are accepted and practised uncritically).

Sexuality

One of the most important themes to emerge from the critique of theories discussed so far is the dismissal of sexuality as something that is innate or biologically determined. Rather, within critical social psychology, sexuality is viewed as socially constructed and negotiated. Foucault (1978) offered an alternative reading of sexuality, presenting it as an historical concept, constructed through a number of discourses including the legal, the religious, the medical and the scientific. The crux of Foucault's theoretical argument was the rejection of sexual identities and practices as resulting from an inner essence (anatomical, psychological or biological): 'sexuality must not be thought of as a kind of natural given which power tries to hold in check, or as an obscure domain which knowledge tries to uncover' (Foucault, 1978: 105).

In Foucault's thesis, sexuality provided a means of controlling the body through legislation on birth control and homosexuality, as well as a means of policing the population as a whole with campaigns against immorality, prostitution and venereal disease. He argued that from the eighteenth century onwards, sexuality increasingly provided the central focus around which social bodies, relationships, positions and practices were organized.

Rather than describing the history of sexuality as repressive Foucault (1978) depicts it as a history of discourses on sex that generated relationships of power and understandings of bodies and their associated pleasures. Charting the inception of our inclination to talk about sex in the penitential practices of the Middle Ages, Foucault develops his main thesis by exploring the defining and redefining of sexuality through later political, economic and technical incitements to converse on sex. Central among the institutions redefining sexual identities and practices was that of science, including medicine, psychiatry and psychology. To illustrate this, Foucault draws on the increasing clinical codification of normal (heterosexual, reproductive) and abnormal (homosexuality, masturbation, hysteria) sexuality in the twentieth century.

Prior to this period, prohibitions on sex had been predominantly of a judicial nature with both transgressions of marriage and deviant sexualities defined under a 'general lawlessness' (Foucault, 1978: 38). Foucault argues that the gradual establishment of heterosexual monogamy as the norm, and the scrutinizing of those whose sexualities did not fit this norm, not only facilitated the establishing of a natural order of desires but created an abnormal annexe of sexuality within which deviant sexualities could be disciplined (or, in the language of Freud and Ellis, cured). New forms of knowledge brought new structures of power through which sexuality could be defined, controlled and disciplined. Consequently the governance of sex became grounded in two systems, and offences became separated into those against the law of marriage and those against 'the regularity of a natural function' (1978: 38). Thus, as Foucault (1978) argued, sexuality came to provide multiple areas of power and control, as it became not only a means of regulating actual sexual behaviour but also a key area in social relations: 'The deployment of sexuality has its reason for being, not in reproducing itself, but in proliferating, innovating, annexing, creating and penetrating bodies in an increasingly detailed way, and in controlling populations in an increasingly comprehensive way' (1978: 107).

Foucault's work on sexuality and discourse more generally has influenced a number of contemporary feminist theorists (see Box 7.6). A good example is Judith Butler whose reading of Foucault's work emphasizes how discourses influence subjectivity so that gender becomes something which is performed and copied from dominant cultural representations of femininity or masculinity, so that people can fit into the roles set down for them (Elliott, 2009: 215–220). As Hepburn (2003: 114–115) notes, Butler's work deconstructs the 'natural realities' surrounding terms such as man, woman, heterosexual and homosexual. 'The idea that there are primary essences of masculinity and femininity emerging from within the body, giving rise to particular identities, is challenged. Instead, masculinity and femininity arise through the performance of gender'.

Box 7.6   Interrogating Foucault

Foucault's writings on the history of sexuality have been widely acclaimed for the insights they provide into the social dimensions of sexuality and issues of power and control (Bartky, 2009; Turner, 1984; Weedon, 1987; Weeks, 1985). Notwithstanding this favourable reception, Foucault's (1978) hesitancy to address issues of gender earned him criticism from some Feminist and Queer theorists. Walby (1990) notes that while Foucault takes into account competing discourses, historical specificity and power, he does not specifically address the issue of gender and power. Penelope (1992) takes this criticism further, accusing Foucault of not only failing to address inequalities relating to power and gender in the construction of sexuality, but of going 'to great lengths to construct a fortuitous history, one in which male domination is reduced to a happenstance intersection of "relationships of force" in which some discourses are privileged (male) while others (female) are silenced' (1992: 25). Furthermore she suggests that Foucault's omission of lesbian sexuality and his subsequent illustrations concentrating on male homosexuality, not only made lesbians invisible but distorted the impact of sexology on this and other aspects of female identity and practice. Similarly, Bleier (1984) argues that while Foucault addressed the issue of power, he did this in a non-direct way where he questions neither the source nor direction of its invention. To counteract this she suggests reading Foucault as a metaphor and applying his analysis to the position of women in the past century. In doing so, it becomes apparent that those who invented the discourses (medical, psychological, religious, legal, etc.) were more than likely men, while those who went to confess, to be cured or punished were women.

A key text challenging the prevalence of heterosexuality as the most 'natural' type of sexuality, and the subordination of women therein, is Adrienne Rich's (1980) *Compulsory Heterosexuality and Lesbian Existence.* Within this work, Rich (1980) challenges representations of heterosexuality (more specifically, definitions of masculinity as different though complementary identities and practices, marriage as the only legitimate expression of sexuality and penetrative sex the most natural sexual relationship) as the 'natural' type of sexuality for women (and by implication men) through two inter-related arguments: the first relating to the socially manufactured and coercive nature of heterosexuality, and secondly, through her dismissal of restrictive clinical definitions of lesbianism in favour of a broader understanding based on the notions of lesbian continuum and lesbian existence. With respect to the naturalness of hetero-sexuality, Rich (1980) presents the ideology of heterosexuality as an extensive socially manufactured matrix that is coercively imposed on many women through a variety of means, including romantic ideol-ogies, the stigmatizing of alternative types of sexuality, and physical and verbal force. Women, she argues, are not born heterosexual but rather are coerced into it through a variety of social mechanisms (e.g. through scientific, legal and educational discourses) that bind them into a 'socially acceptable' sexuality and punish them if they step outside these boundaries.

CRITICAL THINKING BOX: HETEROSEXUALITY

Take time to think about how you experience your sexuality. What types of information did you receive about sexuality in your school, from friends and from your parents? Was there the assumption that you are/were heterosexual? (For example, was there recognition that you might be attracted to a same-sex partner? Were marriage and parenthood talked about as things that would 'naturally' happen when you were older?)

A second theme framing accounts of sexuality within critical social psychology is the relationship between sexuality, language and social practice. Sexuality is viewed as the product of social, cultural and historical discourses. Box 7.7, for example, highlights feminist concerns around the sexualization of women within mass market magazines targeting young men.

Feminists have critiqued the operation of traditional discourses in shaping femininity. For example, Lees (1993) and Thomson and Scott (1991) noted that within the context of school and home, sexuality for many young women has been discussed largely in relation to their future roles of wives and mothers, with married heterosexuality presented as the most natural type of sexuality. More recent feminist analysis has emerged within a more narcissistic, sexualized, consum-er-oriented, individualistic culture (Douglas, 2000). This is sometimes described as 'postfeminism', where women are confronted with new possibilities and dilemmas, ranging from cosmetic surgery to female-targeted pornography, pole dancing, lap dancing and prostitution (Walter, 2010). The postfeminist emphasis is firmly on the celebration of difference, individual choice, the exploration of sexual subjectivity

**Box 7.7   Lads mags and young men's attitudes towards women
and sexual aggression**

Coy and Horvath (2011) provide a review of existing research on mediated sexualized images of women and their likely effects on young men's sexual politics. They point to the popularity of mass market 'lads mags' in the UK (e.g. 'Nuts'; 'Zoo'; 'FHM') and elsewhere, arguing that the 'sexy media diet' (Brown et al., 2006) therein reproduces women as sex objects, is offensive to women and promotes a superficial and dangerous orientation towards women and women's bodies. For example, boys exposed to such magazine content are more likely to see women as sex objects (Peter & Valkenburg, 2007), while young women experience body image problems and pressure to comply with male-centred sexual norms (e.g. Coy, 2009). Such magazines can be situated within a broader sexualization of popular culture where women and men are constructed as body-conscious, erotic objects and consumers (e.g. Gill, 2007; Walter, 2010: 19–38). The authors also point to work which analyses such sexualized material as the mainstreaming of pornography into the mass media (Gill, 2008a; Walter, 2010: 102–118); for example, lads mags portray men as actively endeavouring to manipulate women to attain sex (Taylor, 2005), while pornography often presents aggressive male actors and passive female victims (Matacin & Burger, 1987). Nonetheless, there are differences: total nudity is disavowed in magazines, and other 'masculine' interests are conveyed, broadening the appeal (e.g. sport, cars, alcohol) – the term 'almost porn' has been used in the context of lads mags (Rogers, 2005). One of the difficulties around challenging the content of lads mags, however, is that the content is typically defended as harmless fun delivered with an ironic flourish (Benwell, 2004). How young men respond to such material, and specifically how they view women and sexual relations, is an important research question which the authors are pursuing.

and sexual agency (Gill, 2007, 2008b); there is an assumption that the goals of feminism have been achieved, and that it is legitimate, indeed desirable, for women to embrace appearance-related body practices previously (and to some extent still) rejected by feminism (McRobbie, 2009). Box 7.8 provides an interesting critical analysis of website advertisements aimed at prospective pole dancers.

Box 7.8   Pole dancing, sexuality and 'postfeminist' femininity

Donaghue *et al.* (2011) conducted a discursive analysis of 15 websites based in Australia, focusing on how the business of pole dancing is marketed to potential participants. The analysis draws attention to two main discourses operating within the texts:

1. A postfeminist construction of pole dancing emphasizing women's' sexual agency and assertiveness:

   Your self-confidence will soar as you experience a sense of accomplishment and express yourself through some of the more sensual pole tricks. (Studio Verve)

   The confidence you gain will spill over into everyday life. (Suzie Q)

   ...people gain empowerment and self-confidence through the sensual expression. (Pole Play)

   All the instructors know just how empowering Pole Dancing and the Art of Striptease really are, and they are only too obliged in guiding women into the next revolution of dance. (Pole Divas)

2. An ironic, playful notion of pole dancing as a knowing performance, designed for fun and fitness:

   She-parties are the perfect excuse to get the girls together and laugh yourselves silly as your instructors guide you through a series of pole dance and/or lap dance routines. (She Moves)

   Pole dancing is an entertaining, fun and unusual way to get together and have a laugh with your closest friends. (Pole Revolution)

   This new class of pole dancing is strictly for fun and it is purely for women who want to get fit, have a laugh and discover their sensual side. (Mpole)

The authors proceed to argue that the two discourses present a clash of authenticity against parody, of sexual empowerment versus light relief. The promise of sexual liberation implies that women do not ordinarily enjoy such freedom while the performance dimension allows women to play down or deny any overt sexual motivation (pole dancing can be respecified as fitness or fun). This tension between empowerment and performance discourses is seen to infuse 'raunch culture' more generally, and it is noted that women performers cannot control how their activities are interpreted, leaving themselves open to less flattering judgements (e.g. tacky, slutty, prostitution). The authors conclude that 'the tensions and contradictions between authenticity and parody are revealing of the uneasiness of this postfeminist space, in which bids for "empowerment" are attractive and compelling, yet at the same time contingent, fragile and insecure' (Donaghue et al., 2011: 455; see also Walter, 2010: 39–62).

However this is not to suggest that within critical social psychology, individuals are perceived as passive recipients of social practices. On the contrary, individuals are understood as actively working towards various social positions and representations. For example, McFadden (1995) describes how the women in her study illustrated different forms of resistance to the dominant representations of female sexuality discussed by Fine (1988). These strategies included delaying marriage until they had 'had some fun', choosing to be celibate and seeking alternative sources of information to construct their notions of sexual pleasure and desire. Holland et al. (1991) and Smith (1988) have highlighted similar findings. In her work with lesbian women, Dancey (1994) noted similar resistance among the women interviewed to what they perceived as negative representations of lesbianism. These strategies included empha-sizing the positive benefits associated with a lesbian lifestyle, including the removal of the perceived necessity to conform to role expectations and the solidarity and companionship they experienced living as lesbian women (see also see Clark et al., 2010; Clark & Peel, 2007).

Box 7.9 'Queer' theory (Butler, 1990; 1993)

The pervasiveness of heterosexuality as a cultural norm and the multiple ways in which this is resisted and re-inscribed are dominant strands of feminist (Kitzinger & Wilkinson, 1997a) and gay and lesbian studies (Plummer, 1992; Weeks, 1991). Within the past decade, diver-sification of these themes has occurred in the writings of queer theorists, (most notably Butler, 1993), on sexuality. The main aim of 'queer' theorizing is to destabilize normative understandings of what it is to be a heterosexual wo/man or homosexual wo/man through subversion – the embodiment/representation of the unexpected, for example the macho gay man, female dominatrix, the cross-dresser or the transvestite (Sawicki, 2003).

Drawing on postmodern notions of the 'self' as fragmented, queer theory explicitly challenges the perceived traditional link between sex (fe/male), gender (femininity as passive; masculinity as active) and sexuality (heterosexuality as the most natural mode of sexual expression). Such ideas, however, do not exist unchallenged. Many feminist writers question the reduction of sexuality to the staged personas or performances, believing that such representations contribute to the invisibility of oppressive social and political practices experienced by many so-called straight and gay people. The use of subversive tactics as a political strategy to address prejudice and oppression is also severely questioned. As Segal (1997: 216) notes, 'What seems shocking and disturbing today can become part of the mass media spectacle tomorrow.' In addition, this theoretical perspective has been critiqued for its failure to account for the diversity of oppression mediated through factors such as race and class.

Summary

Feminist and queer scholars have led the way in criticizing mainstream psychobiological accounts of gender and sexuality. This critical work has become more important than ever as biologically determined accounts of sex differences have made a popular comeback due to advances in neuroscience and its enthusiastic reporting by the mass media. The fascination with sex differences within (social) psychology and wider culture has been thoroughly questioned, as have constructions of homosexuality as deviant, and critical work seeks to explore gendered and sexed identities and relationships in diverse contexts. In recent years explorations have focused on the subtle manipulation of feminism by the mass media, marketing and advertising industries, which have co-opted women's desire for greater sexual expression and assertiveness as a way of mainstreaming hyper sexualization and pornography. Critical engagement with classic theories such as psychoanalysis, feminist theory and poststructuralism (e.g. Foucault and Butler), along with work in critical social psychology (e.g. Celia Kitzinger and Sue Wilkinson) seeks to challenge the increasingly subtle manipulation of gender and sexed identities by producing sophisticated socially embedded understandings of masculinities and femininities, as well as gay, lesbian, trans and bisexual lives.

Key references

Clarke, V., Ellis, S., Peel, E. & Riggs, D. (2010). *Lesbian, Gay, Bisexual, Trans and Queer Psychology: An Introduction.* Cambridge: Cambridge University Press.
Clearly written text aimed at undergraduate students covering a range of topics, issues and methods relevant to LGBTQ psychology.

Fine, C. (2010). *Delusions of Gender: How Our Minds, Society and Neurosexism Create Difference.* New York: WW Norton.
A popular and highly regarded critical account of neuro–biological claims around sex differences.

Gill, R. (2007). Postfeminist media culture: elements of a sensibility. *European Journal of Cultural Studies 10*, 147–166.
A clear, critical perspective on sexualization in the media.

Spargo, T. (1999). *Foucault and Queer Theory.* London: Icon Books.
This pocket size books provides an entertaining introduction to the ways in which Foucault's ideas have been used by gay activists to deconstruct the naturalization of sexual behaviour and its links with self-identity.

New references

Archer, J. (2004). Sex differences in aggression in real world settings: a meta-analytic review. *Review of General Psychology, 8*, 291–322.

Baron-Cohen, S. (2005). The essential difference: the male and female brain. *Phi Kappa Phi Forum, 85*(1), 23–27.

Bartky, S. L. (2009). Foucault, femininity, and the modernization of patriarchal power. In R. Weitz (ed), *Politics of Women's Bodies: Sexuality, Appearance, and Behaviour* (3rd edn, pp. 25–45). Oxford: Oxford University Press.

Benwell B (2004). Ironic discourse: evasive masculinity in men's lifestyle magazines. *Men and Masculinities 7*(1), 3–21.

Bordo S (1993). *Unbearable Weight: Feminism, Western Culture, and the Body.* Berkeley, CA: University of California.

Brizendine, L. (2008). *The Female Brain.* London: Transworld.

Brizendine, L. (2011). *The Male Brain.* London: Transworld.

Brown, J. D., L'Engle, K. L., Pardun, C. J., Guo, G., Kenneavy, K. & Jackson, C. (2006). Sexy media matter: exposure to sexual content in music, movies, television, and magazines predicts black and white adolescents' sexual behavior. *Pediatrics, 117*(4), 1018–1127.

Burns M, Tyrer J, & Eating Difficulties Education Network (2009). Feminisms in practice: challenges and opportunities for an eating issues community agency. In H. Malson,, M. Burns (eds) *Critical Feminist Approaches to Eating Dis/Orders* (pp. 221–232). London: Routledge.

Bussey, K., & Bandura, A. (1999). Social cognitive theory of gender development and differentiation. *Psychological Review, 106*(4), 676–713.

Callaghan, J. & Lazard, L. (2011). *Social Psychology.* Exeter, UK: Learning Matters.

Campbell, A. (2008). Attachment, aggression and affiliation: the role of oxytocin in female social behavior. *Biological Psychology, 77*(1), 1–10.

Carey, R.N., Donaghue, N., & Broderick, P. (2011). 'What you look like is such a big factor': Girls' own reflections about the appearance culture in an all-girls' school, *Feminism & Psychology, 21*(3), 299–316.

Chodorow, N. J. (1990). Gender, relation, and difference in psychoanalytic perspective. In C. Zanardi (ed), *Essential Papers on the Psychology of Women* (pp. 420–436). New York: New York University Press.

Chodorow, N. J. (2002). Gender as a personal and cultural construction. In M. Dimen & V. Goldner (eds), *Gender in Psychoanalytic Space: between Clinic and Culture* (pp. 237–261). New York: Other Press.

Clarke, V., Ellis, S., Peel, E. & Riggs, D. (2010). *Lesbian, Gay, Bisexual, Trans and Queer Psychology: An Introduction.* Cambridge: Cambridge University Press.

Clarke, V. & Peel, E. (eds). (2007). *Out in Psychology: Lesbian, Gay, Bisexual, Trans and Queer Perspectives.* John Wiley & Sons.

Connell, R.W. & Messerschmidt, J.W. (2005). Hegemonic masculinity: rethinking the concept, *Gender & Society, 19*(6), 829–859.

Coy, M. (2009). Milkshakes, lady lumps and growing up to want boobies: how the sexualisation of popular culture limits girls' horizons. *Child Abuse Review, 18*(6), 372–383.

Coy, M. & Horvath, M.A.H. (2011).'Lads mags', young men's attitudes towards women and acceptance of myths about sexual aggression. *Feminism & Psychology, 21*(1), 144–150.

Donaghue, N., Whitehead, K. & Kurz, T. (2011). Spinning the pole: a discursive analysis of the websites of recreational pole dancing studios, *Feminism & Psychology, 21*(4), 443–457.

Douglas, S. (2000). Narcissism as liberation. In J. Scanlon (ed), *The Gender and Consumer Culture Reader* (pp. 267–282). New York: New York University Press.

Elliott, A. (2009). *Contemporary Social Theory: An Introduction*. Abingdon, UK: Routledge.

Fine, C. (2010). *Delusions of Gender: How Our Minds, Society and Neurosexism Create Difference*. New York: WW Norton.

Fine, M. (2012). Troubling calls for evidence: a critical race, class and gender analysis of whose evidence counts. *Feminism & Psychology, 22*(1), 3–19.

Finn, M., & Henwood, K. (2009). Exploring masculinities within men's identificatory imaginings of first-time fatherhood. *British Journal of Social Psychology, 48*(3), 547–562.

Gergen, M. M. (2001). *Feminist Reconstructions in Psychology: Narrative, Gender, and Performance*. Thousand Oaks, CA: Sage.

Gill, R. (2012). The sexualisation of culture? *Social & Personality Psychology Compass, 6*(7), 483–498.

Gill R (2008a). Empowerment/sexism: figuring female sexual agency in contemporary advertising. *Feminism & Psychology, 18*, 35–60.

Gill, R. (2008b). Culture and subjectivity in neoliberal and postfeminist times. *Subjectivity, 25*, 432–445.

Gill, R. (2007). Postfeminist media culture: elements of a sensibility. *European Journal of Cultural Studies, 10*, 147–166.

Hall, M. & Gough, B. (2011). Magazine and reader constructions of 'metrosexuality' and masculinity: a membership categorization analysis, *Journal of Gender Studies, 20*(1), 69–87.

Hepburn, A. (2003). *An Introduction to Critical Social Psychology*. London: Sage.

Hiatt, B. (2010). Girls outperform boys across all subjects, *The West Australian*, 16 January, p. 22.

Hines, M. (2005). *Brain Gender*. Oxford: Oxford University Press.

Huesmann, L. R., Moise-Titus, J., Podolski, C., & Eron, L. D. (2003). Longitudinal relations between children's exposure to TV violence and their aggressive and violent behavior in young adulthood: 1977–1992. *Developmental Psychology, 39*(2), 201–221.

Hunt, J. (2011). Girls outperform boys in most subjects again, *Irish Times*, 19 August, p. 7.

Jeffreys, S. (2005). *Beauty and Misogyny: Harmful Cultural Practices in the West*. New York: Routledge.

Jones, D. C., Vigfusdottir, T. H. & Lee, Y. (2004). Body image and the appearance culture among adolescent girls and boys: an examination of friend conversations, peer criticism, appearance magazines, and the internalization of appearance ideals. *Journal of Adolescent Research, 19*, 323–339.

Jordan-Young, R. M. (2011). *Brain Storm: the Flaws in the Science of Sex Differences.* Cambridge, MA: Harvard University Press.

McRobbie A (2009). *The Aftermath of Feminism. Gender, Culture and Social Change.* London: Sage.

Matacin, M.L. & Burger, J.M. (1987). A content analysis of sexual themes in Playboy cartoons. *Sex Roles, 17*(3/4), 179–186.

Muise, A. (2011). Women's sex blogs: challenging dominant discourses of heterosexual desire. *Feminism & Psychology, 22,* 411–419.

Peter, J. & Valkenburg, P.M. (2007). Adolescents' exposure to a sexualized media environment and notions of women as sex objects. *Sex Roles, 56,* 381–395.

Rogers, A. (2005). Chaos to control: men's magazines and the mastering of intimacy. *Men and Masculinities, 8*(2), 175–194.

Sahlins, M.D. (1977). *The Use and Abuse of Biology: An Anthropological Critique of Sociobiology.* Ann Arbor, MI: University of Michigan Press.

Sawicki, J. (2003). Queering Foucault and the subject feminism. In G. Gutting (ed), *The Cambridge Companion to Foucault* (2nd edn, pp. 379–400). Cambridge, UK: Cambridge University Press.

Sevon, E. (2012). 'My life has changed, but his life hasn't': making sense of the gendering of parenthood during the transition to motherhood, *Feminism & Psychology, 22*(1), 60–80.

Shroff, H., Thompson, J.K. (2006). Peer influences, body-image dissatisfaction, eating dysfunction and self-esteem in adolescent girls. *Journal of Health Psychology, 11,* 533–551.

Simpson, M. (1994). Here come the mirror men. *Independent,* 15 November, retrieved 4 January 2008.

Spitzer, R. (1981). The diagnostic status of homosexuality in DSM-III: a reformulation of the issues. *American Journal of Psychiatry, 138*(2), 210–215.

Taylor, L. D. (2005). All for him: articles about sex in American lad magazines. *Sex Roles, 52*(3/4), 153–163.

Taylor, S. E., Klein, L. C., Lewis, B. P., Gruenewald, T. L., Gurung, R. A. R., & Updegraff, J. A. (2000). Biobehavioral responses to stress in females: tend-and-befriend, not fight-or-flight. *Psychological Review, 107*(3), 411–429.

Ussher, J.M. (2006). *Managing the Monstrous Feminine: Regulating the Reproductive Body.* London: Routledge.

Walter, N. (2010). *Living Dolls: the Return of Sexism.* London: Virago.

Wilson, E. (2000). *Sociobiology: the New Synthesis* (25th Anniversary edn). Cambridge, MA: Harvard University Press.

Whitehead, S. (2002). *Men and Masculinities.* Cambridge: Polity Press.

Critical Social Psychology Applied

Part IV

Critical Health Psychology

8

This chapter will highlight:

- Key features of health psychology
- Sample health psychology topics and studies
- Criticisms of mainstream health psychology
- The emergence of critical health psychology (CHP)
- Select CHP perspectives, topics and studies

Introduction

The sub-discipline of health psychology emerged relatively recently, in the 1970s, and has traditionally drawn on ideas and methods from social psychology, particularly in the field of social cognition. Since the rise of critical (social) psychology in the 1990s, however, a number of psychologists working in health-related areas have questioned the reliance on conventional psychological principles and techniques. Indeed, we now have an International Society for Critical Health Psychology whose members look beyond mainstream psychology to understand health and illness. In this chapter we will firstly summarize health psychology before outlining various criticisms and debates. We will then proceed to outline the key assumptions, methods and practices associated with critical health psychology, drawing on recent research examples for illustration.

Health psychology: a critical overview

Psychologists have always been interested in health issues, but as Western societies began to focus attention and resources towards assessing and managing the health of its citizens in the 1970s, a new sub-discipline was born. From its inception, health psychology aligned itself with medical science (and the emerging interdisciplinary field of 'behavioural medicine') and sought to adopt scientific psychological principles and methods in the pursuit of new knowledge. With the rise of neoliberalism and a focus on individual behaviour and responsibility in Western economies, the psychological gaze on the individual matched the prevailing political ideology. Health psychology could promise to measure, predict and control the health behaviours of individuals within a given social setting (see Box 8.1).

Box 8.1 Official depictions of health psychology

The British Psychological Society hosts a Division of Health Psychology, and on their website they provide a succinct characterization of health psychology:

Health Psychology is a branch of Psychology that applies psychological research and methods to:

- the promotion and maintenance of health;
- the prevention and management of illness;
- the identification of psychological factors contributing to physical illness;
- the improvement of the health care system;
- the formulation of health policy.

Typical questions addressed by health psychology research:

- *How do people adapt to chronic illness?*
- *What factors influence healthy eating?*
- *How is stress linked to heart disease?*
- *Why do patients often not take their medication as prescribed?*

http://www.health-psychology.org.uk/

The American Psychological Association also features a Health Psychology Division, and they provide a similar set of aims. On their website, an overview of current directions is provided:

The many areas of research and service delivery illustrate the richness of the field of Health Psychology. Reports by the Surgeon General's Office indicate that the leading causes of mortality in

---

the U.S. have substantial behavioral components. These reports recommend that behavioral risk factors (e.g., drug and alcohol use, high risk sexual behavior, smoking, diet, a sedentary lifestyle, stress) be the main focus of efforts in the area of health promotion and disease prevention.

Given its emphasis on behavior and behavioral change, psychology has a unique contribution to make. For example, Health Psychologists are currently conducting applied research on the development of healthy habits as well as the prevention or reduction of unhealthy behaviors. The impact of behavior on health and the influence of health and disease states on psychological factors are being explored. Psychosocial and physiological linkages in areas such as psychoneuroimmunology, cardiovascular disorders and other chronic diseases are being defined. Ground breaking work is being conducted in psychopharmacology, as the neurological bases of behavior are being mapped.

This is a period of rapid change in health care delivery. Division 38, as part of the American Psychological Association, is working to establish liaisons between legislators, researchers and psychologist practitioners to ensure access to health psychologists as part of quality health care. Active research is being conducted to better understand the impact of health policy and health service delivery reforms on patient health and well being.

http://www.health-psych.org/AboutMission.cfm

There is a clear emphasis on the prevention of disease and the promotion of healthy lifestyles. Numerous models developed within social psychology have been enthusiastically endorsed and used by health psychologists and the quest to explain and predict individual behaviours relating to health, lifestyle and illness. Some of the major models include 'The Health Belief Model', 'The Theory of Reasoned Action' and 'The Transtheoretical Model', and all have been used to investigate a range of topics, such as adherence to medication, smoking initiation, maintenance and cessation, stress and coping, obesity risks and the protective effects of social support. These models tend to assume that health decision making is, or should be, a logical process based on the relevant information and advice available to individuals. The models try to identify those cognitive factors which are thought to influence (un-)healthy decision making and actions, and then devise interventions based on these factors. The Theory of Planned Behaviour (see Conner & Norman, 2005) is perhaps the most popular model in health psychology, drawing on concepts such as attitudes (towards a given behaviour e.g. 'stopping smoking would be good'), subjective norms (perception of local views e.g. 'smoking is bad for your health') and perceived behaviour control (judgements about one's ability to perform a given behaviour e.g. 'I could quit smoking if I wished'). The prediction is that if attitudes and subjective norms are positive (e.g. quitting smoking is a good thing), and perceived behavioural control is strong, then intentions to change behaviour should be strong, leading, ultimately to behaviour change (see Box 8.2 for an example of TPB-informed research).

Box 8.2   A mainstream health psychology study

A recent study published in the *British Journal of Health Psychology* authored by Rivis *et al.* (2011) is entitled 'Understanding young and older male drivers' willingness to drive while intoxicated: the predictive utility of constructs specified by the theory of planned behaviour and the prototype willingness model'. This is a typical theory-driven health psychology study working with specific constructs (here mainly derived from the Theory of Planned Behaviour) and using quantitative methods (questionnaires). The topic is almost secondary: there are many, many studies deploying these and related theories and methods on a range of health behaviours. These studies focus on the amount of variance that can be explained by particular constructs, in this case from two different theories, and discuss implications for the theories in question. Such studies also proceed to make recommendations for health promotion campaigns, in this case anti-drink driving campaigns.

This is a typical example of theory-driven quantitative health psychology research which tests hypotheses relating to (reported) drink driving. Specific variables from the models, which focus on self-perceptions and attitudes, are measured and related to the outcome variable. The power of the models (variables) to explain the dependent variable (willingness to drive while drunk) is then calculated statistically. Here is a selection of journal article titles for a recent issue of the premier APA journal *Health Psychology* to give you a flavour of the types of questions currently of interest to health psychologists:

- Do agonistic motives matter more than anger? Three studies of cardiovascular risk in adolescents.
- Conscientiousness and longevity: an examination of possible mediators.
- Can(not) take my eyes off it: attention bias for food in overweight participants.
- Moderators and mediators of exercise-induced objective sleep improvements in midlife and older adults with sleep complaints.
- Lapse-induced surges in craving influence relapse in adult smokers: an experimental investigation.
- Is self-concealment associated with acute and chronic pain?
- Evidence that self-affirmation reduces alcohol consumption: randomized exploratory trial with a new, brief means of self-affirming.
- Anticipated regret and organ donor registration – a pilot study.

This glimpse into the world of contemporary health psychology highlights a strand of work which suggests that personality traits (e.g. 'conscientiousness') influences health behaviours. Other personality traits thought to be significant include 'optimism', 'health locus of control' and 'perfectionism'. Another strand of work focuses on cognitive (e.g. 'attention bias') factors as predictors of health-related practices and outcomes. Dominant cognitive concepts in health psychology include 'self-efficacy', 'intention implementation' and 'self-regulation'. In particular there is a strong social cognition dimension (e.g. 'anticipated regret'; 'self-affirmation') and a reliance on concepts derived from models such as the Theory of Planned Behaviour.

Although many studies focus on lifestyle, health-related choices and behaviours (e.g. concerning alcohol consumption, smoking, physical exercise), health psychologists are also interested in how people cope with illness – in themselves and significant others. Recent research, for example, has considered stress levels (measured by cortisone patters) in parents of children diagnosed with a mental illness (cortisone is sometimes referred to as the 'stress hormone') (Barker *et al.*, 2012). This study found elevated stress levels for these parents (compared to a control group), and argued for interventions which address the health needs of the parents as well as the affected child. Another recent study highlighted the utility of mobile phone measurements of glucose monitoring and insulin administration in adolescents with diabetes, arguing that such mobile phone indicators help young people to adhere more closely to their medical regime (Mulvaney *et al.*, 2012).

As these examples suggest, and in line with psychology in general, there is a strong orientation towards doing good within health psychology i.e. explaining serious health problems with reference to relevant psychological concepts and offering theory-based interventions to address and alleviate the problem in question (whether to do with drink driving, dealing with a mentally ill child or controlling diabetes symptoms). An overarching commitment to a 'biopsychosocial' model is often cited in health psychology textbooks, suggesting an inclusive, holistic focus on the socially situated embodied person (see O'Connor *et al.*, 2011). The research examples cited above reveal an applied emphasis, a commitment to explaining health behaviours and to designing effective health-promoting initiatives. In Europe and Australia/New Zealand, some health psychologists have drawn upon qualitative research methods. For example, Interpretative Phenomenological Analysis (Smith, 2004) is widely used in UK health and clinical psychology research projects. In general, however, there is a preference towards quantitative methods used to measure and connect biological and psychological phenomena to health-related behaviours. TPB and other research related to social cognition models rely heavily on questionnaire responses, with scales inspired by elements of the model in question (perceived behavioural control, subjective norm, implementation intention etc. – see the Rivis *et al.* [2011] study, Box 8.2). Apart from self-report measures, 'objective' indicators of behaviour or behavioural change may be recorded (e.g. cortisone levels as an index of stress, body mass index, blood alcohol level, number of steps taken as measured by a pedometer etc.). As with psychology in general, experimental designs are privileged, and randomized controlled trials (RCTs) are held in the highest regard, designs which are common in medical research. For example, Cox *et al.* (2012) assigned one group of Hepatitis B patients to a simple intervention where they had to predict if/when they were going to go for a vaccination (low vaccination rates are a problem in this area), while another group did not receive the intervention. Both groups had to complete other measures concerning health beliefs, behaviours and demographic information. They found that the intervention worked for a subgroup of patients who also reported several barriers to vaccination.

The shortcomings of mainstream quantitative research methods have already been covered (see Chapter 3). Suffice to say here that the context and meaning/s of health-related practices are lost in the drive towards measurement, prediction and control. This is not to say that quantitative methods do not have a place, or that they cannot lead to useful health interventions. Rather, such methods cannot help us understand or situate health practices from the inside i.e. the social worlds which patients inhabit, infused with biographies, relationships, constraints and opportunities all of which shape 'individual' preferences and actions. At best, social factors figure only superficially in the formulation of health psychology research. The concept of 'subjective norms' found in the Theory of Planned Behaviour, for example, does seem to suggest an interest in social influences on behaviour; however, the focus is on *individual* perceptions of group/community attitudes and it is assumed that these perceived group norms can be neatly categorized and measured. An individual may be confronted with a wide range of competing and contradictory expectations around, say, smoking (e.g. parents: 'smoking is bad'; some friends: 'smoking is cool'; other friends: 'smoking is stupid' ...) which are difficult, if not impossible, to capture and measure using questionnaire items.

This focus on individual cognitions (attitudes, perceptions, intentions) is questioned by critical health psychologists, as is the implication that individuals alone are responsible for their health-related decisions and actions. By contrast, critical health psychologists situate health practices in relation to relevant social contexts (interpersonal, institutional, cultural ...) which often illuminate social constraints and alternative understandings which inform the health practices of individuals and communities. For example, a family reliant on state support may face limited choices around diet (health foods are often expensive) and exercise (gym membership can be costly); they may also construct 'unhealthy' practices in alternative, positive ways e.g. smoking as a form of stress relief, alcohol as pleasurable, lifestyle as a personal choice and so on. Such representations may seem irrational from a mainstream health psychology perspective, but from an 'insider' family or community angle seem perfectly acceptable and normative. So, the place and meaning of social, emotional and cultural values are central to critical health psychology accounts of health-related practices.

Critical health psychology

Critical health psychology has established itself over the past 10 years or so as a sizeable movement with members from across the globe. There is now an international association which holds conferences every two years (see Box 8.3), textbooks devoted to critical health psychology (e.g. Horrocks & Johnson, 2012; Murray, 2004), and journals which publish qualitative health research and critical perspectives (e.g. *Journal of Health Psychology*).

Box 8.3 What is critical health psychology?

The International Society of Critical Health Psychology (ISCHP) now hosts a website where an outline of CHP is provided:

> Members of the society espouse a variety of theoretical and methodological viewpoints. However, as with other critical psychologists, they share a common dissatisfaction with the positivist assumptions of much of mainstream psychology and its ignorance of broader social and political issues. Instead, they share an interest in various critical ideas (e.g. social constructionism, post-modernism, feminism, Marxism, etc.) and various qualitative and participatory methods of research (e.g. discourse analysis, grounded theory, action research, ethnography, etc.) and their relevance to understanding health and illness. Further, they share an awareness of the social, political and cultural dimensions of health and illness (e.g. poverty, racism, sexism, political oppression, etc.) and an active commitment to reducing human suffering and promoting improved quality of life, especially among those sections of society most in need.

Aims

- To promote increased debate about critical ideas, qualitative and participatory research methods, and social, political and cultural issues within health psychology.
- To facilitate contact and collaboration between critical health psychologists.
- To promote the development of resources and training opportunities in critical health psychology.

http://www.med.mun.ca/ischp/

The 2011 ISCHP conference in Adelaide, Australia advertised the following themes:

> We include presentations on any topic or theme that takes a critical stance on any aspect of health or health care. At the same time, we broadly organised the 2011 conference around five key themes:

- **Time:** health and health care in relation to life-events and life-stages, including child and family health;

- **Place:** health and health care in relation to the different politics, economics and social geographies of location, including, especially, the impact of colonisation (i.e., upon Indigenous health), migration and transition;
- **Face:** health and health care in relation to subjectivities and identities, including those relating to gender, sexuality and embodiment;
- **Governmentality:** health and, especially, health care in relation to strategies of social control, including rhetorics of 'choice', 'risk', 'freedom' and 'consumption';
- **Methods and methodology:** exploring alternative and innovative ways of conducting research in the pursuit of critical interpretations of health and health care.

http://www.adelaide.edu.au/ischp/

Unsurprisingly then, critical health psychologists are influenced by similar perspectives and methods as critical (social) psychologists, they take issue with mainstream (health) psychology, seek to address (health) inequalities and seek to recognize diverse voices and experiences. There is a general critique of liberal consumerist discourses which promote individual 'choice' and responsibility, and a commitment to situate health-related phenomena in appropriate contexts (e.g. temporal, spatial, political).

There is no one dedicated journal which publishes CHP research, but there are health psychology journals which publish some qualitative and critical work (e.g. *Journal of Health Psychology, Psychology & Health*), as well as a number of social and health sciences journals (e.g. *Sociology of Health & Illness; Health*). There are now also some textbooks devoted to critical health psychology, including Crossley (2000), Murray (2004), Lyons & Chamberlain (2006) and Horrocks & Johnson (2012). A wide range of topics are of interest to critical health psychologists (see Box 8.4), and although there is a preference for qualitative research methods, there is much diversity in the ways in which researchers collect and analyse their data. Here is a selection of titles referencing recently published CHP journal articles:

- Health inequalities and homelessness: considering material, spatial and relational dimensions.
- Understanding the impact of HIV diagnosis amongst gay men in Scotland: an interpretative phenomenological analysis.

235

- Emotional inhibition: a discourse analysis of disclosure.
- 'Real men don't diet': an analysis of contemporary newspaper representations of men, food and health.
- Alcohol consumption, gender identities and women's changing social positions.
- Sport, spinal cord injury and body narratives: a qualitative project.
- The social and cultural uses of ketamine.
- Medical and 'new age' approaches to breast cancer: a feminist critique.

CHP: research examples

As the above list of titles suggests, critical health psychologists study a wide range of topics. Here, we present some examples of critical health work: three summaries, and one extended example. The first summary describes a discursive study relating to parental accounts of Attention Deficit Hyperactivity Disorder, the second a qualitative investigation of gendered meanings and practices around binge drinking, while the third concerns a position paper which advocates a social rather than psychiatric understanding of mental health, with a focus on paranoia. The extended example (see Box 8.4) refers to a study with gay 'bears' and their accounts of body shape, lifestyle and health.

Resisting Ritalin: parental talk about treatment medication in childhood ADHD, Carol Gray (2009)

There is controversy around the existence, diagnosis and treatment of Attention Deficit Hyperactivity Disorder (ADHD) in children. This tendency towards the medicalization of childhood difficulties was criticized by Gray, who conducted a discourse analytic study of parents' and teachers' constructions of ADHD. A key finding related to parent's difficulty in challenging the prescription of medications such as Ritalin: they were either positioned as passive and powerless or unhelpfully resistant. Such tensions are complicated by discourses of parenthood which prioritize the protection and welfare of children, so objecting to proposed medical treatment risks being regarded as a 'bad' parent. By raising awareness of parental concerns and discussing alternative, non-medical ways of understanding and addressing challenging childhood behaviours, this critical health psychology work can help dismantle exclusively medicalized constructions of everyday practices.

For more details see:

Gray, C. (2009). 'Resisting' Ritalin: parental talk about treatment medication in childhood ADHD (Attention deficit hyperactivity disorder). Symposium presentation at the 6th International Society for Critical Health Psychology, Lausanne, 8–11 July 2009.

Alcohol consumption, gender identities and women's changing social positions, Antonia C. Lyons and Sara A. Willott (2008)

There is widespread alarm about 'binge drinking' and health effects across many Western societies, especially concerning young people. Young adults, including college students, are drinking more alcohol than ever before, particularly young women. Lyons & Willott set out to explore how young women see their drinking, and what role gender expectations play in drinking practices. To address this question, the authors conducted friendship discussion groups with men and women in their twenties. It was found that these young people regarded binge drinking as unremarkable, 'normal' and fun. At the same time, however, women who were drunk were judged to have transgressed traditional ideals of femininity. This work highlights the complex and sometimes contradictory discourses of femininity and health with which women are faced today, while also contrasting public health discourses (e.g. control) with lay discourses (e.g. pleasure).

For more details see:

Lyons, A. C. & Willott, S.A. (2008). Alcohol consumption, gender identities and women's changing social positions. *Sex Roles*, *59*, 694–712.

Paranoia: a social account, John Cromby & David Harper (2009)

This theoretical paper takes issue with dominant psychological and psychiatric views of distress as individual pathology. Based on experience of working with mental health charities and people struggling with difficult circumstances, as well as psychosocial and discursive perspectives, the authors focus on paranoia as an example of how 'mental illness' can be reconsidered in terms of multiple, mutually influential social and embodied events which come together at a given point. The implications of rejecting medicalized understandings of paranoia, and of promoting a social perspective, are discussed.

For more details see:

Cromby, J. & Harper, D. (2009). Paranoia: a social account. *Theory & Psychology*, *19*(3), 335–361.

Box 8.4 'Celebrating obese bodies...'

In their paper, 'Celebrating "obese" bodies: gay "bears" talk about weight, body image and health', Gough and Flanders (2009) describe a study with gay men who prefer larger bodies and who identify with a 'bear' community. Gay 'bears' tend to reject the thin and stylish ideal for gay men, and instead celebrate big, hairy 'masculine' bodies. In a society (UK) where obesity is commonly viewed as a health 'timebomb', linked with many major diseases such as cardiovascular conditions, diabetes and cancers, those who embrace larger physiques clearly subvert official health promotion advice. From a critical health psychology perspective, gay bears are interesting for occupying such a marginal position; in fact they could be seen as doubly disempowered: on the fringes of mainstream gay society and associated ideals of youth, style and slenderness, and on the periphery of mainstream heterosexist (and sizeist) society as gay men (and medically 'obese' in many cases). So, the study set out to understand a specific bear community, with a particular focus on constructions of body size and shape, health concerns and lifestyle practices. One of the authors (Flanders) identified as a gay bear himself and this 'insider' status helped to recruit participants for interview. Ten interviews were conducted, which were then transcribed and analysed using grounded theory techniques. The data were rich and complex, but one of the themes generated was 'big as healthy' in which the typical equation between slimness and health was subverted. For example, one of the participants, Eddie, says:

> I think because the bear community accepts each other in the way we are, the way we look, and there's not this, it's not as strong, that you have to fit into this, you've got to look like this, you've got to look pretty, you have to wear the latest label clothes, there doesn't seem to be any of that on the 'bear' scene, you get accepted for who you are, without wearing your glad rags, umm, I suppose the twink society, you stand sometimes in [a gay bar] and you see twinks looking at each other's waist and the label and if you have some hairs out of place they would scream their heads off, but with 'bears' they seem to be more masculine, they seem to be more down to earth, bloke next door type, men who just get on with their lives, allow people to be who they are. (244)

Here, thin gay men ('twinks') are portrayed as excessively preoc-cupied with appearance, superficial creatures who do not compare well with more 'masculine', 'down to earth' and mentally healthy bears. The interviewees also explicitly undermined psycho–medical standards of body weight, as Innes explains:

> I think, the 'bear' community does encourage you to remain the weight you are, provided you fit within these ranges, of overweight and obese, not skinny but not too big that you look ridiculous, the society BMI [Body Mass Index] would like me at 12 stone, the 'bear' community wants me to be meaty, the 'bear' community wins hand down because being this size changed my whole outlook on life, because I have, whether it's [name of a northern city], the fact that I've matured, I've got more friends here, than I ever had in my whole life. (249)

Here, bear and medical norms around body weight are contrasted, with the bear version clearly preferred on grounds of bodily comfort, social acceptance and personal development. Medical definitions of normal, healthy bodies are rejected: larger bodies are construed as healthy and attractive within a specific, identity-relevant context. Studies like this help to question automatic or narrow associations between 'obesity' and ill-health, and suggest that definitions of and investments in certain body sizes and shapes will undoubtedly vary between communities. As critical health psychologists, we can further investigate constructions of embodiment and health with other marginalized groups in order to highlight perspectives ordinarily invisible within mainstream behavioural medicine.

Reference:

Gough, B. & Flanders, G. (2009) Celebrating 'Obese' Bodies: Gay 'Bears' Talk about Weight, Body Image and Health, *International Journal of Men's Health*, 8(3), 235–253.

Critical health psychologists are interested in accounts of illness as well as health promotion activities, ranging from psycho-medical and psychiatric categories (such as ADHD, psychosis, depression: see above examples) to established conditions such as cancers, heart disease and diabetes. Often, this work contributes to a critique of narrow medical understandings of the illness in question e.g. questioning the effectiveness of medications (as in Gray's [2009] work on ADHD), highlighting problems with medical definitions, diagnoses and treatments (as in Cromby & Harper's [2009] social account of paranoia) or identifying different constructions of the illness in question (e.g. Horton-Salway's [2007] discursive study of 'chronic fatigue syndrome'). In some cases there may be an agenda to advocate for the perspective and rights of certain patient groups, or simply to present insights into living with a particular condition from an in-depth study. For example, Wilkinson's (2000) focus group study of women with breast cancer focuses on issues of loss, transition and transformation of self and relationships while impressing on the role of social support for women in this position.

The topic of peer support among patients is one which is receiving increasing attention from health researchers, funders and policy-makers. Indeed, patients are now often regarded as experts on their disease; in the UK at least, projects funded by the National Institute of Health Research are required to involve representatives from patient groups and members of the public at all stages (project conception, design, execution and dissemination – see http://www.involve.org.uk/). The phenomenon of patients supporting each other is perhaps apparent on the internet, where online support groups for all manner of illnesses and health issues have flourished. Clearly, internet sites and discussion forums allow flexibility of access, anonymity and the possibility of becoming more informed and empowered (Fletcher & St George, 2011); patients may well feel more inclined to challenge medical opinion following online engagement (Cohen & Raymond, 2011). For example, there are now numerous discussion forums for different types of cancer, and research can help identify how positive support is delivered and how patients benefit from participation in such online discussions (e.g. Gooden & Winefield, 2007). Box 8.5 highlights a recent discursive study by Seymour-Smith (forthcoming) focusing on online support forums concerning testicular cancer.

CHP: theories

As with critical psychology in general, critical health psychologists draw on a wide range of perspectives to help them understand health phenomena. For example, there is a long history of feminist-inspired research on women's' health which has sought to highlight women's' experiences, needs and concerns in health systems which are traditionally male-dominated. Feminist research is not just about raising

Box 8.5   How do men decide whether to have testicular implants for prostate cancer? (Seymour-Smith, forthcoming)

This study analysed discussion 'threads' which featured on four online support forums concerning decision making about testicular implants. A discursive psychology approach was adopted, focusing on how men 'did' support for each other. The importance of attending to the detail of posts and threads was emphasized, as responses to previous posts were 'recipient-designed' i.e. attended to the form and content of the previous post while saying something new or different. So, contributors were careful not to voice criticism of others when doing disagreement, used 'second stories' to affiliate with others (i.e. accounts of similar experiences) and build up credentials for offering advice, and used humour when covering delicate topics. For example, some of the men invoked new identity categories concerning their testicular situation:

> I had a testicle removed nearly 6 years ago and have never missed it. Everything works fine down below, As to being different it's had the opposite effect and possibly made me more confidant such as being proud of only having one. My friends nicknamed me womble (oneball). (Will)

> My feelings on the prosthetic come from a slightly different angle than most, as I am a TC'2er. As a member of the 'flat baggers' club, I get the sensation that no major changes have really taken place. (Frank)

In both cases, novel labels are applied to reconstruct a positive image of having only one testicle (Will) or none (Frank: TC 2'er means that he has had testicular cancer twice). Such categories minimize change and normalize the situation for the men and, arguably, challenge taken-for-granted representations of body image while celebrating diverse body (and testicular) configurations. Contributors were also seen to emphasize personal choice and autonomy in the decision-making process, and to police the expression of emotion, which were linked to the construction and maintenance of masculine identities.

awareness; often feminists advocate change and challenge practices which are thought to marginalize or disempower women in health contexts. Thus feminists do research, but they also advocate activism and intervention in order to improve the experiences and positions of women in health settings. Wilkinson (2004) helpfully summarizes forms of feminist health activism and feminist research traditions. In terms of activism, feminists:

- Organize women-centred institutions, events and publications (e.g. women's health centres);
- Challenge sexist claims and practices within medical science (e.g. about women being more prone to mental illness or over-using health services);
- Agitate for greater representation of women with health professions, and seek change from within (e.g. argue for more female surgeons and health managers);
- Conduct a range of feminist research projects (see below).

In terms of research feminists may utilize:

- Mainstream positivist traditions, whereby conventional scientific methods are adopted in the pursuit of rhetorically powerful knowledge about health phenomena – which can be used to challenge 'malestream' scientific knowledge claims (e.g. about the role of hormones in women's health);
- Experiential traditions, whereby qualitative methods are used to elicit women's personal accounts of health-related experiences, in their own words – which may bring to the forefront a range of voices which have historically been neglected (e.g interview and focus group studies with women who have contracted breast cancer);
- Discursive traditions, whereby dominant health-oriented discourses are identified and challenged, and women's own accounts are examined in order to highlight issues of accountability and morality which are made relevant during social interactions (e.g. questioning discourses of pregnancy and childbirth which position women as solely responsible caregivers; exploring issues of identity, responsibility and significance of anorexia with women diagnosed with this condition).

Critical health psychologists also look to other disciplines (e.g. medical sociology) and interdisciplinary work across the health and social sciences for theoretical resources. For example, Michel Foucault's work on 'govermentality' has been used to help understand the rise of self-surveillance and personal management of health care within Western neo-liberal societies (e.g. Rose, 1996). Indeed, citizens in the UK (and beyond) are strongly encouraged to monitor their intake of un/healthy items such as alcohol (how many units consumed per week, and is this amount within government set limits?), tobacco (what are you doing to cut down or give up cigarettes?) and diet (are you eating your five portions of fruit/vegetables per day?). The focus is very much on individual efforts to assess their lifestyle choices and make changes where they fall short of prevailing advice. A recent book by Sulkunen (2009) applies and updates Foucault's ideas to the arena of health promotion, where government and corporations advertise the importance of self-regulation to achieve fit and healthy bodies.

The work of another French theorist, Pierre Bourdieu, has also been used to help locate health practices in social and community contexts. Bourdieu's (1984) notion of social capital has been particularly influential in analysing the habits of social groups and subcultures: in any given community certain ideals and practices will be valued over others. For example, in some working class and socially deprived environments smoking may well be seen as normal and even desirable as a means of coping with poverty and marginalization (and not smoking may be regarded as odd or anti-social) (Graham, 2012). The consumption of alcohol, particularly beer, is valued by many men for its 'masculine' capital i.e. as a means of bestowing or bolstering male identities in (typically) homosocial situations (de Visser et al., 2009).

Much contemporary social theory focuses on the body, as illustrated by the number of published journal articles covering various aspects of embodiment as well as many books and dedicated journals (e.g. *Body & Society*). We have become a 'somatic society' in the words of Turner (1984), with the body a key resource for making and remaking identities in a consumerist and individualistic culture (Dworkin & Wachs, 2009; Featherstone, 2007; Giddens, 1991; Shilling, 2003). In Bourdieu's (1984) terms, the body is now a source of symbolic capital, a site which signals style, status and substance to others. Certain body shapes and sizes will exude social capital in any given community; for many men, the ideal may be a lean and muscular physique, while women may be encouraged to attain a slim and curvaceous body. Thus, many men and women influenced by such ideals may feel compelled to engage in body work or pursue specific 'body projects' in order to approximate the desired body shape, which could include physical exercise, dieting and cosmetic surgery. The seminal work of

Susan Bordo (1993; 1999) highlighted the pressures and contradictions that confront women and men in the face of consumerist and healthist discourses. The moral imperative that encourages body work places demands and pressures on the consumer that are contradictory. On one hand the consumer is invited to gratify their impulses and indulge in the hedonistic joys of food and passive leisure pursuits while on the other they are disciplined to delay and suppress their desires in order to attain the perfect body. Bordo (1993) notes:

> Consumer culture continually excites and encourages us to 'let go' indulge in our desires – for sugar, fat, sex, mindless entertainment. But at the same time burgeoning industries centered on diet, exercise, and body enhancement glamorize self-discipline and code fat as a symbol of laziness and lack of will power. It's hard to find a place of moderation and stability in all this, easy to fall into disorder. (p. xxi)

Eating disorders such as anorexia are evidence of the extreme measures that some individuals will go to in order to delay and suppress their desires, whereas obesity is an extreme example of giving in to one's desires. 'Both are rooted in the same consumer culture construction of desire as overwhelming and overtaking the self. Given that construction, we can only respond either with total submission or rigid defence' (Bordo, 1993: 201). The mandate for discipline clashes with the mandate for pleasure (Williams & Bendelow, 1998). 'In short, neoliberal governmentality produces contradictory impulses such that the neoliberal subject is emotionally compelled to participate in society as both out-of-control consumer and self-controlled subject' (Guthman & Du Puis, 2006: 444).

In considering the nature and ramifications of a body-conscious consumer culture, much attention has focused on the role of the mass media. Conventional health psychology work focuses on individual pathological variables such as cognitive vulnerability, ridged body schemas, self-focused attention, self-regulation, low self-esteem and attachment avoidance as potential causes (e.g. Strauman et al., 2010). This approach is generally coupled with a focus on the categorization of symptoms into a taxonomy of disorders. The other major problem with social–clinical theory in this area is that it treats social forces such as consumer culture as a merely contributory, facilitating or modulating factor. In response a number of critical feminist scholars argue that the ideology of consumer culture is not simply contributory, but *productive* of eating disorders (e.g. Bordo, 1993; Malson, 2009).

Consumer culture is seen to exert an enormous amount of pressure via inducements that facilitate the internalization of values that emphasize strict bodily surveillance and the linking of self-identity with bodily appearance (Thompson & Hirschman, 1995).

Social psychology's contribution to understanding eating disorders and disturbed body image has enhanced individual psychology's focus on intra-individual factors. It has achieved this by widening its focus by exploring eating disorders in relation to social-identity, group dynamics, social comparisons, attributions and attitudes. While this widened focus has certainly been necessary in gaining a more in-depth understanding of these problems, it still neglects to inquire into the social origins of these problems, and the dominant ideologies in which these disorders arise. For example, analyses that apply social comparison theory to understand eating disorders and disturbed body image (e.g. Dijkstra *et al.*, 2010) have so far failed to explore the historical antecedents of these behaviours and how they have changed over time as a result of changes in social, cultural, political and economic conditions. Secondly, social–clinical research fails to ask why people express a fundamental desire to compare themselves to others in the particular ways they have observed and documented in their research.

Social theorists and critical psychologists argue that it is not the social comparison processes per se that cause distress but their meaning in the context of consumer culture; a culture that commodifies the body (and self-identity), and where achieving the ideal body weight, height and shape have the potential to profoundly effect one's marketability and one's exchange value within peer groups and in society at large. Having the wrong body weight, height and shape can have very real material consequences for the person regardless of their individual predispositions. Bodily appearance has the potential to affect one's sexual desirability, career success, friendships, group memberships and the ability to create positive impressions in the minds of others. The desire to do whatever it takes to achieve the right body shape/image, whether conforming to a strict diet or undertaking cosmetic surgery, is in many respects a rational response to societal pressures. Eating disorders and a disturbed body image are far from being aberrant and idiosyncratic features of pathological individuals; instead they highlight the pressures, incitements, history and structures of power in consumer cultures that reward some and punish others on the basis of the appearance of their bodies (Heyes, 2009). Excessive body fat is punished because it illustrates that the individual is incapable of governing the self by exercising freedom in consumer choice. Such people are unable to take responsibility for the risks to their health that their choices pose and are therefore identified as having little value (Guthman & Du Puis, 2006). Nonetheless, media-generated and health-informed bodily ideals can be resisted (see Box 8.4 on 'gay bears'), and a range of body shapes and practices may be re-viewed in more positive ways in different social settings. In sum, critical health psychologists use concepts from social theory to under-stand and contextualize health-related and embodied ideals and practices, critique dominant discourses around health, lifestyle and the body, and explore alternative meanings and actions in previously subordinated social contexts.

Summary

Critical health psychologists are a mixed bunch – researchers, practi-tioners and community activists – but all are interested in moving beyond narrow psychological (and medical) conceptions of health-related phenomena. Although quantitative methods are not ruled out (e.g. feminist positivist work), there is a preference for qualitative research methods which are designed to promote the perspectives and needs of groups who have been traditionally overlooked or sidelined by mainstream research and service provision. Health practices are situated in relevant social contexts and understood from community and individual perspectives, and such 'insider' knowledge can be valuable in contesting prevailing definitions of health and wellbeing and shifting health policies to better incorporate the needs of margin-alized groups.

Key references

Crossley, M. (2000). *Rethinking Health Psychology*. Buckingham, UK: Open University Press.

Lyons, A.C. & Chamberlain, K. (2006). *Health Psychology: A Critical Introduction*. Cambridge: Cambridge University Press.

Murray, M. (ed.) (2004). *Critical Health Psychology*. Basingstoke, UK: Palgrave Macmillan.
These three textbooks provide students with a clear overview of critical health psychology, including key criticisms of mainstream health psychology and examples of critical research on a range of health-related topics.

New references

Barker, E.T., Greenberg, J.S., Selzer, M.M., Almeida, D.M. (2012). Daily stress and cortisol patterns in parents of adult children with a serious mental illness, *Health Psychology, 31*(1), 130–134.

Bordo, S. (1993). *Unbearable Weight: Feminism, Western Culture and the Body.* Berkeley: University of California Press.

Bordo, S. (1999). *The Male Body.* New York: Farrar, Straus and Giroux.

Bourdieu, P. (1984). *Distinction: a Social Critique of the Judgment of Taste* (Richard Nice, trans.) Cambridge, MA: Harvard University Press.

Cohen, J.H., & Raymond, J.M. (2011). How the internet is giving birth (to) a new social order. *Information, Communication & Society, 14*(6), 937–957.

Conner, M.T. and Norman, P. (eds). (2005). *Predicting Health Behaviour: Research and Practice with Social Cognition Models* (2nd edn). Maidenhead, UK: Open University Press.

Cox, A.D., Cox, D., Cryier, R., Graham-Doston, Y. & Zimet, G. D. (2012). Can self-prediction overcome barriers to Hepatitis B vaccination? A randomized controlled trial, *Health Psychology, 31*(1), 97–105.

Cromby, J., & Harper, D. (2009). Paranoia: a social account. *Theory & Psychology, 19*(3), 335–361.

Crossley, M. (2000). *Rethinking Health Psychology.* Buckingham, UK: Open University Press.

De Visser, Richard O, Smith, Jonathan A & McDonnell, Elizabeth J (2009). 'That's not masculine': masculine capital and health-related behaviour. *Journal of Health Psychology, 14*(7), 1047–1058.

Dijkstra, P., Gibbons, F. X., & Buunk, A. P. (2010). Social comparison theory. In J. E. Maddux & J. P. Tangney (eds), *Social Psychological Foundations of Clinical Psychology* (pp. 195–210). New York: Guilford Press.

Dworkin, S., & Wachs, F. L. (2009). *Body Panic: Gender, Health, and the Selling of Fitness.* New York: New York University Press.

Featherstone, M. (2007). *Consumer Culture and Postmodernism* (2nd edn). London: Sage.

Fletcher, R. & St George, J. (2011). Heading into fatherhood nervously: support for fathering from online dads. *Qualitative Health Research, 21*, 1101–1114.

Giddens, A. (1991). *Modernity and Self-Identity: Self and Society in the Late Modern Age.* Cambridge: Polity Press.

Gooden, R.J. & Winefield, H.R. (2007). Breast and prostate cancer online discussion boards: a thematic analysis of gender differences and similarities. *Journal of Health Psychology, 12*, 103–114.

Gough, B. & Flanders, G. (2009). Celebrating 'obese' bodies: gay 'bears' talk about weight, body image and health, *International Journal of Men's Health*, 8(3), 235–253.

Graham, H. (2012). Smoking, stigma and social class, *Journal of Social Policy*, 41(1), 83–99.

Gray, C. (2009). 'Resisting' Ritalin: Parental Talk about Treatment Medication in Childhood ADHD (Attention deficit hyperactivity disorder). Symposium presentation at the 6th International Society for Critical Health Psychology, Lausanne, 8–11 July 2009.

Guthman, J., & Du Puis, M. (2006). Embodying neoliberalism: economy, culture, and the politics of fat. *Environment and Planning D: Society and Space*, 24(3), 427–448.

Heyes, C. (2009). Diagnosing culture: body dysmorphic disorder and cosmetic surgery. *Body & Society*, 15(4), 73–93.

Horrocks, C., & Johnson, S. (eds). (2012). *Advances in Health Psychology: Critical Approaches*. Basingstoke, UK: Palgrave Macmillan.

Horton-Salway, M. (2007). The ME Bandwagon and other labels: constructing the authentic case in talk about a controversial illness. *British Journal of Social Psychology*, 46(4), 895–914.

Lyons, A. C. & Willott, S.A. (2008). Alcohol consumption, gender identities and women's changing social positions. *Sex Roles*, 59, 694–712.

Malson, H. (2009). Appearing to disappear: postmodern feminities and self-starved subjectivities. In H. Malson & M. Burns (eds) *Critical Feminist Perspectives On Eating Dis/Orders* (pp. 135–145). London: Routledge.

Mulvaney, S.A., Rothman, R.L., Dietrich, M.S. et al. (2012). Using mobile phones to measure adolescent diabetes adherence, *Health Psychology*, 31(1), 43–50.

Murray, M. (ed.). (2004). *Critical Health Psychology*. Basingstoke, UK: Palgrave Macmillan.

O'Connor, D.B., Jones, F.A., Conner, M.T., Abraham, C. (2011). A biopsycho-social approach to health psychology. In G. Davey (ed.). *Introduction to Applied Psychology* (pp. 151–169). Chichester: BPS Wiley-Blackwell.

Rivis, Abraham & Snook (2011). Understanding young and older male drivers' willingness to drive while intoxicated: the predictive utility of constructs specified by the theory of planned behaviour and the prototype willingness model, *British Journal of Health Psychology*, 16(2), 445–456.

Rose, N. (1996). *Inventing Our Selves: Psychology, Power, and Personhood*. Cambridge: Cambridge University Press.

Seymour-Smith (forthcoming). A reconsideration of the gendered mechanisms of support in online interactions about testicular implants: a discursive approach, *Health Psychology.*

Shilling, C. (2003). *The Body and Social Theory* (2nd edn). London: Sage.

Smith, J.A. (2004). Reflecting on the development of interpretative phenomenological analysis and its contribution to qualitative research in psychology. *Qualitative Research in Psychology, 1,* 39–54.

Strauman, T. J., McCrudden, M. C., & Jones, N. P. (2010). Self-regulation and psychopathology: toward an integrative perspective. In J. E. Maddux & J. P. Tangney (eds), *Social Psychological Foundations of Clinical Psychology* (pp. 84–113). New York: Guilford Press.

Sulkunen, P. (2009). *The Saturated Society: Governing Risk and Lifestyles in Consumer Culture.* London: Sage.

Thompson, C. J., & Hirschman, E. C. (1995). Understanding the socialized body: a poststructuralist analysis of consumers' self-conceptions, body images, and self-care practices. *Journal of Consumer Research, 22*(2), 139–153.

Turner, B. (1984). *The Body and Society: Explorations in Social Theory.* London: Sage.

Wilkinson, S. (2004). Feminist contributions to critical health psychology. In M. Murray (ed.). *Critical Health Psychology* (pp. 83–100). Basingstoke, UK: Palgrave Macmillan.

Wilkinson, S. (2000). Feminist research traditions in health psychology: breast cancer research. *Journal of Health Psychology, 5*(3), 353–366.

Williams, S.J. & Bendelow, G. (1998). *The Lived Body: Sociological Themes, Embodied Issues.* London: Routledge.

Critical Work
Psychology

9

This chapter will highlight:

- The history of work psychology
- Some of the social psychological literature applied to the work and organizational context
- Select critical theoretical perspectives, topics and studies applied to work and work psychology

Introduction

Social psychology has enjoyed a long tradition of informing theory, research and practice in the area of work psychology – also known as 'industrial and organizational psychology' (or I/O psychology for short), 'occupational psychology' or 'personnel psychology'. This comes as no surprise given the fundamentally social nature of organizations, which rely to a great extent on interdependent relations and work conducted in groups (or teams).

Work psychologists seek to improve the performance and profitability of organizations by carrying out research and practice in job design and analysis, psychometric testing (such as measuring personality, attitudes and cognitive abilities), motivating for performance, facilitating teamwork, improving decision making, teaching stress management techniques and developing leadership.

In the following discussion we review the history of work psychology, in particular its early successes and some of the research and theoretical perspectives that have come to dominate it. This is then followed by an analysis of social psychological theory that has been applied to the work and organizational context. We then analyse this body of work through a critical theoretical lens which we have divided into three parts: Marxist, Neo-Marxist, and epistemological and ontological criticisms.

History of work psychology

Work psychology first came into being in the early twentieth century as a result of increasing industrialization and the growing size of organizations, both of which presented a new set of challenges for their owners and managers. In many respects work psychology is a product of the twentieth-century Western emphasis on rationality, and the desire of owners/managers for greater efficiency and productivity in the workplace (Vinchur & Koppes, 2010).

The first and most prominent psychologists to apply psychological theories, research and interventions to the workplace included Hugo Munsterberg, James Cattell, Walter Bingham and Walter Dill Scott. In 1913 Munsterberg published *Psychology and Industrial Efficiency* in which he stated: 'Our aim is to sketch the outlines of a new science which is intermediate between the modern laboratory psychology and the problems of economics: the psychological experiment is systematically to be placed at the service of commerce and industry' (Munsterberg, 1913/1973: 3).

In its early years work psychology depended to a large extent on the 'advances in measurement and statistics, particularly the accurate measurement of individual differences'. It was also engaged in conducting research and practice on performance appraisal and training, employee welfare, leadership, motivation and job satisfaction (Vinchur & Koppes, 2010: 5). Braverman (1974) notes:

> The premise of industrial psychology was that, using aptitude tests, it was possible to determine in advance the suitability of workers for various positions by classifying them according to degrees of 'intelligence', 'manual dexterity', 'accident proneness', and general comformability to the 'profile' desired by management. (99)

Although still in its infancy, psychological testing was employed on a mass scale for the first time during the First World War (1914–18). Those in charge of the armed forces in the US and the UK were faced with the problem of how to place large numbers of civilians into military roles where they could best apply their skills and competencies. Testing was used by the military to assist with 'vocational guidance, systematic selection and promotion procedures, job design, (and) equipment design'. The success of these programmes garnered a new found respect for work psychology from both government and private industry as its various techniques for testing intelligence, aptitudes and personality, became accepted forms of workplace management, surveillance and control (Rose, 1999: 81–83).

Box 9.1   Scientific management: a revolutionary approach to job design and analysis

The principles of scientific management were first developed by Fredrick Taylor (1911/1967), an engineer by training whose seminal book *The Principles of Scientific Management* became a highly influential management guide and approach to workplace analysis and design in the early twentieth century. The extension of scientific principles to the workplace became an effective means for achieving increases in efficiency, productivity and profitability. Using a checklist and stopwatch Taylor 'observed and timed work, and then redesigned it, so that tasks could be done more efficiently' (Clegg *et al.*, 2008: 458). Taylor also advocated for the scientific selection and training of employees, and the separation of manual labour from mental labour, the former to be carried out by workers, the latter to be carried out by owners/managers, who by design, were placed in a position to control every aspect of the production process (Clegg *et al.*, 2008: 459).

In order to take advantage of the growing interest in the application of psychological research and theories to the workplace, the interwar period (1919–39) saw the growth in psychologists consulting to organizations. In 1921 the personality psychologist James Cattell founded The Psychological Corporation. It was Cattell's belief that psychology's application to understanding and controlling human behaviour in organizations would be as significant for civilization as the industrial revolution (Baritz, 1960: 192). The Psychological Corporation was set up initially as a public relations exercise to inform industrialists about the utility of applying psychological methods to industry. Slow in its initial growth, The Psychological Corporation eventually grew employing over 100 full-time staff and using the services of over 200 consultant psychologists in the marketing and application of psychological testing in the recruitment, promotion and assessment of employees (Baritz, 1960: 52–53; Vinchur & Koppes, 2010: 9–10).

In the United Kingdom the National Institute of Industrial Psychology was set up in 1921 under the direction of Charles Myer with the support of other leading psychologists, trusts and corporations. The institute sought to address workplace problems such as fatigue, industrial accidents and 'lost time' (Rose, 1999: 66–69).

Box 9.2   The Hawthorne studies and the human relations movement

From 1927 to 1932 the Australian psychologist Elton Mayo became involved in a series of studies conducted at the Hawthorne Plant of the Western Electric company on the outskirts of Chicago. The Hawthorne Studies (as they became known) challenged many of the basic assumptions underpinning scientific management. Mayo believed that greater emphasis on social and psychological techniques:

> could be incorporated into an enlightened management in such a way that the social-emotional needs of workers would be met; thus ending various kinds of irrational hostility in the factory and the 'need' for workers to unite in opposition to management (i.e. via unionization). (1933/1977)

Mayo (1933/1977) pioneered what became known as the 'human relations movement' which came to influence management thinking in the years that followed. His research highlighted the role of social relationships as mediators of productivity, and that a worker's motivation increased when management took a positive interest in them (this became known as the 'Hawthorne Effect'). Mayo's identification of the relational dimension of work stood in contrast to earlier understandings such as scientific management, which sought to control both labour and social processes in the workplace, and which viewed workers as little more than just machines. The Hawthorne Studies also undermined the assumption that workplace behaviour and performance could be accurately predicted by psychologically based testing (Braverman, 1974: 99). Mayo was not simply an indifferent scientific observer, but was concerned about the price paid by the worker in modern society, which he wrote, had destroyed 'the belief of the individual in his social function and solidarity with the group' (Mayo, 1933/1977: 159).

The advent of the Second World War (1939–45) saw work psychology once again play a prominent role in the selection and placement of military personnel. In the 20 years since the end of the First World War work psychologists had greatly refined their various techniques of psychometric testing and selection procedures.

> Each of the two world wars had a major effect on industrial psychology but in a somewhat different way. World War I helped form the profession and give it social acceptance. World War II helped refine it. The next era in the history of I/O psychology saw the discipline evolve into subspecialties and attain higher levels of academic and scientific rigour. (Muchinsky, 2008: 13–14)

Work psychology's growing emphasis on scientific rigour in the period following the Second World War reflected a wider movement in the science of psychology and social psychology at the time, which emphasized the testing of theory using experimental research designs, such as laboratory studies, where variables could be controlled and observed under greater scrutiny. This approach to understanding workplace behaviour solidified its position within the wider psychological sciences.

Box 9.3   Divisions, societies and colleges of work psychology

In Britain the British Psychological Society (BPS) hosts the Division of Occupational Psychology. On the division's website they define occupational psychology as the application of psychological methods to areas of critical relevance to business, including talent management, coaching, assessment, selection, training, organizational development, performance, well-being and work–life balance (http://www.dop.bps.org.uk/).

In the US the American Psychological Association (APA) hosts the Society for Industrial and Organizational Psychology. The APA defines I/O psychology as the application of psychology to all types of organizational and workplace settings, such as manufacturing organizations, commercial enterprises, labour unions and public agencies. Members work in several fields such as testing/assessment, leadership development, staffing, management, teams, compensation, workplace safety, diversity and work–life balance (http://www.apa.org/about/division/div14.aspx).

Applying social psychology to the workplace

In the period following the Second World War social psychological theories began to be applied more directly to the understanding of work and organizational behaviour. One of the earliest landmark applications was Brown's (1954) *Social Psychology and Industry*, which analysed workplace groups and their effects on attitudes, motivation and leadership. Brown also advocated the use of opinion surveys to be used by managers as a tool for understanding worker subjectivity. Brown's book was followed by Katz and Kahn's (1966) *The Social Psychology of Organizations*, which investigated workplace values, roles, motivation, leadership and health. Michael Argyle's (1989) *The Social Psychology of Work* (first published in 1972) continued the theme by analysing the role of technology, social organization and personality differences, and the effect these have on workplace motivation, leadership, training and personnel selection. Argyle argued that it was imperative that researchers draw on social psychology's positivist research tradition if they were to accurately understand organizational behaviour.

More recent applications of social psychology to the workplace include the edited collections *Social Identity at Work* (Haslam *et al.*, 2003), *The Social Psychology of Organizational Behavior* (Thompson, 2003a) and *Social Psychology and Organizations* (De Cremer *et al.*, 2011). All three edited books draw on a range of social psychological theory including personality and individual differences, social identity theory, attitudes, motivation, group dynamics, teamwork, attribution theory, cognitive dissonance and leadership. There are also various chapters devoted to analysing organizational behaviour in edited books on applied social psychology, which draw on similar topics and theories to those noted above (e.g. Brehm *et al.*, 2005: 478–511; Coutts & Gruman, 2005; Van Der Zee & Paulus, 2008).

In our reading of the applied social psychology literature through a critical theoretical lens, four key issues emerged. These include the valorization of a positivist (experimental) epistemology and individualistic ontology, identification with an owner/management perspective on workplace issues and problems, a focus on intra-psychic variables or internal mental states when accounting for organizational problems, and the absence of a clear moral and ethical framework for determining workplace research and practice.

Thompson (2003b), for example, asserts that applied social psychology advances by employing experimental research methodologies, in particular the hypothetico–deductive method. He explains:

'researchers develop a hypothesis derived from theory and then design an experiment that will allow cause-and-effect conclusions from the results. This is in contrast to folk wisdom or qualitative ethnographic research' (Thompson, 2003b: 2). The valorization of the hypothetico–deductive method and the denigration of qualitative methods which Thompson implicitly links to folk wisdom, is given further credence in the final chapter of his edited book, which provides a guide on 'how to read a journal article in social psychology'. At no point in this guide is there any reference to research designs other than those that subscribe to a narrowly conceived positivist epistemology (Jordan & Zanna, 2003).

The second key issue to emerge in the applied social psychology literature is that it takes for granted established relations between the interests of capital regarding organizational behaviour and the interests of the individual employee, usually at the expense of the latter. This can be seen in the way it ignores workplace unions and the power relations that exist between workers and owner/managers. In cases where the issue of power is raised it is understood as a resource attached to positions of authority within an organizational hierarchy. These positions of authority and the power invested in them are treated as naturally occurring phenomenon and accepted as inevitable features of the workplace (e.g. Coutts & Gruman, 2005; Galinsky *et al.*, 2011). In this respect authority and the power relations that maintain them are naturalized and normalized (Clegg, 2011). The question for applied social psychologists is not whether modes of authority and the structures that maintain them are fair and equitable. Instead the question of power is either ignored, isolated to individual influence or becomes one of how best to manage and negotiate it, with a view to gaining optimum efficiency and productivity out of workers.

The third key issue to emerge from the applied social psychological literature is that it focuses almost exclusively on intra-psychic variables or internal mental states in its understanding of organizational behaviour. Issues related to the politics and economics of work are viewed as the domain of sociologists, political scientists and economists (Thompson, 2003b: 2), despite their significant influence on organizational behaviour (e.g. McDonald *et al.*, 2008). The fourth issue to emerge is that the applied social psychological literature lacks a clear moral and ethical framework for determining workplace research and practice. In all of the works cited above there were only fleeting mentions of moral and ethical practice related to research and consulting activities. There was one chapter by Pillutla (2011) that investigated the topic of morals. However, this analysis was taken from the perspective of an individual's potential for moral behaviour in the workplace. Pillutla's chapter is in many respects characteristic of the applied social psychological literature more generally, which views issues of morality and ethical practice as one that pertains solely to the individual worker and their behaviour.

Box 9.4 A mainstream social psychology study applied to work

A recent paper published in the *Journal of Applied Psychology* by Kim and Glomb (2010) is entitled 'Get smarty pants: cognitive ability, personality, and victimization'. This paper examines the relationship between cognitive ability and victimization at work, based on the 'victim precipitation model'. More specifically, it is proposed that people high in cognitive ability are more prone to victimization. The role of personality is also examined, with a focus on agency and communion. The findings support the authors' hypothesis i.e. that high cognitive ability is linked to victimization at work. This relationship is seen to be moderated by personality: agency personality traits strengthen the relationship of cognitive ability and victimization, whereas communion personality traits weaken this relationship.

This is a typical example of a study that employs a hypothetico–deductive research design (a positivist research method) for understanding workplace behaviour related to a core social psychological topic (personality). The purpose of the study is to understand the relationship between cognitive ability and workplace victimization. It asks whether victims of workplace bullying are more likely to be viewed by their fellow employees as 'smart' and 'talented'. The authors then hypothesize that the degree to which a person with a high level of cognitive ability will be victimized will depend on their personality – in particular whether they are high on the personality traits 'agency' and 'communion'. The authors tested each of these variables (cognitive ability, victimization, agency and communion) using a series of pre-established measures/scaled items purported to have high levels of validity (the extent to which the questionnaire collects information reflecting the variable under investigation) and reliability (the extent to which the findings from the questionnaire would be repeated if subsequent tests were retaken at a later stage by the same individuals). The questionnaires were then administered to a sample of employees working in health care homes. The data from the questionnaires were then statistically analysed in order to confirm or disconfirm five different hypotheses proposed at the outset of the study.

Studies of this nature assume that variables like 'cognitive ability' and their casual relationship to other variables are explicable (that is capable of being understood and explained) via statistical analysis. As we will see in the next section critical social psychologists are sceptical of these claims believing that variables like cognitive ability, and personality traits such as agency and communion are not elements of objective reality that have been discovered by social scientists, but are instead ways of interpreting the world that reflect underlying social, cultural, political and economic ideologies. Critical social psychologists would also argue that viewing victimization from the perspective of personality only limits our understanding of the phenomenon. The causes of workplace victimization are likely to be much more complex and multi-dimensional. While victimization will almost certainly have a negative psychological effect on its target, its occurrence may well be caused by a wider range of social forces. For example, a dysfunctional organizational culture, poor leadership, recent cut backs in budgets, external competition or the threat of downsizing as a result of an economic recession.

Critical work psychology

Marxist critiques

Unlike health psychology (see Chapter 8), critiques of work and its analysis have a long and prominent history that began with the nineteenth-century philosopher, economist and social scientist Karl Marx. Marx was highly critical of the degrading workplace conditions that accompanied the growth of capitalism and industrialization in Western Europe during the eighteenth and nineteenth centuries. Marx observed that the organization of work around capitalist economic principles ran counter to healthy social interactions and relations because it denied workers the potential to actualize their creative and spiritual needs (Fromm, 1962/2009). This led to the estrangement of the individual from themselves, others and society, an experience that Marx referred to as 'alienation'. The causes of alienation include the subordination of work to the owners of the workplace (the control of work by a small minority of capitalist owners), the increasing techno-logical means of production, the increase in wealth for the owners of capital at the expense of workers (referred to by Marx as the extraction of 'surplus value') and the increasing 'division of labour' (the division of work into its smallest component parts, which makes it repetitive, dull and frequently dangerous) (Marx, 1844/1964). Under capitalist conditions the subjective experience of work is dominated by political and economic forces that workers have little to no control over. So that alienation (or estrangement) means for Marx:

> that man does *not* experience himself as the acting agent in his grasp of the world, but that the world (nature, others and he himself) remain alien to him. They stand above and against him as objects, even though they may be objects of his own creation. Alienation is essentially experiencing the world and oneself passively, recep-tively. (Fromm, 1961/2004: 37; emphasis added)

This estrangement of the product from the creator (worker) who produced it occurs most acutely in the division of labour because the worker is separated from producing the product in its entirety, from its conception, design, labour, completion and sale to the consumer. The worker under capitalist modes of production completes only a fraction of the overall production process, becoming less a creative agent in control of the work process, and more a small cog in a large imper-sonal machine. The consumer is also separated from the product they purchase because they become isolated from the worker who produced it, so that little importance is attributed to the labour that was used to create it (Marx, 1867/2004). This stands in contrast to the pre-capitalist era where a product or service derived its value from the labour, know-how and ingenuity that went into it; it was understood and valued because of the social interactions and relations invested into it.

Despite the alienation and exploitation that workers experience under capitalist modes of production, Marx observed that workers rarely question the conditions they labour under, accepting them as inevitable outcomes of the system. In his attempt to understand why this might be, Marx developed his theory of ideology to account for the ways in which people think about themselves, others and society. In this theory Marx proposed that thinking is influenced by the ideas that a particular society develops, and these ideas are determined by the economics and politics of that society (Fromm, 1962/2009: 9). For Steger and Roy (2010) ideology is defined as:

systems of widely shared ideas and patterned beliefs that are accepted as truth by significant groups in society ... ideologies organize their core ideas into fairly simple truth games that encourage people to act in certain ways. These claims are assembled by codifiers of ideologies to legitimize certain political interests and to defend and challenge dominant power structures. (11)

Life under the influence of capitalist ideologies creates what Marx's fellow author Fredrich Engels termed 'false consciousness'. Much social psychological theory is based on the assumption that human beings are free thinking, free acting agents, in control of their behaviour, which stems from their own subjective will. In contrast, Marx and Engels observed that social behaviour is largely determined by historical, political and economic forces (Fromm, 1962/2009: 82). The degradation of work for example is falsely conceived as a natural state of affairs, which determines that workers aggressively compete against one another for scarce resources, and that the free market (referred to in contemporary society as 'neoliberalism') allocates these resources in a fair and equitable manner based on an individual's intellect, work ethic and moral resolve. Capitalist historical, political and economic forces, and the values and beliefs they maintain, generate unbridled individualism, aggression, egotism and self-seeking in the workplace, so that workers 'live in an atmosphere of mutual hostility rather than solidarity' (Mandel & Novack, 1970: 77). Therefore it is not workers who are set free by aggression and competition; 'it is, rather capital which is set free' (Marx (1857/1973: 650)). The organization of work around capitalist economic principles is actually antithetical to the concept of society (Augoustinos, 1999).

Aggression and intense competition in the workplace (and that which occurs between groups, organizations and nation states) is beneficial to capital, and the owners of capital, whose ideas of the natural social order exert a 'hegemony' over workers. That is the owners of capital and other business and political elites, subordinate workers to internalize and accept their moral and cultural values, so they become dominated through a mixture of coercion and sponta-neous consent, reinforcing their own servitude (Gramsci, 1971). Business and political elites seek to win the hearts and minds of the people, 'persuading them (without even seeming to do so, or need to do so) that the status quo is natural and inevitable, beneficial for all, and inducing them to identify with it' (Crossley, 2005: 114). Workers and non-workers (the unemployed, pensioners, people with disabil-ities and those suffering mental illness) living on the lower rungs of society come to believe that their station in life is the result of their own lack of moral resolve, accepting their impoverished state.

Neo-Marxist Critiques

Despite the fact that Marx's workplace observations are now over 150-years old and that assembly lines and factories have been replaced with offices, desks and computers, many of his insights are just as relevant today as they were in the ninetieth century, particularly in light of the continuing application of scientific management techniques to the contemporary workplace (Braverman, 1974: 59–85; Ritzer, 2010: Sennett, 2006: 105–115). Scientific management ensures that owners/managers maintain a monopoly over knowledge and decision making, while workers are de-skilled and turned into automatons (Braverman, 1974: 86–95; Edwards, 1979; Morgan, 2006: 22–26). These conditions are maintained by work psychologists whose methods of research and practice are based on managerial assumptions about workplace behaviour. Work psychologists, in conjunction with owner/managers, maintain strict hierarchies of authority; they exercise power that maintains existing inequalities through pre-defined job descriptions and social relations between workers and owner/managers (Islam & Zyphur, 2009; Parker, 2007).

The focus of management (and by default the application of social psychology to the workplace) has always been on the needs of capital (Baritz, 1960: 196–205). The success or otherwise of a manager and their organization is measured, in the first instance, by their contribution to the annual balance sheet. Any intervention designed and implemented by work psychologists is typically justified in terms of its potential to improve the financial bottom line; that such interventions improve the experience of work is secondary (Baritz, 1960; Braverman, 1974; Lefkowitz, 2003). In many cases research and interventions implemented by work psychologists have resulted in the maintenance of degrading workplace conditions. For example, psychologists have worked with managers to weaken the influence of collective bargaining rights in the form of workplace unions and union membership, which has led to union mistrust of psychologists. Zickar (2001) conducted an analysis of personnel management magazines published from 1930 to 1945. He found that managers used personality testing to screen for psychopathologies, which were assumed to be related to a predisposition to union involvement (see also Baritz, 1960: 202). Work psychologists have also conducted research on the predictive relationship between attitudes towards work and level of union activity, in order to provide managers with a measure of employees who are likely to disrupt the workplace with their union involvement (Hamner & Smith, 1978; Schrieshiem, 1978). Huszczo *et al.* (1984: 434–435) found that the privileging of quasi-scientific narratives over the worker's own experience is illustrative of psychology's typical siding with owner/managers. This is due firstly to the emphasis on scientific approaches by managers (efficiency, productivity and profit over human factors), secondly that unions have been largely ignored in psychological research and thirdly, that work psychology interventions have been used to obstruct or bust unions and other forms of collective organizing.

Some work psychologists have hit back at these criticisms describing them as unfair, arguing their research and practice actually functions as a tempering influence on scientific management, and that work psychology has been at the vanguard of promoting more humane approaches to workplace relations (e.g. Vinchur & Koppes, 2010). Despite the efforts of psychologists, however, scientific management continues to exert a significant influence over the contemporary workplace. The prominent American sociologist George Ritzer (2010) has conducted a number of studies into the continuing use of scientific management principles, particularly its application to the service sector where the majority of workers in first world countries are now employed (e.g. transportation, health care, retail, tourism, administration etc.). Ritzer has observed that many service sector organizations use the operations manual of the fast food giant McDonald's as a template to guide job analysis and design. As a result work in many service sector industries has become highly routine, repetitive, temporary and devoid of career characteristics (Gorz, 1989, 1999). Ritzer refers to this process as 'McDonaldization', which applies four highly rational scientific principles to workplace analysis and design. These include: (1) Efficiency (the most optimal method to conduct a workplace task), (2) Calculability (every workplace task should be quantifiable), (3) Predictability (workers provide standardized and uniform services), (4) Control (standardized and uniform workers).

The continued use of scientific management principles in the contemporary workplace however cannot be blamed on work psychologists. However, work psychologists have shown an unwillingness to publicly criticize or lobby against contemporary forms of scientific management. As a result work psychologists have become the maintenance crew for the workers who labour under it. Braverman (1974) notes:

The successors to Taylor are to be found in engineering and work design, and in top management; the successors to Munsterberg and Mayo are to be found in personnel departments and schools of industrial psychology…. Work itself is organized according to Taylorian principles, while personnel departments and academics have buried themselves with the selection, training, manipulation, pacification, and adjustment of 'manpower' to suit the work processes so organized. Taylorism dominates the world of production; the practitioners of 'human relations' and 'industrial psychology' are the maintenance crew for the human machinery. (60)

As Braverman argues, it was the Hawthorne Studies that led to psychologists taking a major stake in the organization of working life. They did this by instituting a therapeutic approach to workplace problems, which assumed that conflicts between management and workers stemmed from problems with individual adjustment and psychopathology, as opposed to the 'defective structural organization of capitalism' (Illouz, 2008: 73). Owners/managers are encouraged by psychologists to help their workers better adjust to the alienating conditions of work, not through direct control and coercion, but in providing for their emotional needs by facilitating open channels of communication and empathy (Illouz, 2008). The control of a workers' body in the form of physical labour has been replaced by the control of a worker's subjectivity, whereby their acceptance of the alienating conditions of work is obtained by encouraging them to internalize desires for a 'career', promotion, monetary gain and in the acquisition of consumer products and services (Beder, 2001; Berardi, 2009).

Ontological and epistemological critiques

In light of the criticisms noted above a key weakness of work psychology (and its use of social psychological theory) is its adherence to a positivist research tradition, which subscribes to a value free science that claims to be impartial and politically neutral. In its attempt to remain 'value free' work psychology has allowed itself to be co-opted by the interests of capital. For example, the measurement of human functioning and performance in the workplace has helped to maintain highly rational capitalist modes of production, which manipulate and exploit workers for the purpose of increasing profit (Carrette, 2003: 73–74; Hollway, 1998; Parker, 2007: 55–73). Not only has work psychology's illusion to an apolitical science created a moral and ethical void in much of its research and practice (Lefkowitz, 2003), but it has also allowed work psychologists to back away from the moral and ethical implications of their work, and to be absolved (at least in their own minds) of the responsibility for their research and consulting activities, which in the majority of cases is contractually defined and controlled by owner/managers representing the interests of capital (Baritz, 1960: 199; Islam & Zyphur, 2009).

Work psychology's adherence to an epistemology based on 'positivist' research methods and an ontology based on 'individualism' has been influenced in large part by its alliance with experimental social psychology. This has meant that work psychology has become un-reflexively caught up in a web of power relations which it ignores. This is despite the recognition by Vinchur and Koppes (2010: 28) that 'the management perspective has been the dominant one in the history of I/O psychology' and that 'this does not necessarily mean that I/O psychologists are anti-worker'. While the majority of work psychologists are genuine in their desire to improve the workers' lot, their research, theories and practice are only as good as the philosophies and theories that underpin them. At present work psychologists show a collective lack of reflexivity in how their research and practice maintains capital and managerial interests at the expense of workers (Baritz, 1960; Blackler & Brown, 1978; Bramel & Friend, 1981; Braverman, 1974; Islam & Zyphur, 2006, 2009; Lefkowitz, 2003).

In his pioneering text *Social Psychology*, published in 1924, Floyd Allport solidified the field's adherence to an individualistic ontology, as the following quote illustrates: 'There is no psychology of groups which is not essentially and entirely a psychology of individuals' (cited in Hogg & Vaughan, 2005: 116). This ontology, which has been applied to the understanding of workplace behaviour by social psychologists (e.g. Thompson, 2003b: 1), effectively separates the individual worker from their organizational and social world. Its singular emphasis on the individual locates the *social* inside the individual's mind (Burr, 2002; Moscovici, 1972), effectively delegitimizing the historical, social, cultural, political and economic forces that influence and shape workplace behaviour.

Work psychology's focus on intra-psychic processes (e.g. personality traits, cognitive abilities, attitudes etc.), lies outside the imperatives of most workers who regard these as having less importance in the workplace when compared to the more dynamic and influential issues of power, justice, equality, politics and ideology (Alvesson & Deetz, 2005; Steffy & Grimes, 1992). Social psychology's positivist approach 'leads to fragmented and specific explanations of organizational phenomena, but does little to increase our understanding of the real complexities of organizational life' (Steffy & Grimes, 1992: 187). Its unwillingness to analyse and better understand the influence that political and economic forces play in organizational behaviour, and moreover its acceptance of them as natural and inevitable, means that it blinds itself to issues that maintain unjust working conditions (see Box 9.5). For example work psychology:

[L]egitimised the individualisation of social and economic relations by working within a (scientific) psychological framework. Political dynamics (like inherent conflicts of interest between owners and workers) became reframed as problems between individuals to be managed using psychological technologies. Accordingly, applied psychology was offering a technical 'fix' for political tensions and the experience of alienated labour was rendered a problem of stress, neurosis or adjustment. (Pilgrim & Treacher, 1992: 30)

Social psychology's influence on work psychology's ontology and epistemology has also greatly constrained its ability to offer effective long-term solutions to workplace problems. Employing positivist research methods has led to delimited definitions of workplace stress, job satisfaction and absenteeism (to name just a few), which are viewed through an intra-psychic prism. Problems such as these are seen to stem from personality traits such as extraversion and neuroticism (Furnham, 1994; Furnham & Heaven, 1999: 196–198; Sterns *et al.*, 1983), a person's locus of control (Burger, 1985) or their level (or lack) of self-efficacy (Jex & Bliese, 1999).

The problem with these studies and others like it is that they narrow their focus of analysis to psychological processes and symptoms only, instead of trying to understand what the origins of these psychological problems are, and to look at ways of changing the wider organizational or external workplace conditions that drive them. Their failure to consider these external factors greatly diminishes its practical utility. The danger is that work psychologists end up attributing workplace stress (as just one example) to a worker's inability to adjust to the alienating conditions of the modern workplace (e.g. Argyle, 1989: 278–284; Haslam & van Dick, 2011). As a result workers end up blaming themselves for political and economic conditions they have little or no control over. Rose (1999) notes:

Whatever their professed concerns, the psychologists of organizations and occupations have colluded in the invention of more subtle ways of adjusting the worker, based upon the happy but not altogether innocent illusion that industrial discontent, strikes, absenteeism, low productivity and so forth do not derive from fundamental conflicts of interest but from ameliorable properties of the psychological relations of the factory. (58)

Box 9.5   Critical management studies

Critical Management Studies (CMS) is a loose amalgam of scholars that draw on a range of critical theoretical perspectives (e.g. Marxism, poststructualism, social constructionism, postcolonialism and feminism), which collectively challenge several key assumptions which underpin the authority and relevance of mainstream thinking and practice related to management, business and organizational studies. CMS proceeds from the assumption that:

> dominant theories and practices of management and organization systematically favor some (elite) groups and/or interests at the expense of those who are disadvantaged by them; and that this systemic inequality or interest-partiality is ultimately damaging for the emancipatory prospects of all groups. (Alvesson *et al.*, 2011: 7).

CMS scholars seek to 'denaturalization' taken-for-granted thinking around the nature of work and are committed to tracing the power relations that structure and maintain inequality in the workplace. CMS scholars are also committed to 'epistemological reflexivity', which states that researchers need to recognize that the production of knowledge around management and organisations by universities, think-tanks, corporations and governments, is influenced by the researcher's own beliefs and values, as well as the beliefs and values of the funding institution, whatever that institution might be. Scientific knowledge is therefore seen as a product of the social, economic, political and cultural forces that underpin a particular society, at a given time in history (Grey & Willmott, 2005: 6; Tadajewski *et al.*, 2011: 3).

Conclusion

From its inception work psychology has functioned by supporting capitalist and now neoliberal modes of workplace analysis and design by instituting methods of quantification and measurement of work related to phenomenon such as personality, cognitive abilities, attitudes and job satisfaction. A critique of this body of work from a Marxist and Neo-Marxist perspective argues that work organized around the principles of capitalist/neoliberal economics is often degrading and alienating for workers. These degrading conditions were found to be unwittingly supported and maintained by work psychologists whose positivist epistemology and individualistic ontology maintains capital and managerial interests at the expense of workers.

A critical approach calls for a reorientation of the basic assumptions that guide work psychology research and practice, starting with a recognition that the workplace is influenced as much by the politics and economics of our respective era as it is by a worker's personality traits, locus of control or their level of self-efficacy. Taking a critical approach to work psychology recognizes the ways in which ideologies and power relations disadvantage and marginalize certain groups in the work context. It also emphasizes the taking of a reflexive stance on its research and practice so that it can move beyond its current limited scope, to an approach which takes account of the external forces which drive workplace conditions as well as making it more aware of its own unconscious or implicit values and political allegiances. Moving beyond an individualistic ontology would lead to more effective and sustainable solutions to workplace problems whose focus would be less about 'fixing the individual' and more about calling for workers to have greater freedom and control over the ways in which work is organized in contemporary society. In this respect, an engagement with critical social psychology not only deconstructs the leading theories in work psychology, but it also has the potential to expand them.

Key references

Hollway, W. (1998). Fitting work: psychological assessment in organizations. In J. Henriques, W. Hollway, C. Urwin, C. Venn & V. Walkerdine (eds), *Changing the Subject: Psychology, Social Regulation and Subjectivity* (Rev edn, pp. 26–59). London: Routledge.
In this chapter Hollway analyses how psychology is used to measure and evaluate individuals in organizations in order to differentiate between them and for the purpose of prediction and control. She argues that psychological technologies such as psychometric testing are used as a form of social regulation in the workplace.

Islam, G., & Zyphur, M. (2006). Critical industrial psychology: what is it and where is it? *Psychology and Society, 34*, 17–30.

Islam, G., & Zyphur, M. (2009). Concepts and directions in critical industrial/ organizational psychology. In D. Fox, I. Prilleltensky & S. Austin (eds), *Critical Psychology: An Introduction* (2nd edn, pp. 110–125). Thousand Oaks, CA: Sage.

In both of these contributions Islam and Zyphur critique I/O psychology for its unspoken managerial assumptions about organizational behaviour. Like Hollway they argue that I/O psychology views individuals in organizations in terms of objective traits and resources, instead of subjective potentials.

Prilleltensky, I. & Nelson, G. (2002). Chapter 10 – Work settings: working critically within the status quo. In Prilleltensky, I., Nelson, G., & Geoffrey, B. (eds), *Doing Psychology Critically: Making a Difference in Diverse Settings*. Basingstoke, UK: Palgrave Macmillan.

Prilleltensky, Nelson and Geoffrey's book takes theory and research in critical psychology and applies it to range of domains. In chapter 10 the authors discuss how critical psychology can be used to guide thinking that deconstructs power discourses in the workplace and practices that aim to reduce inequality through the establishment of partnerships for solidarity.

New References

Alvesson, M., & Deetz, S. A. (2005). Critical theory and postmodern approaches to organizational studies. In S. Clegg, C. Hardy, T. Lawrence & W. R. Nord (eds), *The Sage Handbook of Organization Studies* (2nd edn, pp. 255–283). London: Sage.

Alvesson, M., Bridgman, T., & Willmott, H. (2011). Introduction. In M. Alvesson, T. Bridgman & H. Willmott (eds), *The Oxford Handbook of Critical Management Studies* (pp. 1–26). Oxford: Oxford University Press.

Argyle, M. (1989). *The Social Psychology of Work* (Rev edn). London: Penguin.

Augoustinos, M. (1999). Ideology, false consciousness and psychology. *Theory & Psychology, 9*(3), 295–312.

Baritz, L. (1960). *The Servants of Power: A History of the Use of Social Science in American Industry*. New York: Wiley.

Beder, S. (2001). *Selling the Work Ethic: From Puritan Pulpit to Corporate PR*. London: Zed Books.

Berardi, F. (2009). *The Soul at Work: from Alienation to Authority* (F. Cadel & G. Mecchia, Trans.). Los Angeles: Semiotext.

Blackler, F., & Brown, C. A. (1978). Organizational psychology: good intentions and false promises. *Human Relations, 31*, 333–351.

Bramel, D., & Friend, R. (1981). Hawthorne, the myth of the docile worker, and class bias in psychology. *American Psychologist, 36*, 867–878.

Braverman, H. (1974). *Labor and Monopoly Capital: The Degradation of Work in the Twentieth Century.* New York: Monthly Review Press.

Brehm, S. S., Kassin, S. M., & Fein, S. (2005). *Social Psychology* (6th edn). Boston, MA: Houghton Mifflin.

Brown, J. A. C. (1954). *Social Psychology and Industry: Human Relations in the Factory.* Harmondsworth, UK: Penguin.

Burger, J. (1985). Desire for control and achievement related behaviours. *Journal of Personality and Social Psychology, 46,* 1520–1533.

Burr, V. (2002). *The Person in Social Psychology.* London: Routledge.

Carrette, J. (2003). Psychology, spirituality and capitalism: the case of Abraham Maslow. *Critical Psychology, 8,* 73–95.

Clegg, S. (2011). Power. In M. Tadajewski, P. Maclaran, E. Parsons & M. Parker (eds), *Key Concepts in Critical Management Studies* (pp. 194–197). London: Sage.

Clegg, S., Kornberger, M., & Pitsis, T. (2008). *Managing and Organizations: An Introduction to Theory and Practice* (2nd edn). London: Sage.

Coutts, L. M., & Gruman, J. A. (2005). Applying social psychology to organizations. In F. W. Schneider, J. A. Gruman & L. M. Coutts (eds), *Applied Social Psychology: Understanding and Addressing Social and Practical Problems* (pp. 229–256). Thousand Oaks, CA: Sage.

Crossley, N. (2005). *Key Concepts in Critical Social Theory.* London: Sage.

De Cremer, D., van Dick, R., & Murnighan, K. J. (eds). (2011). *Social Psychology and Organizations.* London: Routledge.

Edwards, R. (1979). *Contested Terrain: The Transformation of the Workplace in the Twentieth Century.* New York: Basic Books.

Fromm, E. (1961/2004). *Marx's Concept of Man* (T. B. Bottomore, Trans.). London: Continuum.

Fromm, E. (1962/2009). *Beyond the Chains of Illusion: My Encounter with Marx and Freud.* New York: Continuum.

Furnham, A. (1994). *Personality at Work: Individual Differences in the Workplace.* London: Routledge.

Furnham, A., & Heaven, P. (1999). *Personality and Social Behaviour.* London: Arnold.

Galinsky, A. D., Rus, D., & Lammers, J. (2011). Power: a central force governing psychological, social, and organizational life. In D. De Cremer, R. van Dick & K. J. Murnighan (eds), *Social Psychology and Organizations* (pp. 17–38). London: Routledge.

Gramsci, A. (1971). *Selections from the Prison Notebooks of Antonio Gramsci* (Q. Hoare & G. Nowell Smith, Trans.). London: Lawrence & Wishart.

Grey, C., & Willmott, H. (2005). Introduction. In C. Grey & H. Willmott (eds), *Critical Management Studies: A Reader* (pp. 1–15). Oxford, UK: Oxford University Press.

Gorz, A. (1989). *The Critique of Economic Reason*. London: Verso.

Gorz, A. (1999). *Reclaiming Work: beyond the Wage-Based Society* (C. Turner, Trans.). Cambridge: Polity Press.

Hamner, W. C., & Smith, F. J. (1978). Work attitudes as predictors of unionization activity. *Journal of Applied Psychology, 63*, 415–421.

Haslam, S. A., & van Dick, R. (2011). A social identity approach to workplace stress. In D. De Cremer, R. van Dick & K. J. Murnighan (eds), *Social Psychology and Organizations* (pp. 325–352). New York: Routledge.

Haslam, S. A., van Knippenberg, D., Platow, M. J., & Ellemers, N. (eds). (2003). *Social Identity at Work: Developing Theory for Organizational Practice*. New York: Psychology Press.

Hogg, M. A., & Vaughan, G. M. (2005). *Social Psychology* (4th edn). Harlow, UK: Pearson.

Hollway, W. (1998). Fitting work: psychological assessment in organizations. In J. Henriques, W. Hollway, C. Urwin, C. Venn & V. Walkerdine (eds), *Changing the Subject: Psychology, Social Regulation and Subjectivity* (Rev edn, pp. 26–59). London: Routledge.

Huszczo, G. E., Wiggins, J. G., & Currie, J. S. (1984). The relationship between psychology and organized labor: past, present and future. *American Psychologist, 39*, 432–440.

Illouz, E. (2008). *Saving the Modern Soul: Therapy, Emotions, and the Culture of Self-Help*. Berkeley: University of California Press.

Islam, G., & Zyphur, M. (2006). Critical industrial psychology: what is it and where is it? *Psychology and Society, 34*, 17–30.

Islam, G., & Zyphur, M. (2009). Concepts and directions in critical industrial/ organizational psychology. In D. Fox, I. Prilleltensky & S. Austin (eds), *Critical Psychology: An Introduction* (2nd edn, pp. 110–125). Thousand Oaks, CA: Sage.

Jex, S. M., & Bliese, P. D. (1999). Efficacy beliefs as a moderator of the impact of work-related stressors: a multilevel study. *Journal of Applied Psychology, 84*(3), 349–361.

Jordan, C. H., & Zanna, M. P. (2003). Appendix: how to read a journal article in social psychology. In L. L. Thompson (ed.), *The Social Psychology of*

Organizational Behavior: Key Readings (pp. 419–428). Hove, UK: Psychology Press.

Katz, D., & Kahn, R. L. (1966). *The Social Psychology of Organizations*. New York: Wiley.

Kim, E., & Glomb, T. M. (2010). Get smarty pants: cognitive ability, personality, and victimization. *Journal of Applied Psychology, 95*, 889–901.

Lefkowitz, J. (2003). *Ethics and Values in Industrial-Organizational Psychology*. Hove, UK: Psychology Press.

Mandel, E., & Novack, G. (1970). *The Marxist Theory of Alienation*. New York: Pathfinder.

Marx, K. (1844/1964). *The Economic and Philosophical Manuscripts of 1844* (R. Livingston & G. Benton, Trans.). London: Lawrence & Wishart.

Marx, K. (1857/1973). *The Grundrisse: Foundations of the Critique of Political Economy* (M. Nicolaus, Trans.). Harmondsworth, UK: Penguin.

Marx, K. (1867/2004). *Capital: Critique of Political Economy* (B. Fowkes, Trans. Vol. 1). Harmondsworth, UK: Penguin.

Mayo, E. (1933/1977). *The Human Problems of An Industrial Civilization*. New York: Arno Press.

McDonald, M., Wearing, S., & Ponting, J. (2008). Narcissism and neo-liberalism: work, leisure and alienation in an era of consumption. *Loisir et Societe (Society and Leisure), 30*, 489–510.

Morgan, G. (2006). *Images of Organization* (Twentieth Anniversary edn). Thousand Oaks, CA: Sage.

Moscovici, S. (1972). Society and theory in social psychology. In J. Israel & H. Tajfel (eds), *The Context of Social Psychology* (pp. 17–68). London: Academic Press.

Muchinsky, P. M. (2008). *Psychology Applied to Work: An Introduction to Industrial and Organizational Psychology* (9th edn). Belmont, CA: Hypergraphic Press.

Munsterberg, H. (1913/1973). *Psychology and Industrial Efficiency*. New York: Arno Press.

Parker, I. (2007). *Revolution in Psychology: Alienation to Emancipation*. Ann Arbor, MI: Pluto Press.

Pillutla, M. M. (2011). When good people do wrong: morality, social identity, and ethical behavior. In D. De Cremer, R. van Dick & K. J. Murnighan (eds), *Social Psychology and Organizations* (pp. 353–369). London: Routledge.

Prilleltensky, I., Nelson, G., & Geoffrey, B. (2002). *Doing Psychology Critically: Making a Difference in Diverse Settings*. Basingstoke, UK: Palgrave Macmillan.

Ritzer, G. (2010). *The McDonaldization of Society* (6th edn). Thousand Oaks, CA: Pine Forge Press.

Rose, N. (1999). *Governing the Soul: the Shaping of the Private Self* (2nd edn). London: Free Association Books.

Schrieshiem, C. A. (1978). Job satisfaction, attitudes towards unions, and voting in a union representation election. *Journal of Applied Psychology, 63,* 251–267.

Sennett, R. (2006). *The Culture of the New Capitalism.* New Haven, CT: Yale University Press.

Steffy, B. D., & Grimes, A. J. (1992). Personnel/organizational psychology: a critique of the discipline. In M. Alvesson & H. Willmott (eds), *Critical Management Studies* (pp. 181–201). London: Sage.

Steger, M. B., & Roy, R. K. (2010). *Neoliberalism: A Very Short Introduction.* New York: Oxford University Press.

Sterns, L., Alexander, R., Barrett, G., & Dambrot, F. (1983). The relationship of extraversion and neuroticism with job preferences and job satisfaction for clerical employees. *Journal of Occupational Psychology, 56,* 145–155.

Tadajewski, M., Maclaran, P., Parsons, E., & Parker, M. (2011). *Key Concepts in Critical Management Studies.* London: Sage.

Taylor, F. W. (1911/1967). *The Principles of Scientific Management.* New York: Norton.

Thompson, L. L. (ed). (2003a). *The Social Psychology of Organizational Behavior: Key Readings.* Hove, UK: Psychology Press.

Thompson, L. L. (2003b). Organizational behavior: a micro perspective. In L. L. Thompson (ed), *The Social Psychology of Organizational Behavior: Key Readings* (pp. 1–6). Hove, UK: Psychology Press.

Van Der Zee, K., & Paulus, P. (2008). Social psychology and modern organizations: balancing between innovativeness and comfort. In L. Steg, A. P. Buunk & T. Rothengatter (eds), *Applied Social Psychology: Understanding and Managing Social Problems* (pp. 271–290). Cambridge, UK: Cambridge University Press.

Vinchur, A. J., & Koppes, L. L. (2010). A historical survey of research and practice in industrial and organizational psychology. In S. Zedeck (ed.), *APA Handbook of Industrial and Organizational Psychology: Building and Developing the Organization* (Vol. 1, pp. 3–36). Washington, DC: American Psychological Association.

Zickar, M. J. (2001). Using personality inventories to identify thugs and agitators: applied psychology's contribution to the war against labor. *Journal of Vocational Behaviour, 59,* 149–164.

Reflections on Critical Social Psychology

10

This chapter will highlight:

- Diversity within critical social psychology
- Ongoing debates, relating to discourse, 'reality' and subjectivity
- The emergence of new movements in mainstream social psychology and their critique

Diversity: critical social psychologies

One message flagged in this book is that contemporary social psychology is a fragmented discipline, beset with difference and often disagreement. Indeed, it might be preferable to speak of social psychologies. Clearly, significant differences exist between 'mainstream' cognitive–experimental and 'critical' forms of social psychology, as we have stressed throughout this book. But there are other branches of social psychology not covered in as much detail here, such as humanistic/experiential social psychology (Stevens, 1996) and psychoanalytic social psychology (Parker & Hook, 2008; Frosh, 1999). This situation is complicated further when we consider differences *within* given brands of social psychology. For example, Stainton-Rogers *et al.* (1995) outlined a number of relatively separate types of (critical) social psychology, and in Box 10.1 we reproduce four brands relevant to critical social psychology.

So, we must be very careful not to regard labels such as 'mainstream' or 'critical' social psychology as reflecting neat, distinct bundles of coherent perspectives, for such thinking would be to mask serious internal debates and conflicts. Although such labels are difficult to avoid and can be useful for teaching purposes, it is important not to imagine critical social psychology as a unified set of concepts and practices. However, we will reiterate here what we feel to be key features of a critical social psychology perspective before moving on to discuss areas where consensus has proved elusive. Some concerns about critical social psychology voiced recently by advocates will then be summarized but we will finish by emphasizing arguments in favour of critical social psychology approaches.

Box 10.1 Critical social psychologies
(Stainton-Rogers et al., 1995)

'Social psychology as social science'

It generally identifies social psychology as inter-disciplinary and accords considerable importance to its sociological roots. Here 'social psychology' is identified with relationships between individuals and social structures (from two-person 'dyads' to organizations and institutions). Individuals are held to be both influenced by and influential upon social structures. Where 'theories' feature, they are likely to be either 'grand theories' (such as structural-functionalism) or interactional models such as 'interactionism'.

'Social psychology as a social constructionist endeavour'

It declares itself early (e.g. in titles like The Social Construction of Death) in a challenge to all pre-emptive attempts to singularize (or even talk of) reality. However, social constructionism has become a buzz term, and you may find you have bought a pragmatist or social scientist underneath the snazzy bodywork? Do not be fooled. Social constructionism offers a powerful challenge to the enterprises listed above (e.g. social psychology as science/humanist endeavour etc.). Social constructionism is not on offer if it is presented as just one approach among many, or called constructivism. This is somebody trying to have their cake and eat it, since constructionism is incompatible with mainstream approaches to social psychology. For example, Jost and Kruglanski's (2002) attempt to reconcile experimental social psychology with social constructionism, while offering a potential rapprochement, is virtually impossible given the profound differences in foundational philosophies between them (Gergen, 2002).

'Social psychology as a postmodern endeavour'

It will shout 'pomo'-speak from the start. You will soon find that its proponents would rather risk incomprehension than being misunderstood. If you don't rapidly find terms like 'deconstruction' being used or any mention of French theorists (like Foucault, Derrida and Deleuze) it must be something else.

'Social psychology as rebellion and resistance'

Sometimes this will be marked for you by the rapid recourse to words like 'feminist', 'Marxist' or 'power'. But even where this does not happen, its polemical tone and rhetorical devices will soon show themselves. It dislikes and distrusts virtually all received social psychology. Some anti-social psychologists think that humanists and postmodernists have either 'sold out' or don't understand that they are being 'used' and that social constructionists are relativists.

Critical social psychology advocates critical theory and practice; indeed, the two are interlinked. The term 'critical' implies a sceptical, questioning attitude towards presented 'knowledge' and the actions promoted thereof and represents the defining feature of social movements such as Marxism, feminism, poststructuralism and social constructionism. A popular 'target' for critical social psychology is the discipline of (social) psychology itself, but more broadly the (psychological) culture from which it derives and which it helps maintain. Rose (1999; 2008) and Parker (1994) use the terms 'psy-disciplines', 'psy-expertise' or 'psy-complex' to denote a powerful contemporary cultural inclination towards deploying individualistic concepts to govern and understand human social experience. Similarly, critical social psychology repudiates accounts or 'discourses' which seek to explain social action in terms of psychological or individualistic categories such as 'personality', 'attitude', 'schema', etc. The argument is that such explanations are often used to oppress individuals and groups and/or to blame them for their predicament. For example, the 'social-class is dead' thesis could easily be used to portray a society of opportunities for all and to place responsibility for 'failure' (e.g. unemployment or poverty) on lazy or unmotivated individuals. This discourse would operate to obscure continuing class-based inequalities in education, health and employment. Previous chapters have presented criticisms of individualistic discourse applied to various topics such as self, prejudice and aggression; critical social psychology is firmly positioned against such a culture of 'self-contained individualism' (Sampson, 1977).

Instead, critical social psychology favours accounts of phenomena which stress the centrality of social relationships and practices. It is argued that socially embedded accounts make for more persuasive and complex insights into the topic in question – did you find this was the case in the previous chapters? For example, gender tends to be regarded as socially constructed within a given culture at a specific historical point and constantly negotiated in interpersonal relationships. In other words, 'femininity' and 'masculinity' are not biological or psychological essences pertaining to women and men respectively, but culturally available discourses which open up and close off certain subject positions. In addition to the focus on language and social construction, the issue of power receives great attention from critical social psychology such that a study of gender would examine how discourses of masculinity and femininity are used in practice – traditionally the 'masculine' is valued (reason, strength, rationality) and the 'feminine' slighted (emotional, weak, irrational), although discourses are emerging which attempt to reverse such thinking ('men as victims', 'career women') (see Chapter 7). In addition to emphasizing the social embeddedness of experience and the operation of power, critical social psychology usually involves a commitment to resistance and social change. There is an affinity with groups identified as marginalized or oppressed and an expressed desire to work towards the betterment of their situation. Such explicitly political and pragmatic work is often labelled 'action research' (or its cousin 'participatory action research').

We have devoted much space in this book to creating an image of critical social psychology as a positive force in opposition to more 'problematic' forms of social psychology and wider culture. This tactic has been useful, even necessary, to render basic 'critical' concepts and themes accessible for a student audience unfamiliar with such vocabulary. However, to construe critical social psychology as a happy family of academics and practitioners who agree on shared policies against common enemies would be to give a mistaken impression, for there is widespread discussion, frequent disagreement and occasional acrimony to be found within critical social psychology texts. In fact, some writers whom we have cited in this book may not be happy with the term 'critical social psychology', preferring alternative labels such as 'discursive psychology' (Edwards & Potter, 1992), 'social constructionism' (Gergen, 1999), 'postmodernism' (Kvale, 1992) or simply 'critical psychology' (Fox et al.,, 2009). The term 'critical social psychology' works for us in the context of this book because it is counter-posed with mainstream cognitive–experimental psychology and emphasizes the 'social' dimension to experience (see also Hepburn, 2003; Tuffin, 2004).

As noted throughout the previous chapters, one of the features that differentiates mainstream social psychology from critical social psychology is the way in which it invokes a range of alternative theoretical perspectives (e.g. Marxism, feminism, poststrucuralism, social constructionism etc.) to deconstruct and expand mainstream social psychological theory. However, a number of critical social psychologists have themselves been critical of how these perspectives are interpreted and applied. For example, Hepburn (1999) argues that key features of Derrida's deconstruction are missing from work in critical social psychology. Parker (2003, 2009) states that elements of Lacanian psychoanalysis and Marxism are philosophically opposed to psychology and these aspects of Marx's work are often evaded, misrepresented or distorted by critical social psychologists in the English-speaking world. Similarly, Hook (2001, 2007) has taken issue with what he regards as the erroneous application of Foucault's conceptualization of discourse by critical social psychologists working in the discursive analysis field. The use and abuse of theoretical perspectives will continue to be an issue for critical social psychology given its relative youth and the nature of inter-disciplinary inquiry, where issues around theoretical interpretation and application are often raised. It is important to keep in mind however that this particular issue is not isolated to critical social psychology, for it also occurs within the theoretical perspectives themselves. For example, there are myriad interpretations of Marx's work and fierce debates between its various proponents have always been a feature of Marxist scholarship. A balance therefore needs to be struck between an ongoing scholarly debate on these various theoretical perspectives and their application to psychology, while not falling into the trap of advocating some form of critical social psychological orthodoxy.

Key issues and debates

In addition to debating how theoretical perspectives should be interpreted, critical social psychologists have also been in debate over other issues revolving around three main key concepts. They include 'discourse', 'reality' and 'subjectivity', which we will now discuss.

1. Discourse

A common activity performed by many critical social psychologists is the analysis of discourse. Discourse analysis is not necessarily a critical practice and other methods have been used for critical purposes, but critically informed discourse analyses have become a mainstay of research projects within critical social psychology. Emerging from the 'turn to language' within contemporary social theory (social constructionism, post-structuralism) and given a critical twist by Foucault and followers (see Hook, 2007; Rose, 1998, 1999), discourse analysis has proved a valuable and versatile tool for deconstructing a range of texts and offering critical readings. There are some valuable texts on discourse analysis available (e.g. Fairclough, 2010; Hepburn & Wiggins, 2007; Parker, 2002; Wetherell *et al.*, 2001) and various book chapters on discourse analysis can be found in books on qualitative research methods (e.g. Arribas-Ayllon & Walkerdine, 2008; Willig, 2008). The chapters in this book also refer to useful papers where discourse analysis has been employed. Students are encouraged to tap into these and other sources in order to grasp how discourse analyses may facilitate the attainment of critical understanding and goals.

Consider the two forms of discourse analysis outlined in Chapter 3. One approach operates at a high level of abstraction, exploring language in relation to ideology and power (Fairclough, 2010), as well as relatively well-bounded areas of social knowledge and the ways in which they subjugate certain elements of the population. This approach is associated with the work of Fairclough (2010), Rose (1998, 1999), Parker and colleagues (Burman & Parker, 1993; Parker, 1992, 2002), Arribas-Ayllon & Walkerdine (2008), and Willig (2008). It is largely influenced by the work of the French philosopher Michel Foucault on the historical subjectification of 'problematic' populations such as criminals, the mentally ill, unemployed, homosexuals etc. An explicitly political project, this approach has been criticized by other discourse analysts for suggesting that people's lives are completely or largely structured by prevailing discourses. For example, a 'medical' discourse would define people as patients subordinate to the knowledge and practices of the medical institution, with little room for effective resistance. Also, it is not clear how discourses are identified or defined and it often seems as if a given discourse is portrayed as a powerful structure or object existing independently of social interaction (see Potter *et al.*, 1990). Such criticisms are valid enough, although Foucauldian approaches to discourse analysis do emphasize resistance and social action. Breeze (2011) outlines a number of other criticisms that have been levelled at 'critical' approaches to discourse analysis; these include:

1. its heterogeneous intellectual inheritance suggests that it operates randomly and is moved by 'personal whim' as opposed to 'well-grounded scholarly principles' (498);
2. textual analysis can often descend into naïve linguistic determinism;
3. it can fall into the trap of analysing text, while ignoring the social context in which it is embedded;
4. tends to be negative in that it deconstructs only, forgetting to reconstruct in the process; and
5. it has become an intellectual orthodoxy in its own right eliminating its reflexive credentials.

The contrasting emphasis of the other form of discourse analysis is on the active or 'performative' quality of everyday talk (see Potter & Wetherell, 1987; Wiggins & Potter, 2008; Wilkinson & Kitzinger, 2008). The focus here tends to be on concrete social interaction as it occurs 'naturally' and the image of the person favoured is that of the social actor and user – rather than subject – of discourse. The term 'interpretative repertoire' is preferred to highlight the specific metaphors and vocabularies used by people during conversation to achieve particular goals. This more interpersonal or conversational level of analysis looks closely at the rhetoric used and the functions which language is made to serve, such as justification of one's actions, presenting self or another in a positive light, avoiding criticism, etc. For example, a game of football might be presented as 'beautiful' or 'poetic' by a speaker in order to fend of criticisms of macho aggression and preserve a positive identity for the speaker as a football fan. This form of discourse analysis has also been criticized, this time on the grounds of lacking a more cultural or political dimension (see Parker, 1990), and that analytic categories such as social class, power, gender and ethnicity 'may be relevant to participants conduct but in ways which are not detected by conversation analysis' (Wooffitt, 2005: 150), although there are examples of such work which do tackle the ideological quality of talk.

The debates between the two camps rumble on but increasingly there are calls for more integrated approaches, and in practice both perspectives are often combined (e.g. Hodgetts & Lecouteur, 2010).

2. 'Reality'

A point worth stressing at once is that critical social psychology does not automatically imply a social constructionist analysis. It is true that many 'critical' theoretical and empirical publications do make use of social constructionist concepts such as the historical and cultural specificity of knowledge, but social constructionist influenced work could just as easily operate in non-critical or even oppressive ways. For example, arguments for equality and non-discrimination could be used by groups traditionally regarded as privileged (e.g. white middle-class males). Conversely, essentialist arguments can be used for critical ends whereby the 'unique' status of a group (women, blacks, the middle-classes, etc.) is emphasized in order to pursue positive outcomes for that group such as independence, freedom from oppression, a distinctive identity, etc. Some feminist authors, for example, have argued that men and women are fundamentally different (e.g. Daly, 1978; Gilligan, 1982) and this idea is firmly embedded in popular culture (e.g. Gray, 1993). The same points can be made with respect to discourse analysis, where an examination of language need not proceed to a political analysis (although some might argue that all talk and text is political in some way – note Parker's analysis of toothpaste instructions, Chapter 3). Similarly, discourse analysis may be used to reinforce or defend positive representations of powerful groups and/or to undermine claims of subordination proffered by minority or powerless groups.

Clearly, the existence of multiple discourses making different and often conflicting claims about 'how things are' makes it difficult to argue for the validity of one version of events over the other. This presents problems for feminist and critical psychologists interested in identifying instances of oppression and inequality, since any account (e.g. the subordination of women) can always be countered by other accounts (e.g. 'it's men who are really oppressed'). This is the key point of tension between some social constructionists and critical psychologists – the issue of relativism (Burr, 2003). Within a postmodern climate, criteria used to judge the 'truth' or value of an account cannot be provided by science, religion, humanism, Marxism or any of the 'grand narratives' of modernism, since these perspectives themselves have been deconstructed as mere stories rather than reflections of reality or truth (see Lyotard, 1984). In other words, just as one person's masterpiece is another's banality, so one construction of reality is simply an interpretation presented from a particular vantage point within a given social context. The problem for feminism is underlined by Jackson (1992), for example, who wonders about the lack of basis for deciding between the rape victim's account of forced sexual intercourse and the rapist's construction of mutually agreeable fun.

So, in accepting poststructuralist ideas, however, it is difficult to say with certainty that certain social groups possess power whilst others lack power. Any one object, say 'men', can be seen as powerful and/or powerless depending on the social context and other sets of relations prevailing, such as social class, sexual orientation, race, etc. By this analysis, some (middle-class) gay men may occupy more powerful social positions compared with (working-class) heterosexual men, though on other occasions macho heterosexuality may work to oppress male homosexuality. The point is that social identities and relationships are complicated by multiple and sometimes conflicting discourses which prevents straightforward allocation of power/lessness to particular groups.

The critical/feminist emphasis on politics, however, urges discourse analysts to move beyond deconstruction in order to articulate positive, political positions. For example, Willig (1998) suggests that discourse analysts are destined to remain observers and commentators if they abstain from adopting particular viewpoints – simply to point up the constructed nature of dominant discourses is less politically effective than actually offering alternative discourses and practices. The task is to adopt a clear position to facilitate political action whilst simultaneously acknowledging the interested or constructed nature of the version presented and the possibility of other interpretations. This 'politics of articulation' recognizes that the community which is being represented (e.g. women) must not be taken as homogeneous ('opening') whilst arguing for the need to stop talking/writing at some point in order to act ('closing') (Wetherell, 1995; see also Jackson, 2005). Similarly, Squire (1995) highlights the way in which feminist discourse analysts may oscillate between a 'pragmatic' use of discourse analysis which privileges specific versions of reality and 'extravagant' deployments which explore the complexities and contradictions pertaining to accounts.

So, critical psychologists who espouse a commitment to left-wing causes tend to straddle both structuralist and poststructuralist perspectives (e.g. Gavey, 1997; Parker, 1992). Using a structuralist framework typical of classic Marxism and socialist feminism, for example, upper middle class and male sections of society enjoy access to power whilst working class and female groups exist in positions of relative powerlessness. In holding on to structuralism, discourse is related to social institutions and practices – gender ideals depicting women as mothers and men as breadwinners can be seen to reinforce patriarchal heterosexuality. The nature of this relation between discourse and social structures is subject to debate, however, with some arguing for the primacy of 'reality' in shaping experience and discourse (e.g. Collier, 1998) and others asserting the power of discourse to define 'reality' and our understanding of it (e.g. Brown *et al.*, 1998).

In the end, the argument goes, we have to convince the reader of the merit and persuasiveness of our own interpretation by providing supporting evidence and discounting competing explanations. Reflexivity is important here, that is, providing information which helps contextualize the reading, although a reflexive account is itself constructed, so that one can easily slide into agonizing contemplation of one's rhetoric rather than promoting the account itself! (Burman & Parker, 1993). So, relativism is not necessarily a barrier to politically motivated inquiry since one's reading of the text can be promoted whilst the status of the reading as one of several possible interpretations is acknowledged (see Box 10.2). For further reading on the realism–relativism issue and related debates see Gavey (1997), Hepburn (2003: 215–223), Raskin (2011), Parker (1992) and Derksen (2010).

Box 10.2   'Politically informed relativism' (Gill, 1995)

Relativists' refusal to deal with questions of value has led to political paralysis. There is no principled way in which they can intervene, choose one version over another, argue for anything. Against this, feminists who have engaged with postmodernism and poststructuralism have taken a rather different position. There is a growing awareness that questions of value are inescapable and must be addressed. In the absence of ontological guarantees, then, values, commitments, and politics must be at the heart of analyses.

We need a relativism which is unashamedly political, in which we, as feminists, can make social transformation an explicit concern of our work. This is something that feminists have always done, but which at present is ruled out by the relative commitments of some discourse analysts.

Discourse analysts should adopt a notion of reflexivity which stresses the need for the analysts to acknowledge their own commitments and to reflect critically upon them. By seeking to explain and justify the basis for their readings or analyses, discourse analysts become accountable for their interpretations and the social and political consequences of these interpretations (Gill, 1995: 177–82).

3. Subjectivity

Although poststructuralism has produced a climate of scepticism regarding structures and essences, the strong view of human experience as entirely framed by language is rejected by a number of writers (see Chapter 6, section 'The problem of subjective experience'). Accepting the arguments for the deconstruction of the core self (or 'unitary, rational subject'), there is nevertheless some dissatisfaction with an image of personhood devoid of emotion and embodiment. Discourse analysis may well help identify those subject positions inhabited by a person and the implications thereof, but there is little said about how it feels for people to occupy those subject positions and relationships with others. As Burr (2003) notes, a woman might accept that current discourses of femininity and motherhood place limits on women's choices but nonetheless may feel a strong desire to have a child. Discourse approaches might connect this desire to powerful social conventions but this account does not seem to adequately capture the emotional experience. Consequently, some writers have looked to other traditions to help complement the insights proffered by social constructionism, notably psychoanalysis.

At first sight there is little common ground between discourse analysis and psychoanalysis since the latter is typically concerned with instinctual, intra-psychic or mental events whilst the former concentrates on social relations. Recent articles by prominent 'critical' writers, however, have revisited psychoanalytic ideas and commented on similarities between discourse analysis and psychoanalysis. For example, both perspectives advocate a split subjectivity, emphasize the centrality of language and interpretation, and are concerned with the relationship between individual and society (see Billig, 1997b; Parker, 1998, 2005). The psychoanalytic work of Jaques Lacan in particular has proved influential for feminist and social constructionist theorists working in the areas of gender and sexuality (e.g. Dimen & Goldner, 2002; Frosh, 1999; Hollway, 1989; Walkerdine, 1991). Lacan highlighted the role of language and culture in producing a subjectivity at once social and emotional. Briefly, the child enters the male-centred Symbolic or cultural order and is dis/placed within positions of gender and sexuality, but to take up these social roles pre-Oedipal infantile desires must be repressed (e.g. a boy must renounce his desire for the mother – and femininity generally). Identity is therefore bound up with loss and (unconscious) desire for a return to earlier fulfilment persists and punctuates the self.

Box 10.3 Subjectivity as defensive and discursive (Hollway, 1984)

According to Hollway (1984, 1989), people are not simply produced by discourse but rather actively identify with (or reject) particular subject positions among those on offer. The 'investment' shown in positions will not necessarily be conscious or rational but may actually involve the operation of defence mechanisms. In applying this analysis to heterosexual relationships, Hollway makes use of Klein's defences of 'splitting', where the 'object' (i.e. person) is divided into good and bad, and 'projection', in which feelings or desires denied by the subject are attributed to another person. These defences are construed as 'relational', as having implications for how the other in a relationship is seen. In the case of projection, for example, a man might locate his own (repressed) feelings of vulnerability on to the woman, thereby constructing her as weak or emotional, and himself as strong and rational. Clearly such a manoeuvre is supported within discourses of gender difference which define masculinity and femininity differently, but cannot be reduced to the effects of these discourses since the individual will already have built up a unique, biographical and largely unconscious set of meanings pertaining to gender difference from childhood. Thus, discourse/s used by individuals will be partially informed by the anxieties and wishes evoked during interpersonal interactions, producing subject positions for self and others which variably reinforce and disrupt those provided by prevailing discourse.

So, Lacan's account emphasizes the connections between language and desire and opens up possibilities for social constructionist writers to incorporate an emotional or experiential dimension to human social interaction. What remains to be worked out, however, is how to combine aspects of discourse analysis and psychoanalysis in practice. For example, can psychoanalytic concepts be used in conjunction with discourse perspectives in order to analyse talk and text? One possibility here relates to defence mechanisms. Instead of regarding defence mechanisms as intra-individualistic practices, as Freud suggested, a more social view would see these as interpersonal, as negotiated in conversation with others (Hollway, 1984). Projection, for example, can be said to operate where feelings and ideas felt to be problematic or taboo are relocated to others, even the targets of the problematic statements. Consider discursive work on prejudice (see Chapter 5), which has studied how people often deny or ward off potential accusations of prejudice and re-place prejudice with the minority groups themselves (i.e. 'blaming the victims'). Such discursive activity could be read as a form of social or conversational projection, working to protect views perceived to be taboo. A lot more work is required in this area, but it is worth knowing that aspects of critical social psychology, discourse analysis and social constructionism are being fruitfully questioned by sympathetic writers and that efforts are being made to forge theories and practices which provide ever more eloquent and convincing accounts of human experience (e.g. Frosh *et al.*, 2003; Parker, 2005).

New challenges for critical social psychology

Positive psychology

Anyone who has followed psychology over the past decade would be well aware of the positive psychology movement. Positive psychology officially emerged in the US at the beginning of 2000 with a special issue published in the American Psychological Association's flagship journal the *American Psychologist*. To re-cap from Chapter 2, the stated aims of positive psychology are to re-dress the balance in psychology from a preoccupation with illness and pathology, towards a 'new science' based on positive subjective experiences, positive individual traits and positive institutions (Seligman & Csikszentmihalyi, 2000: 8).

Despite Seligman and Csikszentmihalyi's claim that positive psychology represents a new school in the science of psychology, it is essentially a facsimile of humanistic psychology, which emerged in the US in the 1950s led by Abraham Maslow and Carl Rogers. Since this time humanistic psychology, in opposition to mainstream psychology, has focused its research and practice on subjective wellbeing, human potential and spirituality. There is however a significant difference between the two movements. Positive psychology subscribes to a restricted individualistic ontology and positivist/experimental epistemology (Taylor, 2001; Christopher & Hickinbottom, 2008; Hodgetts & Lecouteur, 2010), whereas humanistic psychology subscribes to alternative theoretical perspectives including existentialism, phenomenology, human science, transpersonal psychology and poststructuralism.

In effect positive psychology represents a new front in the 'crisis in social psychology'. This ongoing crisis is a struggle between those who want social psychology to continue adhering to natural science methods of inquiry (positivist/experimental epistemology), and those calling for an alternative social psychology that takes the 'social' more seriously, and which is based on new and progressive ontologies and epistemologies. This new front may never have opened up if Seligman had not been so vociferous in his claims that areas of psychology based on alternative theoretical perspectives (that is alternative to the positivist/experimental epistemology) are unscientific (Seligman & Csikszentmihalyi, 2000: 7; Peterson & Seligman, 2004: 4).

Critical social psychologists have two main problems with positive psychology. The first, as was noted, is positive psychology's subscription to an individualistic ontology and positivist/experimental epistemology, which stands in opposition to critical social psychology's theoretical application of Marxism, feminism, poststrucuralism and social constructionism. The second issue is that positive psychology's practical prescriptions for living the 'good life' are based on the promotion of a narrow set of essentialist character traits, which are outlined in the movements taxonomic *Character Strengths and Virtues: A Handbook and Classification* (Peterson & Seligman, 2004). This issue has been analysed by McDonald and O'Callaghan (2008) and Binkley (2011) who invoke the work of Foucault and Nikolas Rose to argue that positive psychology represents a new form of governmentality and 'psy-expertise' that operates in alliance with other types of expertise such as medicine and economics, and societal authorities such as schools and government agencies. This loose amalgamation of expertise tries to shape and regulate subjectivity that is more closely aligned with dominant Western neoliberal economic and political principles. Positive psychology's classifying and categorizing of character strengths and virtues is used as a regulatory tool to promote and reward the benefits of self-governance, particularly the regulation of thinking and emotions that are more positive and productive. It also promotes particular personality traits which are allied to a neoliberal character regime such as independence, enterprising, entrepreneurial, dynamic, flexible and productive. It is important to note however that neoliberal programmes of governmentality and psy-expertise in the form of positive psychology do not seek to control people by directly suppressing freedoms, but instead they 'govern at a distance' by creating subjects capable of economic independence, rational thinking and positive emotional self-regulation.

Social neuroscience

Like positive psychology, the field of social neuroscience (and neuro-science in general) has boomed over the past two decades as evidenced by the growth in academic research, funding and the way it has captured the public's attention. As was argued in Chapter 2, social neuroscience challenges critical approaches to social psychology through its re-biologization of the social world. Social neuroscience (again like positive psychology) subscribes to a positivist/experi-mental epistemology which reduces social behaviour to an individual's biology (Cromby, 2007).

Despite its potential to further knowledge and understanding of human subjectivity, social neuroscience is frequently essentialist, deterministic, decontextualized and reductionist (Cromby *et al.*, 2011: 220). Citing the work of French sociologist Alain Ehrenberg, Meloni (2011: 307) notes the social neurobiological study of empathy, for example, reproduces 'the common naturalistic mistake to exchange a social value ... empathy, for a cognitive mechanism found in our brain'. Social neuroscience begins with the assumption that mental activity and subjectivity must be internal to the person (Meloni, 2011). This presupposes a dualistic conception of social behaviour whereby the individual and their social world are viewed as two separate entities. Employing an individual/social dualism means that problems are located inside the individual, which removes any responsibility from society (Henriques, 1984; Parker *et al.*, 1995: 61).

Social psychologists are drawn to the neurosciences because of its scientific status and because brain research is amenable to natural science methods of investigation. This has led to a neuroscientific imperialism, which claims that anything non-biological in conceptual-ization is unscientific, or worse, antiscientific (Coulter, 2008). The issue of scientific imperialism is an important one because it is invoked not only by social neuroscientists but also by mainstream cognitive social psychologists and positive psychologists, who use it to marginalize alternative movements such as critical social psychology. There are a number of ways in which this is achieved; however, one of the most common is through the use of discourse and rhetoric. To give just one example, Yen (2010) explored the ways in which positive psychology uses rhetoric to position itself within a noble scientific tradition, demarcating itself from its competitors by associating them with lesser non-scientific endeavours (see also McDonald & O'Callaghan, 2008). It is against this current of attempted marginalization that critical social psychologists must continue to swim against.

Box 10.4   Making social science matter: why social inquiry fails and how it can succeed again (Flyvbjerg, 2001)

In this book Bent Flyvbjerg outlines how the social and behavioural sciences will never be able to develop the type of explanatory and predictive theory that has made the natural sciences so successful. As a consequence of its attempted emulation, the social sciences have frequently come under attack for failing to live up to natural science ideals.

The problem in the study of human activity is that every attempt at a context-free definition of an action, that is, a definition based on abstract rules or laws, will not necessarily accord with the pragmatic way an action is defined by the actors in a concrete social situation. (42)

Instead of trying to emulate the natural sciences, Flyvbjerg argues that the social sciences should play to its own unique strengths, which lay in its ability to create a rich and reflexive analysis of values and power. A focus on values and power in human conduct empha-sizes problems of marginality, domination, difference, diversity and the politics of identity. To harness these strengths, Flyvbjerg recom-mends that social science research 'provide concrete examples and detailed narratives of how power works and with what consequences, and to suggest how power might be changed' (140).

While Flyvbjerg's book is aimed at a general social science audience (e.g. economists, planners, social workers, geographers, criminologists etc.), the ideas presented in it go to the heart of what critical social psychology is attempting to do. This includes a break with natural science research methods, addressing issues of social justice by researching discourse, power and ideology, and seeking to institute progressive social change by taking an ethico–political stance.

Summary

In attempting to introduce students to the arena of critical social psychology, it is perhaps inevitable that this book has overlooked or smoothed over some of the complexities and contradictions which are present. By contrasting critical social psychology with 'traditional' or 'mainstream' social psychology we have probably created the impression of a concerted and homogeneous alternative force. This image has perhaps been reinforced by our adherence to the format of conventional social psychology textbooks which cover a range of topics such as social influence, the self, prejudice, gender and applied areas such as health and work. In addition, this structure might serve to suggest clear boundaries between topics when we would actually wish to emphasize the opposite, i.e. that research questions and explanations regarding 'prejudice' might be very similar to those surrounding 'sexualities' (with both perhaps concentrating on discourses which define 'the other'). Similarly, by offering a dedicated chapter on methodology we do not wish to separate out theory from method – we have sought to continually underscore how 'knowledge' is constructed within particular social contexts and therefore always is partial and transitory.

In this last chapter, we hope to have illustrated some of the diversity within critical social psychology by pointing up some issues and debates which inform current thinking, some of which have prompted intense disagreements. The commitment to challenging conventional psychological wisdom is clearly enacted in different ways by different theorists and researchers. Although the preoccupation with discourse is a defining feature of most critical work as we have shown in the book, an exclusive focus on language is increasingly rejected as attempts are made to theorize political and personal 'realities' by drawing on approaches such as structuralism and psychodynamics. Such contributions facilitate healthy and lively discussion and serve to illustrate the depth and breadth of critical social psychology. As the interest in critical social psychology grows further, certain challenges and opportunities are presented. In particular, there is a danger that critical social psychology may become sanitized and institutionalized as just another brand of psychology amongst a variety of alternatives. But by continuing to resist the discipline of psychology and by reflexively questioning the form/s and purpose/es of critical social psychology, we can help ensure a dynamic, stimulating and significant project.

Finally, and in the spirit of the social scientist C. Wright Mills (1959/2000), our hope is that you the reader become a critical social psychologist in your everyday life. That you pass on the insights you've gained from this book and the various readings recommended at end of each chapter to those people and groups we have frequently referred to throughout (e.g. the poor, unemployed, homeless, indigenous, disabled, refugees, mentally ill, homosexuals, single mothers etc.), who may be blaming themselves for those social structures, discourses and ideologies whose existence is the cause of their marginalization.

New references

Arribas-Ayllon, M., & Walkerdine, V. (2008). Foucauldian discourse analysis. In C. Willig & W. Stainton-Rogers (eds), *Sage Handbook of Qualitative Research in Psychology* (pp. 91–108). London: Sage.

Binkley, S. (2011). Happiness, positive psychology and the program of neoliberal governmentality. *Subjectivity, 4*(4), 371–394.

Breeze, R. (2011). Critical discourse analysis and its critics. *Pragmatics, 21*(4), 493–525.

Burr, V. (2003). *Social Constructionism* (2nd edn). Hove, UK: Routledge.

Christopher, J. C., & Hickinbottom, S. (2008). Positive psychology, ethnocentrism, and the disguised ideology of individualism. *Theory & Psychology, 18*(5), 563–589.

Coulter, J. (2008). Twenty-five theses against cognitivism. *Theory, Culture & Society, 25*(2), 19–32.

Cromby, J. (2007). Integrating social science with neuroscience: potentials and pitfalls. *BioSocieties, 2*(2), 149–170.

Cromby, J., Newton, T., & Williams, S. J. (2011). Neuroscience and subjectivity. *Subjectivity, 4*(3), 215–226.

Derksen, M. (2010). Realism, relativism, and evolutionary psychology. *Theory & Psychology, 20*(4), 467–487.

Dimen, M., & Goldner, V. (eds). (2002). *Gender in Psychoanalytic Space: between Clinic and Culture.* New York: Other Press.

Fairclough, N. (2010). *Critical Discourse Analysis: the Critical Study of Language* (2nd edn). Harlow, UK: Longman.

Flyvbjerg, B. (2001). *Making Social Science Matter: Why Social Inquiry Fails and How It Can Succeed Again* (S. Sampson, Trans.). Cambridge, UK: Cambridge University Press.

Fox, D., Prilleltensky, I., & Austin, S. (eds). (2009). *Critical Psychology: An Introduction* (2nd edn). Thousand Oaks, CA: Sage.

Frosh, S., Phoenix, A., & Pattman, R. (2003). Taking a stand: using psychoanalysis to explore the positioning of subjects in discourse. *British Journal of Social Psychology, 42*(1), 39–53.

Gergen, K. J. (2002). Beyond the empiricist/constructionist divide in social psychology. *Personality and Social Psychology Review, 6*(3), 188–191.

Henriques, J. (1984). Social psychology and the politics of racism. In J. Henriques, W. Hollway, C. Urwin, C. Venn & V. Walkerdine (eds), *Changing the Subject: Psychology, Social Regulation and Subjectivity* (pp. 60–89). New York: Methuen.

Hepburn, A. (1999). Derrida and psychology: deconstruction and its ab/uses in critical and discursive psychologies. *Theory & Psychology, 9*(5), 639–665.

Hepburn, A. (2003). *An Introduction to Critical Social Psychology.* London: Sage.

Hepburn, A., & Wiggins, S. (eds). (2007). *Discursive Research in Practice: New Approaches to Psychology and Interaction.* Cambridge, UK: Cambridge University Press.

Hodgetts, K., & Lecouteur, A. (2010). Gender and disadvantage in the Australian parliamentary inquiry into the education of boys. *Feminism & Psychology 20*(1), 73–93.

Hook, D. (2001). Discourse, knowledge, materiality, history: Foucault and discourse analysis. *Theory & Psychology, 11*, 521–547.

Hook, D. (2007). *Foucault, Psychology and the Analytics of Power.* Basingstoke, UK: Palgrave Macmillan.

Jackson, S. (2005). 'I'm 15 and desperate for sex': 'doing' and 'undoing' desire in letters to a teenage magazine. *Feminism & Psychology, 15*(3), 295–313.

Jost, J. T., & Kruglanski, A. W. (2002). The estrangement of social constructionism and experimental social psychology: history of the rift and prospects for reconciliation. *Personality and Social Psychology Review, 6*(3), 168–187.

Lyotard, J.-F. (1984). *The Postmodern Condition: A Report on Knowledge.* Manchester, UK: Manchester University Press.

McDonald, M., & O'Callaghan, J. (2008). Positive psychology: a Foucauldian critique. *Humanistic Psychologist, 36*(2), 127–142.

Meloni, M. (2011). Philosophical implications of neuroscience: the space for a critique. *Subjectivity, 4*(3), 298–322.

Mills, W. C. (1959/2000). *The Sociological Imagination* (Fortieth Anniversary edn). Oxford, UK: Oxford University Press.

Parker, I. (1992). *Discourse Dynamics: Critical Analysis for Social and Individual Psychology.* London: Routledge.

Parker, I. (ed.). (2002). *Critical Discursive Psychology.* Basingstoke, UK: Palgrave Macmillan.

Parker, I. (2003). Jacques Lacan, barred psychologist. *Theory & Psychology, 13*(1), 95–115.

Parker, I. (2005). Lacanian discourse analysis in psychology: seven theoretical elements. *Theory & Psychology, 15*(2), 163–182.

Parker, I. (2009). Critical psychology and revolutionary Marxism. *Theory & Psychology, 19*(1), 71–92.

Parker, I., Georgaca, E., Harper, D., McLaughlin, T., & Stowell-Smith, M. (1995). *Deconstructing Psychopathology*. London: Sage.

Parker, I., & Hook, D. (2008). Psychoanalysis and social psychology: historical connections and contemporary applications. *Journal of Community & Applied Social Psychology, 18*(2), 91–95.

Peterson, C., & Seligman, M. E. P. (2004). *Character Strengths and Virtues: A Handbook and Classification*. Washington, DC: American Psychological Association.

Raskin, J. D. (2011). On essences in constructivist psychology. *Journal of Theoretical and Philosophical Psychology, 31*(4), 223–239.

Rose, N. (1998). *Inventing Ours Selves: Psychology, Power, and Personhood*. Cambridge, UK: Cambridge University Press.

Rose, N. (1999). *Governing the Soul: the Shaping of the Private Self* (2nd edn). London: Free Association Books.

Rose, N. (2008). Psychology as a social science. *Subjectivity, 25*(4), 446–462.

Seligman, M. E. P., & Csikszentmihalyi, M. (2000). Positive psychology: an introduction. *American Psychologist, 55*(1), 5–14.

Taylor, E. (2001). A reply to Seligman on positive psychology. *Journal of Humanistic Psychology, 41*(1), 13–29.

Tuffin, K. (2004). *Understanding Critical Social Psychology*. London: Sage.

Wetherell, M., Taylor, S., & Yates, S. J. (eds). (2001). *Discourse as Data: A Guide for Analysis*. London: Sage.

Wiggins, S., & Potter, J. (2008). Discursive psychology. In C. Willig & W. Stainton-Rogers (eds), *The Sage Handbook of Qualitative Research in Psychology* (pp. 73–90). London: Sage.

Wilkinson, S., & Kitzinger, C. (2008). Conversation analysis. In C. Willig & W. Stainton-Rogers (eds), *The Sage Handbook of Qualitative Research in Psychology* (pp. 54–72). London: Sage.

Willig, C. (2008). Discourse analysis. In J. A. Smith (ed.), *Qualitative Psychology: A Practical Guide to Research Methods* (2nd edn, pp. 160–185). London: Sage.

Wooffitt, R. (2005). *Conversation Analysis and Discourse Analysis: A Comparative and Critical Introduction*. London: Sage.

Yen, J. (2010). Authorizing happiness: rhetorical demarcation of science and society in historical narratives of positive psychology. *Journal of Theoretical and Philosophical Psychology, 30*(2), 67–78.

Postscript

We hope that this book has proved a stimulating and rewarding introduction to critical social psychology and related fields. In attempting to make complex concepts and debates accessible, we have probably not done justice to the broad and fragmented arena of critical social psychology, but in pursuing the recommended readings alongside this preliminary text you will undoubtedly have attained a firm grasp of the material. Critical social psychology does not lend itself naturally to clear and unproblematic teaching or writing and our own experience of teaching critical social psychology and writing this text would reinforce this view. Perhaps in the future you will take on other 'critical' courses during your studies and will have the opportunity to conduct a research project informed by critical literature and using methods such as discourse analysis. Chapter 3, on methods, is an obvious starting place, but you would do well to consult other texts on (qualitative) research methods in general and discourse analysis in particular (e.g. Willig, 2008; Smith, 2008).

It is also a good idea to consult a range of journal articles where critical work is published. Journals such as *Discourse & Society* and *Feminism & Psychology* are fine places to start, but it is worth browsing other sociological and inter-disciplinary periodicals (e.g. *Sociological Review*; *Theory & Psychology*). In addition, dedicated critical titles are available, such as the *Annual Review of Critical Psychology*, *Subjectivity* and *Radical Psychology*. The latter is also published on the internet and is part of a larger website devoted to the presentation and discussion of critical issues in psychology and society (http://www.radpsynet.org/). There are other critical psychology websites which serve similar functions, notably one co-ordinated by Denis Fox, editor of two Critical Psychology texts (1997; 2009), which is very user-friendly (http://www.dennisfox.net/critpsy/) and provides links to numerous other critical psychology groups and sites. One of the advantages of these sites is the advice and encouragement offered to students and researchers interested in pursuing critical goals at work and in society generally.

New references

Fox, D. & Prilleltensky, I. (1997). (eds) *Critical Psychology: An Introduction.* Thousand Oaks, CA: Sage.

Fox, D., Prilleltensky, I. & Austin, S. (eds). (2009). *Critical Psychology: An Introduction* (2nd edn). Thousand Oaks, CA: Sage.

Smith, J. (2008) (Ed) *Qualitative Psychology: A Practical Guide to Research Methods.* London: Sage

Willig, C. (2008) *Introducing Qualitative Research in Psychology* (2nd edn). Buckingham: Open University Press.

Glossary

Agency Emphasizes individuals as active in negotiating their social worlds and directly challenges traditional notions of the individual as a passive recipient of social structures, dictates and regulations.

Aggression This is a broad term that situates aggression not in the actions of the individual but rather as a set of social, cultural and historically located activities.

Alienation A term used by Marx to describe the feelings of isolation and estrangement experienced by workers when they are separated from the products they create. Alienation occurs in conditions where workers have little or no control over the production process. The term is also used to describe a more general condition where an individual is estranged from themselves, others and society.

Androgyny An androgynous individual is said to possess high levels of both 'masculine' and 'feminine' characteristics, but Bem's (1974) concept has been criticized for failing to account for the social construction of gender.

Class Refers to the system of social stratification based on the economic status of the individual or group. The class one is born into will influence one's material life chances so that inequality becomes a fundamental characteristic of class-based societies.

Collectivism Cultural ideals prioritizing the group over the individual as expressed in norms such as duty and self-discipline common in 'Eastern' societies (contrast with Western individualism).

Compulsory heterosexuality A term used to challenge prevalent representations of heterosexuality as 'natural' and to encourage notions of heterosexuality as socially constructed and managed.

Conformity Within critical social psychology, conformity is redefined as a socially produced and managed activity. This is in contrast to traditional social psychological perspectives which define conformity at the level of the individual.

Consumer culture The culture of consumer society where 'consumption' has come to replace 'production' as the primary means by which socio–economic status is determined, self-identity is constructed, and where the aim of life centres on the purchase of products, services and their experiences.

Continuum of sexual violence   In contrast to the traditional definitions of sexual violence as rape, the continuum emphasizes the everyday abuse of women (and some men) through sexist jokes, harassment, marital rape, domestic violence and murder.

Deconstructionism   A joining together of destruction and construction which marks a critical stripping away of assumptions underlying a 'text' (e.g. a theory).

Determinism   A criticism levelled at various theories in social psychology which present the individual as shaped (or 'determined') by forces outside their control.

Discourse analysis   A general term applied liberally to various forms of textual analysis, but the term 'discourse' is often traced to Foucault and associated with the identification of 'top-down' historical/cultural representations (e.g. discourses of medicine, science, individualism, etc.).

Empiricism   A commitment to gathering data in a systematic manner in order to produce 'valid' knowledge.

Essentialism   A view proclaiming the existence of an 'essential' core within individuals (and things) which can be identified; it has been used to argue that men and women are 'naturally' different.

Feminisms   A recent term which highlights differences and debates within feminism in the light of the increasing range of experiences and positions articulated by women.

Governmentality   A term used by Foucault to describe a particular rationality for governing populations in neoliberal democracies where 'governing at a distance' replaces more direct forms of intervention. Neoliberal democracies seek to produce 'self-governing individuals' who are rational, productive, responsible, independent and enterprising.

Hegemony   Most often associated with the work of Italian theorist Antonio Gramsci, hegemony refers to the ways in which the ruling classes dominate society by setting its intellectual and moral parameters. These values are consented to by the rest of society who are persuaded that status quo is natural, inevitable and beneficial for all.

Homophobia   Homophobia refers to practices that oppress gay, lesbian and bisexual people and derives from discourses that represent heterosexuality as the only natural, normal and acceptable sexuality.

Ideology   Political and economic ideas that are taken for granted by the majority and which promote particular ways of thinking and behaviour. Ideologies are used to serve and legitimize inequalities and the power that maintains them.

Individualism A focus on the individual or parts of individuals (e.g. memory systems, genes, etc.), the main unit of analysis found in mainstream social psychological theories.

Interpretative repertoire Used by Potter and Wetherell (1987) in their landmark text to signify a relatively discrete set of metaphors and images drawn upon in talk to construct a particular object (e.g. 'the self as an actor on the stage of life') and associated with their 'bottom-up' form of discourse analysis where individual creativity is apparent.

Masculinities Emphasizes the range of 'masculine' subject positions available to men in contemporary society; challenges the idea of masculinity as something fixed or essential.

Neoliberalism A political and economic ideology which proposes that human wellbeing and the distribution of resources is most effectively and efficiently achieved through the 'free market' as opposed to government intervention. Neoliberal economic policies include the deregulation of financial institutions, the privatization of government/national enterprises, reduction in government funding, reduction in taxation and the undermining of collective labour movements.

'New' racism A term coined by Billig (1988), it refers to new more subtle types of racist activity where, in their talk, people often present racist sentiments while denying their prejudice at the same time.

Oedipal complex A Freudian term used to describe the feelings of hatred young children experience for their mother around the age of 3 or 4.

Post-modernism Often used alongside or as a substitute term for post-structuralism and signals a break with 'modernist' ideals such as truth, meaning and progress in favour of celebrating diverse (and equally valid) perspectives.

Post-structuralism A scepticism towards claims about underlying 'reality' such as those found in structuralist theories and a view of meaning as multi-faceted, partial and debatable.

Power/Knowledge A theory of power developed by Foucault which proposes that power and knowledge directly imply one another. How we come to know ourselves is influenced by knowledge which stems from the dominant ethical and moral codes of our culture.

Prejudice This term refers to oppressive social activities against an individual or individuals. In contrast to traditional psychological definitions of prejudice, critical definitions explicitly recognize the socially legitimized and power dimensions associated with prejudiced activities.

Psychosocial Studies An interdisciplinary field that seeks to investigate how individual subjectivity is influenced by biographical, social and cultural forces.

'Queer' theory A recent theoretical paradigm that aims to destabilize social norms and practices which present heterosexuality as natural and correct.

Realism A commitment to some notion of the 'real', whether this is said to exist independently of discourse or bound up with discourse; 'critical realists' accept constructionist arguments but argue that some constructions refer to reality (e.g. ethnic minorities as oppressed).

Reductionism An objection to mainstream psychological methods which tend to empty or reduce concepts of their meaning in order to render them measurable.

Reflexivity A practice popular with qualitative and many critical researchers whereby the constructed nature of one's analysis is made visible through highlighting personal and theoretical ideas which have informed the research process and outcomes.

Relativism A position following from post-structuralism and constructionism which rejects established notions of truth and reality and which, some argue, may lead to an inability to convincingly advocate or apply a particular political stance.

Sex roles Social psychological concept which explains gender (difference) in terms of socialization rather than biology but which neglects power relations and discourse.

Sexism Discourses and practices used to construct wo/men as inferior.

Sexology The scientific study of human sexual functioning and behaviour. Sexuality as an innate characteristic of human development forms a central assumption of this paradigm.

Sexual invert A term coined by Ellis to define homosexual individuals as biologically abnormal.

Slag A complex, derogatory term (predominately applied to women) and used to control sexual/social identities and activities.

Social Constructionism A broad perspective which locates meaning within social/linguistic processes, emphasizes a critique of 'common sense' and highlights the plurality of constructions or interpretations.

Social control This term explicitly recognizes the functions of conformity/obedience as a means of controlling the social practices of populations.

Structuralism Explains human behaviour in terms of 'structures', which can be 'external', such as 'capitalism', 'patriarchy'
or language, or internal, such as the unconscious, cognitive or
biological systems.

Subject positions Those 'slots' made available by discourses which
people may take up, re-work or reject, depending on resources and
circumstances.

Subjectivity A term which avoids the individualism and realism
implied in terms such as 'personality' and which emphasizes the
self as an almost continuous process of construction.

Subversion Highlights one of the ways in which individuals resist
oppressive social practices – that is, by re-working taken-for-granted
social representations to produce more positive social meanings.

Working-class femininities Emphasizes the complex interaction of
social class and gender in identity negotiation.

References

Adams, G. & Salter, P.S. (2007) Health psychology in African settings: a cultural-psychological analysis, *Journal of Health Psychology, 12*(3), 539–548.

Adlam, D., Henriques, J., Rose, N., Salfield, A., Venn, C. & Walkerdine, V. (1977) Psychology, ideology and the human subject, *Ideology & Consciousness, 1*, 5–56.

Adorno, T.W., Frenkel-Brunswick, E., Levinson, D.J. & Sanford, N. (1950) *The Authoritarian Personality*, New York: Harper Row.

Allport, G.W. (1968) The historical background of modern social psychology. In G. Lindzey & E. Aronson (eds), *The Handbook of Social Psychology* (2nd edn, Vol. 1), Reading, MA: Addison-Wesley.

Althusser, L. (1984) *Essays on Ideology*, London: Verso.

Alvesson, M., & Deetz, S. A. (2005). Critical theory and postmodern approaches to organizational studies. In S. Clegg, C. Hardy, T. Lawrence & W. R. Nord (eds), *The Sage Handbook of Organization Studies* (2nd edn, pp. 255–283). London: Sage

Alvesson, M., Bridgman, T., & Willmott, H. (2011). Introduction. In M. Alvesson, T. Bridgman & H. Willmott (eds), *The Oxford Handbook of Critical Management Studies* (pp. 1–26). Oxford: Oxford University Press.

Amir, M. (1971) *Patterns of Forcible Rape*, Chicago: University of Chicago Press.

Ancis, J.R. & Szymanski, D.M. (2001) Awareness of white privilege among white counseling trainees, *Counseling Psychologist, 29*, 549–550.

Anderson, R. (1988) *The Power and the Word: Language, Power and Change*, London: Paladin.

Andrews, M., Squire, C., & Tamboukou, M. (2008) (eds). *Doing Narrative Research*. London: Sage.

Antaki, C., Billig, M., Edwards, D., & Potter, J. (2003). Discourse analysis means doing analysis: a critique of six analytic shortcomings. *Discourse Analysis Online, 1*(1).

Archer, J. (2004) Sex differences in aggression in real world settings: a meta-analytic review. *Review of General Psychology, 8*, 291–322.

Archer, J. & Lloyd, B.B. (1985) *Sex and Gender*, Cambridge: Cambridge University Press.

Arfken, M. (2011). Marxist scholarship and psychological practice. *Annual Review of Critical Psychology, 9*, 6–7.

Argyle, M. (1989). *The Social Psychology of Work* (Rev edn). London: Penguin.

Argyris, C. (1975) Dangers in applying results from experimental social psychology, *American Psychologist, 30*, 469–485.

Armistead, N. (1974) *Reconstructing Social Psychology*, Harmondsworth: Penguin.

Armstrong, G. (1998) *Football Hooligans: Knowing the Score,* New York: Berg.

Aron, A. & Corne, S. (1994) (eds). *Ignacio Martín-Baró: Writings For A Liberation Psychology.* Cambridge, MA: Harvard University Press.

Aronson, E. (1988) *The Social Animal* (5th edn), New York: Freeman.

Arribas-Ayllon, M., & Walkerdine, V. (2008). Foucauldian discourse analysis. In C. Willig & W. Stainton-Rogers (eds), *Sage Handbook of Qualitative Research in Psychology* (pp. 91–108). London: Sage.

Asch, S. (1952) *Social Psychology,* Englewood Cliffs, NJ: Prentice-Hall.

Augoustinos, M. (1999). Ideology, false consciousness and psychology. *Theory & Psychology, 9*(3), 295–312.

Augoustinos, M. & Every, D. (2007). The language of 'race' and prejudice: a discourse of denial, reason, and liberal-practical politics. *Journal of Language and Social Psychology,* 26: 123–144.

Augoustinos, M., Tuffin, K. & Every, D. (2005). New racism, meritocracy, and individualism: constraining affirmative action in education. *Discourse & Society, 16,* 315–339.

Austin, J. (1962) *How to Do Things with Words,* London: Oxford University Press.

Australian Law Reform Commission (ALRC). (1987). Traditional Aboriginal society and its law. In W.H. Edwards (ed.), *Traditional Aboriginal Society:A Reader* (pp. 189–202) Melbourne: Macmillan.

Baker, C.D. (2000) Locating culture in action: membership categorization in texts and talk. In A. Lee & C. Poynton (eds) *Culture and Text: Discourse and Methodology in Social Research and Cultural Studies* (pp. 99–113). London: Routledge.

Ballaster, R., Beetham, M. Frazer, E. & Hebron, S. (1991) *Women's Worlds: Ideology, Femininity and the Woman's Magazine,* Basingstoke, UK: Palgrave Macmillan.

Bandura, A. (1973) *Aggression: A Social Learning Analysis,* New Jersey: Prentice-Hall.

Bandura, A. (1977) *Social Learning Theory,* Englewood Cliffs: Prentice-Hall.

Bandura, A. (1983) Psychological mechanisms in aggression. In R. Geen & L. Donnerstein (eds), *Aggression: Theoretical and Empirical Reviews,* vol. 1. New York: Academic Press.

Banister, P., Burman, E., Parker, I., Taylor, M. & Tindall, C. (1994) *Qualitative Methods in Psychology: A Research Guide,* Buckingham: Open University Press.

Banister, P., Bunn, G., Burman, E., et al. (2011). *Qualitative Methods in Psychology: a Research Guide* (2nd edn). Maidenhead, UK: Open University Press.

Baritz, L. (1960). *The Servants of Power: a History of the Use of Social Science in American Industry.* New York: Wiley.

Barker, E.T., Greenberg, J.S., Selzer, M.M., Almeida, D.M, (2012) Daily stress and cortisol patterns in parents of adult children with a serious mental illness, *Health Psychology, 31*(1), 130–134.

Barker, M. & Petley, J. (1997) *Ill-Effects: The Medial Violence Debate,* London: Routledge.

Barker, R., Dembo, T. & Lewin, K. (1941) Imitation of film-mediated aggressive models, *Journal of Abnormal and Social Psychology, 66*, 3–11.

Baron, A. (1977) *Human Aggression,* New York: Plenum.

Baron-Cohen, S. (2005) The essential difference: the male and female brain. *Phi Kappa Phi Forum, 85*(1), 23–27.

Baron, R.A. & Byrne, D. (1999) *Social Psychology: Understanding Human Interaction,* Boston: Allyn & Bacon.

Bartky, S. L. (2009). Foucault, femininity, and the modernization of patriarchal power. In R. Weitz (ed.), *Politics of Women's Bodies: Sexuality, Appearance, and Behaviour* (3rd edn, pp. 25–45). Oxford, UK: Oxford University Press

Bateson, P. (1989) Is aggression instinctive? In J. Groebel & R.A. Hinde (eds), *Aggression and War: Their Biological and Social Bases,* New York: Cambridge University Press.

Baumeister, R.F. (1988) Should we stop studying sex differences altogether? *American Psychologist, 42*: 1092–1095.

Becker, D., & Marecek, J. (2008). Positive psychology: history in the remaking? *Theory & Psychology, 18*(5), 591–604.

Beder, S. (2001). *Selling the Work Ethic: From Puritan Pulpit to Corporate* pr. London: Zed Books.

Bem, S.L. (1974) The measurement of psychological androgyny, *Journal of Consulting and Clinical Psychology, 42*, 155–162.

Bem, S.L. (1981) Gender schema theory: a cognitive assessment of sex-typing, *Psychological Review, 88*, 354–364.

Bem, S. (1985) Androgyny and gender schema theory: a conceptual and empirical integration. In T.N. Sonderegger (ed.), *Nebraska Symposium on Motivation 1984: Psychology and Gender,* Lincoln, NE: University of Nebraska Press.

Bem, S. (1987) Gender schema theory and the romantic tradition. In P. Shaver & C. Hendrick (eds), *Sex and Gender,* Newbury Park: Sage.

Bem, S.L., Martyna, W. & Watson, C. (1976) Sex-typing and androgyny: further explorations of the expressive domain, *Journal of Personality & Social Psychology, 33*, 48–54.

Benbow, C.P. & Stanley, J.C. (1980) Sex differences in mathematical ability: fact or artifact? *Science, 210*, 1262–1264.

Ben-Ner, A., McCall, B.P., Stephane, M. & Wang, H. (2009) Identity and in-group and out-group differentiation in work and giving behaviours: experimental evidence, *Journal of Economic Behaviour and Organization, 72*, 153–170.

Benwell B (2004) Ironic discourse: evasive masculinity in men's lifestyle magazines. *Men and Masculinities, 7*(1), 3–21.

Berardi, F. (2009). *The Soul at Work: From Alienation to Authority* (F. Cadel & G. Mecchia, Trans.). Los Angeles: Semiotext.

Berger, P.L. & Luckman, T. (1967) *The Social Construction of Reality,* Harmondsworth: Penguin.

Berkowitz, L. (1962) *Aggression: A Social Psychological Analysis,* New York: McGraw-Hill.

Berkowitz, L. (1974) Some determinants of impulsive aggression: role of mediated associations with reinforcement for aggression, *Psychological Review*, 81(2), 165–176.

Berkowitz, L. & Geen, R. (1966) Film violence and the cue properties of available targets, *Journal of Personality and Social Psychology*, 3, 525–530.

Bhavnani, K. K. & Phoenix, A. (1994) Special issue: shifting identities shifting racisms, *Feminism & Psychology*, 4(1).

Billig, M. (1976) *Social Psychology and Intergroup Relations*, London: Academic Press.

Billig, M. (1978) *Fascists: A Social Psychological View of the National Front*, London: Harcourt Brace Jovanovich.

Billig, M. (1982) *Ideology and Social Psychology*, Oxford: Blackwell.

Billig, M. (1985) Prejudice, categorization and particularization: from a perceptual to a rhetorical approach, *European Journal of Social Psychology*, 15, 79–103.

Billig, M. (1988) The notion of prejudice: some rhetorical and ideological aspects, *Text*, 8, 91–110.

Billig, M. (1990) Rhetoric of social psychology In I. Parker & J. Shotter (eds), *Deconstructing Social Psychology*, London: Routledge.

Billig, M. (1992) *Talking of the Royal Family*, London: Routledge.

Billig, M. (1995) *Banal Nationalism*. London: Sage.

Billig, M. (1996). Remembering the particular background of social identity theory. In W. P. Robinson (ed.), *Social Groups and Identities: Developing the Legacy of Henri Tajfel* (pp. 337–358). Oxford, UK: Butterworth-Heinemann.

Billig, M. (1997a) Rhetorical and discursive analysis: how families talk about the royal family. In N. Hayes (ed.), *Doing Qualitative Analysis in Psychology*, London: Psychology Press.

Billig, M. (1997b) The dialogic unconscious: psychoanalysis, discursive psychology and the nature of repression, *British Journal of Social Psychology*, 36(2), 139–160.

Billig, M. (1999). *Freudian Repression: Conversation Creating the Unconscious*. Cambridge, UK: Cambridge University Press.

Billig, M. (2001) Humour and hatred: the racist jokes of the Ku Klux Klan, *Discourse & Society*, 12, 267–289.

Billig, M. (2002). Henri Tajfel's 'cognitive aspects of prejudice' and the psychology of bigotry. *British Journal of Social Psychology*, 41, 171–188.

Billig, M. (2003). Political rhetoric. In D. O. Sears, L. Huddy & R. Jervis (eds), *Oxford Handbook of Political Psychology* (pp. 222–251). Oxford: Oxford University Press.

Billig, M. (2011). Writing social psychology: fictional things and unpopulated texts. *British Journal of Social Psychology*, 50(1), 4–20.

Billig, M., Condor, S., Edwards, D., Gane, M., Middleton, D. & Radley, A. (1988) *Ideological Dilemmas: A Social Psychology of Everyday Thinking*, London: Sage.

Binkley, S. (2011). Happiness, positive psychology and the program of neoliberal governmentality. *Subjectivity*, 4(4), 371–394.

Bishop, E. C., & Shepherd, M. L. (2011). Ethical reflections: examining reflexivity through the narrative paradigm. *Qualitative Health Research, 21*(9), 1283–1294.

Blackler, F., & Brown, C. A. (1978). Organizational psychology: good intentions and false promises. *Human Relations, 31,* 333–351.

Blackman, L., Cromby, J., Hook, D., Papadopoulos, D. & Walkerdine, V. (2008) Creating subjectivities (editorial), *Subjectivity, 22,* 1–27.

Blackwell, J. C., Smith, M. E. G., & Sorenson, J. S. (2003). *Cultures of Prejudice: Arguments in Critical Social Science* (2nd edn). Peterborough, Canada: Broadview Press.

Blakemore, J., Young, J., Dilorio, J. & Fairchild, D. (1997) Exploring the campus climate for women faculty. In N. Benokraitus (ed.), *Subtle Sexism: Current Practices and Prospects for Change,* London: Sage.

Bleier, R. (1984) *Science and Gender: A Critique of Biology and Its Theories on Women,* London: Pergamon.

Blood, S. K. (2005). *Body Work: The Social Construction of Women's Bodies.* London: Routledge.

Bocock, R. (1976). *Freud and Modern Society: An Outline and Analysis of Freud's Sociology.* New York: Holmes and Meier.

Bocock, R. (1993). *Consumption.* London: Routledge.

Bocock, R. (2002). *Sigmund Freud* (2nd edn). London: Routledge.

Bond, M.H. & Cheung, T.S. (1983) The spontaneous self-concept of college students in Hong Kong, Japan and the United States, *Journal of Cross-Cultural Psychology, 14,* 153–171.

Bordo, S. (1993). *Unbearable Weight: Feminism, Western Culture, and the Body.* Berkeley, CA: University of California Press.

Bordo, S. (1999) *The Male Body.* New York: Farrar, Straus and Giroux.

Bostock, J., & Freeman, J. (2003). No limits: doing participatory action research with young people in Northumberland. *Journal of Community & Applied Social Psychology, 13*(6), 464–474.

Bourdieu, P. (1984) *Distinction: A Social Critique of the Judgment of Taste* (Richard Nice, trans.), Cambridge, MA: Harvard University Press.

Boyle, M. (1996) 'Schizophrenia' re-evaluated. In T. Heller, J. Reynolds, R. Gomm, R. Muston & S. Pattison (eds), *Mental Health Matters: A Reader,* Basingstoke: Palgrave Macmillan.

Bramel, D., & Friend, R. (1981). Hawthorne, the myth of the docile worker, and class bias in psychology. *American Psychologist, 36,* 867–878.

Brannigan, A. (2004). *The Rise and Fall of Social Psychology: An Iconoclast's Guide to the Use and Misuse of the Experimental Method.* Piscataway, NJ: Aldine Transaction.

Braverman, H. (1974). *Labor and Monopoly Capital: The Degradation of Work in the Twentieth Century.* New York: Monthly Review Press.

Breeze, R. (2011). Critical discourse analysis and its critics. *Pragmatics, 21*(4), 493–525.

Brehm, S. & Kassin, S. (1993) *Social Psychology,* Boston: Houghton Mifflin.

Brehm, S. S., Kassin, S. M., & Fein, S. (2005). *Social Psychology* (6th edn). Boston: Houghton Mifflin.

Brewer, M.B. (2001) In-group identification and intergroup conflict: when does in-group love become out-group hate? In R. Ashmore, L. Jussim & D. Wilder (eds) *Social Identity, Intergroup Conflict and Conflict Reduction.* New York: Oxford University Press.

Brewster-Smith, M. (1983) The shaping of American social psychology: a personal perspective from the periphery, *Personality and Social Psychology, 9,* 165–180.

Brittan, A. (1987) *Masculinity and Power,* London: Blackwell.

Brizendine, L. (2008). *The Female Brain.* London: Transworld.

Brizendine, L. (2011). *The Male Brain.* London: Transworld.

Brown, H. (1996) Themes in experimental research on groups from 1930s to the 1990s. In M. Wetherell (ed.), *Identities, Groups and Social Issues,* London: The Open University.

Brown, J. A. C. (1954). *Social Psychology and Industry: Human Relations in the Factory.* Harmondsworth, UK: Penguin.

Brown, J. D,, L'Engle, K. L., Pardun, C. J., Guo, G., Kenneavy, K. & Jackson, C. (2006) Sexy Media Matter: Exposure to Sexual Content in Music, Movies, Television, and Magazines Predicts Black and White Adolescents' Sexual Behavior. *Pediatrics, 117*(4), 1018–1127.

Brown, L. (1997) New voices, new visions: towards a lesbian/gay paradigm for psychology. In M. Gergen & S. Davis (eds), *Towards a New Psychology of Gender: A Reader.* London: Routledge.

Brown, P. (1974) *Radical Psychology,* London: Tavistock.

Brown, S.R. (1980) *Political Subjectivity: Applications of Q Methodology in Political Science,* New Haven, CT: Yale University Press.

Brown, S. D. (2007). Intergroup processes: social identity theory. In D. Langdridge & S. Taylor (eds), *Critical Readings in Social Psychology* (pp. 133–162). Maidenhead, UK: Open University Press.

Brown, S.D. & Pujol, J. with Curt, B. (1998) As one in a web? Discourse, materiality and the place of ethics, in I. Parker (ed.), *Social Constructionism, Discourse and Realism,* London: Sage.

Brown, R. & Hewstone, M. (2005) An integrative theory of intergroup contact. In M. Zanna (ed.) *Advances in Experimental Social Psychology, 37,* 255–343.

Brownmiller, S. (1976) *Against Our Will: Men, Women and Rape,* Harmondsworth: Penguin.

Brydon-Miller, M. (1997). Participatory action research: psychology and social change. *Journal of Social Issues, 53*(4), 657–666.

Buckingham, D. (1993) Boys' talk: television and the policing of masculinity. In D. Buckingham (ed.), *Reading Audiences: Young People and the Media,* Manchester: Manchester University Press.

Bull, P. (2007). Political language and persuasive communication. In A. Weatherall, B. M. Watson & C. Gallois (eds), *Language, Discourse and Social Psychology* (pp. 255–275). Basingstoke, UK: Palgrave Macmillan.

Burger, J. (1985). Desire for control and achievement related behaviours. *Journal of Personality and Social Psychology, 46,* 1520–1533.

Burger, J. (2009). Replicating Milgram: would people still obey? *American Psychologist, 64*(1), 1–11.

Burke, C. (1980) cited in Hudson, B. (1984) Femininity and adolescence. In A. McRobbie & M. Nava (eds), *Gender and Generation,* London: Macmillan.

Burke, S. & Goodman, S. (2012) 'Bring back Hitler's gas chambers': Asylum-seeking, Nazis and Facebook – a discursive analysis, *Discourse & Society, 23*(1), 19–33.

Burman, E. (1990) *Feminists and Psychological Practice,* London: Sage.

Burman, E. (1991) What discourse is not, *Philosophical Psychology, 4*(3), 325–342.

Burman, E. (1998) *Deconstructing Feminist Psychology,* London: Sage.

Burman, E. (2003). Discourse analysis means analysing discourse. *Discourse Analysis Online,* http://extra.shu.ac.uk/daol/current/

Burman, E. & Parker, I. (1993) *Discourse Analytic Research. Repertoires and Readings of Text in Action,* London: Routledge.

Burman, E., Alldred, P., Bewley, C., Goldberg, B., Heenan, C., Marks, D., Marshall, J., Taylor, K., Ullah, R. & Warner, S. (1995) *Challenging Women: Psychology's Exclusions, Feminist Possibilities,* Buckingham: Open University Press.

Burns, M., Tyrer. J. & Eating Difficulties Education Network (2009) Feminisms in practice: challenges and opportunities for an eating issues community agency. In Malson H, Burns, M (eds) *Critical Feminist Approaches to Eating Dis/Orders* (pp. 221–232). London: Routledge.

Burr, V. (1995) *An Introduction to Social Constructionism,* London: Routledge.

Burr, V. (1998) *Gender and Social Psychology,* London: Routledge.

Burr, V. (2002). *The Person in Social Psychology,* London: Routledge.

Burr, V. (2003). *Social Constructionism* (2nd edn). London: Routledge

Burton, M., & Kagan, C. (2005). Liberation social psychology: learning from Latin America. *Journal of Community & Applied Social Psychology, 15*(1), 63–78.

Buss, A. (1961) *The Psychology of Aggression,* New York: Wiley.

Bussey, K., & Bandura, A. (1999). Social cognitive theory of gender development and differentiation. *Psychological Review, 106*(4), 676–713.

Butler, J. (1990) *Gender Trouble: Feminism and the Subversion of Identity,* London: Routledge.

Butler, J. (1993) *Bodies That Matter: On the Discursive Limits of Sex,* New York: Routledge.

Cairns, E. & Mercer, G. (1984) Social identity in Northern Ireland, *Human Relations, 37*(12), 1095–1102.

Callaghan, J. & Lazard, L. (2011). *Social Psychology.* Exeter: Learning Matters.

Cameron, D. (1992) *Feminism and Linguistic Theory* (2nd edn), Basingstoke: Palgrave Macmillan.

Campbell, A. (2008). Attachment, aggression and affiliation: the role of oxytocin in female social behavior. *Biological Psychology, 77*(1), 1–10.

Canaan, J. (1996) 'One thing leads to another': drinking, fighting and working-class masculinities. In M. Mac An Ghaill (ed.), *Understanding Masculinities: Social Relations and Cultural Arenas,* Milton Keynes: Open University Press.

Capdevila, R. & Callaghan, J. (2008) 'It's not racist, it's common sense': a critical analysis of political discourse around asylum and immigration in the UK. *Journal of Community and Applied Social Psychology, 18,* 1–16.

Caprara, G., Barbaranelli, C., Pastorelli & Perugini, M. (1994) Individual differences in the study of human aggression, *Aggressive Behaviour, 1,* 61–74.

Carey, R. N., Donaghue, N., & Broderick, P. (2011). 'What you look like is such a big factor': Girls' own reflections about the appearance culture in an all-girls' school. *Feminism & Psychology, 21*(3), 299–316.

Carlson, S. (2010). In defense of queer kinships: Oedipus recast. *Subjectivity, 3*(3), 263–281.

Carrette, J. (2003). Psychology, spirituality and capitalism: the case of Abraham Maslow. *Critical Psychology, 8,* 73–95.

Cartwright, D. (1979) Contemporary social psychology in historical perspective, *Social Psychology Quarterly, 42,* 82–93.

Cash, J. (2002). Troubled times: changing the political subject in Northern Ireland. In V. Walkerdine (ed.), *Challenging Subjects: Critical Psychology for a New Millennium* (pp. 88–100). Basingstoke, UK: Palgrave Macmillan.

Cashmore, E. (1987) cited in Wetherell, M. (ed.) (1996) *Identities, Groups and Social Issues,* London: Sage.

Castillejo, I. de (1973) *Knowing Woman: A Feminine Psychology,* London: Hodder & Stoughton.

Cherry, F. (2009). Social psychology and social change. In D. Fox, I. Prilleltensky, I., & S. Austin (eds), *Critical Psychology: An Introduction* (2nd edn, pp. 93–109). Thousand Oaks, CA: Sage.

Chiu, C.-Y., & Cheng, S. Y. Y. (2007). Toward a social psychology of culture and globalization: some social cognitive consequences of activating two cultures simultaneously. *Social and Personality Psychology Compass, 1*(1), 84–100.

Chodorow, N. (1978) *The Reproduction of Mothering,* Berkeley: University of California Press.

Chodorow, N. J. (1990). Gender, relation, and difference in psychoanalytic perspective. In C. Zanardi (ed.), *Essential Papers on the Psychology of Women* (pp. 420–436). New York: New York University Press.

Chodorow, N. J. (2002). Gender as a personal and cultural construction. In M. Dimen & V. Goldner (eds), *Gender in Psychoanalytic Space: between Clinic and Culture* (pp. 237–261). New York: Other Press.

Choi, P.Y.L. (1994) Women's raging hormones. In P.Y.L. Choi & P. Nicolson (eds), *Female Sexuality: Psychology, Biology and Social Context,* New York: Harvester Wheatsheaf.

Christopher, J. C., & Hickinbottom, S. (2008). Positive psychology, ethnocentrism, and the disguised ideology of individualism. *Theory & Psychology, 18*(5), 563–589.

Cixous, H. (1975), cited in Minsky, R. (1996) *Psychoanalysis and Gender,* London: Routledge.

Clarke, V. & Peel, E. (2007) *Out in Psychology: Lesbian, Gay, Bisexual, Trans and Queer Perspectives.* Chichester, UK: John Wiley & Sons.

Clarke, V., Ellis, S., Peel, E. & Riggs, D. (2010) *Lesbian, Gay, Bisexual, Trans and Queer Psychology: An Introduction.* Cambridge: Cambridge University Press.

Clegg, S. (2011). Power. In M. Tadajewski, P. Maclaran, E. Parsons & M. Parker (eds), *Key Concepts in Critical Management Studies* (pp. 194–197). London: Sage.

Clegg, S., Kornberger, M., & Pitsis, T. (2008). *Managing and Organizations: An Introduction to Theory and Practice* (2nd edn). London: Sage.

Cohen, J.H., & Raymond, J.M. (2011). How the internet is giving birth (to) a new social order. *Information, Communication & Society, 14*(6), 937–957.

Collier, A. (1998) Language, practice and realism. In I. Parker (ed.), *Social Constructionism, Discourse and Realism,* London: Sage.

Condor, S. (1988) 'Race Stereotypes' and racist discourse, *Text, 8,* 69–91.

Connell, R.W. (1987) *Gender and Power,* Cambridge: Polity.

Connell, R.W. (1995) *Masculinities,* Cambridge: Polity.

Connell, R.W. & Messerschmidt, J.W. (2005). Hegemonic masculinity: rethinking the concept, *Gender & Society, 19*(6), 829–859.

Conner, M.T., Norman, P. (eds) (2005) *Predicting Health Behaviour: Research and Practice with Social Cognition Models* (2nd edn). Maidenhead, UK: Open University Press.

Cooper, D. (1967). *Psychiatry and Anti-Psychiatry.* London: Paladin.

Coulter, J. (2008). Twenty-five theses against cognitivism. *Theory, Culture & Society, 25*(2), 19–32.

Coutts, L. M., & Gruman, J. A. (2005). Applying social psychology to organizations. In F. W. Schneider, J. A. Gruman & L. M. Coutts (eds), *Applied Social Psychology: Understanding and Addressing Social and Practical Problems* (pp. 229–256). Thousand Oaks, CA: Sage.

Cox, A.D., Cox, D., Cryier, R. *et al.* (2012) Can self-prediction overcome barriers to Hepatitis B vaccination? A randomized controlled trial, *Health Psychology, 31*(1), 97–105.

Coy, M. (2009) Milkshakes, lady lumps and growing up to want boobies: how the sexualisation of popular culture limits girls' horizons. *Child Abuse Review, 18*(6), 372–383.

Coy, M. & Horvath, M.A.H. (2011).'Lads mags', young men's attitudes towards women and acceptance of myths about sexual aggression. *Feminism & Psychology, 21*(1), 144–150.

Coyle, A. & Kitzinger, C. (2001) *Lesbian and Gay Psychology,* Leicester: BPS Books.

Crawford, M. & Unger, R. (2004) *Women and Gender: A Feminist Psychology.* London: McGraw-Hill.

Cromby, J. (2007). Integrating social science with neuroscience: potentials and pitfalls. *BioSocieties, 2*(2), 149–170.

Cromby, J., & Harper, D. (2009). Paranoia: a social account. *Theory & Psychology, 19*(3), 335–361.

Cromby, J., Newton, T., & Williams, S. J. (2011). Neuroscience and subjectivity. *Subjectivity, 4*(3), 215–226.

Crossley, M. (2000). *Rethinking Health Psychology*. Buckingham, UK: Open University Press.

Crossely, M. L. (2000). *Introducing Narrative Psychology: Self, Trauma and the Construction of Meaning*. Buckingham UK: Open University Press.

Crossley, N. (2005). *Key Concepts in Critical Social Theory*. London: Sage.

Cúellar, D. P. (2010). *From the Conscious Interior to An Exterior Unconscious: Lacan, Discourse Analysis and Social Psychology*. London: Karnac Books.

Curt, B. C. (1994) *Textuality and Tectonics: Troubling Social and Psychological Science*, Buckingham: Open University Press.

Cushman, P. (1995). *Constructing the Self, Constructing America: A Cultural History of Psychotherapy*. Cambridge, MA: Da Capo Press.

Dafermos, M. & Marvakis, A. (2006). Critiques in psychology – critical psychology. *Annual Review of Critical Psychology, 5*, pp. 1–20.

Dahrendorf, R. (1973) *Homo Sociologicus*, London: Routledge & Kegan Paul.

Daly, M. (1978) *Gyn/Ecology: The Metaethics of Radical Feminism*, London: The Woman's Press.

Dancey, C. (1994) Lesbian Identities. In P. Choi, P. Nicolson, B. Alder, C. Dancey, L. Gannon, E. McNeill & J. Usher (eds), *Female Sexuality*, New York: Harvester Wheatsheaf.

Daniluk, J. (1991) Female sexuality: an enigma, *Canadian Journal of Counselling, 25*(4), 433–446.

Danziger, K. (1997). *Naming the Mind: How Psychology Found Its Language*. London: Sage.

Danziger, K. (2000). Making social psychology experimental: a conceptual history. *Journal of the History of the Behavioural Sciences, 36*(4), 329–347.

Davies, B. & Harré, R. (1990) Positioning: the discursive production of selves, *Journal for the Theory of Social Behaviour, 20*(1), 43–63.

Day, K. (2000) Women and alcohol: discourses around femininity and pleasure in contemporary Britain, unpublished doctoral thesis, Sheffield: Hallam University.

Dean, M. (2010). *Governmentality: Power and Rule in Modern Society* (2nd edn). London: Sage.

De Beauvoir, S. (1962). *The Second Sex* (H. M. Parshley, Trans.). Harmondsworth U.K.:

De Cremer, D., van Dick, R., & Murnighan, K. J. (eds). (2011). *Social Psychology and Organizations*. London: Routledge.

Delman, J. (2012). Participatory action research and young adults with psychiatric disabilities. *Psychiatric Rehabilitation Journal, 35*(3), 231–234.

Denzin, N. K., & Lincoln, Y. S. (2005). Introduction: the discipline and practice of qualitative research. In N. K. Denzin & Y. S. Lincoln (eds), *The Sage Handbook of Qualitative Research* (3rd edn, pp. 1–32). Thousand Oaks, CA: Sage.

Derksen, M. (2010). Realism, relativism, and evolutionary psychology. *Theory & Psychology, 20*(4), 467–487.

Deutsch, M. & Gerrard, H.B. (1955) A study of normative and informational social influence upon individual judgement, *Journal of Abnormal and Social Psychology, 51*, 629–636.

De Visser, Richard, O., Smith, Jonathan A. & McDonnell, Elizabeth J. (2009) 'That's not masculine': masculine capital and health-related behaviour. *Journal of Health Psychology, 14*(7), 1047–1058.

De Vos, J. (2012). *Psychologisation in Times of Globalisation*. London: Routledge.

Dijkstra, P., Gibbons, F. X., & Buunk, A. P. (2010). Social comparison theory. In J. E. Maddux & J. P. Tangney (eds), *Social Psychological Foundations of Clinical Psychology* (pp. 195–210). New York: Guilford Press.

Dimen, M., & Goldner, V. (eds). (2002). *Gender in Psychoanalytic Space: Between Clinic and Culture*. New York: Other Press.

Dixon, J.A. & Durrheim, K. (2003) Contact and the ecology of racial division: some varieties of informal segregation, *British Journal of Social Psychology, 42*, 1–24.

Dixon, J., & Levine, M. (2012). Introduction. In J. Dixon & M. Levine (eds), *Beyond Prejudice: Extending the Social Psychology of Conflict, Inequality and Social Change* (pp. 1–23). Cambridge: Cambridge University Press.

Dixon, J., & Levine, M. (eds). (2012). *Beyond Prejudice: Extending the Social Psychology of Conflict, Inequality and Social Change*, Cambridge, UK: Cambridge University Press.

Dollard, J., Doob, L., Miller, N., Mowrer, O. & Sears, R. (1939) *Frustration and Aggression,* New Haven, CT: Yale University Press.

Donaghue, N., Whitehead, K. & Kurz, T. (2011) Spinning the pole: a discursive analysis of the websites of recreational pole dancing studios, *Feminism & Psychology, 21*(4), 443–457.

Douglas, S. (2000). Narcissism as liberation. In J. Scanlon (ed.), *The Gender and Consumer Culture Reader* (pp. 267–282). New York: New York University Press.

Dua, A. (2006). *Feminist Psychology*. New Delhi: MD Publications.

Duckitt, J. (1992) *The Social Psychology of Prejudice*. Westport, CT: Praeger.

Duckitt, J. (2003) Prejudice and intergroup conflict. In D.O. Sears, L. Huddy & R. Jervis (eds) *Oxford Handbook of Political Psychology* (pp. 559–601). New York: Oxford University Press.

Duriez, B. & Soenens, B. (2009). The intergenerational transmission of racism: the role of right wing authoritarianism and social dominance orientation. *Journal of Research in Personality, 43*(5), 906–909.

Durrheim, K. (2012). Implicit prejudice in mind and interaction. In J. Dixon & M. Levine (eds), *Beyond Prejudice: Extending the Social Psychology of Conflict, Inequality and Social Change* (pp. 179–199). Cambridge: Cambridge University Press.

Durrheim, K., Hook, D., & Riggs, D. W. (2009). Race and racism. In D. Fox, I. Prilleltensky & S. Austin (eds), *Critical Psychology: An Introduction* (2nd edn, pp. 197–214). Thousand Oaks, CA: Sage.

Dworkin, S., & Wachs, F. L. (2009). *Body Panic: Gender, Health, and the Selling of Fitness*. New York: New York University Press.

Ebbesen, E. G., Duncan, B. & Konecni, V. J. (1975) Effects of content of verbal aggression on future verbal aggression: a field experiment, *Journal of Experimental Social Psychology, 11,* 192–204.

Edley, N. (2006). Never the twain shall meet: a critical appraisal of the combination of discourse and psychoanalytic theory in studies of men and masculinity. *Sex Roles, 55,* 601–608.

Edley, N. & Wetherell, N. (1995) *Men in Perspective: Practice, Power and Identity,* Hemel Hempstead: Prentice Hall/Harvester Wheatsheaf.

Edwards, D. (2005). Discursive psychology. In K. L. Fitch & R. E. Sanders (eds), *Handbook of Language and Social Interaction* (pp. 257–273). Mahwah, NJ: Lawrence Erlbaum.

Edwards, D. & Potter, J. (1992) *Discursive Psychology,* London: Sage.

Edwards, D. & Potter, J. (1993) Language and causation: a discursive action model of description and attribution, *Psychological Review, 100,* 23–41.

Edwards, D. & Potter, J. (2005) Discursive psychology, mental states and descriptions. In H. te Molder & J. Potter (eds) *Conversation and Cognition* (pp. 241–260), Cambridge: Cambridge University Press.

Edwards, D., Ashmore, M. & Potter, J. (1995) Death and furniture: the rhetoric, politics and theory of bottom line arguments against relativism, *History of the Human Sciences, 8*(2), 25–44.

Edwards, R. (1979). *Contested Terrain: The Transformation of the Workplace in the Twentieth Century.* New York: Basic Books.

Elliott, J. (1991). *Action Research for Educational Change.* Milton Keynes: Open University Press.

Elliott, A. (2009). *Contemporary Social Theory: An Introduction.* Abingdon, UK: Routledge.

Elliott, A. M. (2002). *Psychoanalytic Theory: An Introduction* (2nd edn). Basingstoke, UK: Palgrave Macmillan.

Elliott, R., Fischer, C. T., & Rennie, D. L. (1999). Evolving guidelines for publication of qualitative research studies in psychology and related fields. *British Journal of Clinical Psychology, 38*(3), 215–229.

Ellis, H. (1913) *Studies in the Psychology of Sex,* Philadelphia: F.A. Davis.

Ellis. H (1936) *Studies in the Psychology of Sex,* New York: Random House.

Emerson, P., & Frosh, S. (2009). *Critical Narrative Analysis in Psychology* (Revised edn). Basingstoke, UK: Palgrave Macmillan.

Every, D. & Augoustinos, M. (2007) Constructions of racism in the Australian parliamentary debates on asylum seekers. *Discourse & Society, 18*(4), 411–436.

Ewen, S. (2001). *Captains of Consciousness: Advertising and the Social Roots of Consumer Culture* (Rev edn). New York: Basic Books.

Eysenck, H.J. (1952) *The Scientific Study of Personality,* London: Routledge.

Eysenck, H. & Nias, D. (1980) *Sex, Violence and the Media,* London: Paladin.

Faderman, L. (1991) *Odd Girls and Twilight Lovers,* London: Penguin.

Fagot, B. (1974) Sex differences in toddlers' behaviour and parental reaction, *Developmental Psychology, 4,* 554–558.

Fairclough, N. (2010). *Critical Discourse Analysis: The Critical Study of Language* (2nd edn). Harlow, UK: Longman.

Faludi, S. (1992) *Backlash: The Undeclared War Against Women,* London: Chatto & Windus.

Featherstone, M. (2007) *Consumer Culture and Postmodernism* (2nd edn). London: Sage.

Ferguson, A. (1982) Patriarchy, sexual identity and the sexual revolution. In N. Keohane, Z. Rosaldo & B. Gelpi (eds), *Feminist Theory: A Critique of Ideology,* Chicago: University of Chicago Press.

Ferguson, M. (1983) *Forever Feminine: Women's Magazines and the Cult of Femininity,* London: Heinemann.

Feshbach, S. (1964) The function of aggression and the regulation of aggressive drive, *Psychological Review, 71,* 57–72.

Figes, E. (1970) *Patriarchal Attitudes,* New York: Stein & Day.

Fine, C. (2010) *Delusions of Gender: How Our Minds, Society and Neurosexism Create Difference.* New York: WW Norton.

Fine, M. (1988) Sexuality, schooling and adolescent females: the missing discourse of desire, *Harvard Educational Review, 58,* 29–53.

Fine, M. (2012) Troubling calls for evidence: a critical race, class and gender analysis of whose evidence counts. *Feminism & Psychology, 22*(1), 3–19.

Fine, M., & Torre, M. E. (2006). Intimate details: participatory action research in prison. *Action Research, 4*(3), 253–269.

Finlay, L. & Gough. B. (eds) (2003) Reflexivity: a practical guide for researchers in health and social science, Oxford: Blackwell Publishing.

Finn, M., & Henwood, K. (2009). Exploring masculinities within men's identificatory imaginings of first-time fatherhood. *British Journal of Social Psychology, 48*(3), 547–562.

Fishwick, N. (1986) *From Clegg to Clegg House: The Official Century of the Sheffield and Hallamshire County Football Association 1886–1986,* Sheffield: The Sheffield and Hallamshire County Football Association.

Fishwick, N. (1989) *English Football and Society,* Manchester: Manchester University Press.

Fiske, S.T., Gilber, D.T., & Lindzey, G. (2010) (eds) *Handbook of Social Psychology* (5th edn). New York: Wiley.

Fletcher, R. & St George, J. (2011). Heading into fatherhood nervously: support for fathering from online dads. *Qualitative Health Research, 21,* 1101–1114.

Florance, I., Mullensiefen, D., & Carter, S. (2011). How to get ahead in the psychology of advertising. *Psychologist, 24*(6), 462–465.

Flowers, P., & Buston, K. (2001). 'I was terrified of being different': Exploring gay men's accounts of growing-up in a heterosexist society. *Journal of Adolescence, 24*(1), 51–65.

Flyvbjerg, B. (2001). *Making Social Science Matter: Why Social Inquiry Fails and How It Can Succeed Again* (S. Sampson, Trans.). Cambridge: Cambridge University Press.

Ford, A. (1985) *Men,* London: Weidenfeld & Nicolson.

Foucault, M. (1954). *Mental Illness and Psychology* (A. Sheridan, Trans.). Berkeley, CA: University of California Press.

Foucault, M. (1961). *Madness and Civilization: a History of Insanity in the Age of Reason* (R. Howard, Trans.). London: Routledge.

Foucault, M. (1972) *The Archaeology of Knowledge,* London: Tavistock.

Foucault, M. (1976) *The History of Sexuality,* Vol. 1, London: Allen.

Foucault, M. (1977) *Discipline and Punish: The Birth of the Prison,* Harmondsworth: Peregrine.

Foucault, M. (1978) *The History of Sexuality: An Introduction,* London: Penguin Press.

Foucault, M. (1980) *Power/Knowledge,* Sussex: Harvester Press.

Foucault, M. (1988) *The Care of the Self. Vol.& The History of Sexuality,* London: Penguin Press.

Fox, D. & Prilleltensky, I. (1997) *Critical Psychology: An Introduction,* London: Sage.

Fox, D., Prilleltensky, I., & Austin, S. (eds). (2009). *Critical Psychology: An Introduction* (2nd edn). Thousand Oaks, CA: Sage.

Freeman, M. (1993) *Re-writing the Self,* London: Routledge.

Freud, S. (1908) *Character and Anal Eroticism.* In J. Strachey (ed.), *Standard Edition of the Complete Psychological Works of Sigmund Freud Vol. 9,* London: Hogarth Press.

Freud, S. (1920) *Beyond the Pleasure Principle.* In J. Strachey (ed.) *Standard Edition of the Complete Psychological Works of Sigmund Freud Vol. 18,* London: Hogarth Press.

Freud, S. (1923) *The Ego and the Id,* in J. Strachey (ed.) *Standard Edition of the Complete Psychological Works of Sigmund Freud Vol. 19,* London: Hogarth Press.

Freud, S. (1931) *Female Sexuality.* In J. Strachey (ed.), *Standard Edition of the Complete Psychological Works of Sigmund Freud, Vol. 21,* London: Hogarth Press.

Freud, S. (1933) *New Introductory Lectures on Psychoanalysis,* London: Hogarth Press.

Friday, N. (1980) *Men in Love: Men's Sexual Fantasies,* New York: Arrow Books.

Frodi, A., Macaulay, J. & Thome, P. (1977) Are women always less aggressive than men? A review of the experimental literature, *Psychological Bulletin, 84*(4), 634–661.

Fromm, E. (1956/1991). *The Sane Society.* London: Routledge.

Fromm, E. (1961/2004). *Marx's Concept of Man* (T. B. Bottomore, Trans.). London: Continuum.

Fromm, E. (1962/2009). *Beyond the Chains of Illusion: My Encounter with Marx and Freud.* New York: Continuum.

Frosh, S. (1987) *Psychology and Psychoanalysis,* London: Sage.

Frosh, S. (1989). *Psychoanalysis and Psychology: Minding the Gap.* London: Macmillan.

Frosh, S. (1991). *Identity Crisis: Modernity, Psychoanalysis and the Self.* London: MacMillan.

Frosh, S. (1993) The seeds of male sexuality. In J. Usher & C. Baker (eds), *Psychological Perspectives on Sexual Problems,* London: Routledge.

Frosh, S. (1997) *For and Against Psychoanalysis,* London: Routledge

Frosh, S. (1999). *The Politics of Psychoanalysis.* Basingstoke, UK: Palgrave Macmillan.

Frosh, S. (2002). Racism, racialised identities and the psychoanalytic other. In V. Walkerdine (ed.), *Challenging Subjects: Critical Psychology for a New Millennium* (pp. 101–110). Basingstoke, UK: Palgrave Macmillan.

Frosh, S. (2010). *Psychoanalysis Outside the Clinic: Interventions in Psychosocial Studies.* Basingstoke, UK: Palgrave Macmillan.

Frosh, S., Phoenix, A. & Pattman, R. (2002) *Young Masculinities: Understanding Boys in Contemporary Society.* Basingstoke, UK: Palgrave Macmillan.

Frosh, S., Phoenix, A., & Pattman, R. (2003). Taking a stand: using psychoanalysis to explore the positioning of subjects in discourse. *British Journal of Social Psychology, 42*(1), 39–53.

Frosh, S., & Baraitser, L. (2008). Psychoanalysis and psychosocial studies. *Psychoanalysis, Culture and Society, 13,* 346–365.

Furnham, A. (1994). *Personality at Work: Individual Differences in the Workplace.* London: Routledge.

Furnham, A., & Heaven, P. (1999). *Personality and Social Behaviour.* London: Arnold.

Galinsky, A. D., Rus, D., & Lammers, J. (2011). Power: a central force governing psychological, social, and organizational life. In D. De Cremer, R. van Dick & K. J. Murnighan (eds), *Social Psychology and Organizations* (pp. 17–38). London: Routledge.

Gallagher, A.M. (1988) Identity and ideology in Northern Ireland: a psychological perspective, *Irish Review, 4*(7), 7–14.

Garfinkel, H. (1967) *Studies in Ethnomethodology,* Englewood Cliffs, NJ: Prentice Hall.

Garvey, C. (1977) *Play,* Cambridge, MA: Harvard University Press.

Gavey, N. (1993) Technologies and effects of heterosexual coercion. In S. Wilkinson & C. Kitzinger (eds), *Heterosexuality: A Feminism & Psychology Reader,* London: Sage.

Gavey, N. (1997) Feminist poststructuralism and discourse analysis. In M. Gergen & S. Davis (eds), *Toward A New Psychology of Gender: A Reader,* London: Routledge.

Gavey, N. (2011). Feminist poststructuralism and discourse analysis revisited. *Psychology of Women Quarterly, 35*(1), 183–188.

Geen, R. (1978) The effects of attack and uncontrollable noise on aggression, *Journal of Research in Personality, 12,* 15–29.

Geen, R. (1990) *Human Aggression,* Milton Keynes: The Open University Press.

Geen, R., Stonner, D. & Shope, G. (1975) The facilitation of aggression by aggression: evidence against the catharsis hypothesis, *Journal of Personality and Social Psychology, 31,* 721–726.

Geertz, C. (1974) From the native's point of view: on the nature of anthropological understanding. In K. Basso & H. Selby (eds), *Meaning in Anthropology,* Albuquerque, NM: University of New Mexico Press.

Gergen, K. (1989) Warranting voice and the elaboration of the self. In J. Shotter & K.J. Gergen (eds), *Texts of Identity,* London: Sage.

Gergen, K. (1991) *The Saturated Self: Dilemmas of Identity in Contemporary Life,* New York: Basic Books.

Gergen, K. (1999) *An Invitation to Social Construction,* London: Sage.

Gergen, K.J. (1973) Social psychology as history, *Journal of Personality and Social Psychology,* 26, 309–320.

Gergen, K. J. (2002). Beyond the empiricist/constructionist divide in social psychology. *Personality and Social Psychology Review, 6*(3), 188–191.

Gergen, K. J. (2010). Beyond the enlightenment: relational being. In S. R. Kirschner & J. Martin (eds), *The Sociocultural Turn in Psychology: The Comtextual Emergence of Mind and Self* (pp. 68–87). New York: Columbia University Press.

Gergen, K. J. (2012). The social dimension of social psychology: a historical analysis. In A. W. Kruglanski & W. Stroebe (eds), *Handbook of the History of Social Psychology* (pp. 137–157). Hove, UK: Psychology Press.

Gergen, M. M. (2001). *Feminist Reconstructions in Psychology: Narrative, Gender, and Performance.* Thousand Oaks, CA: Sage.

Giddens, A. (1991). *Modernity and Self-Identity: Self and Society in the Late Modern Age.* Stanford, CA: Stanford University Press.

Gill, R. (1993) Justifying injustice: broadcaster's accounts of inequality. In E. Burman & I. Parker (eds), *Discourse Analytic Research: Repertoires and Readings of Texts in Action,* London: Routledge.

Gill, R. (1995) Relativism, reflexivity and politics: interrogating discourse analysis from a feminist perspective. In S. Wilkinson & C. Kitzinger (eds), *Feminism and Discourse,* London: Sage.

Gill, R. (2007) Postfeminist media culture: elements of a sensibility. *European Journal of Cultural Studies 10,* 147–166.

Gill, R. (2008a) Empowerment/sexism: figuring female sexual agency in contemporary advertising. *Feminism & Psychology,* 18, 35–60.

Gill, R. (2008b). Culture and subjectivity in neoliberal and postfeminist times. *Subjectivity, 25,* 432–445.

Gill, R. (2012) The sexualisation of culture? *Social & Personality Psychology Compass, 6*(7), 483–498.

Gilligan, C. (1982) *In a Different Voice,* Cambridge, MA: Harvard University Press.

Goffman, E. (1959) *The Presentation of Self in Everyday Life,* New York: Doubleday.

Goldberg, S. (1977) *The Inevitability of Patriarchy,* London: Temple-Smith.

Gooden, R.J. & Winefield, H.R. (2007). Breast and prostate cancer online discussion boards: a thematic analysis of gender differences and similarities. *Journal of Health Psychology, 12,* 103–114.

Goodley, D. (2010). *Disability Studies: An Interdisciplinary Introduction*. London: Sage

Goodman, S. (2008). Justifying the harsh treatment of asylum seekers on the grounds of social cohesion. *Annual Review of Critical Psychology 6*, 110–124.

Goodman, S. (2010). 'It's not racist to impose limits on immigration': constructing the boundaries of racism in the asylum and immigration debate. *Critical Approaches to Discourse Analysis across Disciplines 4*(1), 1–17.

Goodman, S. & Burke, S. (2011) Discursive deracialization in talk about asylum seeking. *Journal of Community and Applied Social Psychology, 21*(2), 111–123.

Gordo, A., & De Vos, J. (2010). Psychologism, psychologisation and de-psychologisation. *Annual Review of Critical Psychology, 8*, 3–7.

Gorz, A. (1989). *The Critique of Economic Reason*. London: Verso.

Gorz, A. (1999). *Reclaiming Work: beyond the Wage-Based Society* (C. Turner, Trans.). Cambridge: Polity Press.

Gough, B. (1998) Men and the discursive reproduction of sexism: repertoires of difference and equality, *Feminism & Psychology, 8*(1), 25–49.

Gough, B. (2001) Heterosexual masculinity and homophobia. In A. Coyle & C. Kitzinger (eds), *Lesbian and Gay Psychology*, Leicester: BPS Books.

Gough, B. (2004). Psychoanalysis as a resource for understanding emotional ruptures in the text: the case of defensive masculinities. *British Journal of Social Psychology, 43*(2), 245–267.

Gough, B. (2009) A psycho-discursive approach to analysing qualitative interview data, with reference to a father-son relationship, *Qualitative Research, 9*(5), 527–545.

Gough, B. & Edwards, G. (1998) The beer talking: four lads, a carry out and the reproduction of masculinities, *Sociological Review, 46*(3), 409–435.

Gough, B. & Flanders, G. (2009) Celebrating 'obese' bodies: gay 'bears' talk about weight, body image and health, *International Journal of Men's Health, 8*(3), 235–253.

Gough, B. & Madill, A. (in press) Subjectivity in psychological science: from problem to prospect, *Psychological Methods*.

Gough, B. & Peace, P. (2000) Reconstructing gender in the 1990s: men as victims, *Gender & Education, 12*(3), 385–399.

Gough, B., Robinson, S., Kremer, J. & Mitchell, R. (1992) The social psychology of intergroup conflict: an appraisal of Northern Ireland research, *Canadian Psychology, 33*(3), 645–651.

Gould, J. & Gould, C. (1989) *Sexual Selection*, New York: Scientific American Library.

Graham, H. (2012) Smoking, stigma and social class, *Journal of Social Policy, 41*(1), 83–99.

Gramsci, A. (1971). *Selections from the Prison Notebooks of Antonio Gramsci* (Q. Hoare & G. Nowell Smith, Trans.). London: Lawrence & Wishart.

Graumann, C. F. (2001). Introducing social psychology historically. In M. Hewstone & W. Stroebe (eds), *Introduction to Social Psychology* (3rd edn, pp. 3–22). Malden, MA: Blackwell.

Gray, C. (2009). 'Resisting' Ritalin: Parental Talk about Treatment Medication in Childhood ADHD (Attention deficit hyperactivity disorder). Symposium presentation at the 6th International Society for Critical Health Psychology, Lausanne, 8–11 July 2009.

Gray, J. (1993) *Men are from Mars, Women are from Venus : A Practical Guide for Improving Communication and Getting What You Want in Your Relationships,* London: Thorsons.

Gray, J.A. (1981) A biological basis for the sex differences in achievement in science? In A. Kelly (ed.) *The Missing Half: Girls and Science Education,* Manchester: Manchester University Press.

Greenwood, J. D. (2000). Individualism and the social in early American social psychology. *Journal of the History of the Behavioral Sciences, 36*(4), 443–455.

Greenwood, J. D. (2004a). *The Disappearance of the Social in American Social Psychology.* Cambridge, UK: Cambridge University Press.

Greenwood, J. D. (2004b). What happened to the 'Social' in Social Psychology? *Journal for the Theory of Social Behaviour, 34*(1), 19–34.

Grey, C., & Willmott, H. (2005). Introduction. In C. Grey & H. Willmott (eds), *Critical Management Studies: a Reader* (pp. 1–15). Oxford: Oxford University Press.

Griffin, C. (1991) Experiencing power: dimensions of gender, 'race' and class, *BPS Psychology of Women Newsletter, 8,* 43–58.

Griffin, C. (1993) *Representations of Youth: The Study of Youth and Adolescence in Britain and America,* Cambridge: Polity Press.

Griffin, C. (1995) *Feminism, Social Psychology and Qualitative Research,* The Psychologist, BPS, March.

Gross, G. (1974) Unnatural selection. In N. Armistead (ed.), *Reconstructing Social Psychology,* Harmondsworth: Penguin.

Guillaumin, C. (1995) *Racism, Sexism, Power and Ideology,* London: Routledge.

Guimarães, A.S.A. (2003) Racial Insult in Brazil, *Discourse & Society 14,* 133–151.

Gunter, B. (1986) *Television and Sex Role-Stereotyping,* London: John Libbey.

Guthman, J., & Du Puis, M. (2006). Embodying neoliberalism: economy, culture, and the politics of fat. *Environment and Planning D: Society and Space, 24*(3), 427 – 448.

Habermas, J. (1968/1987). *Knowledge and Human Interests* (J. J. Shapiro, Trans.). Cambridge: Polity.

Hall, J.M. (2011) Narrative methods in a study of trauma recovery, *Qualitative Health Research, 21*(1), 3–13.

Hall, S. (1990) Cultural identity and diaspora. In J. Rutherford (ed.), *Identity: Community, Culture and Difference,* London: Lawrence & Wishart.

Hall, M. & Gough, B. (2011) Magazine and reader constructions of 'metro-sexuality' and masculinity: a membership categorisation analysis, *Journal of Gender Studies, 20*(1), 69–87.

Halpern, D.F. (1992) *Sex Differences in Cognitive Abilities* (2nd edn), Hillsdale, NJ: Erlbaum.

Hamilton, D. & Trolier, T. (1986) Stereotypes and stereotyping: an overview of the cognitive approach. In J. Dovidio & S. Gaertner (eds), *Prejudice, Discrimination and Racism,* Orlando: Academic Press.

Hammersley, M. (1989) *The Dilemma of Qualitative Method: Herbert Blamer and the Chicago Tradition,* London: Routledge.

Hamner, W. C., & Smith, F. J. (1978). Work attitudes as predictors of unionization activity. *Journal of Applied Psychology, 63,* 415–421.

Hampson, E. (1990) Variation in sex related cognitive abilities across the menstrual cycle, *Brain & Cognition, 14,* 26–43.

Hansen, S., McHoul, A., & Rapley, M. (2003). *Beyond Help: a Consumers' Guide to Psychology.* Ross-on-Wye, UK: PCCS Books.

Hare-Mustin, R.T. (1991) Sex, lies and headaches: the problem is power. In T.J. Godrich (ed.), *Women and Power: Perspectives for Therapy,* New York: Norton.

Hare-Mustin, R.T. & Marecek, J. (1997) Abnormal and clinical psychology: the politics of madness. In D. Fox and I. Prilleltensky (eds), *Critical Psychology: An Introduction,* London: Sage.

Hare-Mustin, R. T., & Marecek, J. (2009). Clinical psychology: the politics of madness. In D. Fox, I. Prilleltensky & S. Austin (eds), *Critical Psychology: An Introduction* (2nd edn, pp. 75–92). Thousand Oaks, CA: Sage.

Harmon-Jones, E., & Devine, P. G. (2003). Introduction to the special section on social neuroscience: promise and caveats. *Journal of Personality and Social Psychology, 85*(4), 589–593.

Harré, R. (1979) *Social Being: A Theory for Social Psychology,* Oxford: Basil Blackwell.

Harré, R. (1989) Language games and the texts of identity. In J. Shotter & K.J. Gergen (eds), *Texts of Identity,* London: Sage.

Harré, R. & Secord, P.F. (1972) *The Explanation of Social Behaviour,* Oxford: Basil Blackwell.

Haslam, A. S., van Knippenberg, D., Platow, M. J., & Ellemers, N. (eds). (2003). *Social Identity at Work: Developing Theory for Organizational Practice.* New York: Psychology Press.

Haslam, S. A., & van Dick, R. (2011). A social identity approach to workplace stress. In D. De Cremer, R. van Dick & K. J. Murnighan (eds), *Social Psychology and Organizations* (pp. 325–352). New York: Routledge.

Hattenstone, S. (2012). Stephen Lawrence verdict does not end debate on police racism. *Guardian,* 6 January. Retrieved 15 May, 2012, from http://www.guardian.co.uk/commentisfree/2012/jan/06/stephen-lawrence-verdict-police-racism.

Harvey, D. (2005). *a Brief History of Neoliberalism.* Oxford, UK: Oxford University Press.

Hayes, N. (1997) *Doing Qualitative Analysis in Psychology,* London: Psychology Press.

Heaven, P.C.L. & St Quintin, D. (2003) Personality factors predict racial prejudice, *Personality and Individual Differences, 34,* 625–634.

Heelas, P. (1986) Emotion talk across cultures. In R. Harré (ed.), *The Social Construction of Emotion,* (pp. 234–266), Oxford: Blackwell.

Heller, T., Reynolds, J., Gomm, R., Muston, R. & Pattison, S. (1996) *Mental Health Matters: A Reader,* Basingstoke: Palgrave Macmillan.

Henriques, J. (1984). Social psychology and the politics of racism. In J. Henriques, W. Holloway, C. Urwin, C. Venn, and V. Walkerdine (eds) *Changing the Subject: Psychology, Social Regulation, and Subjectivity* (pp. 11–25), London: Methuen.

Henwood, K. & Pidgeon, N. (1992) Qualitative research and psychological theorizing, *British Journal of Psychology, 83*(1), 97–111.

Hepburn, A. (1999). Derrida and psychology: deconstruction and its ab/ uses in critical and discursive psychologies. *Theory & Psychology, 9*(5), 639–665.

Hepburn, A. (2000) On the alleged incompatibility between feminism and relativism, *Feminism & Psychology, 10*(1), 91–106.

Hepburn, A. (2003). *An Introduction to Critical Social Psychology.* London: Sage.

Hepburn, A., & Wiggins, S. (eds). (2007). *Discursive Research in Practice: New Approaches to Psychology and Interaction.* Cambridge, UK: Cambridge University Press.

Herzlich, C. (1973) *Health and Illness: A Social Psychological Analysis,* London: Academic Press.

Heyes, C. (2009). Diagnosing culture: body dysmorphic disorder and cosmetic surgery. *Body & Society, 15*(4), 73–93.

Hiatt, B. (2010). Girls outperform boys across all subjects, *West Australian,* 16 January, p. 22.

Hill, D.B. (2006). Theory in applied social psychology: past mistakes and future hopes. *Theory & Psychology, 16*(5), 613–640.

Hines, M. (2005). *Brain Gender.* Oxford: Oxford University Press.

Hodgetts, D., Drew, N., Sonn, C., Stolte, O., Nikora, L. W., & Curtis, C. (2010). *Social Psychology and Everyday Life.* Basingstoke, UK: Palgrave Macmillan.

Hodgetts, K., & Lecouteur, A. (2010). Gender and disadvantage in the Australian parliamentary inquiry into the education of boys. *Feminism & Psychology 20*(1), 73–93.

Hogg, M.A. & Abrams, D. (1988) *Social Identifications: A Social Psychology of Intergroup Behaviour and Group Processes,* London: Routledge.

Hogg, M. A., & Vaughan, G. M. (2005). *Social Psychology* (4th edn). Harlow, UK: Pearson.

Holland, J., Ramazanoglu, C. & Scott, S. (1990) *Sex, Risk, Danger: AIDS Education Policy and Young Women's Sexuality,* London: The Tufnell Press.

Holland, J., Ramazanoglu, C., Scott, S., Sharpe, S. & Thomson, R. (1991) *Pressure, Resistance and Empowerment: Young Women and the Negotiation of Safer Sex,* London: The Tufnell Press

Hollway, W. (1983) Heterosexual sex, power and desire for the other. In S. Cartledge & J. Ryan (eds), *Sex and Love: New Thoughts on Old Contradictions,* London: Women's Press.

Hollway, W. (1984) Gender difference and the production of subjectivity. In J. Henriques, W. Hollway, C. Urwin, C. Venn & V. Walkerdine (eds), *Changing the Subject: Psychology, Social Regulation and Subjectivity,* London: Methuen.

Hollway, W. (1989) *Subjectivity and Method in Psychology: Gender, Meaning and Science,* London: Sage.

Hollway, W. (1998). Fitting work: psychological assessment in organizations. In J. Henriques, W. Hollway, C. Urwin, C. Venn & V. Walkerdine (eds), *Changing the Subject: Psychology, Social Regulation and Subjectivity* (Rev edn, pp. 26–59). London: Routledge.

Hollway, W., & Jefferson, T. (2005). Panic and perjury: a psychosocial exploration of agency. *British Journal of Social Psychology, 44,* 147–163 (plus commentaries).

Holly, L. (1989) *Girls and Sexuality,* Milton Keynes: Open University Press.

Hook, D. (2001). Discourse, knowledge, materiality, history: Foucault and discourse analysis. *Theory & Psychology, 11,* 521–547.

Hook, D. (2007). *Foucault, Psychology and the Analytics of Power.* Basingstoke, UK: Palgrave Macmillan.

Hook, D. (2011). a *Critical Psychology of the Postcolonial: The Mind of Apartheid.* Hove, UK: Psychology Press.

Horney, K. (1924a) On the genesis of the castration complex in women. In J. Miller (ed.), *Psychoanalysis and Women,* New York: Brunner/Mazel.

Horney, K. (1924b) On the genesis of the castration complex in woman, *International Journal of Psychoanalysis, 5,* 50–60.

Horrocks, C., & Johnson, S. (eds). (2012). *Advances in Health Psychology: Critical Approaches.* Basingstoke, UK: Palgrave Macmillan.

Horton-Salway, M. (2007). The ME Bandwagon and other labels: constructing the authentic case in talk about a controversial illness. *British Journal of Social Psychology, 46*(4), 895–914.

Housden, M. (1997) *Resistance & Conformity in the Third Reich,* London: Routledge.

Howarth, C., & Hook, D. (2005). Towards a critical social psychology of racism: points of disruption. *Journal of Community & Applied Social Psychology, 15*(6), 425–431.

Huesmann, L.R. & Eron, L.D. (eds) (1986) *Television and the Aggressive Child: A Cross-Cultural Comparison,* Mahwah, NJ: Lawrence Erlbaum.

Huesmann, L. R., Moise-Titus, J., Podolski, C., & Eron, L. D. (2003). Longitudinal relations between children's exposure to TV violence and their aggressive and violent behavior in young adulthood: 1977–1992. *Developmental Psychology, 39*(2), 201–221.

Hunt, J. (2011). Girls outperform boys in most subjects again, *Irish Times,* 19 August, p. 7.

Huszczo, G. E., Wiggins, J. G., & Currie, J. S. (1984). The relationship between psychology and organized labor: past, present and future. *American Psychologist, 39,* 432–440.

Hutt, C. (1972) *Males and Females,* Harmondsworth: Penguin.

Hyde, J. S., & Jaffee, S. R. (2000). Becoming a heterosexual adult: the experiences of young women. *Journal of Social Issues, 56*(2), 283–296.

Ibáñez, T. (1990) Henri, Serge and the next generation, *BPS Social Psychology Newsletter, 24*, 5–14.

Ibáñez, T. & Íñiguez, L. (1997) *Critical Social Psychology*, London: Sage.

Illouz, E. (2008). *Saving the Modern Soul: Therapy, Emotions, and the Culture of Self-Help*. University of California Press: Berkeley, CA.

Imperato-McGinley, J., Peterson, R.E., Gautier, T. & Sturla, E. (1979) Androgens and the evolution of male-gender identity among male pseudohermaphrodites with 5 alpha reductase deficiency, *New England Journal of Medicine, 300*, 1233–1237.

Ingleby, D. (1972) Ideology and the human sciences: some comments on the role of reification in psychology and psychiatry. In T. Pateman (ed.), *Counter Course: A Handbook for Course Criticism*, Harmondsworth: Penguin.

Ingleby, D. (1985) Professionals as socializers: the 'psy complex', *Research in Law, Deviance and Social Control, 7*, 79–109.

Islam, G., & Zyphur, M. (2006). Critical industrial psychology: what is it and where is it? *Psychology and Society, 34*, 17–30.

Islam, G., & Zyphur, M. (2009). Concepts and directions in critical industrial/organizational psychology. In D. Fox, I. Prilleltensky & S. Austin (eds), *Critical Psychology: An Introduction* (2nd edn, pp. 110–125). Thousand Oaks, CA: Sage.

Jackson, L., Gardner, P. & Sullivan, L. (1992) Explaining gender differences in self-pay expectations: social comparison standards and perceptions of fair play, *Journal of Applied Psychology, 77*, 651–663.

Jackson, M. (1984a) Sexology and the social construction of male sexuality (Havelock Ellis). In L. Coveney (ed.), *The Sexuality Papers*, London: Hutchinson.

Jackson, M. (1984b) Sexology and the universalisation of male sexuality (from Ellis to Kinsey and Masters and Johnson). In L. Coveney (ed.), *The Sexuality Papers*, London: Hutchinson.

Jackson, M. (1989) Sexuality and struggle: feminism, sexology and the social construction of sexuality. In C. Jones & P. Mahony (eds), *Learning Our Lines: Sexuality and Social Control in Education* (pp. 1–22), London: The Women's Press.

Jackson, M. (1994) *The Real Facts of Life: Feminism and the Politics of Female Sexuality 1850–1940*, London: Taylor & Francis.

Jackson, S. (1992) The amazing deconstructing woman, *Trouble and Strife, 25*, 25–31.

Jackson, S. (2005). 'I'm 15 and desperate for sex': 'doing' and 'undoing' desire in letters to a teenage magazine. *Feminism & Psychology, 15*(3), 295–313.

Jahoda, G. (1988). Critical notes and reflections on 'social representations'. *European Journal of Social Psychology, 18*, 195–209.

Jahoda, G. (2007). *A History of Social Psychology: From the Eighteenth-Century Enlightenment to the Second World War*. Cambridge: Cambridge University Press.

Jahoda, M., Lazarsfield, P.F. & Zeisel, H. (1972) *Marienthal: The Sociography of an Unemployed Community*, London: Tavistock (first published 1933).

Jaspers, J. (1986) Forum and focus: a personal view of European social psychology, *European Journal of Social Psychology*, 16, 343–349.

Jefferson, G. (1990). List construction as a task and resource. In G. Psathas (ed.) *Interaction Competence*. Lanham, MD: University Press of America.

Jefferson, T. (1994) Theorising masculine subjectivity. In T. Newburn & E.A. Stanko (eds), *Just Boys Doing Business?* (pp. 10–31), London: Routledge.

Jeffreys, S. (1984) Free from the uninvited touch of man: women's campaigns around sexuality 1880–1914. In L. Coveney (ed.), *The Sexuality Papers*, London: Hutchinson.

Jeffreys, S. (1986) *The Spinster and her Enemies: Feminism and Sexuality 188–1930*, London: Pandora.

Jeffreys S (2005) *Beauty and Misogyny: Harmful Cultural Practices in the West*. New York: Routledge.

Jenkins, R. (2008). *Social Identity* (3rd edn). London: Routledge.

Jex, S. M., & Bliese, P. D. (1999). Efficacy beliefs as a moderator of the impact of work-related stressors: a multilevel study. *Journal of Applied Psychology*, 84(3), 349–361.

Johnson, R.A. (1976) *She: Understanding Feminine Psychology*, New York: Harper & Row.

Johnson, T.A. (1987) Premenstrual syndrome as a western culture-specific disorder, *Culture, Medicine and Psychiatry*, 11, 337–356.

Jones, D. C., Vigfusdottir, T. H. & Lee, Y. (2004) Body image and the appearance culture among adolescent girls and boys: an examination of friend conversations, peer criticism, appearance magazines, and the internalization of appearance ideals. *Journal of Adolescent Research*, 19, 323–339.

Jones, O. (2011a). *Chavs: The Demonization of the Working Class*. London: Verso.

Jones, O. (2011b). The poor against the poor: feral underclass or economically excluded. *Le Monde Diplomatique (English Edition)*, September, pp. 12–13.

Jones, R.L. (1991) (ed.) *Black Psychology*. Berkeley, CA: Cobb & Henry.

Jordan, C. H., & Zanna, M. P. (2003). Appendix: how to read a journal article in social psychology. In L. L. Thompson (ed.), *The Social Psychology of Organizational Behavior: Key Readings* (pp. 419–428). Hove, UK: Psychology Press.

Jordan-Young, R. M. (2011). *Brain Storm: The Flaws in the Science of Sex Differences*. Cambridge, MA: Harvard University Press.

Jost, J. T., & Kruglanski, A. W. (2002). The estrangement of social constructionism and experimental social psychology: history of the rift and prospects for reconciliation. *Personality and Social Psychology Review*, 6(3), 168–187.

Jourard, S.M. (1972) Psychology for control and for liberation of humans, paper presented to the BPS Annual Conference, Nottingham.

Kagan, C., Burton, M., & Siddiquee, A. (2008). Action research. In C. Willig & W. Stainton Rogers (eds), *The Sage Handbook of Qualitative Research in Psychology* (pp. 32–53). London: Sage.

Kagan, C., Burton, M., Duckett, P., Lawthom, R., & Siddiquee, A. (2011). *Critical Community Psychology: Critical Action and Social Change.* Hoboken, NJ: John Wiley & Sons.

Kaminer, D. & Dixon, J. (1997) The reproduction of masculinity: a discourse analysis of men's drinking talk, *South African Journal of Psychology, 25*(3), 168–174.

Katz, D., & Kahn, R. L. (1966). *The Social Psychology of Organizations.* New York: Wiley.

Kelly, L. (1988a) *Surviving Sexual Violence,* London: Polity Press.

Kelly, L. (1988b) How women define their experiences of violence. In K. Yllo & M. Bograd (eds), *Feminist Perspectives on Wife Abuse* (pp. 114–132), Newbury Park, CA: Sage.

Kemmis, S., & McTaggart, R. (2005). Participatory action research: community action and the public sphere. In N. K. Denzin & Y. S. Lincoln (eds), *The sage handbook of qualitative research* (3rd edn, pp. 559–603). Thousand Oaks, CA: Sage.

Kim, E., & Glomb, T. M. (2010). Get smarty pants: cognitive ability, personality, and victimization. *Journal of Applied Psychology, 95,* 889–901.

Kimball, M. (1994) The worlds we live in: gender similarities and differences, *Canadian Psychology, 35,* 388–404.

Kimura, D. (1987) Are men's and women's brains really different? *Canadian Psychology, 28,* 133–147.

Kinder, D.R. & Kam, C.D. (2009). *Us against Them: Ethnocentric Foundations of America Public Opinion.* Chicago, IL: University of Chicago Press.

Kirschner, S. R., & Martin, J. (2010). The sociocultural turn in psychology: an introduction and invitation. In S. R. Kirschner & J. Martin (eds), *The Sociocultural Turn in Psychology: The Contextual Emergence of Mind and Self* (pp. 1–27). New York: Columbia University Press.

Kirsta, A. (1994) *Deadlier than the Male: Aggression in Women,* Glasgow: HarperCollins.

Kitzinger, C. (1986) Introducing and developing Q as a feminist methodology: a study of accounts of lesbianism. In S. Wilkinson (ed.), *Feminist Social Psychology: Developing Theory and Practice,* Milton Keynes: Open University Press.

Kitzinger, C. (1987) *The Social Construction of Lesbianism,* London: Sage.

Kitzinger, C. (1994) Problematizing pleasure: radical feminist deconstructions of sexuality and power. In H.L. Radtke & H.J. Stam (eds), *Gender and Power,* London: Sage.

Kitzinger, C. (1997) Lesbian and gay psychology: a critical analysis. In D. Fox & I. Prilleltensky (eds), *Critical Psychology: An Introduction,* London: Sage.

Kitzinger, C. (2000). Doing feminist conversation analysis. *Feminism & Psychology 10*(2), 163–193.

Kitzinger, C. (2002). Doing feminist conversation analysis. In P. McIlvenny (ed.), *Talking Gender and Sexuality* (pp. 49–78). Amsterdam: John Benjamins Publishing.

Kitzinger, C. & Frith, H. (1999) Just say no? The use of conversation analysis in developing a feminist perspective on sexual refusal, *Discourse & Society*, *10*(3), 293–316.

Kitzinger, C. & Wilkinson, S. (1997a) Validating women's experience? Dilemmas in feminist research, *Feminism & Psychology*, *7*(4), 566–577.

Kitzinger, C. & Wilkinson, S. (1997b) Virgins and queers: rehabilitating heterosexuality. In M. Gergen & S. Davis (eds), *Towards a New Psychology of Gender: A Reader* (403–420), London: Routledge.

Kitzinger, C., Wilkinson, S. & Perkins, R. (1992) Special Issue on Heterosexuality, *Feminism & Psychology*, *2*(3).

Klama, J. (1988) *The Myth of the Beast Within*, New York: Wiley & Sons.

Klein, M. (1952). The origins of transference, *International Journal of Psychoanalysis*, *33*, 433–438.

Kleiner, B. (1998) The modern racist ideology and its reproduction in 'pseudo-argument', *Discourse & Society*, *9*(2), 187–215.

Kline, P. (1988) *Psychology Exposed*, London: Routledge.

Kohlberg, L (1969) Stage and sequence: the cognitive-developmental approach to socialization. In D.A. Goslin (ed.) *Handbook of Socialization Theory and Research* (pp. 347–480), Chicago: Rand McNally.

Kremer, J., Barry, R. & McNally, A. (1986) The misdirected letter and the quasi-questionnaire: unobtrusive measures of prejudice in Northern Ireland, *Journal of Applied Social Psychology*, *16*(4), 303–309.

Kretschmer, E. (1925) *Physique and Character*, New York: Harcourt.

Krippendorff, K. (2004). *Content Analysis: An Introduction to Its Methodology* (2nd edn). London: Sage.

Kuhn, T. (1970) *The Structure of Scientific Revolutions* (2nd edn), Chicago: University of Chicago Press.

Kvale, S. (ed.) (1992) *Psychology and Postmodernism*, London: Sage.

Lacan, J. (1968). *The Language of the Self: The Function of Language in Psycho-analysis* (A. Wilden, Trans.). Baltimore, MA: John Hopkins University Press.

La Framboise, T., Helye, A. & Ozer, E. (1990) Changing and diverse roles of women in American Indian cultures, *Sex Roles*, *22*, 455–486.

Laing, R.D. (1960) *The Divided Self*, London: Tavistock.

Laing, R.D. (1967) *The Politics of Experience and The Bird of Paradise*, Harmondsworth: Penguin.

Lakoff, G. (1987) *Women, Fire and Dangerous Things: What Categories Reveal About the Mind*, Chicago: University of Chicago Press.

Langdridge, D. (2007). *Phenomenological Psychology: Theory, Research and Method*. Harlow, UK: Pearson.

Langdridge, D. (2008). Phenomenology and critical social psychology: directions and debates in theory and research. *Social and Personality Psychology Compass*, *2*(3), 1126–1142.

Langdridge, D., & Butt, T. (2004). A hermeneutic phenomenological investigation of the construction of sadomasochistic identities. *Sexualities*, *7*(1), 31–53.

Larkin, J. & Popaleni, K. (1994) Heterosexual courtship violence and sexual harassment: the private and public control of young women, *Feminism & Psychology, 4*(2), 213–227.

Larsen, K. (1974) Conformity in the Asch experiment, *Journal of Social Psychology, 94*, 303–304.

Lasch, C. (1979). *The Culture of Narcissism: American Life in An Age of Diminishing Expectations.* New York: W.W. Norton & Company.

Latane, B. & Darley, J.M. (1970) *The Unresponsive Bystander: Why Doesn't He Help?* Englewood Cliffs, NJ: Prentice Hall.

Lather, P. (1988) Feminist perspectives on empowering research methodologies, *Women's Studies International Forum, 11*, 569–581.

Lather, P. (1992) Postmodernism and the human sciences. In S. Kvale (ed.), *Psychology & Postmodernism* (pp. 88–109), London: Sage.

Layton, L. (2008). What divides the subject? Psychoanalytic reflections on subjectivity, subjection and resistance. *Subjectivity, 22*(1), 60–72.

Leahey, T.H. (1992) *A History of Psychology: Main Currents in Psychological Thought* (3rd edn), Englewood Cliffs: Prentice Hall.

Le Bon, G. (1895) cited in R. Stainton-Rogers, W. Stainton-Rogers & P. Stenner (1995) *Social Psychology: A Critical Agenda,* London: Polity Press.

Lees, S. (1993) *Sugar and Spice: Sexuality and Adolescent Girls,* London: Penguin.

Lees, S. (1998) *Ruling Passions: Sexual Violence, Reputation and the Law,* Milton Keynes: Open University Press.

Lefkowitz, J. (2003). *Ethics and Values in Industrial-Organizational Psychology.* Hove, UK: Psychology Press.

Lincoln, Y. S., & Guba, E. G. (1985). *Naturalistic Inquiry.* Newbury Park, CA: Sage.

Lindesmith, A. R., Strauss, A. L., & Denzin, N. K. (1999). *Social Psychology* (8th edn). Thousand Oaks, CA: Sage.

Lippman, W. (1922) *Public Opinion,* New York: Harcourt Brace.

Lorenz, K. (1966) *On Aggression,* London: Methuen.

Lubek, I. (1997) Reflexively recycling social psychology: a critical autobiographical account of an evolving critical social psychological analysis of social psychology. In T. Ibáñez & L. Íñiguez (eds), *Critical Social Psychology* (pp. 195–229), London: Sage.

Lynn, N. & Lea, S. (2003). A phantom menace and the new apartheid: the social construction of asylum-seekers in the United Kingdom. *Discourse & Society, 14*(4), 425–452.

Lyotard, J.-F. (1984). *The Postmodern Condition: a Report on Knowledge.* Manchester, UK: Manchester University Press.

Lyons, A.C. & Chamberlain, K. (2006). *Health Psychology: A Critical Introduction.* Cambridge: Cambridge University Press.

Lyons, A. C. & Willott, S.A. (2008). Alcohol consumption, gender identities and women's changing social positions. *Sex Roles, 59*, 694–712.

Macan Ghaill, M. (ed.) (1996) *Understanding Masculinities: Social Relations and Cultural Arenas,* Milton Keynes: Open University Press.

McKinlay, A. & Potter, J. (1987). Social representations: a conceptual critique. *Journal for the Theory Of Social Behaviour, 17*(4), 471–487. doi:10.1111/j.1468-5914.1987.tb00109.x.

MacMillan, K. (2003) The next turn: reflexively analysing reflexive research. In Finlay, L. & Gough, B. (2003) (eds) *Reflexivity: a Practical Guide for Researchers in Health & Social Sciences.* Oxford: Blackwell.

Maccoby, E. & Jacklin, C.N. (1974) *The Psychology of Sex Differences,* London: Oxford University Press.

Mahony, P. (1985) cited in Hester, M. (1992) *Lewd Women and Wicked Witches: A Study of the Dynamics of Male Domination,* London: Routledge.

Malson, H. (2009). Appearing to disappear: postmodern feminities and self-starved subjectivities. In Malson, H. & Burns, M. (eds), *Critical Feminist Perspectives On Eating Dis/Orders* (pp. 135–145). London: Routledge.

Mandel, E., & Novack, G. (1970). *The Marxist Theory of Alienation.* New York: Pathfinder.

Marcuse, H. (1964/2002). *One Dimensional Man: Studies in the Ideology of Advanced Industrial Society.* London: Routledge.

Marecek, J., & Hare-Mustin, R. T. (2009). Clinical psychology: the politics of madness. In D. Fox, I. Prilleltensky & S. Austin (eds), *Critical Psychology: An Introduction* (pp. 75–92). London: Sage.

Markus, H. & Kitayama, S. (1991) Culture and the self: implications for cognition, emotion and motivation, *Psychological Review, 98*: 224–254.

Marsh, P. & Campbell, A. (1982) *Aggression and Violence,* Oxford: Blackwell.

Marsh, P., Rosser, E. & Harré, R. (1978) *The Rules of Disorder,* London: Routledge & Kegan Paul.

Marx, K. (1844/1964). *The Economic and Philosophical Manuscripts of 1844* (R. Livingston & G. Benton, Trans.). London: Lawrence & Wishart.

Marx, K. (1857/1973). *The Grundrisse: Foundations of the Critique of Political Economy* (M. Nicolaus, Trans.). Harmondsworth, UK: Penguin.

Marx, K. (1867/2004). *Capital: Critique of Political Economy* (B. Fowkes, Trans. Vol. 1). Harmondsworth, UK: Penguin.

Maslow, A. (1954). *Motivation and Personality.* New York: Harper & Row.

Masters, M.S. & Sanders, B. (1993) Is the gender difference in mental rotation disappearing? *Behaviour Genetics, 23,* 337–341.

Mastroianni, G. R. (2002). Milgram and the holocaust: a re-examination. *Journal of Theoretical and Philosophical Psychology, 22*(2), 158–173.

Matacin, M. L. & Burger, J. M. (1987) A content analysis of sexual themes in Playboy cartoons. *Sex Roles 17*(3/4), 179–186.

Mayo, E. (1933/1977). *The Human Problems of An Industrial Civilization.* New York: Arno Press.

Maze, J. R. (2001). Social Constructionism, Deconstructionism and Some Requirements of Discourse. *Theory & Psychology, 7*(3), 393–417.

McCreanor, T. (1996) Why strengthen the city wall when the enemy has poisioned the well? An assay of anti-homosexual discourse in New Zealand, *Journal of Homosexuality, 3,* 75–105.

McDermott, E. (2006). Surviving in dangerous places: lesbian identity performances in the workplace, social class and psychological health. *Feminism & Psychology, 16*(2), 193–211.

McDonald, M., & O'Callaghan, J. (2008). Positive psychology: a Foucauldian critique, *Humanistic Psychologist, 36*(2), 127–142.

McDonald, M. & Wearing, S. (2012). *Social Psychology and Theories of Consumer Culture: a Political Economy Perspective*. London: Routledge.

McDonald, M., Wearing, S., & Ponting, J. (2008). Narcissism and neoliberalism: work, leisure and alienation in an era of consumption. *Loisir et Societe (Society and Leisure), 30*(1), 489–510.

McFadden, M. (1995) Female Sexuality in the Second Decade of AIDS, unpublished doctoral thesis, The Queen's University, Belfast.

McFadden, M. & Sneddon, I. (1998) Sexuality. In K. Trew & J. Kremer (eds), *Gender and Psychology*, London: Arnold.

McGhee, P. (1996) Defining social psychology. In R. Sapsford (ed.), *Issues for Social Psychology*, Milton Keynes, The Open University.

McKenna, K. Y. A., & Bargh, J. A. (2000). Plan 9 from cyberspace: the implications of the internet for personality and social psychology. *Personality and Social Psychology Review, 4*(1), 57–75.

McKinlay, A., & McVittie, C. (2008). *Social Psychology and Discourse*. Oxford, UK: Wiley-Blackwell.

McNaughten, P. (1993) Discourses of nature: argumentation and power. In E. Burman & I. Parker (eds), *Discourse Analytic Research* (pp. 52–75), London: Routledge.

McPherson, W. (1999). The Stephen Lawrence Inquiry: Report of an Inquiry by Sir William Macpherson of Cluny London: The Stationery Office.

McRobbie, A. (1991) *Feminism and Youth Culture: From Jackie to Just Seventeen*, London: Macmillan.

McRobbie A (2009) *The Aftermath of Feminism. Gender, Culture and Social Change*. London: Sage.

Mead, G.H. (1934) *Mind, Self & Society*, Chicago: University of Chicago Press.

Meloni, M. (2011). Philosophical implications of neuroscience: the space for a critique. *Subjectivity, 4*(3), 298–322.

Messner, M. (1997) *Politics of Masculinities: Men in Movements*, Thousand Oaks, CA: Sage.

Midgley, N. (2006). Psychoanalysis and qualitative psychology: complementary or contradictory paradigms? *Qualitative Research in Psychology, 3*(3), 213–231.

Milgram, S. (1974) *Obedience to Authority: An Experimental View*, New York: Harper & Row.

Miller, G. (1969) Psychology as a means of promoting human welfare, *American Psychologist, 24*, 1063–1075.

Miller, P. & Fowlkes, M. (1980) Social and behavioural constructions of female sexuality, *Signs: Journal of Women in Culture and Society, 5*(4), 256–273.

Miller, P., & Rose, N. (1997). Mobilizing the consumer: assembling the subject of consumption. *Theory, Culture & Society, 14*(1), 1–36.

Millett, K. (1970) *Sexual Politics,* London: Virago.

Mills, W. C. (1959/2000). *The Sociological Imagination* (Fortieth Anniversary edn). Oxford, UK: Oxford University Press.

Minard, R.D. (1952) Race relationships in the Pocahontas coal fields, *Journal of Social Issues, 25,* 29–44.

Minsky, R. (1996) *Psychoanalysis and Gender,* London: Routledge.

Mischel, W. (1966) A social learning view of sex differences in behaviour. In E.E. Maccoby (ed.), *The Development of Sex Differences* (pp. 56–81), Stanford, CA: Stanford University Press.

Mitchell, J. (1974) *Psychoanalysis and Feminism,* London: Allen Lane.

Moane, G. (1998) Violence. In K. Trew & J. Kremer (eds), *Gender & Psychology,* London: Arnold.

Moghaddam, F. M. (1998) The self in culture. In F.M. Moghaddam, *Social Psychology: Exploring Universals Across Cultures,* New York: Freeman.

Moloney, P., & Kelly, P. (2008). Beck never lived in Birmingham: why cognitive behaviour therapy may be a less helpful treatment for psychological distress than is often supposed. In R. House & D. Loewenthal (eds), *Against and for* cbt*: Toward a Constructive Dialogue* (pp. 278–288). Ross-on-Wye, UK: PCCS.

Morgan, G. (2006). *Images of Organization* (Twentieth Anniversary edn). Thousand Oaks, CA: Sage.

Moscovici, S. (1972). Society and theory in social psychology. In J. Israel & H. Tajfel (eds), *The Context of Social Psychology* (pp. 17–68). London: Academic Press.

Moscovici, S. (1981) On social representation. In J.P. Forgas (ed.), *Social Cognition: Perspectives on Everyday Life* (pp. 181–209), London: Academic Press.

Moscovici, S. (1984) The phenomenon of social representations. In R. Farr & S. Moscovici (eds), *Social Representations* (pp. 3–69), Cambridge: Cambridge University Press.

Muchinsky, P. M. (2008). *Psychology Applied to Work: An Introduction to Industrial and Organizational Psychology* (9th edn). Belmont, CA: Hypergraphic Press.

Muise, A. (2011) Women's sex blogs: challenging dominant discourses of heterosexual desire, *Feminism & Psychology, 22,* 411–419.

Muldoon, O. & Reilly, J. (1998) Biology. In K. Trew & J. Kremer (eds), *Gender & Psychology: A European Text,* London: Arnold.

Mulvaney, S.A., Rothman, R.L., Dietrich, M.S. et al. (2012) Using mobile phones to measure adolescent diabetes adherence, *Health Psychology, 31*(1), 43–50.

Munsterberg, H. (1913/1973). *Psychology and Industrial Efficiency.* New York: Arno Press.

Murray, M. (2002). Connecting narrative and social representation theory in health research. *Social Science Information, 41*(4), 653–673.

Murray, M. (2003). Narrative psychology and narrative analysis. In P. Camic, J. E. Rhodes & L. Yardley (eds), *Qualitative Research in Psychology:*

Expanding Perspectives in Methodology and Design (pp. 95–112). Washington, DC: American Psychological Association.

Murray, M. (2004) (ed.) *Critical Health Psychology.* Basingstoke, UK: Palgrave Macmillan.

Murray, M. (2007). Narrative psychology. In J. A. Smith (ed.), *Qualitative Psychology: a Practical Guide to Research Methods* (2nd edn, pp. 111–132). London: Sage.

Naus, P. (1987) cited in Daniluk, J. (1991) Female sexuality: an enigma, *Canadian Journal of Counselling, 25*(4), 433–446.

Nicolson, P. (1992) Feminism and academic psychology: towards a psychology of women. In K. Campbell (ed.), *Critical Feminisms: Argument in the Disciplines,* Buckingham: The Open University Press.

Nicolson, P. (1994) Anatomy and destiny: sexuality and the female body. In P. Choi, P. Nicolson, B. Alder, C. Dancey, L. Gannon, E. McNeill & J. Ussher (eds), *Female Sexuality,* New York: Harvester Wheatsheaf.

Nightingale, D. & Neilands, T. (1997) Understanding and practising critical psychology. In D. Fox & I. Prilleltensky (eds), *Critical Psychology: An Introduction* (pp. 68–84), London: Sage.

Oakley, A. (1979) cited in Hudson, F. & Ineichen, B. (1991), *Taking It Lying Down: Sexuality and Teenage Motherhood,* London: Macmillan.

Ochsner, K. N., & Lieberman, M. D. (2001). The emergence of social cognitive neuroscience. *American Psychologist, 59*(9), 717–734.

O'Connor, J. (1996) *The Irish Male at Home and Abroad,* Dublin: New Island Books.

O'Connor, D.B., Jones, F.A., Conner, M.T., Abraham, C. (2011) a biopsychosocial approach to health psychology. In G. Davey (ed.). *Introduction to Applied Psychology* (pp. 151–169). Chichester, UK: BPS Wiley-Blackwell.

Oishi, S., Kesebir, S., & Snyder, B. H. (2009). Sociology: a lost connection in social psychology. *Personality and Social Psychology Review, 13*(4), 334–353.

Okazaki, S., & Abelmann, N. (2008). Colonialism and psychology of culture. *Social and Personality Psychology Compass, 2*(1), 90–106.

Orne, M. (1962) On the social psychology of the psychological experiment, *American Psychologist, 17*(11), 776–783.

Ostrove, J. M., & Cole, E. R. (2003). Privileging class: toward a critical psychology of social class in the context of education. *Journal of Social Issues, 59*(4), 677–692.

Ottmann, G., Laragy, C., Allen, J., & Feldman, P. (2011). Co-production in practice: participatory action research to develop a model of community aged care. *Systemic Practice and Action Research, 24*(5), 413–427.

Overstreet, M. (1999) *Whales, Candlelight, and Stuff Like That: General Extenders in English Discourse.* Oxford: Oxford University Press.

Oyama, S. (1997) Essentialism, women and war: protesting too much, protesting too little. In M. Gergen & S. Davis (eds), *Towards a New Psychology of Gender* (pp. 521–532), London: Routledge.

Pakulski, J., & Waters, M. (1996). *The Death of Class.* London: Sage.

Pancer, S. M. (1997). Social psychology: the crisis continues. In D. Fox & I. Prilleltensky (eds), *Critical Psychology: An Introduction* (pp. 150–165). Thousand Oaks CA: Sage Publications.

Parker, I. (1989) *The Crisis in Social Psychology, and How to End It*, London: Routledge.

Parker, I. (1990) Discourse: definitions and contradictions, *Philosophical Psychology, 3*, 189–204.

Parker, I. (1992) *Discourse Dynamics: Critical Analysis for Social and Individual Psychology*, London: Routledge.

Parker, I. (1994) Discourse analysis. In P. Banister, E. Burman., I. Parker, M. Taylor & C. Tindall (eds), *Qualitative Methods in Psychology: A Research Guide* (pp. 92–107), Buckingham: Open University Press.

Parker, I. (1997) *Psychoanalytic Culture: Psychoanalytic Discourse in Western Society*, London: Sage.

Parker, I. (1998) *Social Constructionism, Discourse and Realism*, London: Sage.

Parker, I. (1999) Critical psychology: critical links, *Annual Review of Critical Psychology, 1*, 3–18 (concurrently published in *Radical Psychology*).

Parker, I. (ed.). (2002). *Critical Discursive Psychology*. Basingstoke, UK: Palgrave Macmillan.

Parker, I. (2003). Jacques Lacan, barred psychologist. *Theory & Psychology, 13* (1), 95–115.

Parker, I. (2004). Criteria for qualitative research in psychology. *Qualitative Research in Psychology, 1*(2), 95–106.

Parker, I. (2005a). Lacanian discourse analysis in psychology: seven theoretical elements. *Theory & Psychology, 15*(2), 163–182.

Parker, I. (2005b) *Qualitative Psychology: Introducing Radical Research*. London: Routledge.

Parker I. (2007). *Revolution in Psychology: Alienation to Emancipation*. London: Pluto Press.

Parker, I. (2011) Discursive social psychology now, *British Journal of Social Psychology*, DOI: 10.1111/j.2044–8309.2011.02046.x

Parker, I., & Hook, D. (2008). Psychoanalysis and social psychology: historical connections and contemporary applications. *Journal of Community & Applied Social Psychology, 18*(2), 91–95.

Parker, I. & Shotter, J. (1990) *Deconstructing Social Psychology*, London: Routledge.

Parker, I. & Spears, R. (1996) *Psychology & Society: Radical Theory & Practice*, London: Pluto.

Parker, I., Georgaca, E., Harper, D., McLaughlin, T. & Stowell-Smith, I. (1995) *Deconstructing Psychopathology*, London: Sage.

Parlee, M.B. (1975) Review essay: psychology, *Signs, 1*, 119–138.

Parsons, T. (1954) *Essays in Sociological Theory*, New York: The Free Press.

Penelope, J. (1992) *Call Me Lesbian: Lesbian Lives, Lesbian Theory*, Freedom, CA: The Crossing Press.

Percy, C. (1998) Feminism. In K. Trew & J. Kremer (eds), *Gender & Psychology: A European Text*, London: Arnold.

Perrin, S. & Spencer, C.P. (1981) Independence or conformity in the Asch experiment as a reflection of cultural and situational factors, *British Journal of Social Psychology, 20,* 205–209.

Peter, J. & Valkenburg, P.M. (2007) Adolescents' exposure to a sexualized media environment and notions of women as sex objects. *Sex Roles, 56,* 381–395.

Peterson, C., Maier, S. & Seligman, M. (1993) *Learned Helplessness: A Theory for the Age of Personal Control,* New York: Oxford University Press.

Peterson, C., & Seligman, M. E. P. (2004). *Character Strengths and Virtues: a Handbook and Classification.* Washington, DC: American Psychological Association.

Pettigrew, T.F. (1958) Personality and sociocultural factors in intergroup attitudes: a cross-national comparison, *Journal of Conflict Resolution, 2,* 29–42.

Phoenix, A., Woollett, A. & Lloyd, E. (eds) (1991) *Motherhood: Meanings, Practices and Ideologies,* London: Sage.

Pilgrim, D., & Treacher, A. (1992). *Clinical Psychology Observed.* London: Routledge.

Pillutla, M. M. (2011). When good people do wrong: morality, social identity, and ethical behavior. In D. De Cremer, R. van Dick & K. J. Murnighan (eds), *Social Psychology and Organizations* (pp. 353–369). London: Routledge.

Pleck, J. (1987) American fathering in historical perspective. In M.S. Kimmel (ed.), *New Directions in Research on Men and Masculinities* (pp. 83–97), Englewood Cliffs, NJ: Prentice Hall.

Plummer, K. (1992) *Modern Homosexuality: Fragments of Lesbian and Gay Experiences,* New York: Routledge.

Plummer, D. (1999). *One of the Boys: Masculinity, Homophobia, and Modern Manhood.* London: Routledge.

Polkinghorne, D. (1988). *Narrative Knowing and the Human Sciences.* Albany, NY: State University of New York Press.

Potter, J. (1996) *Representing Reality: Discourse, Rhetoric and Social Construction,* London: Sage.

Potter, J. (1997) Discourse and critical social psychology. In T. Ibáñez & L. Íñiguez (eds), *Critical Social Psychology,* (pp. 55–66), London: Sage.

Potter, J. (ed.). (2007). *Discourse and Psychology: Theory and Method* (Vol. 1). London: Sage.

Potter, J. (ed.). (2007). *Discourse and Psychology: Discourse and Social Psychology* (Vol. 2). London: Sage.

Potter, J. (ed.). (2007). *Discourse and Psychology: Discursive Psychology* (Vol. 3). London: Sage.

Potter, J. (2012). Discourse analysis and discursive psychology. In H. Cooper, P. M. Camic, D. L. Long, A. T. Panter, D. Rindskopf & K. J. Sher (eds), apa *Handbook of Research Methods in Psychology: Research Designs: Quantitative, Qualitative, Neuropsychological, and Biological* (Vol. 2, pp. 119–138). Washington, DC: American Psychological Association.

Potter, J. & Wetherell, M. (1987). *Discourse and Social Psychology: Beyond Attitudes and Behaviour,* London: Sage.

Potter, J., Wetherell, M., Gill., R. & Edwards, D. (1990) Discourse – noun, verb or social practice? *Philosophical Psychology, 3,* 205–217.

Prilleltensky, I. (1999). Critical psychology praxis. In InterAmerican Society of Psychology (ed.), *La psicologia al fin del siglo* (pp. 279–304). Caracas, Venezuela: Sociedad Interamericana de Psicologia.

Prilleltensky, I., Nelson, G., & Geoffrey, B. (2002). *Doing Psychology Critically: Making a Difference in Diverse Settings.* Basingstoke, UK: Palgrave Macmillan.

Ramazanoglu, C., & Holland, J. (eds). (2002). *Feminist Methodology: Challenges and Choices.* London: Sage.

Rapley, M. (1998). 'Just an ordinary Australian': self-categorization and the discursive construction of facticity in 'new racist' political rhetoric. *British Journal of Social Psychology, 37*(3), 325–344.

Raskin, J. D. (2011). On essences in constructivist psychology. *Journal of Theoretical and Philosophical Psychology, 31*(4), 223–239.

Ratner, C. (2006). *Cultural Psychology: a Perspective on Psychological Functioning and Social Reform.* Mahwah NJ: Lawrence Erlbaum.

Reavey, P. (1999) Child sexual abuse: professional and everyday constructions of female sexuality, unpublished doctoral thesis, Sheffield Hallam University.

Reavey, P. & Gough, B. (2000) Dis/locating blame: survivors' constructions of self and sexual abuse, *Sexualities, 3*(3), 325–346.

Renzetti, C. & Curran, D. (1992) Sex role socialisation In J.A. Kournay, J.P. Sterba & R. Tong (eds), *Feminist Philosophies,* Englewood Cliffs, NJ.: Prentice Hall.

Rheinharz, S. (1992) *Feminist Methods in Social Research,* Oxford: Oxford University Press.

Rich, A. (1980) Compulsory heterosexuality and lesbian existence, *Signs: Journal of Women in Culture and Society, 5*(4), 631–657.

Richardson, F. C., & Fowers, B. J. (2010). Hermeneutics and sociocultural perspectives in psychology. In S. R. Kirschner & J. Martin (eds), *The Sociocultural Turn in Psychology: the Comtextual Emergence of Mind and Self* (pp. 113–136). New York: Columbia University Press.

Ricoeur, P. (1984). *Time and Narrative* (K. McLaughlin & D. Pellauer, Trans. Vol. 1, 2 & 3). Chicago: University of Chicago Press.

Ring, K. (1967). Some sober questions about frivolous values. *Journal of Experimental Social Psychology, 3,* 113–123.

Ritzer, G. (2010). *The McDonaldization of Society* (6th edn.). Thousand Oaks, CA: Pine Forge Press.

Rivis, A., Abraham, C. & Snook, S. (2011) Understanding young and older male drivers' willingness to drive while intoxicated: the predictive utility of constructs specified by the theory of planned behaviour and the prototype willingness model, *British Journal of Health Psychology, 16*(2), 445–456.

Rogers, A. (2005) Chaos to control: men's magazines and the mastering of intimacy. *Men and Masculinities 8*(2), 175–194.

Rogers, C. (1961). *On Becoming a Person: a Therapist's View of Psychotherapy.* Boston, MA: Houghton Mifflin.

Rose, N. (1979) The psychological complex: mental measurement and social administration, *Ideology & Consciousness*, 5, 5–68.

Rose, N. (1985) *The Psychological Complex: Psychology, Politics and Society in England 1869–1939*, London: Routledge and Kegan Paul.

Rose, N. (1989) *Governing the Soul: The Shaping of the Private Self*, London: Routledge.

Rose, N. (1998). *Inventing Our Selves: Psychology, Power, and Personhood*. Cambridge, UK: Cambridge University Press.

Rose, N. (1999). *Governing the Soul: the Shaping of the Private Self* (2nd edn). London: Free Association Books.

Rose, N. (2008). Psychology as a social science. *Subjectivity*, 25(4), 446–462.

Rossi, B. (1977) A biosocial perspective on parenting, *Daedalus*, 106, 1–32.

Rothbart, M. (1981) Memory processes and social beliefs In D. Hamilton (ed.), *Cognitive Processes in Stereotyping and Intergroup Behaviour* (pp. 145–181), Hillsdale: Erlbaum.

Sahakian, W.S. (1982) *History and Systems of Social Psychology*, London: McGraw-Hill.

Sahlins, M. D. (1977). *The Use and Abuse of Biology: An Anthropological Critique of Sociobiology*. Ann Arbor, MI: University of Michigan Press.

Salter, P. & Adams, P (2011) A critical race psychology is not yet born. *Connecticut Law Review*, 43(5), 1355–1377.

Sampson, E.E. (1977) Psychology and the American ideal, *Journal of Personality & Social Psychology*, 35, 767–782.

Sampson, E. E. (1989). The challenge of social change for psychology: globalization and psychology's theory of the person. *American Psychologist*, 44(6), 914–921.

Sampson, E.E. (1993) *Celebrating The Other: A Dialogic Account of Human Nature*, New York: Harvester Wheatsheaf.

Santa Ana, O.S. (1999) 'Like an animal I was treated': anti-immigrant metaphor in US public discourse, *Discourse & Society*, 10(2), 191–224.

Sapsford, R. (1996) *Issues for Social Psychology*, Buckingham: Open University Press.

Sapsford, R. & Dallos, R. (1996) Resisting social psychology. In R. Dallas (ed.), *Issues for Social Psychology*, Buckingham: Open University Press.

Sarbin, T. (ed.) (1986). *Narrative Psychology: The Storied Nature of Human Conduct*. New York: Praeger.

Sass, L.A. (1992) The epic of disbelief: the postmodernist turn in contemporary psychoanalysis. In S. Kvale (ed.), *Psychology & Postmodernism* (pp. 166–182), London: Sage.

Sawicki, J. (2003). Queering Foucault and the subject feminism. In G. Gutting (ed.), *The Cambridge Companion to Foucault* (2nd edn, pp. 379–400). Cambridge, UK: Cambridge University Press.

Scharff, C. (2011). 'It is a colour thing and a status thing, rather than a gender thing': negotiating difference in talk about feminism. *Feminism & Psychology*, 21(4), 458–476.

Schegloff, E.A. (1998) 'Whose text? Whose context?' *Discourse & Society*, 8(2), 165–188.

Schrieshiem, C. A. (1978). Job satisfaction, attitudes towards unions, and voting in a union representation election. *Journal of Applied Psychology, 63*, 251–267.

Seale, C. (1999) *The Quality of Qualitative Research*, London: Sage.

Sedgwick, P. (1974) Ideology in modern psychology. In N. Armistead (ed.), *Reconstructing Social Psychology* (pp. 29–38), Harmondsworth: Penguin.

Segal, L. (1987) *Is the Future Female? Troubled Thoughts on Contemporary Feminism*, London: Virgo.

Segal, L. (1990/1994) *Slow Motion: Changing Masculinities, Changing Men*, London: Virago.

Segal, L. (1997) Sexualities. In K. Woodward (ed.), *Identity and Difference* (pp. 183–239), London: Sage.

Segal, L. (1999). *Why Feminism? Gender, Psychology and Power*. Cambridge, UK: Polity

Seligman, M. E. P. (2003). *Authentic Happiness: Using the New Positive Psychology to Realize Your Potential for Lasting Fulfillment*. Sydney: Random House.

Seligman, M. E. P., & Csikszentmihalyi, M. (2000). Positive psychology: an introduction. *American Psychologist, 55*(1), 5–14.

Semin, G. & Rubini, M. (1990) Unfolding the concept of person by verbal abuse, *European Journal of Social Psychology, 20*, 463–474.

Senn, C.Y. (1996) Q-methodology as feminist methodology: women's views and experiences of pornography. In S. Wilkinson (ed.), *Feminist Social Psychologies: International Perspectives* (pp. 201–217), Buckingham: Open University Press.

Sennett, R. (2006). *The Culture of the New Capitalism*. New Haven, CT: Yale University Press.

Sevón, E. (2011). 'My life has changed, but his life hasn't': making sense of the gendering of parenthood during the transition to motherhood. *Feminism & Psychology, 22*(1), 60–80.

Seymour-Smith (forthcoming). A reconsideration of the gendered mechanisms of support in online interactions about testicular implants: a discursive approach, *Health Psychology*.

Sherif, M. (1935) *The Psychology of Social Norms*, New York: Harper & Row.

Sherif, M., & Sherif, C. W. (1953). *Groups in Harmony and Tension: An Integration of Studies of Intergroup Relations*. Oxford, UK: Harper & Brothers.

Sherif, M. & Sherif, C. (1969) *Social Psychology*, New York: Harper & Row.

Shields, S.A. & Crowley, J.J. (1996) Appropriating questionnaires and rating scales for a feminist psychology: a multi-method approach to gender and emotion. In S. Wilkinson (ed.), *Feminist Social Psychologies: International Perspectives* (pp. 218–232), Buckingham: Open University Press.

Shilling, C. (2003). *The Body and Social Theory* (2nd edn). London: Sage.

Shotter, J. (1993a) *Conversational Realities*, London: Sage.

Shotter, J. (1993b) *Cultural Politics of Everyday Life*, Buckingham: Open University Press.

Shotter, J. & Gergen, K.J. (1988) *Texts of Identity*, London: Sage.

Shotter, J. & Parker, I. (1990) (eds) *Deconstructing Social Psychology* (London: Routledge)

Shroff, H. & Thompson, J. K. (2006) Peer influences, body-image dissatisfaction, eating dysfunction and self-esteem in adolescent girls. *Journal of Health Psychology, 11,* 533–551.

Shweder, R. & Bourne, E. (1982) Does the concept of the person vary cross-culturally? In A. Marsella & G. White (eds), *Cultural Conceptions of Mental Health and Therapy* (pp. 97–137), Boston: Dordrecht.

Siann, G. (1985) *Accounting for Aggression,* London: Allen & Unwin.

Siddiquee, A., & Kagan, C. (2006). The internet, empowerment, and identity: an exploration of participation by refugee women in a Community Internet Project (CIP) in the United Kingdom (UK). *Journal of Community & Applied Social Psychology, 16*(3), 189–206.

Silverman, I. (1977). Why social psychology fails. *Canadian Psychological Review, 18,* 353–358.

Simpson, M. (1994) Here come the mirror men. *Independent,* 15 November, retrieved 4 January 2008.

Sloan, T. (2009). Doing theory. In D. Fox, I. Prilleltensky & S. Austin (eds), *Critical psychology: An introduction* (2nd edn, pp. 319–334). Thousand Oaks, CA: Sage.

Smail, D. (2005). *Power Interest and Psychology: Elements of a Social Materialist Understanding of Distress.* Ross-on-Wye, UK: PCCS.

Smith, D. (1988) Femininity as discourse. In L. Roman & L. Christian (eds), *Becoming Feminine: The Politics of Popular Culture,* London: Falmer.

Smith, J.A. (2004). Reflecting on the development of interpretative phenomenological analysis and its contribution to qualitative research in psychology. *Qualitative Research in Psychology, 1,* 39–54.

Smith, J. A. (ed.). (2007). *Qualitative Psychology: a Practical Guide to Research Methods* (2nd edn). London: Sage.

Smith, M. (1994). Selfhood at risk: postmodern perils and the perils of postmodernism, *American Psychologist, 49*(5), 405–411.

Smith, B. & Sparkes, A. (2011). Multiple responses to a chaos narrative. *Health: An Interdisciplinary Journal for the Social Study of Health, Illness & Medicine, 15*(1), 38–53.

Smith, P.B. & Bond, M.H. (1993) *Social Psychology Across Cultures: Analysis and Perspectives,* Hemel Hempstead: Harvester Wheatsheaf.

Smith, P. B., Bond, M. H., & Kagitcibasi, C. (2006). *Understanding Social Psychology across Cultures: Living and Working in a Changing World.* London: Sage.

Smith, R., Miller, D.A., Maitner, A.T., Crump, S.A., Garcia-Marques, T. & Mackie, D.M (2006) Familiarity can increase stereotyping, *Journal of Experimental Social Psychology, 42,* 471–478.

Spargo, T. (1999). *Foucault and Queer Theory.* London: Icon Books.

Spence, J.T. & Helmreich, R.L. (1978) *Masculinity and Femininity: Their Psychological Dimensions, Correlates and Antecedents,* Austin, TX: University of Texas Press.

Spence, J.T., Helmreich, R.L. & Stapp, J. (1974) The Personal Attributes Questionnaire: a measure of sex role stereotype and masculinity-femininity, *JSAS: Catalog of Selected Documents in Psychology, 4*(43), (Ms No 617).

Spender, D. (1980) *Man Made Language,* London: Routledge.

Speer, S. A. (2000). Let's get real? Feminism, constructionism and the realism/relativism debate. *Feminism & Psychology, 10*(4), 519–530.

Spitzer, R. (1981). The diagnostic status of homosexuality in DSM-III: a reformulation of the issues. *American Journal of Psychiatry, 138*(2), 210–215.

Squire, C. (1995) Pragmatism, extravagance and feminist discourse analysis. In S. Wilkinson & C. Kitzinger (eds), *Feminism & Discourse: Psychological Perspectives* (pp. 145–164), London: Sage.

Stainton-Rogers, W. (2003). *Social Psychology: Experimental and Critical Approaches.* Maidenhead, UK: The Open University Press.

Stainton-Rogers, R., Stenner, P., Gleeson, K. & Stainton-Rogers, W. (1995) *Social Psychology: A Critical Agenda,* Cambridge: Polity Press.

Stanko, E. (1985) *Intimate Intrusions: Women's Experience of Male Violence,* London: Routledge & Kegan Paul.

Stanley, L. (1990) *Feminist Praxis: Research, Theory and Epistemology in Feminist Sociology,* London: Routledge.

Steffy, B. D., & Grimes, A. J. (1992). Personnel/organizational psychology: a critique of the discipline. In M. Alvesson & H. Willmott (eds), *Critical Management Studies* (pp. 181–201). London: Sage.

Steger, M. B., & Roy, R. K. (2010). *Neoliberalism: a Very Short Introduction.* New York: Oxford University Press.

Stephens, C. (2011). Narrative analysis in health psychology research: personal, dialogical, and social stories of health. *Health Psychology Review, 5*(1), 62–78.

Sterns, L., Alexander, R., Barrett, G., & Dambrot, F. (1983). The relationship of extraversion and neuroticism with job preferences and job satisfaction for clerical employees. *Journal of Occupational Psychology, 56*, 145–155.

Stevens, R. (1996) *Understanding the Self,* Buckingham: Open University Press/Sage.

Still, A. (1996) Historical origins of social psychology. In R. Sapsford (ed.), *Issues for Social Psychology,* Buckingham: Open University Press.

Stokoe, E. (2010). Gender, conversation analysis, and the anatomy of membership categorization practices. *Social and Personality Psychology Compass, 4*(7), 428–438.

Stokoe, E. & Edwards, D. (2007) 'Black this: black that': racial insults and reported speech in neighbour complaints and police interrogations, *Discourse & Society, 18*(3), 337–372.

Storr, A. (1970) *Human Aggression,* Harmondsworth: Penguin.

Stratton, P. (1997) Attributional coding of interview data: meeting the needs of long-haul passengers. In N. Hayes (ed.), *Doing Qualitative Analysis in Psychology* (pp. 115–143), London: Psychology Press.

Strauman, T. J., McCrudden, M. C., & Jones, N. P. (2010). Self-regulation and psychopathology: toward an integrative perspective. In J. E. Maddux & J. P. Tangney (eds), *Social Psychological Foundations of Clinical Psychology* (pp. 84–113). New York: Guilford Press.

Sulkunen, P. (2009). *The Saturated Society: Governing Risk and Lifestyles in Consumer Culture.* London: Sage.

Swann, J. (1992) *Girls, Boys and Language,* Oxford: Blackwell.

Synder, M. & Uranowitz, S.W. (1978) Reconstructing the past: some cognitive consequences of person perception, *Journal of Personality and Social Psychology, 33,* 941–950.

Szasz, T. (1961) *The Myth of Mental Illness,* New York: Harper & Row.

Tadajewski, M., Maclaran, P., Parsons, E., & Parker, M. (2011). *Key Concepts in Critical Management Studies.* London: Sage.

Tajfel, H. (1978) *Differentiation between Social Groups: Studies in Intergroup Behaviour.* London: Academic Press.

Tajfel, H. (1981) *Human Groups and Social Categories.* Cambridge: Cambridge University Press.

Tajfel, H. & Billig, M. (1973) Social categorization and intergroup behaviour, *European Journal of Social Psychology, 1,* 149–178.

Tajfel, H. & Turner, J.C. (1979) An integrative theory of intergroup conflict. In W. Austin & S. Worchel (eds), *The Social Psychology of Intergroup Relations* (pp. 33–47), California: Brooks-Cole.

Tajfel, H. & Turner, J.C. (1985) The social identity theory of intergroup behaviour. In S. Worchel & W. Austin (eds), *Psychology of Intergroup Relations* (pp. 2–24), Chicago: Nelson-hall.

Tavris, C. and Wade, C. (1984) *The Longest War: Sex Differences In Perspective,* New York: Harcourt Brace Jovanovich.

Taylor, E. (2001). A reply to Seligman on positive psychology. *Journal of Humanistic Psychology, 41*(1), 13–29.

Taylor, F. W. (1911/1967). *The Principles of Scientific Management.* New York: Norton.

Taylor, L. D. (2005). All for him: articles about sex in American lad magazines. *Sex Roles, 52*(3/4), 153–163.

Taylor, S. E., Klein, L. C., Lewis, B. P., Gruenewald, T. L., Gurung, R. A. R., & Updegraff, J. A. (2000). Biobehavioral responses to stress in females: tend-and-befriend, not fight-or-flight. *Psychological Review, 107*(3), 411–429.

Terman, L. & Miles, C. (1936) *Sex and Personality,* New York: McGraw-Hill.

Terry, G., & Braun, V. (2012). Sticking my finger up at evolution: unconventionality, selfishness, and choice in the talk of men who have had 'preemptive' vasectomies. *Men and Masculinities, 15*(3), 207–229.

Thompson, C. J., & Hirschman, E. C. (1995). Understanding the socialized body: a poststructuralist analysis of consumers' self-conceptions, body images, and self-care practices. *Journal of Consumer Research, 22*(2), 139–153.

Thompson, J. (1984) *Studies in the Theory of Ideology,* Cambridge: Polity.

Thompson, L. L. (ed.). (2003a). *The Social Psychology of Organizational Behavior: Key Readings.* Hove, UK: Psychology Press.

Thompson, L. L. (2003b). Organizational behavior: a micro perspective. In L. L. Thompson (ed.), *The Social Psychology of Organizational Behavior: Key Readings* (pp. 1–6). Hove, UK: Psychology Press.

Thomson, R. & Scott, S. (1991) *Learning About Sex: Young Women and the Social Construction of Sexual Identity,* London: The Tufnell Press.

Tiffin, J., Knight, F.B. & Josey, C.C. (1940) *The Psychology of Normal People,* Boston, MA: Heath.

Toffler, A. (1981) *The Third Wave,* London: Pan Books.

Trew, K. & Kremer, J. (1998) *Gender & Psychology: A European Text,* London: Arnold.

Triandis, H. C. (2001). Individualism-collectivism in personality. *Journal of Personality, 69*(6), 907–924.

Triplett, N. (1898) The dynamogenic factor in pace-making and competition, *American Journal of Psychology, 9,* 507–533.

Trivers, R. (1985) *Social Evolution,* Menlo Park, CA: Benjamin/Cummings Publishers.

Tuffin, K. (2004). *Understanding Critical Social Psychology.* London: Sage.

Turner, B. (1984) *The Body and Society,* Oxford: Blackwell.

Turner, C.W. & Goldsmith, D. (1976) Effects of toy guns on children's antisocial free play behaviour, *Journal of Experimental Child Psychology, 21,* 303–315.

Turner, J.C. (1982) Towards a cognitive re-definition of the social group. In H. Tajfel (ed.) *Social Identity and Intergroup Relations* (pp. 15–41), Cambridge University Press.

Turner, J.C., Hogg, M.A., Oakes, P.J., Reicher, S.D. & Wetherell, M. (1987) *Rediscovering the Social Group: A Self-Categorization Theory,* Oxford: Blackwell.

Unger, R. K. (1996) Using the master's tools: epistemology and empiricism. In S. Wilkinson (ed.), *Feminist Social Psychologies: International Perspectives* (pp. 165–181), Buckingham: Open University Press.

Ussher, J. (1991) *Women's Madness: Misogyny or Mental Illness,* London: Harvester Wheatsheaf.

Ussher, J. (2005). *Managing the Monstrous Feminine: Regulating the Reproductive Body* (New edn). London: Routledge.

Ussher, J. (2011). *The Madness of Women: Myth and Experience.* London: Routledge.

Vance, C. (1984) *Pleasure and Danger: Exploring Female Sexuality,* London: Routledge.

Van Der Zee, K., & Paulus, P. (2008). Social psychology and modern organizations: balancing between innovativeness and comfort. In L. Steg, A. P. Buunk & T. Rothengatter (eds), *Applied Social Psychology: Understanding and Managing Social Problems* (pp. 271–290). Cambridge, UK: Cambridge University Press.

Van den Berg, H., Wetherell, M. & Houtkoop-Steenstra, H. (eds) (2003) *Analysing Race Talk: Multidisciplinary Approaches to the Interview.* Cambridge: Cambridge University Press.

van Dijk, T. (1984) *Prejudice in Discourse: An Analysis of Ethnic Prejudices in Cognition and Conversation,* Amsterdam: John Benjamins.

van Dijk, T. A. (1993) Denying racism: elite discourse and racism. In J. Solomos & J. Wrench (eds) *Racism and Migration in Western Europe* (pp. 179–193). Oxford: Berg.

Vinchur, A. J., & Koppes, L. L. (2010). A historical survey of research and practice in industrial and organizational psychology. In S. Zedeck (ed.), *apa Handbook of Industrial and Organizational Psychology: Building and Developing the Organization* (Vol. 1, pp. 3–36). Washington, DC: American Psychological Association.

Waddell, N. & Cairns, E. (1986) Situational perspectives on social identity in Northern Ireland, *British Journal of Social Psychology, 25,* 25–31.

Walby, S. (1990) *Theorising Patriarchy,* Oxford: Blackwell.

Walkerdine, V. (1981) Sex, power and pedagogy, *Screen Education,* 38, 14–23. Reprinted in M. Arnot & G. Weiner (eds) (1987) *Gender and The Politics of Schooling,* London: Hutchinson.

Walkerdine, V. (1987) No laughing matter: girls' comics and the preparation for adolescent sexuality. In J.M. Broughton (ed.), *Critical Theories of Psychological Development,* New York: Plenum Press.

Walkerdine, V. (1991) *Schoolgirl Fictions.* London: Verso.

Walkerdine, V. (1996) Special Issue on social class, *Feminism & Psychology,* 6(3).

Walter, N. (2010). *Living Dolls: The Return of Sexism.* London: Virago.

Weatherall, A. (2002). *Gender, Language and Discourse.* London: Routledge.

Weatherall, A. (2012) Discursive Psychology and feminism, *British Journal of Social Psychology, 51*(3), 463–470.

Wearing, S., Wearing, M. & McDonald, M. (2010). Understanding local power and interactional processes in sustainable tourism: exploring village-tour operator relations on the Kokoda Track, Papua New Guinea. *Journal of Sustainable Tourism, 18*(1), 61–76.

Wearing, S., McDonald, M. & Wearing, M. (in press). Consumer culture, the mobilisation of the narcissistic self, and adolescent deviant leisure. *Leisure Studies.*

Weedon, C. (1987) *Feminist Practice and Post-Structuralist Theory,* London: Blackwell.

Weeks, J. (1977) *Coming Out: Homosexual Politics in Britain from the Nineteenth Century to the Present Day,* London: Quartet Books.

Weeks, J. (1981) *Sex, Politics and Society: The Regulation of Sexuality since 1800,* London: Longmans.

Weeks, J. (1985) *Sexuality and Its Discontents,* London: Tavistock Publications.

Weeks, J. (1991) *Against Nature: Essays on History, Sexuality and Identity,* London: Rivers Oram.

Weisstein, N. (1993) Psychology constructs the female; or the fantasy life of the male psychologist (with some attention to the fantasies of his friends, the male biologist and the male anthropologist), *Feminism & Psychology,* 3(2), 195–210. (First published 1968.)

West, D., Roy, C. & Florence Nichols (1978) *Understanding Sexual Attacks,* London: Heinemann.

Wetherell, M. (1982) Cross-cultural studies of minimal groups: implications for the social identity theory of intergroup relations. In H. Tajfel (ed.),

Social Identity and Intergroup Relations (pp. 207–240), Cambridge University Press.

Wetherell, M. (1995) Romantic discourse and feminist analysis: interrogating investment, power and desire. In S. Wilkinson & C. Kitzinger (eds), *Feminism & Discourse: Psychological Perspectives* (pp. 128–145), London: Sage.

Wetherell, M. (1996) *Identities, Groups and Social Issues,* London: Sage/Open University Press.

Wetherell, M. (1997) Linguistic repertoires and literary criticism: new directions for a social psychology of gender. In M. Gergen & S. Davis (eds), *Towards a New Psychology of Gender: A Reader* (pp. 149–171), London: Routledge.

Wetherell, M. (1998) Positioning and interpretative repertoires: conversation analysis and post-structuralism in dialogue. *Discourse & Society, 9*(3), 387–416.

Wetherell, M. (2003) Paranoia, ambivalence and discursive practices: concepts of position and positioning in psychoanalysis and discursive psychology. In R. Harre & F. Moghaddam (eds) *The Self and Others: Positioning Individuals and Groups in Personal, Political and Cultural Contexts* (pp. 99–120), New York: Praeger/Greenwood Publishers.

Wetherell, M. & Edley, N. (1999) Negotiating hegemonic masculinity: imaginary positions and psycho-discursive practices, *Feminism & Psychology, 9*(3), 335–357.

Wetherell, M. & Griffin, C. (1991) Feminist psychology and the study of men and masculinity: Part one: Assumptions and perspectives, *Feminism and Psychology, 1*, 361–393.

Wetherell, M. & Maybin, J. (1996) The distributed self: a social constructionist perspective. In R. Stevens (ed.), *Understanding the Self* (pp. 219–280), London: Sage/Open University Press.

Wetherell, M. & Potter, J. (1992) *Mapping the Language of Racism: Discourse and the Legitimation of Exploitation,* Hemel Hempstead: Harvester Wheatsheaf.

Wetherell, M., Stiven, H. & Potter, J. (1987) 'Unequal egalitarianism': a preliminary study of discourses concerning gender and employment opportunities, *British Journal of Social Psychology, 26*, 59–71.

Wetherell, M., Taylor, S., & Yates, S. J. (eds). (2001). *Discourse as Data: A Guide for Analysis* London: Sage.

Wetherell, M., Taylor, S., & Yates, S. J. (eds). (2001). *Discourse Theory and Practice: A Reader* London: Sage.

Wetherell, M., & Mohanty, C. T. (eds). (2010). *The Sage Handbook of Identities.* London: Sage.

Whaley, A.L. (1997) Ethnicity/race, paranoia, and psychiatric diagnoses: clinician bias versus sociocultural differences, *Journal of Psychopathology and Behavioural Assessment, 19*, 1–17.

White, J. (1970) *Toward a Black Psychology, Ebony* magazine.

Whitehead, S. (2002) *Men and Masculinities.* Cambridge: Polity Press.

Wiggins, S., & Potter, J. (2008). Discursive psychology. In C. Willig & W. Stainton Rogers (eds), *The Sage Handbook of Qualitative Research in Psychology* (pp. 73–90). London: Sage.

Wilder, D.A. (1990) Some determinates of the persuasive power of in-group and out-groups: organization of information and attribution of independence, *Journal of Personality & Social Psychology, 59*, 1202–1213.

Wilkinson, S. (ed.) (1986) *Feminist Social Psychology: Developing Theory & Practice*, Milton Keynes: Open University Press.

Wilkinson, S. (1988) The role of reflexivity in feminist psychology, *Women's Studies International Forum, 11*, 493–502.

Wilkinson, S. (1991) Feminism and psychology: from critique to reconstruction, *Feminism & Psychology, 1*(1), 5–18.

Wilkinson, S. (ed.) (1996) *Feminist Social Psychologies: International Perspectives*, Buckingham: Open University Press.

Wilkinson, S. (1997) Prioritising the political: feminist psychology. In T. Ibáñez & L. Íñiguez (eds), *Critical Social Psychology* (pp. 178–194), London: Sage.

Wilkinson, S. (2000). Feminist research traditions in health psychology: breast cancer research. *Journal of Health Psychology, 5*(3), 353–366.

Wilkinson, S. (2004). Feminist contributions to critical health psychology. In M. Murray (ed.). *Critical Health Psychology* (pp. 83–100). Basingstoke: Palgrave Macmillan.

Wilkinson, S. & Kitzinger, C. (1993) *Heterosexuality: A Feminism & Psychology Reader*, London: Sage.

Wilkinson, S. & Kitzinger, C. (1994) The social construction of heterosexuality, *Journal of Gender Studies, 3*(30), 307–316.

Wilkinson, S. & Kitzinger, C. (1995) *Feminism and Discourse*, London: Sage.

Wilkinson, S., & Kitzinger, C. (2008). Conversation analysis. In C. Willig & W. Stainton Rogers (eds), *The Sage Handbook of Qualitative Research in Psychology* (pp. 54–72). London: Sage.

Williams, J. (1984) Gender and intergroup behaviour: towards an integration, *British Journal of Psychology, 23*, 311–316.

Williams, R. (2009) The health experiences of African-Carribean and White working-class fathers. In B. Gough & S. Robertson (eds) *Men, Masculinities & Health: Critical Perspectives*. Basingstoke: Palgrave Macmillan.

Williams, L., Labonte, R., & O'Brien, M. (2003). Empowering social action through narratives of identity and culture. *Health Promotion International, 18*, 33–40.

Williams, J., & Lykes, M. B. (2003). Bridging theory and practice: using reflexive cycles in feminist participatory action research. *Feminism & Psychology, 13*(3), 287–294.

Williams, S.J. & Bendelow, G. (1998) *The Lived Body: Sociological Themes, Embodied Issues*. London: Routledge.

Williams, T.P. & Sogon, S. (1984) Group composition and conforming behaviour in Japanese students, *Japanese Psychological Research, 26*, 231–234.

Willig, C. (1998) Social constructionism and revolutionary socialism: a contradiction in terms? In I. Parker (ed.), *Social Constructionism, Discourse and Realism* (pp. 91–104), London: Sage.

Willig, C. (1999) *Applied Discourse Analysis: Social and Psychological Interventions,* Buckingham: Open University Press.

Willig, C. (2008a). *Introducing Qualitative Research in Psychology* (2nd edn.). Maidenhead, UK: Open University Press.

Willig, C. (2008b). Discourse analysis. In J. A. Smith (ed.), *Qualitative Psychology: a Practical Guide to Research Methods* (2nd edn, pp. 160–185). London: Sage.

Willig, C., & Stainton-Rogers, W. (eds). (2008). *The Sage Handbook of Qualitative Research in Psychology.* London: Sage.

Willis, P. (1977) *Learning to Labour: How Working-Class Kids Get Working-Class Jobs,* Farnborough, Hants: Saxon House.

Willott, S. & Griffin, C. (1997) 'Wham, bam, am i a man?', unemployed men talk about masculinities, *Feminism & Psychology, 7*(1), 107–128.

Wilson, E.O. (1975) Human decency is animal, *New York Times Magazine,* 12 October, pp. 38–50.

Wilson, E.O. (1978) *On Human Nature,* Cambridge, MA: Harvard University Press.

Wilson, E. (2000). *Sociobiology: the New Synthesis* (25th Anniversary edn.). Cambridge, MA: Harvard University Press.

Wilson, G. (1994) Biology, sex roles and work. In C. Quest (ed.), *Liberating Women ... From Modern Feminism* (pp. 60–69), London: Institute of Economic Affairs, Health & Welfare Unit.

Winterson, J. (1985) *Oranges Are Not the Only Fruit,* London: Vintage.

Woodward, K. (1997). *Identity and Difference.* Thousand Oaks, CA; Maidenhead, BRK, England: Sage Publications, Inc.

Wooffitt, R. (2005). *Conversation Analysis and Discourse Analysis: a Comparative and Critical Introduction.* London: Sage.

Wowk, M. T. (2007). Kitzinger's feminist conversation analysis: critical observations. *Human Studies, 30*(2), 131–155.

Yardley, L. (2000). Dilemmas in qualitative health research. *Psychology and Health, 15,* 215–228.

Yardley, L. (2008). Demonstrating validity in qualitative psychology. In J. A. Smith (ed.), *Qualitative Psychology: a Practical Guide to Research Methods* (2nd edn, pp. 235–251). London: Sage.

Yen, J. (2010). Authorizing happiness: rhetorical demarcation of science and society in historical narratives of positive psychology. *Journal of Theoretical and Philosophical Psychology, 30*(2), 67–78.

Zajonc, R.B. (1965) Social facilitation, *Science, 149,* 269–274.

Zickar, M. J. (2001). Using personality inventories to identify thugs and agitators: applied psychology's contribution to the war against labor. *Journal of Vocational Behaviour, 59,* 149–164.

Zillman, D. (1979) *Hostility and Aggression,* Hillsdale, NJ: Lawrence Erlbaum Associates.

Zimmerman, D.H. (2005) Introduction: conversation analysis and social problems, *Social Problems, 52*(4), 445–448.

Zizek, S. (2000). *The Spectre Is Still Roaming Around.* Zagreb: Arkzin.

Index